959.7

I N A

FORMOSA

● Hong Kong

HAINAN

I N A

S E A

IPPINES

LUZON

N

0 50 100 150 200 250 300

Scale of Miles

Robert Shaplen

THE LOST REVOLUTION: VIETNAM 1945–1965

ANDRE DEUTSCH

FIRST PUBLISHED 1966 BY
ANDRE DEUTSCH LIMITED
105 GREAT RUSSELL STREET
LONDON WCI
COPYRIGHT © 1955, 1962, 1963, 1964 AND 1965
BY ROBERT SHAPLEN
ALL RIGHTS RESERVED
PRINTED PHOTOLITHO IN GREAT BRITAIN BY
EBENEZER BAYLIS AND SON LTD
THE TRINITY PRESS, WORCESTER, AND LONDON

Endpapers by Tom Funk

A portion of this book originally appeared,
in somewhat different form, in *The New Yorker*.

This book is dedicated to my wife,
June Herman Shaplen, with love
and gratitude

Contents

Acknowledgments

This book is primarily based on my own experience and research in the former Indochina area over a twenty-year period. Largely, it is the result of what I saw and heard; much of it comes from Vietnamese sources. There were, of course, many Americans who provided me with original material and who themselves were valuable sources. My Vietnamese friends and acquaintances are too numerous to mention; most of their names appear in the book, and many of them have played principal roles in Vietnam. Among the Americans who were particularly helpful, and to whom I wish to express my thanks, were former Ambassador Edmund Gullion, now Dean of the Fletcher School of Diplomacy; the late Robert Blum, of the Council on Foreign Relations; Major General Edward Lansdale (retired); former Ambassador Kenneth Young; and Roger Hilsman, of Columbia University and formerly Assistant Secretary of State for the Far East. There were many others who extended help of various sorts, including some whose names I am not at liberty to mention.

In writing some of the historical background, a number of books were useful. They include *The Struggle for Indochina*, by Ellen Hammer; *The Two Viet-Nams*, by Bernard Fall; *No Peace for Asia*, by Harold Isaacs; and *Vietnam, a Diplomatic Tragedy*, by Victor Bator. Documents furnished me by Vietnamese and American officials were also helpful. A great deal of valuable editorial counsel was furnished me by William Knapp and Robert Gerdy, of the editorial staff of *The New Yorker*, and by Miss Acy Glasser. I wish to thank the editors of *Newsweek*, for whom I worked when I first arrived on the Asian mainland in the fall of 1945,

ix

after having been a war correspondent for that magazine in the Pacific; the editors of *The Reporter*, for permission to include two articles written in the nineteen-fifties; and particularly William Shawn, the editor of *The New Yorker*, for the numerous opportunities he has given me to report from the Far East. Finally, I wish to express my deepest thanks to my wife, June Herman Shaplen, for her editorial guidance and for the sheer mechanical labor she devoted to the completion of the book.

R.S.

Introduction

This book is both a history of events and a memoir of a personal association that began twenty years ago with a part of the world very few Americans cared or even knew about at the time. When I first arrived in Saigon, in French Indochina, in July, 1946, less than a year after the war in the Pacific and on the Asian mainland had ended, there were only a few Americans in the country—a slim diplomatic staff headed by a Consul General; an information officer named Joe Robinson, who was the first American I ever met with that special fondness for the Vietnamese people, and for things Vietnamese, that so many Americans, myself included, have come to acquire; a Graves Registration Team, whose ghoulish task it was to recover the bodies of American fliers lost in the Indochina jungle during the war; and a number of intelligence officers. Ten months before I came, one of the latter, Lieutenant Colonel Peter Dewey, while riding in his jeep on a road outside Saigon, had been shot to death by a band of men supposedly attached to the Vietminh.

What was the Vietminh? Who was this strange little man who wore a scraggly goatee and called himself Ho Chi Minh? What, in fact, was Indochina, and of what possible importance could it be to America and to Americans, so many tens of thousands of whom were only too happy to say goodbye to the Pacific and to Asia after the long and difficult Japanese war?

If Indochina was not important to the United States, there was no doubt of its importance to France, which had taken possession of its 287,000 square miles during the second half of the nineteenth century and divided what is now the Vietnamese part of it—for nearly a thousand years under Chinese domination and then intermittently a precarious independent kingdom—into three separate colonial areas, Tonkin, Annam, and Cochin China, and the rest of it into Cambodia and Laos. Much has been written about the colonial period in Indochina, about the failure of the French to prepare the Vietnamese for any independent national role—administratively, let alone, politically—and about their odd mixture of surface racial, or sexual, tolerance and a basic contempt for a subject people that frequently led to demonstrations of gross cruelty against whole villages as well as individuals. But to me one fact has always stood out above all others—that at the end of the Second World War, despite the French cultural and educational impact on Indochina, which was not negligible at the higher levels, eighty per cent of the Vietnamese people were illiterate, and that this was a higher percentage of illiteracy than in the early years of the nineteenth century. Despite these imperfections, or perhaps because of them, and because of the profits that were obtained from Indochina's rubber and rice, opium and alcohol, the French, with their national pride deeply injured as a result of their defeat by the Nazis in Europe, and the humiliation to which they were subjected by the Japanese in Asia, were the most reluctant of all the imperial powers to give up the prizes of their prewar empire. In the late summer of 1945, the French returned to Indochina with the help of British and Chinese occupation troops, but their freedom of movement was initially limited to the south; in the north, the newly created Republic of Vietnam, headed by President Ho Chi Minh, the leader of the Vietminh (a contraction of the Vietnam Doc Lap Dong Minh, the League for the Independence of Vietnam), had taken over in Hanoi as an independent government. In March, 1946, chiefly in order to assure the withdrawal of the Chinese occupation forces in the north and the re-entry of a limited number of French troops there, France recognized the Republic of Vietnam as "a free country with a separate government, a separate legislative body, and separate finances within the Indochinese Federation and the French Union." However, the French refused to follow through on their recognition by providing the new government with suitable guarantees and economic assistance; and in contravention of agreements they had made with Ho Chi Minh to hold a referendum in the south, they established their own new puppet regime in what was then still Cochin China but is now part of South Vietnam.

Neither the proposed Indochina Federation nor the French Union, which were little more than contrived theoretical devices by which the French hoped to regain their military, political, and economic position in Indochina, ever became viable in the Far East. If the French had accepted the fact that the war had drastically altered the old colonial dispensation, and if they had sought honestly and unselfishly to encourage the attachment of new and genuine native nationalist governments to a really legitimate union of former French possessions, an association akin to the British Commonwealth might have been established. The fact that they failed to do so was essentially their own fault, but part of the blame, and the responsibility for the turmoil that followed, belongs to the United States, which during the Second World War had repeatedly enunciated the principle of postwar independence for colonial peoples. After the war, we seemed to forget about most of these promises, or we hedged on them.

The premise on which the various sections of this book were written, dealing as they do with different periods of the last two decades but largely with the events of the last three years, is essentially the same throughout—that a revolutionary condition existed in Indochina all along, one that should have been regarded from the start by the Western nations for what it was, a truly Asian revolution, representing the legitimate hopes of people throughout the region to be free of any domination, either that of their former colonial masters, of old or new native tyrants or satraps, or that of the Communists. Unfortunately, while the Communists were quick to take advantage of the revolutionary opportunities in Indochina, the Western nations, especially France, did not face up to the realities of the situation.

In November, 1946, the Indochina war was triggered by a minor incident over customs patrols in the North Vietnamese port of Haiphong, followed a month later by an all-out French response to Vietminh acts of terror in the native quarter of Hanoi. The brutal conflict, which lasted eight years and cost the French colonial forces 174,000 casualties, and which the United States financed and supported, culminated in the great French defeat at Dienbienphu in May, 1954, immediately followed by the French surrender and by the settlements at the Geneva Conference that summer. Under the terms of these agreements, North and South Vietnam were recognized as two separate nations, with capitals in Hanoi and Saigon, and the independence of Cambodia and Laos, which had been painfully but more peacefully evolving through long negotiations, was also guaranteed. A referendum was supposed to take place in 1956 in both parts of Vietnam, whereby unification of the two halves under a chosen President was to be brought about, but the new South Vietnamese government of President Ngo Dinh Diem refused to hold the vote. President Diem's reasons, while violently objected to by the North Vietnamese, were justified in the opinion of many neutral observers. Diem claimed that, in the first place, South Vietnam had not signed the Geneva accords; that, in the second place, the tight Communist control in the north made an honest vote impossible there; and that, furthermore, the continued presence of armed Communist guerrillas in the south, who were to have been withdrawn to the north after the Geneva Conference but a considerable number of whom went underground, made a fair election impractical, if not impossible, in South Vietnam as well. It is probably true that if an honest election could have been held in both parts of Vietnam at this time, it would have been won by Ho Chi Minh, whose popularity as an ardent and active nationalist leader over many painful years of struggle was greater than the popularity of Diem, who had spent several years in exile and had returned to Vietnam only in 1954. In the two first years of his regime, Diem had done remarkably well in establishing a new government against numerous political obstacles, but it cannot be said that he had ever captured the imagination of the Vietnamese as Ho had.

By 1958, the Communist guerrillas in South Vietnam had become more active and what is termed the "second Indochina War"— actually an insurrection that became a revolutionary civil war—began. In this conflict, beyond financing the South Vietnamese and supplying them with arms and economic assistance, the United States soon came to play a more active role by sending military advisers to the Diem government, and later to the successors of that government. Under the rather obscure terms of the Geneva protocols, such advisers were to be limited to a few hundred, but in view of the fact that the Communists had violated the Geneva agreement by leaving their underground agents in the south, the United States felt it was justified in sending additional military personnel to support the South Vietnamese when they asked for it. This step-up, which had begun under the Eisenhower administration, was increased immeasurably by Presidents Kennedy and Johnson. By midsummer of 1965, some 125,000 American military men were in South Vietnam or en route there, including 30,000 Marines; all or part of several Army infantry, airborne and paratroop divisions, and their supporting elements; about 30,000 military advisers and their administrative and supporting contingents; and numerous Marine and Army air force units. The task initially assigned to the American fighting elements was to guard key bases in the northern and central sectors of the country, but they increasingly undertook actual combat assignments, either in conjunction with Vietnamese forces in seeking out the Vietcong, or on their own. While no unified over-all joint command had yet been established, regional joint commands were created, and a more clearly defined American command role seemed to be evolving. It was expected that, if the war continued, the total American commitment would soon approach 200,000 ground forces, or close to the maximum 275,000 the United States had in Korea.

As this influx of combat troops increased, the earlier role of advisers became more anomalous and harder to define. Even before the additional American troops were brought in as defensive or offensive elements, the advisers—only about 5,500 of whom were actually in the field assigned to Vietnamese units from battalions on up through the level of corps—had found it ever harder to draw the line between rendering "advice" and actually participating in the conflict; more and more, the advisers had found themselves engaged in offensive as well as defensive actions as they accompanied Vietnamese troops into battle, but they had all along been handicapped by the lack of any command function. By mid-1965, the advisers began to be assimilated into the new command structure of the American fighting troops being brought into Vietnam, although they still retained their advisory role.

Originally, American pilots were designated to fly helicopters carrying Vietnamese troops into battle and to pilot fighter and bomber planes in the course of instructing Vietnamese; as the pace of the war grew, these functions, too, had invariably brought about a more direct American involvement. As a result, American casualties, while not large in relation to those suffered by the Vietnamese, began to mount, reaching a little over five hundred killed in direct combat by the end of July, 1965.

Though the prime factor in the American build-up was the increased scope and intensity of the Vietcong attacks in the South Vietnamese countryside, the more dramatic aspects of America's greater involvement in the war had been incited by North Vietnamese attacks on American warships in the Gulf of Tonkin and by Vietcong attacks on American installations in the south. These had resulted in the first retaliatory sea and air assaults by the United States on bases in North Vietnam in the summer of 1964 and early in 1965, and they were soon followed by consistent American air attacks on Vietcong bases, supply lines, and troop concentrations in South Vietnam, and on lines of communication in neighboring Laos, along which men and material sent by North Vietnam to the Vietcong regularly passed. By March, 1965, joint American and Vietnamese air raids on Communist bases and on highways, bridges, and radar installations in North Vietnam were taking place almost daily, while the Vietcong in the south were also subjected to steady raids.

As the Vietcong troops demonstrated their ability to attack in battalion and even multi-battalion strength, as they had done toward the end of the war against the French, it seemed more and more apparent that the protracted and tragic conflict in South Vietnam could not be "won," in the final analysis, by either the Communists or the American-backed South Vietnamese forces. Although the war, in the most important sense, was a political one, in military terms the advantage the Vietcong held on the ground was countered for a time by the American-Vietnamese advantage in the air and at sea. However, as the Vietcong grew in strength and the government's fighting capability diminished, the guerrillas' position steadily improved, and even the influx of American troops did not provide the ratio of eight- or ten-to-one superiority to a guerrilla force that military men consider necessary to defeat such an enemy. Furthermore, the instability of the Saigon government, which had begun with the overthrow in November, 1963, of what had become the Diem dictatorship, and had resulted in a series of shaky military and civilian administrations thereafter, remained one of the most significant factors in the inability of the South Vietnamese to prosecute the war more successfully in the countryside. The Americans, themselves rather inexperienced in counter-insurgency, were unable to persuade the South Vietnamese to employ the strategy and tactics of guerrilla warfare. Although the government forces were better equipped with arms and ammunition, modern weapons, and planes, the Vietcong guerrillas seemed to have the far greater will to win—the same sort of fanatic dedication that they had learned from the Chinese Communists, developed against the French, and refined for themselves after 1958.

So long as the United States continued to help the South Vietnamese, however, it seemed likely that the Saigon government would be able to hold out, though by the spring of 1965 there were those who had seriously begun to question this; the inability of the South Vietnamese to rally themselves, especially to establish a stable central government, and the continued inability of the Americans to guide them politically, to avert repeated coups or attempts at coups, and to inspire them militarily created a chronic condition of uncertainty in the country. In the United States, there was growing confusion about our role in South Vietnam, and differences of opinion as to whether we should remain there or get out became intense. A vocal body of public opinion, expressed in Congress, in academic circles, and in the press, seemed to be in favor of pulling out and negotiating the best possible settlement. Other influential leaders, including the administration's policymakers, continued to maintain that the war had to be fully prosecuted and that the air attacks on the north had to be sustained as a legitimate reprisal for Hanoi's direction and support of the guerrilla movement in the south and as a way to force the North Vietnamese to the conference table. A documentation of the alleged direction of the southern guerrillas by the North Vietnamese was issued in February, 1965, in the form of an American White Paper, which purported to prove in considerable detail that Hanoi had continuously infiltrated men and supplies into the south and that it was giving military as well as political orders to the National Liberation Front, the clandestine group in the southern jungle that claimed to be an independent revolutionary body. While there was no doubt that North Vietnam was infiltrating soldiers and supplies into South Vietnam, and that it was probably furnishing the grand strategy, it was a fact that the Vietcong was still very much a southern revolutionary force in its own right, and that many of the arms the guerrillas were using were American weapons being captured from the South Vietnamese forces. However, beginning late in 1964, new Soviet-type arms manufactured in China began flowing into South Vietnam, and these improved weapons, as well as some shipped from Communist Europe, were vital additions to the guerrillas' arsenal.

The likelihood of further commitment of American forces in South Vietnam, and of the extension of the air attacks on North Vietnam, entailed the obvious risk of inciting the Chinese Communists, who for many years had been assisting the North Vietnamese, to take a more active part in the war, especially as China felt its own borders threatened. Though most military experts did not believe the Chinese would enter the war on a large scale because of their essential economic and military weakness, particularly in the air, the mere prospect of such an eventuality, or of the commitment of the North Vietnamese regular army units, was viewed with dismay, not only because it could lead to a world war of nuclear dimensions but because, ever since the Korean War, American military leaders had been strongly against any use of large numbers of American ground forces on the Asian mainland. Ultimately, even though the North Vietnamese showed little willingness to enter negotiations during the summer of 1965, as their Vietcong disciples held the upper hand in South Vietnam, it seemed obvious that some sort of negotiated settlement to end the protracted Vietnamese conflict would have to take place. The climate for negotiation was created in April, 1965, when President Johnson delivered an important address in which he expressed the willingness to enter "unconditional discussions" as a preliminary to negotiations. While making it clear that the United States would not withdraw its support of South Vietnam or enter "meaningless" negotiations, the President expressed an eagerness to support an area-wide Southeast Asia economic recovery program, including the full development of the Mekong River Valley, if the North Vietnamese ceased their aggression in the south and peace was established. The reaction of Hanoi and of the Vietcong, and of other Communist governments, notably the Chinese, to the Johnson offer, and to numerous subsequent overtures made by the President, while not encouraging, nevertheless seemed to indicate that all those concerned were willing to have the hostilities end—but each only on his own specific terms. There were signs that the North Vietnamese were being hurt by bombings, but not enough to lessen their determination to oppose the American presence in South Vietnam; Hanoi constantly reiterated its demand that the Americans cease bombing the north and withdraw their forces from the south before any negotiations could be held.

Beyond the question of negotiations was the larger problem of what might happen afterward—how to guarantee any settlement that might eventually be made and how to protect South Vietnam from renewed Communist subversion in the future. The problem was one that might well be pondered, both in the light of the history of the postwar period, especially the failures of the 1954 Geneva Conference, and of a subsequent one held in 1962 on Laos, and with a view to the dark possibilities of the future. In most respects, it seemed almost impossible to police any kind of settlement in a manner that would preclude an ultimate attempt by the Communists, or at least by Communist-oriented neutralists, to take over all of Vietnam; nor did the outlook for Laos and Cambodia, and eventually for Thailand and Burma, look much better. Too much time had been lost, and the possibilities of creating and sustaining viable nationalist states able to stand on their own feet and resist the impact of Communism, either locally inspired or deriving its inspiration from Communist China, no longer seemed very promising. The best that one might hope for, perhaps, was an eventual settlement of differences between China and the United States, which, in turn, might restrain a new generation of Chinese leaders from imperialist adventures in Southeast Asia. Should that happen, the nations of that region, including a reunified Vietnam, might in time form themselves into a truly neutral bloc. This remained a long-term prognosis, and one about which, in the difficult summer of 1965, it was hard to be sanguine.

Since 1945, the role of the United States in Vietnam, and in all of Southeast Asia, has not, in the author's opinion, been one on which we can pride ourselves. The chance to guide the Asian revolution along legitimate nationalist lines surely existed after the end of the Second World War; our failure to take advantage of it was basically due to ignorance and to our anxiety to disentangle ourselves from situations we did not then regard as vital to our interests. To be sure, we did become embroiled in China, which we had historically considered a vital Asian area of interest, and in 1946 we made an effort to create a coalition government between the Communists and the Nationalists—an attempt that the author, who was in China at the time, felt was essentially futile but one that might have effectively provided time to develop and support bona-fide nationalist movements in Southeast Asia if, again, we had seized the opportunity. Surely one way *not* to encourage the growth of an anti-Communist nationalist movement in Indochina was to support an outworn and despised French colonial regime. This is not to say that the United States could or should have directly involved itself in revolutionary movements in Indochina or elsewhere in Southeast Asia and made them turn out the way we wanted, in American terms; this was as impossible as it was undesirable. But there were many things we might have done, for instance, to help some of the nationalist leaders in what is now the two halves of Vietnam establish sincere dialogues with the French and reach the sort of independent solutions many of them were groping for; had we done so, had we at least tried, with imagination and foresight, we might have helped immeasurably to avoid the two decades of bloodshed, civil war, and disillusion that have followed, and our own prestige in Asia might have been much higher than it is today.

It is because of the many Western failures of omission and commission—failures that do not exonerate those of anti-Communist Vietnamese and other native nationalist leaders—that I have entitled this book "The Lost Revolution." The principal losers, of course, have been the Vietnamese people, some thirty million of them, more or less equally divided between South and North Vietnam. If one includes the period of the Pacific war, during which they were an ostensible part of the Japanese Co-Prosperity Sphere, the Vietnamese have now been involved in war, with all its terrible economic, social, cultural, and psychological consequences, for twenty-five years. The Vietnamese are, in many respects, the most sophisticated and courageous people in Southeast Asia, and the fact that they were never given the opportunity to create a unified nation, with the promise of playing a meaningful role in the world community, stands today as one of the great postwar democratic failures. In this sense, "the lost revolution" is as much an American loss as it is a French one, and the irony therein is obvious, for the United States and France were the two modern nations whose revolutions served to inspire millions of people throughout the world, including the Vietnamese, offering them an alternative to Communist moves to subvert their longing for freedom.

ROBERT SHAPLEN

New York City
August, 1965

THE LOST REVOLUTION

CHAPTER I

∾∽∾

The Return of the French
1945-1946

Saigon in the summer of 1946 had the misleading appearance of a tranquil city. It slumbered in the tropical sun until, in midafternoon, the monsoonal showers cooled it off and left a soft, fresh breeze circulating. Handsome French and graceful Vietnamese women moved along the tree-lined Rue Catinat, drifting in and out of the stylish shops. In the Jardin d'Enfants, in the square in front of the American Consulate, half-clad native children frolicked with their *amahs*. At the Cercle Sportif, the French club, where one might have spent the siesta hours swimming or napping in a comfortable reclining chair, the tennis players arrived for a set or two on the quickly drying courts before the cocktail hour began. But then, as dusk fell, a change occurred; a strange stillness permeated the unfolding darkness, and a sense of tension slowly mounted. If one dined out—at the Red Mill, for instance, an excellent French restaurant on the outskirts of town—one ate in a grille-covered outdoor cage (with a lock on it) erected to ward off grenades; and the Corsican *patron* opened his cage only to the white men he knew, mostly Frenchmen and their wives or mistresses. It was a unique experience to eat some of the finest food in the world in a kind of prison, but one got used to the idea, and as the wine flowed behind the iron bars, there was a

1

feeling almost of coziness. Even the sound of artillery a few miles away in the jungle, or the occasional nearby crackle of rifle fire, did not diminish the warm glow; in fact, the sporadic shooting provided a certain zest to the meal, and the awareness that imminent danger was lurking in the night outside increased the appetite.

The danger was real, for the tranquility of day had given way to nocturnal terror. Under the cover of darkness, members of the Vietminh front, many of whom were daytime peasants, had grabbed their guns and set out to assassinate designated enemies, either French or Vietnamese who were known supporters of the French, in the villages around Saigon or in the city itself. The night before I arrived, fifteen murders had taken place, and this, I discovered, was an average toll. On my first morning, I had surveyed the area in a light plane and had seen scores of burnt-out houses in the villages—this, too, was part of the campaign of terror, and of its inevitable consequence, reprisal. There were already more than fifty thousand French colonial troops in the country, including some twelve thousand members of the famous French Foreign Legion, about a tenth of whom, mostly Germans, had deserted to the Vietminh.

The French by now had made it clear that they would not succumb easily to the Vietminh attempt to keep them from re-establishing their control in Cochin China; the country roads bristled with armed jeeps and reconnaisance cars or trucks, many of which, as well as the fighters and bombers that roamed the skies, still bore "U.S.A." markings, having been shipped in a hurry from the theaters of the Second World War to deal with the situation in Indochina. Even now, at this early date, America was popular neither with the French nor with the Vietminh. The former blamed us for having arranged a deal whereby Chinese Nationalists troops had temporarily occupied Tonkin in the north, where the new Republic of Vietnam, the instrument of the Vietminh, had previously established itself; and the Vietminh naturally resented the use of American equipment to help restore the defeated and discredited French to colonial power in the south.

What had happened, in the short space of a year, to create this confused situation, a situation that would serve as a prelude to at least twenty more years of bitter warfare, first colonial and then fratricidal—a complex conflict in which the United States would become increasingly and inextricably involved?

In the north, immediately after V-J day, events had moved swiftly. On August 19, 1945, a few days after hostilities ended, and even before the arrival of the Chinese forces who were to disarm the Japanese 21st Division, the provisional Vietnam Republic headed by Ho Chi Minh, the creator and unchallenged leader of the Vietminh, had taken over. There had been a few skirmishes with the Japanese, but no substantial effort on their part to interfere with the seating of the new government in Hanoi. Emperor Bao Dai, who had been the prewar puppet ruler of Annam under the French and had briefly served, in the last days of the war, as a Japanese puppet in Tokyo's attempt to unify Cochin China, Annam, and Tonkin, had willingly abdicated and, as a simple private citizen, become a counselor of state to President Ho. In Saigon, on August 25th, six days later, the Vietminh ordered a huge popular demonstration; more than a hundred thousand Vietnamese marched in orderly fashion past the old stucco French government buildings in celebration of the apparent nationalist ascendancy. Harold Isaacs, who was my colleague on *Newsweek* magazine, arrived in Saigon at this time and noted that the Vietnamese seemed to be taking over in the south almost as easily as they had in the north. In his prophetic book, *No Peace for Asia,* Isaacs subsequently wrote:

In the cities and countryside there was order. Markets thrived, utilities and public services continued to function. In government bureaus Annamites [Vietnamese] set about the exciting business of creating a government of their own. There were scarcely any incidents. In all the month of August, by subsequent official French acknowledgement, only one Frenchman was killed in a street clash. The Vietnam government opened wide the prison gates. Thousands of political prisoners came blinking into the light from the sordid dungeons of Saigon and Hue and Hanoi and other cities. . . . It seemed indeed, for a breathless interval, that the new dispensation had come. The Annamites believed that what they had won for themselves the victorious Allies would never take away. "We are convinced," they said in their declaration of independence, "that the Allies who recognized the principles of equality at the conferences of Teheran and San Francisco cannot fail to recognize the independence of Vietnam."

Actually, the situation in the south was considerably more confused politically than it was in the north, where the Vietminh front from the outset had managed to control and dominate a revolutionary and nationalist movement that was compounded of a variety of different parties and factions, not all of which were by any means Communist. In the south, there had been a longer history of left-wing factionalism, and the Vietminh's position was not as strong. It depended for its support chiefly on the Indochinese Communist Party, headed by Tran Van Giau, who had been educated in Moscow and had returned to Cochin China in the early thirties, and on the Advance Guard Youth, a paramilitary Marxist force led by Pham Ngoc Thach. However, since the thirties there had also been an active group of Trotskyists in Cochin China headed by a young intellectual named Ta Thu Thau, who had studied in France. The Trotskyists themselves had soon split into two factions, one of which had gradually co-operated with Giau's Communists in Cochin China while the other, which became more active in the north, had remained anti-Stalinist. To a considerable degree, in this early period, the Indochina Communist Party had operated without the close supervision of Moscow, but after a conference in 1935 in the Portuguese colony of Macao, near Hong Kong, the party re-established its firm links with the Comintern. A year later, when the first period of the Popular Front began in France, the Indochina Communists had joined with more moderate groups legally seeking to redress colonial grievances by appealing to the French Socialist leadership in Paris and its local representatives. For a time, in the Popular Front period, the Trotskyists and the Stalinists had continued to work together in Cochin China, creating joint "action committees" to improve labor conditions, and so on; but then they had split, and as the Stalinists became faction-ridden, the Trotskyists briefly became the dominant left-wing group. After the end of the Popular Front, in 1938, both the Trotskyists and the Stalinists had gone underground. Many of their leaders were jailed, and they had remained in jail during the long war against Japan.

In August, 1945, when the Vietminh, following up on its success in the north, tried to take over in Cochin China, too, it was opposed by the Trotskyists, still headed by Ta Thu Thau, and by various other nationalists and religious groups, including members of the Hoa Hao and Cao Dai sects. These dissident revolutionists organized themselves into a United National Front, which held its own demonstrations in Saigon. The Vietminh, seeking to become the all-embracing nationalist force, as it was up north, had established what it called the Committee of the South, headed by Tran Van Giau, and this Committee took over public buildings and set about establishing a government in Saigon. It recognized the authority of the new Republic of Vietnam in Hanoi, but, for the time being, functioned rather independently. In seeking to foster its nationalist authority, and to win as much worker-peasant popularity as possible, the Committee maintained the position that independence could be won by negotiation. The Trotskyists and the other radical nationalists, including some of the religious sect leaders, did not agree; their views were strengthened when, on September 2nd, a few days after the first British representatives arrived in Saigon to prepare the way for British occupation forces, another tremendous celebration organized by the Vietminh to welcome the Allies resulted in a sudden outburst of shooting, during which several Frenchmen and a number of Vietnamese were killed. The French blamed the Vietnamese and the Vietnamese blamed the French, charging that they had used drunken, still-armed Japanese soldiers as *provocateurs,* which was probably the case; at any rate, as reports spread that the British were planning to bring the French back to power, the Trotskyists denounced as an act of treason the Vietminh's decision to welcome the British troops. The Vietminh thereupon cracked down on the Trotskyists and on the other opposition leaders, breaking up their meetings and forcing them into hiding. A few weeks later, on orders of Tran Van Giau, Ta Thu Thau was murdered, and in the weeks and months that followed, the Vietminh murdered a number of other opposition nationalist leaders.

The Vietnamese Communists in Cochin China had to contend with external as well as internal problems. They suffered from a tremendous sense of isolation. Both Tran Van Giau and Ho Chi Minh admitted that they stood "quite alone" and could not expect help from any quarter, not even from the Russians, who, as Giau complained, seemed to be indulging in "an excess of ideological compromise." The Soviet Union, concentrating on extending its strength through military might in Europe, apparently did not look upon the small Vietnamese Communist movement in Cochin China as serving any useful purpose —not at the moment, anyway. As for the French Communists, the Vietnamese regarded them as "Frenchmen and colonialists first and Communists after," and it was significant that of twenty active French Communists in Saigon in the fall of 1945, only one supported the local Communist movement. A document that the French Communists prepared for their Vietnamese cousins actually warned them not to engage in any "premature adventures" in behalf of independence that "might not be in line with Soviet perspectives," such as an effort by Moscow to obtain the support of France in Europe. It was suggested that the Vietnamese Communists restrain themselves until after the French elections, in October, 1945, when the French Communist Party hoped to win more strength. As a result of these unexpected admonitions, the Vietnamese Communists decided to dissolve themselves as a party and to work, for the time being, as individuals in the Vietminh front. As for the Americans, from whom so much help had been hoped for in the fight for independence, the Vietnamese were reluctantly forced to conclude that these hopes engendered by the gaudy statements in the Atlantic Charter and other documents, and the rolling declarations of American leaders, especially those of President Roosevelt, were just dreams; they would soon be totally blasted by the announcement that the French would be allowed to buy a hundred and sixty million dollars' worth of surplus United States war equipment.

The first British occupation troops, practically all of them Indian, arrived in Saigon on September 12, 1945. They entered a strange emotional and political climate. The Vietminh's Committee of the South was occupying all government buildings and to all intents and purposes was running a government. About five thousand French troops were being confined to barracks by the Japanese, where they had been since they were interned on Tokyo's orders the previous March—there were still seventy thousand armed Japanese in Cochin China. Now the British, under Major General Douglas Gracey, wasted no time in carrying out their mission to "restore order in the south." They threw the Vietminh out of a number of government buildings and took over most of the city's police stations. Within two weeks, they freed and began to rearm the French forces, ultimately giving them twelve thousand automatic weapons. They were in no hurry to disarm the Japanese; in fact, even two months later only five per cent of the seventy thousand Japanese had been disarmed, and many Japanese soldiers were used as a transportation corps to ferry the occupation forces around the country by air and by truck. (There were reports, circulated by the French, that the Japanese had armed the Vietminh and that, under Tokyo orders, they were supporting the Vietminh bid for independence, but these stories were patently untrue. Rumors that large numbers of Japanese soldiers were deserting to the Vietminh were equally false; American intelligence officers in Saigon at the time estimated that, at most, two thousand Japanese deserted and were roving the countryside, and while some were undoubtedly working with the Vietminh, most of them had simply become bandits.)

The end came for the short-lived Vietnamese government in Saigon on September 23rd. Early that morning, some fifteen hundred troops under the command of Colonel H. J. Cedile, who was the new French Commissioner in Cochin China, executed a *coup d'état* against the Committee of the South. Cedile, who had parachuted into Cochin China a month before and formed a nucleus of a hundred and fifty commandos, had been quietly trying to persuade the Committee that the French were determined to welcome the Vietnamese into the proposed Indochina Federation and the French Union, the details of which supposedly were still being worked out in Paris. The Vietnamese remained uninterested; as far as they were concerned, they had declared and proved their competence to maintain their own independence. Now, with the help of the first rearmed French troops, Cedile moved quickly and with cold efficiency to destroy the fledgling Vietnamese administration. He seized the Hotel de Ville, the main government building, and took control of the other government offices not already taken over by the British. In the process, a number of Vietnamese were killed and others were badly beaten. There was some resistance and fighting in the streets, but by midmorning the French tricolor was once more flying from most important buildings.

Parts of the city, however, were still held by groups of Vietnamese, not necessarily revolutionists but members of armed bands, including those of the Binh Xuyen, an underground gangster-like organization. As the French population, numbering about twenty thousand, went wild with joy and insulted, molested, and arrested Vietnamese at random in the downtown area, some of the Vietnamese bands elsewhere in the city struck back and attacked any unarmed French they could find. For two days, there was complete chaos; for the most part, the British and the Japanese simply stood by and allowed events to take their course. When the Vietnamese called a general strike, all commercial activity ceased, and the power and water supplies were cut off. Saigon then became a dead, as well as a barricaded, city. Finally, on October 3rd, a truce was worked out by the British; some of the Committee of the South leaders who had fled into the countryside when the *coup d'état* took place reappeared to take part in discussions, under guarantees given them by General Gracey. They insisted that their independence be fully restored to them, but the French offered only some vague pledges of limited autonomy. Inevitably, the negotiations collapsed, and a week later British and French forces, still with the help of the Japanese, began a campaign to clear the area around Saigon of Vietminh elements. On October 17th, the Vietminh launched a counterattack within Saigon itself that came close to succeeding in its aim of recapturing some government buildings; but the attack was repulsed, and the revolutionists again fled the city, this time for good.

The mission of the British was accomplished. On the surface, at least, the French were back in power in Cochin China and their troops, under General Jacques Philippe Leclerc, the first of many French commanders, were about to launch the fatal adventure of trying to recapture all of Indochina. The long nights of terror had begun.

The French Guard Re-emerges

By mid-1946, the pattern of French reconquest in Cochin China had been pretty well established. Leclerc had been replaced by General Jean Etienne Valluy, but the military policy was firmly fixed, fore-shadowing the whole French campaign; the colonial forces were clearing the roads and occupying narrow strips on either side, and, insofar as they could with the limited number of troops at their disposal, they were dividing small areas of the countryside into squares, within which they sought, for the most part vainly, to clear out the Viet-minh and then spread their control out farther in what was a fore-runner of the "oil slick" theory (to be attempted on a larger scale, without much more success, nearly two decades later by the South Vietnamese Army and the Americans). Then, as now, however, it was the Vietminh (now called the Vietcong) that dominated the rural areas; the guerrillas, the daytime peasants who became nighttime partisans, poorly armed as they were in comparison to the French, were already probing the French outposts strung out along the roads and adjacent to them. For eight long years, the French would follow this defensive strategy, and the theory of the fixed position, of the armed camp, led to the final tragic dénouement of Dienbienphu in May, 1954.

While the French armed forces were attempting to gain military control in Cochin China, the French administration in Saigon was seeking, with somewhat more success, to regain political and economic control of the colony. The chief instruments in accomplishing this were Admiral Thierry D'Argenlieu, the new French High Commissioner in Indochina, and Colonel Cedile, who remained the Cochin China Commissioner. Admiral D'Argenlieu was a Carmelite monk when he wasn't fighting for his country; an imposing, dedicated man, he was imbued with a historic sense of French grandeur on which was now superimposed the goad of injured patriotic pride. At first, D'Argenlieu, and particularly the more conciliatory Cedile, maintained an ambivalent position on the matter of autonomy or independence for the Vietnamese, but they both soon adopted a more inflexible view. They were obviously influenced by the group of old-line colonial administrators in Cochin China, many of whom had been part of the wartime Vichy regime countenanced by the Japanese until close to the end; these men, as well as the commercial class of *colons,* who sought the reascendancy of the Bank of Indochina and the re-estab-

B

lishment of French economic supremacy, especially the reopening of the lucrative rubber plantations, were fast regaining their prewar dominant roles. There was a concomitant native factor: Cochin China had been the first area conquered by the French, and the only one of the Indochinese subdivisions that had become an outright colony—the others were protectorates or kingdom-protectorates—and consequently the Cochin Chinese had always been more malleable than the Vietnamese in other parts of Indochina; they had been most strongly influenced by all aspects of French culture and teaching, and by the whole French social fabric and administrative structure, and they now fell easily into a pattern of postwar puppetry.

Beneath its charm and beauty, Saigon, in these days when I first saw it, was an emotionally torn city. In contrast to the re-emerging old colonial guard were the "new" men, fresh from the French Maquis, who had been sent out to Indochina without any Asian experience. For the most part, they were youngsters in their twenties to whom the Resistance had been their university, its romantic liberation cause their total *raison d'être*. There were also some men in their late thirties and forties, former *fonctionnaires,* journalists, or academicians, with a more solid liberal heritage dating back to the prewar years. These ex-Maquis elements had been assigned to Indochina often because there had been no place for them back home; their liberal ideas about a new French Republic, and about independence for France's former colonies, had been an embarrassment back in Paris, and it was easier to send them abroad, where their views would soon be submerged in a more "practical" or "realistic" climate. Their "re-education" in the resurgent colonial atmosphere of Saigon was painful to watch, and one of my clearest and saddest memories is of the disillusion of this group of men, who had come to believe, in their heroic underground years, that there really would be a new postwar world, and a new France to play a proud part in it.

Night after night, in the sidewalk cafés, they sat over their drinks, shaking their heads in disbelief at what was happening, wondering aloud what cruel fate had sent them here to take part in the shabby reappearance of a discredited empire. Within a short time, despite the pretense as expressed by Cedile that "there never was a gap between the old-timers and the newcomers," a number of these men I knew were forced to resign from their jobs in the new Cochin China administration because they refused to adopt the new line. Others went through the motions of fulfilling their assignments, becoming more apathetic each day, while still others made their compromise and became withdrawn and cynical. After five o'clock, these lost souls sat around the Club de la Presse, an informal and congenial gathering place, and drowned their disillusion in *rhum et citronnade*. They watched, among other things, the slow disintegration of the Saigon press. At first, after the French return, there was a mild form of censorship, but this soon gave way to complete control by the new colonial bureaucracy. Shortly before my arrival, the outspoken French-edited *Justice*, which had supported recognition of the Republic of Vietnam, ceased publication after a band of French soldiers had raided its plant, while two Vietnamese papers, whose views had been no more than moderate on the question of independence, were indefinitely suspended and never reappeared. There remained three reactionary dailies, part Vietnamese and part French, and they firmly espoused the new policy. In many respects, they were worse than the most conservative papers in Paris. When Léon Blum, the Socialist leader, went to Washington to negotiate a loan for France, one of them described him as "a disgusting gypsy."

Even before they signed the March, 1946, agreement recognizing Ho Chi Minh's Republic of Vietnam in the north, the French had begun to play upon the natural anti-Tonkinese sentiments of the Cochin China population. Parades were staged in Saigon, and hired coolies, directed by megaphones, marched through the streets with placards reading, "COCHINCHINE POUR LES COCHINCHINOIS." In mid-February, Commissioner Cedile appointed a Consultative Council of twelve members to take the place of the prewar Colonial Council; four of the twelve were Frenchmen, and the remaining were trusted Vietnamese, all but one being naturalized French citizens. In mid-April, the issue of Cochin China versus Tonkin, really the issue of renewed French presence versus independence for Vietnam, came to a head at a conference called in the resort town of Dalat, north of Saigon, in the southern part of Annam. This conference was to precede a meeting in France that was to spell out the March accord. In many respects, Dalat proved to be more important than the latter meeting, which opened in Fontainebleau, near Paris, early in July, for it was at Dalat that the wide gulf between the French and the Vietnamese became clear and the stage for the Indochina war was really set.

Essentially, what the French sought to do at Dalat was to define their idea of the proposed Indochina Federation. What they envisaged was the joining of the central part of Indochina, including some tribal areas, with Cochin China, tied closely together with Cambodia and Laos into a combination of shadow republics and controlled kingdoms, which the northern Republic of Vietnam could or could not join, as it saw fit. This amounted to an attempt to isolate the Vietnamese in the north and to force them into line by applying economic pressure; though the north was rich in minerals, Cochin China was the richest rice area. While they continued to pay lip service to the pledge of holding a referendum that might bring all the Vietnamese parts of Indochina together, the French insisted no such vote could be held until the guerrilla resistance ceased in Cochin China. More significant was the French proposal that their High Commissioner, who would be the head of the Federation, should remain in charge of all federal services, execute all laws, and operate in effect like a prewar Governor General, except that he would now have some native advisers. An Assembly of sixty—ten for each of the five Indochina subdivisions, Tonkin, Annam, Cochin China, Cambodia, and Laos, and ten representing "French interests"—would have some limited budgetary and legislative functions. In even this restricted chosen body, the Republic of Vietnam, consisting of Tonkin and part of Annam, would be outvoted.

The representatives of the Vietnamese Republic at Dalat, headed by Vo Nguyen Giap, a lawyer and onetime teacher who was to become a brilliant military leader in the war against the French, insisted that they be allowed to run their own customs and coin their own money, and they also demanded a degree of military independence from France. In cultural matters, the north Vietnamese were willing to recognize the right of the French to maintain a vital interest in Indochina, but they insisted on owning their own colleges and having the right to determine language requirements in secondary schools. As things turned out, nothing was settled at Dalat, and this was in part a reflection of prior French haziness about what the Indochina Federation and the French Union were really supposed to be. Perhaps more importantly, the failure at Dalat was due to the success the French felt they were already having in recovering their position in Cochin China. Even so, Ho Chi Minh, who was in a mood of compromise, a mood he maintained in the face of rising opposition within his own ranks through all that fateful summer of 1946, commented hopefully when the conference ended, "We agree on the principle of the creation of a federal organism, providing it allows the members of the federation to prosper freely while remaining interdependent," and he spoke of the continued willingness of the Vietnamese to make concessions, especially economic ones, in the interest of "collaboration with France." But, as Ellen Hammer, author of *The Struggle for Indochina* and one of the foremost students of this period, wrote, "It was difficult to be optimistic after Dalat. The conference had only shown up more clearly the basic disagreements between the two peoples. Vo Nguyen Giap wept when it was over."

The final blow came on June 1st, just as Ho Chi Minh left for France for a vacation in advance of the conference at Fontainebleau. On that date, Admiral D'Argenlieu sponsored the creation of the "Provisional Government of Cochin China." D'Argenlieu declared that the creation of the government was a necessary answer to the continuing Vietminh terrorism, and the French argued that, after all, Cochin China was doing nothing more than what Tonkin had done before, in establishing the provisional Republic of Vietnam. But all independence-minded Vietnamese saw the move for what it was—an effort to renounce the past pledges the French had made for a referendum and to torpedo the Fontainebleau conference before it began. The President of the provisional Republic was Dr. Nguyen Van Thinh, a physician and a French citizen, on whose head the Republic of Vietnam had already placed a price as a traitor. When I arrived in Saigon, the French were busily engaged in the fiction of promoting the new republic. The Consultative Council previously set up had grown to a membership of forty-two, all of whom were appointed by Dr. Thinh, with the approval of Admiral D'Argenlieu. It consisted of fourteen Frenchmen and twenty-eight Vietnamese, who were either French citizens or of clear French persuasion—mostly French-trained professional people, doctors, pharmacists, dentists, lawyers, and so on. The pretense that they had actually been elected was maintained by the French, since some of them had initially been nominated by groups of village notables in "safe" districts where the terrorists were not too active. If the Council members did not openly represent the Bank of Indochina or the big commercial trusts, neither, by any stretch of imagination, did they represent the people of Cochin China, the predominant peasant population or the workers. Dr. Thinh told me, however, that they expressed "the natural anti-Tonkinese sentiments of the south."

Dr. Thinh was the first of a long line of pitiful postwar figures through whom the French sought to maintain their rule in Cochin China. A tiny man, he spent most of the time in his home, a small place that looked like a gingerbread house; his office in one of the old colonial palaces was a bare room with a single glass-topped desk, on which, when I visited him, there were no papers—nothing. He wore a white suit. He spoke hopefully of being able to hold elections in the villages as soon as possible for "headmen," who would in turn elect members of a new Council, which would sit until a new Parliament of a hundred members could be more broadly elected. Dr. Thinh spoke critically of the government in the north and said it was impossible for Cochin China to think of federating with it. He spoke vaguely, like the French, of each of the former Indochina areas becoming "autonomous" under some sort of continuing French protection, but then he added, in a brief burst of authority, that both from an economic and a social aspect French laws and French ways were no longer applicable to an Oriental society. "A suit that is made for a tall man is not made for a small man," he said, with a smile that seemed almost self-mocking, as if he were looking in a mirror. Dr. Thinh's remarks were prophetic. Four months later, in November, after telling members of his Cabinet the night before that "I am heartbroken to have led you on this adventure," the little doctor hanged himself.

A Vietminh Agent Speaks Out

During this period, when the French were setting up their puppet regime in Cochin China, the Vietminh was still attempting to consolidate itself as the dominant force in the resistance movement. In the early months of 1946, it was continuing to receive some opposition from members of the radical United National Front, and the Hoa Hao and Cao Dai religious sects. And the Communists, still under the leadership of Tran Van Giau, were still employing harsh methods to crush these rebellious elements, murdering some and terrorizing others into silence. At the time of the Dalat Conference, the Vietminh government in Hanoi sent a top organizer named Nguyen Binh to Cochin China to co-ordinate the resistance movement in the south, and he succeeded, in a matter of months, in establishing general unity, although some discordant elements remained. At this time, according to estimates I was given in Saigon, the guerrillas in Cochin China had about twenty thousand weapons of various kinds, mostly old French rifles and some Japanese guns. They operated in groups of ten or twelve men, and had already created small suicide squads, called *can tu*, which usually carried grenades and concentrated on hit-and-run tactics against French detachments or outposts. By the summer of 1946, the guerrillas were using terrorists in Saigon fairly regularly, and most of the cafés and restaurants, like the Red Mill, had put up some kind of protection. It was considered wise to choose seats in the rear of such places, where the grenades, frequently tossed by teen-age youngsters dashing past on bicycles, were less likely to penetrate.

In these days in Saigon, it was not difficult to make contact with members of the Vietminh, although a rendezvous had to be arranged discreetly and careful precautions had to be taken, especially as the colonial *sûreté* and the French military extended their patrols around the city. I had asked a French friend of mine, one of the disillusioned ex-Maquis whose sense of romanticism outweighed his caution, to arrange a meeting with a Vietminh agent, and one evening, at the Club de la Presse, he whispered to me that it was all set. At eight-thirty the following morning, we climbed into a pair of cyclos, bicycle-propelled rickshas, and rolled down Rue Catinat, past the cafés and the fine perfume and jewelry shops that were being unlocked and opened for business. As we moved away from the business area, the shops were replaced by the wide-windowed, rose-colored stucco homes and spacious gardens of the French residential sections. Overhead, in the azure sky, French fighter planes roared out on their daily anti-guerrilla strafing runs. When we approached the east suburbs of the city, the comfortable-looking homes gave way to wood and straw huts and the paved streets turned into dirt roads.

In the dusty yards in front of the huts, skinny, bare youngsters played in the dirt; sleeping infants hung backward over the shoulders of their mothers in the custom of the East, while others were being suckled. Cats and dogs, and even pigs and goats, sniffed among the huts and clusters of people. We passed an outdoor native market and smelled the pungent blends of raw meats and fowl and ripe fruits and vegetables. After a half-hour ride, my French companion directed our cyclo drivers to make a few false turns, and we then debarked in front of a small Vietnamese café with a tiny stone terrace. "Wait," my friend whispered, and he ambled off down the road.

He came back fifteen minutes later, still alone. "C'est bien," he said. "They'll be right here—they're in one of the huts a few hundred yards away." A short time later, a young girl accompanied by a man who looked anywhere from twenty-five to forty years old strolled by, nodded at my friend, and joined us as if they had just happened to be walking past and had recognized us. The man was about five feet six and was dressed completely in black. He wore a shirt and trousers of cotton and silk called au baba in Vietnamese, roughly translatable as dress pajamas. As soon as he sat down, he brought from his pocket a tin of Burley & Bright tobacco and lit a pipe. The girl, who was just under five feet tall and looked very young, had on a faded white blouse and black slacks, both of which were clean but well-worn, and she was wearing two tiny, round, low-quality jade earrings.

Brushing the flies away, we began our conversation. I asked questions in English, which my friend translated into French for the man; the girl spoke only Vietnamese. The man explained, with a warm and apologetic smile, that he could not give us their real names for reasons of security. He offered the alias of Hoang Thanh Kieu and said he was thirty-nine years old. The girl's name he gave as Nguyet Anh, and he said she was seventeen. Officially, he said, he was a member of one of the secret Vietminh village committees a few kilometers from Saigon, but actually he took part in some military actions against the French, and he had actively joined in or witnessed about a dozen ambush attacks in the last few months. He described the girl as a former Vietminh Red Cross worker who was now a liaison agent, or message carrier.

Men like Hoang and young girls like Nguyet, who once they became Vietminh members almost never saw their families again, for mutual protection, were in most respects typical of the many thousands of underground workers fighting the French in Cochin China. Sitting across from Hoang on this particular morning, and watching him as he talked and puffed at his pipe, I was immediately struck by the combination of his devotion to the cause, for which he seemed quite ready to die, and the quality in him of restrained fatalism. The latter served to temper his fanaticism without weakening his idealistic fervor or his reservoir of confidence. In fact, the more he spoke, the more convinced he seemed of the inevitability of his movement's eventual success.

Hoang told me he had been living in Cochin China for ten years and that for the last three he had had his own small farm near Saigon, where he was staying part of the time with his second wife and their two children. With a little rice, some vegetables, a few chickens, and some fruit trees, they had barely enough to get by, especially since his Vietminh activities kept him from farming. Whenever he came into the city, he made it a point never to eat or sleep in the same place twice in a row. His usual practice was to check in with an underground friend in a different hut each night, and he never stayed in Saigon more than one week at a stretch. The rest of the time, he wrote and distributed propaganda among the people of his village and other villages nearby, except for the occasional sorties he made with the Vietminh troops.

When I asked him if he would trace his revolutionary career for me, he smiled and the hidden wrinkles in his face came suddenly to life. There were twenty children in his family, he began, of whom he was the eldest, and he had been born in the northern Annam province of Thanh Hoa, where his father, an educated man, worked as a station-master for the French railway. The seeds of discontent were probably sown in his soul at the age of two, Hoang said, when his father had a fight with his French employers over his refusal to pay a special "tax," which amounted to a bribe to keep his job. So his father quit, went out into the country to become a rice grower, and joined an early secret nationalist organization called Van Thanh, which was more of a cultural group dedicated to the study of letters and to philosophic discussion than a cell of political action. Actually, Hoang explained, with a touch of revolutionary smugness, the members of the Van Thanh were merely ultranationalist patriots who had no sense of democracy and at bottom revered the old Annam monarchy. "At least it was a beginning, because they started to find out about themselves and ask questions," Hoang said patronizingly.

When Hoang was four years old, his father's rice fields were inundated by a great flood. The family moved north to Hanoi, where the father became a watchmaker and Hoang began going to school, studying French and arithmetic in the next few years. As he grew older, he learned a little about watchmaking and helped his father in the shop, but it was not until he was seventeen and left home to go to work on a farm in North Annam that he acquired any real political consciousness. As he came to this part of his story, Hoang looked at me intently across the café table and bent forward, lowering his voice. His face literally seemed to grow darker with reminiscent anger, and even the girl, who had understood nothing except by implication, leaned over and watched him as he tapped a finger fitfully against the metal table top. He was describing to us the first time he was beaten up. It had happened one day after work, he said, when he had felt like taking a walk through the orchards instead of returning immediately to the laborers' quarters. His French boss intercepted him and asked him what he was doing, and when Hoang replied truthfully, the man struck him over the back with a heavy stick and sent him stumbling almost senseless to the coolie shack. About this time, he also began hearing stories of the bad treatment of coolies on a big French coffee plantation a few miles away, of how they had been conscripted from far-off places without being told for what, of the over-crowded and filthy conditions under which they lived, and the sixteen or eighteen hours they worked each day, beginning at three in the morning. "I occasionally met some of these people, or their friends, in the nearby village," Hoang said, "and I heard of the savage beatings which were a matter of custom on such plantations. The coolies there were treated like animals. Naturally, I wanted to see the injustices removed." These events seemed to have become so real and permanent a part of Hoang's life that he trembled as he spoke of them.

When he was twenty-one, in 1929, he went on, he joined the VNQDD—the Vietnam Quoc Dan Dang, or People's Fatherland Front. This was the largest and most active nationalist organization in Indochina until the formation of the Vietminh front in 1939. Although still relatively amorphous, it had dropped the cultural trimmings of its discussion-club predecessors and was wholeheartedly dedicated to correcting the evils of French colonial rule, and it was one of the first groups that were prepared to use force—usually the weapon of assassination—to attain its ends. In 1930, when Hoang had returned to Hanoi and started writing his first propaganda tracts, he was living with a friend who was arrested one day by the French police for having tossed a grenade at a public meeting. Hoang himself was taken into custody for "suspicious activity." He was put in the Hanoi jail for three years; he was never tried, although the sûreté questioned him repeatedly about his VNQDD accomplices. When he refused to divulge anything, he was beaten on the soles of his feet with sticks by the half-caste and Indian guards at the prison. There were also times when he was suspended in the air upside down and water was poured in his nostrils to make him talk. Finally released, he resumed his propagandizing for Vietnamese freedom, but he had to be doubly careful because the number of French police had increased and he was by now a marked revolutionist. Sometimes, at night, he would walk the patrolled streets of Hanoi for an hour or more before finally shaking off someone he knew was a spy or a member of the secret police.

Anyone caught was subjected to torture or was killed outright.

Two of Hoang's friends were machine-gunned to death on one occasion in Annam for leading a coolie demonstration, and another time four village VNQDD leaders were dragged to death behind a bus for miles along a bumpy dirt road. Hoang's recitation of these events was all the more poignant and real for me because I had spoken with Frenchmen in Saigon who sadly admitted abuses that had gone on in years past. I had heard of whole villages being wiped out in reprisal for the acts of one or two patriotic individuals. Despite his nationalist zeal, however, Hoang grew disillusioned when the Japanese swarmed into Indochina in 1940 because many VNQDD members were not averse to trading in rice and other goods with the new enemies, who, as far as Hoang was concerned, were no better than the French, despite their promises of co-prosperity and ultimate independence for the Vietnamese.

By 1944, Hoang had stopped attending VNQDD meetings, and he eventually dropped out of the party completely. After the death of his first wife, he returned to Cochin China and worked as an itinerant laborer in villages near Saigon. Once in a while, he would come into the city by bicycle or in a *boîte d'allumettes,* a small horse-drawn carriage meaning "matchbox." Once, he almost got into serious trouble with the dreaded *kempetai,* the Japanese police, when he saw some white war prisoners he thought were Dutch being marched along the Saigon waterfront. When the procession was halted at an intersection, Hoang found himself standing next to one of the prisoners. Suddenly overwhelmed by a feeling of pity, he held a cigarette in his hands behind his back for the man to take. One of the *kempetai* saw him and he was dragged away to the military jail. He was held there for four days and questioned about his activities. Several times he was slapped in the face by his Japanese inquisitors, who kept him during the day in an open pen under the broiling sun, but finally he was let go when he convinced them he had not been trying to help the Allied cause but had only been offering relief to a suffering fellow man. After this incident, Hoang stayed pretty much in the village where he was eventually able to buy his own small farm.

As Hoang got further into his story, he grew more and more intense and his voice became louder, so that my friend, sitting at his side, had to nudge him several times and tell him to quiet down. By now, two or three other men were sitting in the café and regarding our group with interest. When we pointed them out to Hoang, he glanced at them and said he thought they were all right and there was nothing to worry about. As we ate lunch, Hoang continued his account more quietly. Although he had quit the VNQDD, Hoang emphasized that he remained a passionate nationalist, and when the amalgam Vietminh front began to take shape early in 1945, he joined it. At first, it was a loosely organized group of men who met informally. Gradually, however, it became the source of a new flow of nationalist propaganda, expressing the universal disappointment at the "freedom" that the Japanese had offered but not introduced, and after a few months some of its members showed up with revolvers or guns. By March, 1945, when the Japanese did away with the puppet French administration and took over themselves with the help of Bao Dai and other Vietnamese puppets, Hoang was writing propaganda tracts fast and furiously again and having them mimeographed or printed—on ancient flat-bed presses hidden in farmhouses—and distributed surreptitiously all over Cochin China. He was still doing this when the war ended in August.

On August 25th, Hoang was among those who took part in the parade organized by the Vietminh in Saigon, and he marched past the old French palaces brandishing the new Vietnamese flag—a yellow star on a red field. After the parade, Hoang returned to his village, where he became one of its underground administrators. He was in Saigon again on September 23rd, when the French executed their *coup d'état* against the month-old Vietminh regime, and after that he stayed in the city four months, hiding out by day in the hut of a friend in the suburbs, where he pounded out fresh propaganda aimed at arousing the people against what was now termed the dual treachery of the British and the French. He still regarded the Americans as friends, although in an increasingly dim and distant way, somewhat like angels who had failed to keep an appointment. For the first time, Hoang now had a gun, an American .45, which his friend claimed to have bought from a Chinese. "Everyone—all of us—had now become combatants," Hoang said.

One night in early October, Hoang got to use his gun for the first time. Five kilometers from Saigon, near the village of Go Vap, the British had installed some Gurkha troops, who, according to the Vietminh, were looting while ostensibly searching for members of the underground. On the dirt road leading into the village, the Gurkhas had established a guard post alongside an ancient pagoda. Just at dusk on this particular evening, as the sun was dipping over the paddies, two groups of fifteen Vietminh fighters attacked the post with light guns and grenades. They were able to make only one solid thrust before the fifty Gurkhas on duty, well-armed with automatic rifles, turned them back. The Vietminh attempt was led by two grenade-throwing members of the *can tu*, the underground's death volunteers. Hoang recalls firing his gun from the cover of a nearby paddy ditch, but the counterattack came so swiftly that he and the men with him had to withdraw without ascertaining what damage, if any, they had caused. Two of the Vietminh were killed and three wounded, and one of the dead was one of Hoang's best friends. A few nights later, Hoang went out again, on an ambush of some trucks carrying Gurkha reinforcements to an area east of Saigon. This time, Hoang accompanied three members of the *can tu* who were to toss grenades at the passing trucks from the side of the road.

"It was a very dark night, without stars," he recounted, "and the trucks were late in coming, although we had had word when they had left Saigon. Finally, we heard them from far off and saw their headlights glimmer on the road. We crouched down in the gully where we were hiding, and when the first truck came by, our *can tu* fighters threw about six grenades up at it. There was a lot of explosion and great shouts and cries. By the time the next truck—it must have been about fifty yards behind—caught up, we had escaped over the paddies. It was impossible to tell for certain, but I am sure we must have killed quite a few."

As the fighting in the south grew increasingly violent and General Leclerc's troops moved farther out along the roads into the countryside, Hoang told me, he used to watch the flames billow into the dark tropic sky at night when the French were burning the hide-outs of *les terroristes*. "I used to sit in front of my door with my wife," he said, "and smoke my pipe, and suddenly we would see a burst of orange light shoot up and then die down again, first in one direction and then in another. There was a terrible stillness to the air, and a dry smell, and all over the village there would be other families of Vietnamese silently watching, too. Very little was ever said." I asked Hoang to tell me of the biggest engagement in which he had taken part. "In January, 1946, the Vietminh headquarters for the eastern part of Cochin China were on the island of Au Phu Dong, in the Saigon River near here," he began. "This island is about four miles long and a mile wide and is covered with cocoa trees and water palms. We had a group of sixteen hundred men and women there, including part of the Red Cross, of which Nguyet"—he motioned at the girl still sitting quietly at the table—"was a member. On the morning of the fifteenth, at about seven, we ran out of our houses when we suddenly heard whooshing noises overhead. At first we didn't know what it was; it was the first time we had ever heard mortar. The shelling went on for two hours at intervals and then a small plane came over and flew low, and we knew they had spotted us. As quickly as we could, we got together the women and children and old people and took them to the mainland across a temporary bridge we had built. About four hundred remained, but only half of us had any arms. Just before noon, we could see lots of small boats being lined up in the river, and an hour later they began moving down toward us. When they were a hundred yards away, the firing began. They were Gurkhas again, and they were using machine guns and rifles. We stayed down in trenches in the brush and held our fire as long as we could because we were so short on ammunition. There must have been about a thousand of them, but after half an hour of wild shooting they retired back upriver without landing. We considered ourselves lucky. If they had known more about how to handle their boats and had not tried to land on the wrong side of the island, we would have been finished. This was one of the biggest mass engagements we fought. The next day we continued to evacuate the island, carrying out our wounded by sampan. Since then, the French have occupied Au Phu Dong several times, but they have never kept any troops there, so our people keep on coming back. All the houses are now destroyed and there are only huts left."

As Hoang talked of these events, his voice was almost matter-of-fact and calm and not nearly as loud or emotional as it had been when he was telling of the abuses his people had suffered. He seemed to consider it perfectly normal and natural that once the French and British had ousted the peacefully instituted Vietnamese government in Saigon, the Vietnamese had the right to take matters into their own hands and fight back in any way they could. "You see," he said, "this is not just a matter of a sudden conspiracy. We are like a spring that has been sat upon for nearly a hundred years and now has been released. Acts of 'terrorism' for us have become a part of war, although we do not approve of throwing grenades so that innocent people are hurt or killed. Nevertheless, the people of Indochina, despite mistakes we may make, support us because they will not accept the return of the French. This is true of the young people and the old ones. Children of ten and twelve are even trusted by us as liaison agents. Women help in our Red Cross and troop kitchens. Men who are too old to fight, or too ill, can often help by spying, or just by raising rice on their farms."

Hoang stopped talking and mopped his brow with his handkerchief. It had become oppressively hot in the café. As we were silent a moment, two Vietnamese approached and sat down at the table next to ours. They smoked cigarettes and drank small glasses of orange juice, and they kept staring at us so that Hoang looked back at them. Finally, he leaned over. "I am not sure about those two," he whispered. "Perhaps we had better go." My French friend suggested a split departure. Hoang and the girl arose first and we shook hands all around, pretending goodbyes. Then they left. Ten minutes later, with the pair of Vietnamese still at the table alongside, my friend and I got up and went out. Making sure we were not being followed, we strolled leisurely around the block and continued on for two more blocks, where we found Hoang and Nguyet in the back room of a small frame house. The room was furnished only with a decrepit-looking wooden table and a few straight-backed chairs. Hoang sat at the table writing. The girl lay on a straw mat on the floor, her eyes closed, with one knee drawn up, but as we came in she looked up and smiled. A small boy brought four cups of steaming tea and we all sat down. I asked about the girl, who throughout our four-hour conversation had sat immobile in the café, understanding little or nothing but seeming, by the delicate flickers of expression on her oval face, to have comprehended a great deal. Now, when she spoke in Vietnamese, it was in a soft, shy voice that could hardly be heard, and her deep brown eyes darted from one of us to the other. She said that her brother had been killed the year before as a Vietminh partisan. As she said this, she brought out from her dress a picture of herself with him. Although he was nineteen when he died, he looked pathetically young and small. Hoang explained Nguyet's duties to me. "She is really a runner now," he said. "Sometimes she travels eighty miles in five days, walking through the wild panther regions of the Moi country in Annam. There is no transportation—she has to walk. Usually she goes barefoot because she has only the one pair of shoes she is wearing and one extra dress. That, you see, is her dowry."

We had more tea and in a short time my French friend and I got up to go. We walked, in the gathering dusk, halfway back to the center of the city before we found two cyclos. As we rode along, a light breeze began to play about our moist faces. It was siesta time but we found a café, where we stopped for a drink. We did not talk much about where we had been, and I did not see Hoang and Nguyet again, but some days later my friend, who seemed to know a great deal about what the Vietminh was up to—not surprisingly, he was shipped back to France a few weeks later—told me that Hoang had returned to his village and that the girl had left for the north on a courier mission. "She told Hoang to please say goodbye to the American," my friend said.

I have often wondered what happened to Hoang and Nguyet. They were typical of the early Vietminh, in the days when the Communists, though they already dominated the movement in both the north and the south, had not yet succeeded in eliminating all the non-Communist nationalist elements that had joined the broad resistance front. By now, if Hoang is still alive, the chances are that in the normal course of events he would have been expelled from the Vietminh ranks because, as an ex-member of the VNQDD and a non-Communist, he would certainly have come under suspicion. It may be that he embraced Communism and survived, but I somehow doubt it, for I came to know many men like Hoang through the years, ardent nationalists who in 1945 and 1946 gravitated naturally to the Vietminh because it was the most active dynamic center of attraction. It is harder to guess what might have happened to Nguyet. She may have married and settled in what has since become Vietcong territory in the south, or, after the 1954 partition of Vietnam, she may have drifted back to the north. Somehow, more than in the case of Hoang, I have the feeling that she may have become a fullfledged Communist, perhaps even one of the female cadres serving with a Vietcong platoon in the south today. At any rate, I doubt that if she is still around, she would be solicitous enough in 1965 to "say goodbye to the American."

CHAPTER II

∽ॐ∾

Ho Chi Minh—the Untried Gamble

If the relationship between the Americans and the Vietminh in Cochin China was never more than a tentative one, it was much closer in the north, both in the months preceding the end of the war and in the period immediately afterward. There are moments in history when certain events, however obscure and fragmentary they may seem in retrospect, nevertheless serve as an endless source of speculation: *if* they had been approached in another way, *if* they had been allowed to run their course, would the whole chain of events that followed have perhaps been different? There is certainly some reason to believe that this might have been true about the relations between Ho Chi Minh and a number of Americans in 1945 and 1946, and, more significantly, about Ho's relations with a small group of French politicians and diplomats. It is easy now to dismiss these events and their meaning as unimportant if one assumes that the Communists, and Ho in particular, never had any other intention than to create a Communist state in Vietnam. However, in the opinion of those who, with varying degrees of political sophistication, lived through this early postwar period and helped form part of its history, such broad assumptions are over-simplifications of what was a highly tenuous and complicated set of political circumstances.

I have always shared the belief of many, if not most, observers who were in Indochina at the time that a serious mistake was made by both the French and the Americans, especially by the dominant French policymakers in Paris, in not dealing more realistically with Ho in 1945 and 1946, when there was a strong possibility that he might have been "Titofied" before Tito and Titoism were ever heard of; that the whole course of events might thereby have been altered and a great deal of bloodshed averted; and that today a unified Vietnam, even under some form of left-wing leadership, might have been the bulwark of a neutral bloc of Southeast Asian states seeking, above all, to avoid Chinese Communist domination. Some of the highest American officials have privately told me, in recent years, that they now believe the gamble with Ho should have been taken; in fact, a considerable number of them are again talking about Vietnam becoming a Southeast Asian Yugoslavia, a possibility that seems to me now rather remote. History, contrary to the popular belief, seldom does repeat itself, and second chances are seldom offered. It is one of the particular tragedies of American postwar policy that so many first chances have been missed.

There are many facets to the story of Ho's relations with the West during and after the Second World War. Let us start with the somewhat naïve but at the same time revealing account of a former young lieutenant in the United States Army—I shall have to refer to him only as John—who in May, 1945, parachuted into Ho's jungle headquarters near the village of Kim Lung in northern Tonkin on a mission to establish an underground that would help Allied personnel escape to freedom. Kim Lung lies on the edge of a heavy rain forest, thickly underlaid by brush. Amid sugar-loaf formations of mountains lie tiny valleys, and it was in one of these, near a small stream halfway up a tall hill, that Ho Chi Minh's camp, consisting of four huts, lay sequestered. Each of the huts was twelve feet square, set four feet off the ground on bamboo stakes, and Ho's was as bare as the others.

In this crude revolutionary cradle, deep in Japanese territory, John had the unique experience of living and working with Ho for several months. He found Ho completely co-operative in lending the support of his guerrillas for scouting and raiding parties, including one to rescue some French internees near the China border. John used his portable radio to put Ho in preliminary touch with French negotiators who were in Kunming, China, and who would soon be debating Indochina's postwar future with Ho in Hanoi, but John himself played a more immediate role in Vietnamese affairs by informally helping Ho frame a Declaration of Independence.

"He kept asking me if I could remember the language of our Declaration," John says. "I was a normal American, I couldn't. I could have wired up to Kunming and had a copy dropped to me, of course, but all he really wanted was the flavor of the thing. The more we discussed it, the more he actually seemed to know about it than I did. As a matter of fact, he knew more about almost everything than I did, but when I thought his demands were too stiff, I told him anyway. Strange thing was he listened. He was an awfully sweet guy. If I had to pick out one quality about that little old man sitting on his hill in the jungle, it was his gentleness."

He and John exchanged toasts and shared stewed tiger livers. John now admits his naïveté in being ready to believe that Ho was not a Communist. But even if he was, John felt certain that Ho was sincere in wanting to co-operate with the West, especially with France and the United States. Some of Ho's men impressed John less. "They go charging around with great fervor shouting 'independence,' but seventy-five per cent of them don't know the meaning of the word," he wrote in his diary. John still has two letters in English Ho sent him in the jungle. One of them, written soon after the Japanese surrender, when the Vietminh was about to seize control of the nationalist movement, reads as follows:

DEAR LT. [John],
I feel weaker since you left. Maybe I'd have to follow your advice—moving to some other place where food is easy to get, to improve my health. . . .
I'm sending you a bottle of wine, hope you like it.
Be so kind as to give me foreign news you got.
. . . Please be good enuf to send to your H.Q. the following wires.

1. Daiviet [an anti-Vietminh nationalist group] plans to exercise large terror against French and to push it upon shoulder of VML [Vietminh League]. VML ordered 2 millions members and all its population be watchful and stop Daiviet criminal plan when & if possible. VML declares before the

world its aim is national independence. It fights with political & if necessary military means. But never resorts to criminal & dishonest act.

Signed—NATIONAL LIBERATION COMMITTEE
OF VML

2. National Liberation Committee of VML begs U.S. authorities to inform United Nations the following. We were fighting Japs on the side of the United Nations. Now Japs surrendered. We beg United Nations to realize their solemn promise that all nationalities will be given democracy and independence. If United Nations forget their solemn promise & don't grant Indochina full independence, we will keep fighting until we get it.

Signed—LIBERATION COMMITTEE OF VML
Thank you for all the troubles I give you. . . . Best greetings!

Yours sincerely, Hoo [sic]

What spells the difference between 1945 and 1965, between John's jungle love feast with Ho Chi Minh—the vast prestige America then enjoyed in Asia—and the complex tragedy of the war in Vietnam today, in which Americans are engaged in bombing Ho's country? Those who insist that we should have tried to win Ho to our side maintain this even though they were aware of the fact that he had never wavered from a straight Marxist-Leninist course. Despite his orthodox ideological convictions (or perhaps because they were so orthodox), and because Indochina was a long way from Stalin's Moscow, Ho had already written his own unique revolutionary case history. He was, at this time, less a potential apostate than a kind of old Bolshevik maverick, a last Marxist Mohican in the anti-colonial wilderness of Southeast Asia. If it appears that he simply bewitched a handful of Americans in an atmosphere of dangerous and rollicking camaraderie late in the war and the months afterward, there is considerable more evidence than John's alone to substantiate the theory that Ho meant what he said, that he very much wanted the friendship of liberal Americans and liberal Frenchmen, with whose help he hoped to steer a moderate course to Vietnamese freedom. Was it only a game he was playing, as a superb actor, and did he just use this small group of foreign friends to further his own burning cause in Moscow's image? There is enough proof of his sincerity to doubt this over-simplified conclusion. Not only was Moscow far off, with a record of having done little to help Ho concretely in the difficult years gone by, but, significantly, Communist China did not yet exist. Who, then, more than the Americans, professing themselves to be ardently against colonialism in the projected postwar world, were in a position to help him win liberty from France and simultaneously ward off Chinese penetration?

Official wartime American policy had been alternately positive and vague about Indochina. President Roosevelt had obtained the tentative approval of Stalin and Chiang Kai-shek for a postwar Indochina trusteeship, though both had expressed themselves as favoring ultimate independence for the Vietnamese. Churchill's reaction to the trusteeship proposal had been negative, and Roosevelt had chided him as an old imperialist. Roosevelt had been somewhat ambivalent himself, however, when it came to doing anything to pave the way for Vietnam's independence. In October, 1944, he had told Secretary of State Cordell Hull that "we should do nothing in regard to resistance groups in Indochina," and when a Free French mission to Kandy, Ceylon, sought help from the Allied Southeast Asia Command, Roosevelt gave orders that "no American representatives in the Far East, whether civilian or military, are authorized to make any decisions on political questions with the French or anyone else."

The "anyone else" presumably included Ho Chi Minh, although Roosevelt may never even have heard of him. Ho had long been a man of mystery and many names. For the moment, one need only go back to 1939, when Ho was still known as Nguyen Ai Quoc (Nguyen, the Patriot). In that year, following the fall of the Popular Front in France, the Indochina Communist Party Ho had welded together was disbanded and went underground. When the Japanese swept into Tonkin in September, 1940, the Communists and the non-Communist nationalists launched uprisings against both the French and the Japanese, but they were quickly crushed. In May, 1941, after the Japanese had established their puppet regime of Vichy Frenchmen, Ho and other Vietnamese Communists met with other nationalists at Tsin-li, just across the Tonkinese border in China. They reorganized their scattered ranks into the Vietnam Doc Lap Dong Minh—Vietminh for short—and the guiding spirit, the man selected as General

Secretary, was bearded little Nguyen Ai Quoc, who had unexpectedly shown up at the meeting, though many had thought he had died of tuberculosis years before in the jungle. Without any flexing of Communist muscles, Ho and his friends concentrated on creating a common nationalist front to continue the fight against both Japan and France and to gain Vietnamese freedom.

At the end of 1941, Nguyen Ai Quoc was arrested by the Kuomintang secret police. They knew he was a Communist but chose to describe him as "a French spy" and threw him into jail at Liuchow. Eying Tonkin, as the Chinese had for many years, the Kuomintang had its own plans to build an anti-French "independence" movement around picked pro-Chinese Vietnamese. They soon discovered, however, that it was Nguyen Ai Quoc's Communist guerrillas of the Vietminh front who had the only real experience in Indochina. No one else, with one exception, had a network of agents there. The exception, oddly enough, was a civilian group headed by a dozen Allied businessmen, each of whom had his private organization of French, Chinese, and Vietnamese operatives; their original purpose had been to do what could be done to protect Allied assets and property in the Far East, and after Pearl Harbor this unique group had started working with Ho's guerrillas to gather intelligence for Allied air forces based in China and in India.

Early in 1943, Nguyen Ai Quoc sent a message from his prison cell to the southern Chinese warlord, Chang Fa Kwei, who, while an important leader of the Kuomintang, had frequently fought for power with Chiang Kai-shek and had his own ideas about Indochina. Nguyen Ai Quoc told Chang Fa Kwei that if he were set free, he would re-gather his intelligence network in Indochina and, presumably, work in Chang's behalf. Chang thereupon ordered his release from the Liuchow jail, and did so without telling Chiang Kai-shek. It was at this point that Nguyen Ai Quoc adopted the name of Ho Chi Minh (He Who Shines), primarily to hide his identity from Chiang Kai-shek's secret-police chief, Tai Li. As Ho, he became the directing head of the umbrella organization of Vietnamese revolutionary groups called the Dong Ming Hoi, which the Kuomintang was sponsoring and of which the Communist-dominated Vietminh was at first simply a part.

Ho received and disbursed a hundred thousand Chinese Nationalist dollars a month to carry on espionage and sabotage in Indochina. During 1943 and 1944, the Vietminh built up its own political strength at the expense of the other Dong Minh Hoi organizations, and by the end of 1944 it had an independent army of ten thousand rebels under the command of the young lawyer and teacher, Vo Nguyen Giap, who had already begun to demonstrate a remarkable military talent. Inevitably, as a result of the Vietminh's growing independence, relations between Ho and the Kuomintang in Chungking and Kunming became strained; under the circumstances, there was little his guardian angel, Chang Fa Kwei, could do about it. Equally unhappy about Ho were both the Vichy and the Free French, who buried their differences long enough to exchange secret information about him.

In the second half of 1944, Ho began to look to the Americans; what took place over the next two years, including the strange jungle romance between Ho and young soldiers like John, had overtones of comic opera, although the story had a sad ending. Ho, on four separate occasions, came secretly to the office of Strategic Services in Kunming, late in 1944 and early in 1945, seeking arms and ammunition in return for intelligence, sabotage against the Japanese, and continued aid in rescuing shot-down Allied pilots. He was rejected each time. According to Paul E. Helliwell, who was O.S.S. intelligence chief in China at the time and who has since denied that O.S.S. in any way "managed" Ho, "O.S.S. China was at all times consistent in its policy of giving no help to individuals such as Ho, who were known Communists and therefore obvious postwar sources of trouble." At the same time, however, and despite President Roosevelt's expressed policy of hands off the Indochina resistance movement—Helliwell says he was personally unaware of any direct orders—the decision not to help Ho was principally based, he adds, on Ho's refusal to pledge that any arms he received would be used only against the Japanese and not against the French.

Ho kept on trying. Helliwell finally gave him six .38-caliber revolvers and twenty thousand rounds of ammunition, but this was simply a token of appreciation for Vietminh assistance in bringing out three American pilots. Later, Ho wrote to Richard Heppner, who was chief of O.S.S. in China late in the war, requesting the help of the United States, which had already pledged the Philippines their freedom, in pressuring the French to grant Indochina independence. The fact is Ho did get some assistance from O.S.S. and from other American and Allied agencies over and above Helliwell's six pistols, although the material aid he received was not as great as the inspirational encouragement he was unofficially accorded. As a subsequent American intelligence chief in the Far East put it, "Ho offered to be our man, and we never grabbed his hand because we couldn't bankroll him."

Ho tried several Allied sources. Major General Claire Chennault, head of the 14th Air Force, who was warned by his Kuomintang friends to steer clear of him, at one point unwittingly had Ho introduced to him as "an old Vietnamese guide." Nothing came of that, but the British were somewhat more helpful and dropped some supplies to Free French and Vietminh guerrillas in November, 1944, after Ho had secretly moved back into Tonkin with about two hundred of his Vietminh followers. With him came a representative of the civilian group of former American businessmen in Indochina, who had for some time been co-operating with Ho's men. This hush-hush group had been under the wing of the O.S.S. at first but was now unofficially attached to another American Army group, the Air Ground Aid Service (AGAS). The arms that Ho and his handful of Vietnamese carried with them into Tonkin at this point are known to have come partly from O.S.S. supplies, although they had not been initially distributed for that purpose, and partly from some other American arsenals.

In the northern Tonkin jungle, in a mixed-up area where Chinese bandits, Free French and American paratroopers, and various groups of nationalists were all active, Ho Chi Minh set up his revolutionary headquarters. Vietminh troops, under young Giap, successfully harassed the Japanese, proselytized on behalf of Vietnamese freedom, and helped rescue additional Allied pilots. An American who was with Ho at his forest headquarters during this period remembers above all "his strength of character and his single-mindedness." His appraisal of Ho was as follows: "You've got to judge someone on the basis of what he wants. Ho couldn't be French, and he knew he could fight the French on his terms. He was afraid of the Chinese, and he couldn't deal with them because they'd always demand their pound of flesh. Moscow, so far away, was good at blowing up bridges, but not much good at building them again. If it weren't for the war, of course, Ho wouldn't have had a chance against the long background of French colonialism. But now he was in the saddle, although it wasn't clear what horse he was riding. For the moment, surely, he was helping us, on the ground. We and the French were in a position to help him in the future. I think he was ready to remain pro-West."

From Cabin Boy to Premier

There is admittedly a lot in Ho's past to contradict this assumption. Nevertheless, in spite of his basic Communist pedigree, the key to his character adds up to a rare combination of a disciplined doctrinaire party loyalist and a supremely passionate and proud individually-minded Asian nationalist, whose strategy and tactics have always been his own as much as Moscow's or Peking's.

He was born on May 19, 1890 (some sources say 1891 or 1892), in Kim Lien, a part of Annam known for its revolutionaries. His real name was Nguyen Van Thanh and he was the son of a poor native prefect who, though he eventually passed the mandarin examinations for a job in the imperial civil service, was privately an anti-French nationalist and eventually had his rank and job taken away from him. In 1911, after having attended high school in Hué, Ho briefly became a substitute teacher in a small fishing village and then shipped as a cabin boy aboard a vessel bound for France. For the next three years, he traveled around the world, usually as a cook's helper under the name of Ba, and managed in his spare time to read everything he could lay his hands on, from Shakespeare and Tolstoy to Marx. His wandering also helped develop his extraordinary linguistic talents—Ho learned French, English, Russian, German, Czech, Japanese, and three Chinese and various Annamese dialects. At some point, he apparently paid one or two brief visits to New York; he has been known to reminisce about Harlem and the abject poverty of the

Negroes he saw there, and to declaim against the "irony" of the Statue of Liberty.

In 1914, he debarked at Le Havre and, having decided to devote his life to the revolution, adopted his underground name of Nguyen Ai Quoc. He went to London, where he joined a secret revolutionary group called the Overseas Workers. He stoked furnaces and did other menial jobs for a living—for a time he worked as a dish washer in the Carlton Hotel kitchen, where he became a favorite of the famous Chef Escoffier. During the war, he turned up in Paris and, after studying photography, set himself up in a tiny Montmartre room and studio, advertising, for forty-five francs, "good portraits, beautiful frames."

Ho soon joined the Ninth Section of the French Socialist Party, and got to know men like Léon Blum, Marius Moutet, and Jean Longuet, who was Karl Marx's grandson and who invited the intense but shy little Annamite to write for *Le Populaire*. With apparent deliberateness, Ho divided his time between small cultural clubs, chiefly the Club du Faubourg, and various radical political groups. At the former, he heatedly debated such subjects as hypnotism and astronomy, and particularly enjoyed the endless discussions about dreams, the soul, and death. Once he argued vehemently with Dr. Coué, the self-perfectionist. He even wrote a play, *The Bamboo Dragon,* about an ignorant, abused chief of an Asian nation; although the play has never been heard of since, a critic at the time described it as "animated by an Aristophanic verve." A French member of the club recalls Ho as a man who had no time for women or drink; his one vice was American cigarettes. "He was reserved but not timid," this man says. "He was *sympathique* but not not at all fanatic, and very witty. He seemed always to be mocking the world and at the same time to be mocking himself."

As Ho improved his speaking abilities, he stepped up his agitation among the hundred thousand Vietnamese living in France and began to appear at Communist as well as Socialist meetings. In 1919, wearing a rented dress suit, he showed up at the Versailles Peace Conference, seeking to deliver a modest appeal for Vietnamese freedom; he was not accorded a hearing. The next year, when the Socialist Party met at Tours, deeply divided on its future course of action, Ho voted with the left majority to break away and join Marcel Cachin, the founder of the new French Communist Party. The year after that, he helped organize the Intercolonial Union, a group of subject peoples of the world, and became the editor of a Communist paper concentrating on colonial affairs. He was allowed considerable leeway by his sponsors, the colonial section of the Communist Youth, and since the newly organized Communist International was itself divided on the question of Moscow control, Ho got away with expressing his opinions freely. He traveled quite a bit around Europe, making speeches in which he took the side of the anti-Moscow independents without openly joining any faction, and went so far as to favor a gradualism that would lead from a "bourgeois democratic" regime for "conscientious" elements of all classes to "a Socialist state." Ruth Fischer, a well-known former German Communist who knew Ho during this period, has written, "It was Ho Chi Minh's nationalism which impressed us European Communists born and bred in a rather grey kind of abstract internationalism."

In 1922, he made his first pilgrimage to Moscow, to attend the Fourth Comintern Congress and then the International School of Marxism. At the Congress, he came into contact for the first time with such important leaders as Lenin, Trotsky, and Bukharin, and with many Communist leaders from other nations. After preliminary training, he helped organize the Southeast Asia Bureau of the Comintern and attended the University for Toilers of the East in Moscow. One of his early associates-in-training was the Indian M. N. Roy, one of the few men Ho failed to charm. "When I knew him as a novice in Moscow, Ho was anything but an impressive personality or a diligent student," Roy later wrote. Nevertheless, Ho was impressing more important men, who soon recognized him as a worthy addition to the international *apparat*. After attending the 1924 Congress of International Peasantry (Krestintern) as a French Communist delegate, Ho remained in Moscow to complete his revolutionary course. There is some evidence that he was then sent for a brief time to Boston with a Soviet economic mission. In the spring of 1925, after having attended the Fifth Congress of the Comintern, where he further established himself as an expert on colonial affairs, he was taken to Canton by Michael Borodin, the top Soviet adviser to the Kuomintang. Working closely with Borodin, as a translator and interpreter, young Ho, who then called himself Ly Thuy, had ample opportunity to observe how the collaboration between the Communists and the Kuomintang was fashioned, and how it later disintegrated. At the same time, he was secretly setting up the Thanh Nien (Association of Revolutionary Annamite Youth), the first real Communist organization in Indochina. He also organized a League of Oppressed Peoples of Asia, which became the genesis of the South Seas Communist Party that ran all Communist activities in Southeast Asia for the Comintern. In 1927, after the Kuomintang-Communist split in China, Ho fled back to Moscow via Hankow, but he left behind a solid network of two hundred and fifty Annamite Communists, most of whom had received some training in Moscow or at Chiang Kai-shek's Whampoa Academy in Canton. This original Vietnamese group of Communists kept in touch with the world Communist movement through underground liaison centers in China ports; so long as they directed their activities against French imperialism only, the Kuomintang left them alone, and eventually most of them were infiltrated into Indochina, where they became the nucleus of Ho's cadre. One of them was Pham Van Dong, who was to become the Prime Minister of North Vietnam.

Back in Moscow, Ho came to be accepted as an Asian expert by such Comintern luminaries as Zinoviev and Trotsky. Significantly, he kept out of internecine party battles and thus stepped easily into the world of Stalin after the purges; but there is no evidence to indicate that his personal standing with Stalin was anywhere near as high as it had been with the old Leninist guard. (In fact, there was more reason to suppose that Stalin grew to mistrust Ho but accepted him with qualifications as a technician rather than a theoretician—and in accordance with the then greater latitude still being allowed Asian Communists to develop in their own way.) For a time, once more, Ho traveled through Europe, attending various Communist conferences; in 1928, he went to Siam (Thailand), where, frequently disguised as a Buddhist monk, he quietly organized thousands of local Annamites and at the same time acted as agent of the Third International in the Far East. Under the aegis of the Shanghai Bureau, he directed "agitprop" (agitation and propaganda) in Siam, Malaya, and the Dutch East Indies.

Early in 1930, he went secretly to Hong Kong to reunify elements of the Thanh Nien he had created back in 1925, which had become split into factions fighting for Comintern recognition within Indochina. At this time, he formed the new Vietnamese Communist Party, which the Comintern promptly accepted, and which that fall, after taking in some Cambodian and Laotian elements, became the Indochina Communist Party. Its headquarters were shifted from Hong Kong to Indochina, but Ho remained in the British crown colony in his over-all Comintern capacity. He made brief trips to Hanoi, however, and on one occasion narrowly escaped from the French *sûreté* by stripping to the waist, grabbing a ricksha, and pulling an old lady with vegetables in her lap beyond the security cordon. The French were discouraged. "It is useless to try to buy him, he is 'completely disinterested,' " a *sûreté* report declared. At the instigation of the French, however, who had information from an important French Comintern agent they had captured, the British arrested Ho in Hong Kong in June, 1931. He was kept in prison for about a year and nearly died of tuberculosis. After his release, British officials in London revoked an "agreement" whereby he was to be turned over to the French (which would have meant death or life imprisonment) and ordered that he be kept in British jurisdiction instead, as a legitimate political refugee. Shortly thereafter, Ho "escaped" to Amoy. There is a story that he agreed to work for British intelligence, and for a time at least this was likely.

Now come the most obscure years in Ho Chi Minh's life, from 1933 until he suddenly showed up in south China in 1941. During this time, he is said to have married or taken on a regular concubine, by whom he had a daughter who later worked anonymously for the Vietminh and then disappeared. (The mother died in China during the war.) Ho, over this eight-year span, was variously reported in Shanghai, where he is said to have taught school briefly, in Siam, in Java, in France, in Portuguese East Africa, and in Moscow, where he attended more party schools. After an indefinite time recovering his health in northern Indochina hideouts, he resumed his career as an underground organizer of Communist cells in Southeast Asia; despite the fact that his earlier efforts had mostly collapsed, and that many of his earlier associates had been arrested or purged by the Comintern under Stalin's orders, Ho apparently was still in Moscow's good graces. During the period of the Popular Front, when Ho was under orders to tone down the activity of his Communists, and when the Trotskyists made strong inroads in the Indochina Communist Party (in opposition to Stalin's policy of favoring a French alliance over supporting the fight of France's colonies for independence), Ho bided his time. Subsequently, in 1946 and 1947, he was to have his troubles eliminating the vestiges of Trotskyism.

The extent of Ho's disciplined behavior in the thirties remains a matter of some debate. The French insist he continued to carry out Moscow's orders, and this was probably so, although he apparently moved slowly and cautiously. "I do not think Ho has ever been a free man," one high French official says. On the other hand, Maurice Thorez, the French Communist chief, is known to have remarked, "We cannot trust Ho—he is a Trotskyist himself at heart." Ho has made no bones about his obligations as a Communist, on an international plane. When, as a Comintern agent, he once told a French Communist friend, "I am a professional revolutionary, I am always on strict orders, my itinerary is always carefully prescribed, and you can't deviate from the route, can you?"—he surely meant it. But there remained the dynamic dream that has always been the supreme passion of his life: a free Vietnam.

Ho Dickers with France

In the light of the above summary of Ho's career as a long-time trusted worker in Communist vineyards, let us return to the jungle and to the months, just before the end of the war in 1945, when he sounded out the French in Kunming over the radio of the young American lieutenant, John.

The messages John sent out for Ho reached Léon Pignon, a political career man of the French who was later to be High Commissioner of Indochina, and Major Jean Sainteny, a Free French Army officer who became the chief French representative in North Vietnam. After reading Ho's demands for guaranteed independence from France in five to ten years, Pignon and Sainteny replied that they were willing to negotiate, but no time or place was set. The Americans by this time were posing a new problem for the French. When Roosevelt's orders against helping the underground in Indochina were lifted, early in April, the Office of Strategic Services had begun to retrain and equip some two thousand French soldiers who had made their way to Kunming after the Japanese take-over. The plan was to drop Franco-American teams back into Indochina, with supplies to follow if guerrilla resistance bands could be organized. In point of fact, while willingly taking any material help they could get, the French wanted to avoid any direct American involvement. Helliwell, the former O.S.S. intelligence head, later said: "It was perfectly obvious by June of 1945 that the French were infinitely more concerned with keeping the Americans out of Indochina than they were in defeating the Japanese or in doing anything to bring the war to a successful conclusion in that area."

Not too many Americans did get into Tonkin, but several O.S.S. teams were dropped into the jungle, and with their help Ho's forces managed to augment their supplies with a small number of tommy guns and carbines. At the war's end, replenishing their arsenal with captured or surrendered Japanese equipment, Vietminh troops moved swiftly to carry out Ho's orders of a general insurrection. All over Indochina, there was rising support for the independence movement. Under Giap, now a self-styled General, the Vietminh troops moved into Hanoi on August 17, 1945. A week later, Major Sainteny parachuted into the city from a Free French bomber, with Major Archimedes Patti, of the O.S.S. Patti's mission was to liberate war prisoners, for which he had to obtain the co-operation of the Japanese, since the Chinese occupation forces had not yet arrived. Sainteny found himself immediately hamstrung by the Vietminh and by the Japanese, who, with Patti's apparent blessing, completely restricted his movement, on the grounds of his personal safety, and kept several

c

hundred French citizens virtually locked up in the Hotel Metropole. Sainteny was incensed, and five days after his arrival he telegraphed Calcutta: "We are before a collusive Allied maneuver with the purpose of throwing the French out of Indochina." He had a point, but it was far more accidental than collusive.

Within a period of weeks, other American officers arrived in Hanoi, among them some top officers of the China Combat Command. At the same time came a number of American correspondents. Their open sympathies, in typical American fashion of supporting the underdog, were clearly with the Vietminh, and especially with Ho. Major Patti made no bones about favoring Vietnamese independence; French sources say he even offered to help Ho get arms, and that an American general on the scene indicated he had some business connections back home that would sell the new regime heavy equipment for rebuilding the country. That Ho needed help was obvious. My *Newsweek* associate, Harold Isaacs, saw Ho in November, and Ho expressed his readiness to permit the French to maintain their economic position in Vietnam if they recognized Vietnamese independence. "Why not?" Ho asked. "We've been paying out our life's blood for decades. Suppose it costs us a few hundred million more piastres to buy our freedom?"

Recalling his long struggles, his years in Chinese and British prisons, Ho was full of humility and neither looked nor played the part of a head of government. He wore a faded khaki jacket and trousers, a white shirt, and old slippers. "They call me 'Excellency.' Funny, eh?" he remarked.

The sympathy Americans had for Ho late in 1945 and early in 1946 found expression in the formation of the Vietnam-American Friendship Association. Its first meeting in Hanoi was attended by an American general and his officers. After listening to Vietnamese professions of esteem and fondness for America, the general returned the compliments and looked forward to such things as student exchanges. Major Sainteny, who had suffered the further indignity of being arrested by the Japanese while riding in his jeep, which carried a French flag, and having an American colonel obtain his release, later referred to the Americans' "infantile anti-colonialism, which blinded almost all of them." Despite his dismay, it was Sainteny who, more than any other Frenchmen, was to sympathize with Ho Chi Minh and try to promote a real policy of co-operation with him.

After two meetings with Ho, late in September and early in October, Sainteny felt that he was "a strong and honorable personality." Subsequently, in his book, *The Story of a Lost Peace, 1945–1947*, Sainteny wrote that "this ascetic man, whose face revealed at once intelligence, energy, cleverness, and fineness, was a personality of the highest order who would not be long in placing himself in the foreground of the Asian scene." Pignon, who was more interested in building up other nationalists than in adopting Ho, was also impressed but was less sure of his sincerity. From the outset, Pignon had no illusions about "Ho's Communist face" and considered him "a great actor." Nevertheless, both Frenchmen regarded Ho as "a man of peace," and Pignon's reservations about Ho's honesty did not include skepticism about Ho's preference for moderation and for compromise over killing. The two French negotiators differed most strongly perhaps on their assessment of Ho's humility and pride: Sainteny was always impressed with the first; Pignon flashed warning signals about the second.

Sainteny did most of the negotiation with Ho that led to the agreement of March 6, 1946, whereby the Republic of Vietnam was recognized as an independent part of the French Union, with French troops permitted to return to Tonkin. During the period of the negotiations, Sainteny has written, Ho "aspired to become the Gandhi of Indochina." Ho is quoted as saying: "While we want to govern ourselves . . . I need your professional men, your engineers, and your capital to build a strong and independent Vietnam." Ho, says Sainteny, wanted the French Union to be constructed with "a Vietnamese cornerstone. . . . He wanted independence for his country, but it was to France herself that he wanted to owe it. . . . It is certainly regrettable that France minimized this man and was unable to understand his value and the power he disposed of." Sainteny points out that China was Vietnam's age-old enemy, that Ho's overtures to the Americans had already proved "rather disappointing," and that, "against the wishes of an important faction of his party," Ho was not inclined to look for aid in Moscow, "which he knew too well." Sainteny, nevertheless, was realistic enough to admit that Ho's prefer- ence for French backing was partly predicated on the expectations of a Communist victory in France.

When the Communists in France lost out, Sainteny says, Ho felt he needed the support of French liberals and moderates more than ever if he was successfully to "muzzle his opposition" in Vietnam, which had begun to cause him some trouble. This particularly in- cluded some of the old Chinese Dong Minh Hoi groups, which Ho had subjugated in the late-war jungle days, when the Vietminh had become the dominant part of the underground front. The Chinese in Hanoi sought to reactivate these organizations, notably the Dong Minh Hoi and the more important Vietnam. Quoc Dan Dang (VNQDD), the leading Vietnamese national party; they specifically wanted Ho to include representatives of these groups in his govern- ment.

The Chinese in the northern part of Vietnam had several ob- jectives. In the first place, they were there for profit, if not for out- right loot, and they succeeded—by inflating the Chinese dollar at the expense of the Indochina piastre; by making off with huge amounts of opium, which they seized both in Laos and in Vietnam; and by engaging in heavy black-market operations in Hanoi and Haiphong, where there was a large Chinese mercantile population. In the second place, the Chinese had no use for the French or the Vietnamese, and they did not hesitate to terrorize the local French and Vietnamese citizens. The fact that many of their occupation troops were more rag- tail than professional encouraged this, and in the winter of 1945 things became so bad that Sainteny cabled Paris to ask for a United Nations investigation of the conduct of the Chinese forces; both the British and the American representatives in Hanoi supported him. As events turned out, this was not necessary, since the French finally managed to get the Chinese out of the north by renouncing their extraterritorial and other rights in China and by granting numerous concessions to the Chinese in Vietnam, including a free zone for Chinese goods at Haiphong and certain customs exemptions for goods shipped in over the railroad from Kunming.

Though the Chinese agreed to leave by mid-March, 1946, they actually didn't pull out the bulk of their troops until the summer. In the meantime, they kept up their political offensive, and they obtained some advantage from the fact that initially the Vietminh's strength was largely concentrated in Hanoi itself and in a few other cities but not yet in the countryside, where both the Dong Minh Hoi and the VNQDD had previously built up considerable support, especially in the areas near the Chinese border. Much of the Vietminh's support, despite its Communist leadership, came from non-Communist Vietnamese, whose passionate desire for independence was a powerful factor in enabling Ho Chi Minh to form his original broad front in his own dynamic image. In order to stress his nationalist feelings more than his Communist background and doctrine, and also as a result of the orders that had come from the French Communist Party, Ho, in mid-November, 1945, dissolved the Indochina Communist Party in the north. (A small group of Communist extremists, including Giap and Dang Xuan Khu—better known today as Truong Chinh, the strongest pro-Peking man among the Hanoi Communists—formed what they called Marxist Study Groups, which later became the nucleus of the Laodang, or Workers, Party, the successor of the old Communist Party in Indochina.)

To obtain the support of as many groups as possible for the agreement he was about to sign with Sainteny, Ho selected the chief of the Dong Ming Hoi to be his Vice-President, and he gave three top Cabinet jobs to VNQDD men, including the Ministry of Foreign Affairs. At the same time, to pacify the Chinese further, he dropped Giap and one other leading Communist from the Cabinet. As the Vietminh began organizing People's Committees to replace the old Councils of Notables in the villages, it made further temporary concessions to the Chinese parties, promising the VNQDD fifty seats and the Dong Minh Hoi twenty out of a total of three hundred and fifty in the assembly elections that were to be held in January, 1946. The vote took place on a limited basis only, in some parts of the country, and about half of those elected, as it turned out, were non-political-party people, though the Vietminh did well by controlling the vote in many villages, and in Hanoi Ho received an alleged ninety-eight per cent of the ballots. Ho had other reasons for wanting to go slow politically. He had an extremely difficult economic situation on his hands. There had been a famine early in 1945, followed by floods that had swept over the broken dikes of the Red River Delta. Then came a severe drought. The breakdown of the Vietnamese transportation system had made it impossible to ship rice from the south, which was having its own troubles. In 1945 and through the early part of 1946, it was estimated that a million Vietnamese died of starvation in the north.

Modus Vivendi Is Signed

In the face of all these difficulties, Ho's eagerness in wanting to conclude the March, 1946, agreement with Sainteny can better be understood. When he signed it, he made a direct and dramatic appeal to the Vietnamese people at a big outdoor meeting in Hanoi. "Fellow countrymen, who have followed me up to now," he asked, "follow me once more. I would prefer death a hundred times to betraying my country."

Two months later, as the French were doing their best to sabotage Ho by holding the separatist conference at Dalat, in the south, and by getting ready to set up their independent puppet regime in Cochin China, Ho left for France with a small delegation to negotiate what he hoped would be a full implementation of the March contract he had made with Major Sainteny. During the summer, while he was away, and with both Sainteny and Pignon out of Hanoi, too, the extremist group among the Communists, led by Giap and Dang Xuan Khu, rode roughshod over the non-Communist nationalists. As in the south, terror also struck the country, and many pro-French Vietnamese as well as Frenchmen were assassinated. There are those who say that this was all part of the game, that Ho went to France and remained there as the pretender of peace, tortuously seeking an agreement, while the extremists were given a free hand back in Vietnam. Sainteny, among others, vehemently denies that this was the case.

In Biarritz, where he first rested, in Paris and then at the conference in Fontainebleau, Ho enjoyed huge personal success. He charmed everyone, especially the press. He distributed roses to girl reporters, signed his name in blood for an American male correspondent. He was widely compared to Confucius, to the Buddha, to St. John the Baptist, to anyone's doting grandfather, and it was noted that he was an ascetic, since, among other things, he refused to take a drink. Everywhere he went, whether to the opera, to a fancy reception, to a picnic, or to a press conference, he appeared in his simple, high-buttoned linen work suit. "As soon as one approaches this frail man, one shares the admiration of all men around him, over whom he towers with his serenity acquired from wide experience," wrote one reporter. Noting his "tormented face and his eyes of blue which burn with an inner light," another declared that he "hides a soul of steel behind a fragile body." His wit, his Oriental courtesy, his *savoir-faire,* his mixed profundity and playfulness in social intercourse, his open love for children, above all his seeming sincerity and simplicity, captured one and all.

Unfortunately, in point of accomplishment Ho's trip was far less successful. The fault, now generally admitted, was chiefly that of the French, who, while the conference went on, continued to violate its spirit by further fostering the idea of the separate south and central federation in Indochina. In Paris, the shakiness of the national government delayed the start of the sessions with Ho. He stayed at Biarritz to wait and go fishing. "The conference was fishy from the start," one of his delegates remarked. Sainteny later wrote that Ho was "reticent and nervous," but after playing pelota, roaming the countryside, and visiting Lourdes, he "found his smile again" and was "as affable and simple as before." When three leading Communists, including the Minister of Air, paid him a visit and commented, for propaganda purposes, about the "indescribable conditions" in which Ho was quartered at Biarritz, Ho announced that, on the contrary, he was "enchanted" by his stay on the Basque coast.

When he and Sainteny finally flew up to Paris for the start of the talks, Sainteny described him as "pale, eyes brilliant, and tight-throated," and he quoted Ho as saying, when the plane was settling down, "Above all, don't leave me, whatever you do." As the conference dawdled in the shadow of defeat, by now the result of the activities of the Vietminh extremists in Hanoi as well as of the French maneuvers in Cochin China, Ho grew more and more restless. Sainteny agreed he ought to return to Hanoi as soon as possible. "What would I be able to do if I went home empty-handed?" Ho asked. "Don't let me leave this way," he begged Sainteny and Marius Moutet, the Socialist Minister of Overseas Territories. "Arm me against those who would seek to displace me. You will not regret it." It was a significant plea, as significant as what Ho said on another evening to Sainteny and Moutet, "If we have to fight, we will fight. You will kill ten of our men and we will kill one of yours, and in the end it will be you who will tire of it."

At midnight on September 14, 1946, the frail figure of Ho Chi Minh, in its military tunic, walked out of the Hotel Royal-Monceau in Paris (the Fontainebleau sessions had ended) and strolled to Moutet's house nearby. There Ho and Moutet signed a *modus vivendi*, which, while it underlined Vietnamese (and some French) concessions for safeguarding French rights in Indochina, only postponed agreement on basic political questions; it at least placed upon the French the responsibility for restoring order in Cochin China. This was nothing more than had been agreed to in the spring and been vitiated since, but Ho publicly called the *modus vivendi* "better than nothing." He murmured to a security officer who accompanied him back to the hotel early in the morning, however, "I have just signed my death warrant."

Despite the failure of his mission, Ho, in his true cosmopolitan fashion, had enjoyed his stay in Paris, a city he had always loved. Years before, standing on a bridge across the Seine, he had remarked to a Communist comrade, "What a wonderful city, what a wonderful scene!" When his friend had replied that Moscow was also beautiful, Ho had said, "Moscow is heroic, Paris is the joy of living." During the 1946 conference, Ho had revisited some of his former haunts and, mixing socially with several foreign correspondents, had talked freely about himself and his politics. "Everyone has the right to his own doctrine," he had said. "I studied and chose Marx. Jesus said two thousand years ago that one should love one's enemies. That dogma has not been realized. When will Marxism be realized? I cannot answer. . . . To achieve a Communist society, big industrial and agricultural production is necessary. . . . I do not know when that will be realized in Vietnam, where production is low. We are not yet in a position to meet the conditions."

Ho's self-analysis, in relation to Indochina's development, is a markedly honest one, in Marxist terms. From the outset, Marxism was far more than a blueprint for him. It was a *logique,* and as one of the keenest Indochina scholars, Paul Mus, has pointed out, it was acquired by Ho as a vital Western weapon, an arsenal in fact, with which, as an Asian, he could combat his French masters. Ho, as a Marxist, was quick to appreciate how his country was being robbed, kept in economic penury by a purposefully unimaginative colonial power. While the French took out rubber or rice or whatever else they wanted and sold it in the world market at a high profit, the Vietnamese lived under a system in which only human labor and not money, in any international sense, counted; goods were in effect bartered for subsistence. Such an economic condition became the fulcrum of Ho's anger and drove him way back, almost inevitably, to Marxism and thence to Communism. "Ho had to build on what every Asian must build *per se,*" Mus says, "a Western logic to deal with us Europeans. Whether it be a profession such as the law or medicine or what have you, an Asian must find this *logique* or be lost. Ho found it first in Marxism and he became a Leninist, since Lenin was faced in Russia with the same problem of the vacuum at the village level. Ho was successful because he remained true to Leninism and Marxism. In this sense, straightforward according to *his* view, he belongs to a proper fraternity."

Along with Sainteny, Mus is one of those Frenchmen who admit that France and the Western world missed a proper opportunity with Ho in 1946. Mus himself, as a French negotiator, met Ho a year later, and he has the same queer fondness for him most men who knew him have retained. "I have no reason, as a Frenchman, to like Ho for what he has done," Mus told me long afterward, "but still I like him. I am not afraid to say so. I like him for his strong mind. Although he is a great actor—one cannot afford to be naïve with him—he does not go back on his word. He believes in the truth as he sees it. *But* he is a Marxist, and that is where we part company." He quotes Ho as telling him, in 1947, "My only weapon is anger.

. . . I won't disarm my people until I trust you." Ho's willingness to deal with the French, Mus believes, was largely predicated on his need for French advice, above all for financial advisers. "Marxist doctrine calls for the proletarian state to use, at least temporarily, the accountancy of the bourgeois-capitalist countries," Mus says. Because of the inbred economy imposed by the Bank of Indochina, Ho knew that Vietnam could not stand on its own feet, either in terms of money or trade. He also knew he could not rely on the colonial French. His political approach was through metropolitan France. He wasn't convinced that this was his only chance, but he was determined to play the possibilities. He wavered between his affection and regard for France, which had given him his self in the Marxist image, and his new disillusion of 1946. "If we had supported him more strongly then," Mus added, "we might have won. . . . We thought we could crush him if it came to war. We did not appreciate how hard he could fight. But we must not forget that he really wanted an agreement with France at the time of Fontainebleau because it would have served him. That part of his motivation afterward died, of course, but we should understand that it existed at the time and that he was truly disappointed."

When Ho returned to Vietnam from France at the end of that sad 1946 summer, he was confronted with a difficult internal political situation. While the conflict between himself and the extremists was perhaps exaggerated, there is no doubt that the younger men around Ho, especially Giap and Dang Xuan Khu, had disapproved of his moderation and patience at Fontainebleau. They almost certainly wanted to move on to violence at once. Considerable conjecture about Ho's troubles with this group soon arose, and then shifted to speculation that ranged from rumors of Ho's retirement into mere figurehead status to the increasingly heard report, of which the French sporadically claimed proof, that he was dead. It is a fact that for many months he was not seen and was hardly mentioned, but what seems to have happened was this:

Ho became quite ill when he arrived back in Hanoi. He stayed in bed for several weeks. During this period, he may have been under some protective form of house arrest (British sources insist this was so); apparently he was surreptitiously moved in and out of a nearby jungle headquarters. Various elements within the Vietminh and out —among them the old pro-Chinese groups, for their own obvious purposes—openly accused Ho of having sold out to France with the *modus vivendi,* and tracts distributed in the Hanoi area bitterly attacked him. "When a man remains in foreign countries for a long while, he becomes their slave," one of them read. These were probably nothing more than the dying gasp of the pro-Chinese Vietnamese leaders, some of whom had already fled to China when Giap, with the departure of Chinese troops, unrestrainedly cracked down on them.

If Ho was temporarily and perhaps deliberately kept in the background, his eclipse did not last long. His policy of moderation was surely in evidence once more in the fall of 1946, when a constitution of surprising temperance, by Communist terms, was adopted. Two months later, in December, following the incident over customs control in Haiphong harbor and the outbreak of Vietminh terror and French Army reprisals in Hanoi, the war between the French and the Vietminh began. Both sides by then seemed not only ready but anxious to fight. Ho and his government fled into the jungle. However, by April, 1947, Ho's position as the commanding figure in the Vietminh was again supreme. It was in that month that Paul Mus traveled through the forest as a French emissary to meet Ho and offer him what amounted to terms of unconditional surrender. When Ho asked Mus if he—were he in Ho's place—would accept them, Mus admitted he wouldn't. "In the French Union there is no place for cowards," Ho then declared. "If I accepted those conditions, I should be one." Mus says it was completely obvious to him that Ho was running his own show, and that he had the power to reject the French offer without even having to consult the Tong Bo, the five-man Vietminh "politburo."

Even if Ho had had trouble with the extremists, if he had still at that time been a moderate hoping for a *rapprochement* with France, this would not have meant that he was not also, as he always has been in the final analysis, Moscow's man; the two Ho's were not incompatible, and much of what has since happened in the postwar world would seem to corroborate this. Moscow, as a matter of fact, may very well have intervened secretly to restore fully Ho's power and prestige; in substantiation of this theory is the belief that some of the other Vietminh leaders, notably Dang Xuan Khu, have always been under the influence of the Chinese Communists rather than Moscow-orientated. If Ho was torn, within himself and with relation to his followers, a little Moscow glue may have put him together again.

An interesting comment on Ho came at this time from none other than Bao Dai, whose brief tenure as Ho's adviser ended when he fled to Hong Kong, from which place the French would soon resurrect him to head an opposition government in the south. "During the few months I was in Hanoi as Supreme Counselor," Bao Dai said, "I saw Ho Chi Minh suffer. He was fighting a battle within himself. Ho had his own struggle. He realized Communism was not best for our country, but it was too late. Ultimately, he could not overcome his allegiance to Communism."

After Paul Mus's 1947 visit, no non-Communist Westerner is believed to have seen Ho in the jungle until late in 1954. On several occasions, however, he replied telegraphically to questions sent him by Western correspondents. What gradually evolved was a somewhat altered version of him. While he became more cynical and coy, he also became more folksy. "Uncle Ho," the patriarch, emerged. And as he increasingly became more anti-American, he hewed closer than ever to the Communist line, as handed down by Moscow and later by Peking as well. He continued, however, to speak the truth about himself, in his own peculiar lights. "When I was young, I studied Buddhism, Confucianism, Christianity, as well as Marxism," he once told a United Press questioner. "There is something good in each doctrine." Asked his opinion of American intentions in Asia, Ho snapped back, "Marshallization of the world." The Russians, he said, were "against Marshallization of the world." In the next breath, with sad truth, he declared that American aid "is a good thing if it goes directly to the people," thereby touching a sore spot inasmuch as the United States aid to the Vietnamese became a sensitive issue with the French in the south. Ho denied vehemently that Vietnam was or could become Russia's or anyone else's "satellite." He kept insisting he could remain neutral, "like Switzerland," in the world power struggle. "If the Chinese Communists offer you artillery and heavy mortars, would you accept them?" he was subsequently asked. Ho fell back on coyness. "What friendly advice would you give us in that case?" he wired back to his questioner. To a Siamese journalist who inquired, "Is there any truth in the rumors that Mao Tse-tung and you have set up a close relationship and that you favor Communism of the Moscow kind," Ho replied—with an odd quality of dishonesty vis-à-vis his Asian questioner—"What is astonishing is that many intelligent foreigners believe these French slanders."

Events themselves belied Ho's last answer. There was no doubt that after 1950 he moved swiftly and snugly into the Moscow-Peking ideological camp.

As it evolved, the Vietminh emphasized the dominant role of the working class, in accordance with the decisions of the Asian and Australian Trade Union Conference held at Peking in November and December, 1949. Ho and Mao exchanged cables at that time, and soon thereafter eight hundred Vietnamese labor leaders met in rebel Indochina territory and, among panoplied pictures of Stalin, Mao, and Ho, demonstrated their total allegiance to Communism. Titoism was attacked, although when Yugoslavia quickly recognized Ho's regime, along with Soviet Russia and China, Ho had some embarrassing moments; he solved them typically, by pointing out that he had announced his readiness to establish relations with "any government" while at the same time continuing to blast Tito on the Vietminh jungle radio.

Early in 1951, when the Communists resumed their open leadership of the Vietminh movement, Ho lapsed into another period of silence. It was then that rumors of his death in the jungle again were heard. From time to time, Dang Xuan Khu, who became General Secretary of the new party, or someone else in the hierarchy, would publicly extol him. The tone grew reverential; a Ho myth in the milder image of a Stalin myth was reared, and a much tougher, more rigid Ho than he had ever made himself out to be slowly emerged. In 1953, Joseph Starobin, correspondent of the *Daily Worker* in New York, met Ho in the Tonkin jungle. He was not unexpectedly charmed by "the legendary president," who wore such simple peasant clothes and who knew so much about the world. Starobin rhapsodized: "As we sat there that first evening, these facets of the president's personality emerged. He was the world traveler, in whom each recollection of a crowded past was still vivid. He was the old-timer, the Communist leader of an older generation, for whom the lamps of memory needed only the reburnishing of conversation to become shiny and bright. There was also the Uncle Ho who works his own garden, types his own messages, teaches the four virtues— 'industriousness, frugality, justice and integrity'—to the youth." Starobin was with Ho when Stalin died. He described the rapt jungle scene: "Crude benches illumined by candles set in a makeshift candelabra made out of bamboo; at the front was a portrait of Stalin wreathed in flowers . . . two violins played softly."

This touching bit of pastoral Stalinoidism was real enough in the context of the time, or real enough, at least, for so stalwart a Stalinist as Starobin; but it seems somehow doubtful that Ho took it quite so seriously or regarded it so poignantly. He was far too clever for that, and he had seen far too many of his old comrades purged by Stalin to render such an unqualifiedly touching response to the old tyrant's death. Nevertheless, it was certainly true that by this time the die had been cast, and that Ho, rejected by the West, no longer had any option—if one may assume that he had one earlier—but to attach himself firmly to the Communist camp. The wandering minstrel of Southeast Asia was home again, but there were to be many moments in the future when his relationship to the Communists, especially after the Sino-Soviet split, would once again be tenuous and difficult to define. Perhaps no one anywhere in the world would be called upon to perform such a unique balancing act between Moscow and Peking as the adroit old guerrilla, Nguyen Ai Quoc. For the moment, however, it is sufficient to re-emphasize "what might have been" in that crucial year between August, 1945, when the big war ended, and July-September, 1946, when the abortive conference at Fontainebleau preceded by a few months the start of the Indochina war. This was the first important turning point in the unfortunate history of Indochina, and this, perhaps more than any other time, was when "the lost revolution" was actually lost.

CHAPTER III

╰∿╯

The Critical Period
1947–1953

Historical speculation, it has been argued, is basically fruitless, since history, including war and revolution, is the predictable product of negative and positive forces, and the events they cause are incontrovertible, whether actively opposed or responded to passively. The Russian and Chinese revolutions, in this sense, can be called inevitable, and on a smaller scale so can what has happened in Indochina since 1945. Much of what has occurred there, and in North and South Vietnam, Cambodia, and Laos, into which it was broken up, has resulted from positive revolutionary action. Almost as much has been the result of what did *not* take place. The time factor was invariably important, and what might have occurred and didn't— or, in contradistinction, what might have been avoided but wasn't —was as often attributable to the miscalculations of one side as it was to purposeful decisions of the other. If one accepts the theory of action and reaction, the outcome was still inevitable; the historical determinist admits of no contingencies that, in terms of human error or choice, could really alter the result. One may thus conclude that because Ho Chi Minh was a Communist, fashioned by his background and environment, he was bound to do what he did, no matter what transpired before and after the Fontainebleau Conference in the summer of 1946, and that therefore speculation that he might have done otherwise, or been made into something else, is as futile as it is naïve. It is here that the anti-Communists become as rigid in their thinking as the Marxists. From the vantage point of Communist doctrine, on the other hand, it can further be maintained—as, in fact, it has been—that, colonialism and capitalist imperialism being what they were, the decline of the French and their defeat in 1954, followed by their departure from Indochina, were also inevitable, and that it was equally so that the task of temporarily filling the vacuum should have fallen upon the United States. I say "temporarily" because, to follow the revolutionary dialectic through to its logical conclusion, the victory of the Communists remains certain, and, no matter what sort of negotiations ultimately end the present war, the pendulum cannot be swung back. Many experts, non-Communist as well as Marxist, believe this to be true. Others disagree strongly, and still others, myself included, are simply not certain, though no one can afford to be optimistic. It is sadly apparent, in view of what has already happened in the last twenty years in the Indochina area and in all of Southeast Asia, that the prospects of avoiding further Communist penetration are not bright so long as the free world refuses to face up to the revolutionary challenge that exists in purely Asian and not necessarily Communist or Marxist terms.

The theory propounded in this book is based on the proposition that the events that have occurred in Indochina to date were not inevitable, that they could have been foreseen and avoided by the Western democracies, and that therefore a certain amount of speculation about them is justified and may still be useful in planning and looking ahead. If the opportunity to deal with Ho in 1945–46 represented at best a gamble—but one that, as I have suggested, should have been at least attempted—the chance that was lost, almost exactly at mid-century, between the years 1948 and 1953, to create, in the southern part of Vietnam, a challenging alternative to the emerging Communism in the north was an even greater tragedy, because its denial represented a foolish neglect, and even a wilful rejection, of the possibilities that existed. In this lost opportunity, the United States was almost as much to blame as France, the power directly responsible;

perhaps, in a certain sense, the Americans were more to blame, because, while not as deeply involved, they had more ways to apply pressure.

Bao Dai—Center Stage

The years 1947–48 in Indochina, before Ho Chi Minh and the Vietminh adopted their irreconcilable Communist position and when they were still on the defensive militarily, was a time of subtle political maneuvering behind the scenes of the physical conflict. As soon as the war began, and the Vietminh forces retreated to the countryside and the jungle, Ho and the other Communist leaders, whatever differences they might have had during and after Fontainebleau, readopted their earlier tactics of creating a broad resistance front among the various nationalist groups, including some of the pro-Chinese elements. Domestically, Ho's Vietnam Republic rallied the population to increase the production of rice, maize and sweet potatoes, to repair dikes and bridges, and to maintain its successful drive against illiteracy. Abroad, the Vietminh went out of its way to cultivate support for its cause. "The world is aware that it was not the Vietnamese who started the fighting—it is obvious we were not in a position to do so—and much sympathy had been paid to Vietnam in every country," one statement declared, with modest righteousness. As for the French, Ho sought to maintain at least the posture of cordial relations. He bemoaned the failures at Fontainebleau, alluded hopefully to new negotiations, pledged that the war would stop as soon as independence was granted, did not renounce potential membership in the French Union, and promised that not only would French economic and cultural interests be guaranteed after peace was established but that new French as well as other foreign capital would be welcomed.

The French were not interested in being conciliated. As their troops laid siege to Hanoi and Haiphong, captured most of the important cities and towns of northern and central Vietnam, and gained control of virtually all strategic highways and waterways and of the area along the Chinese border, their attitude was one of complete confidence. "There is no military problem any longer in Indochina," Paul Coste-Floret, the Minister of War, said in Paris in May, 1947. "The success of French arms is complete." It was no coincidence that the already referred-to mission of Paul Mus to Ho's headquarters in the jungle two months earlier amounted to a demand for unconditional surrender. In September, General Valluy, the French Commander in Chief, began amphibious and paratroop offensives on the central coast and in the northern mountains that were supposed to signal the final big offensive. But the great victory never took place. Slowly, the Vietminh pockets of resistance that were thought to have been eliminated came back to life, and the guerrillas began their concentrated campaign of sabotage against the French lines of communication and against the French outposts along the roads. And as the French mounted what they called "punitive and mopping-up operations," they found themselves suddenly on the defensive against the unseen enemy. It was obvious, as the French soon acknowledged, that the Vietminh controlled most of the countryside and that to dislodge the guerrillas would, according to Coste-Floret's estimate, require half a million men or more. By the middle of 1947, despite Valluy's bold intentions, the French leaders back home realized that they would never be able to reconquer Indochina solely by military means, and they became aware that their hope lay in mounting a political offensive as a corollary to a policy of military containment.

In Saigon, the imperious Admiral D'Argenlieu was replaced as High Commissioner by Emile Bollaert, a veteran Radical Socialist parliamentarian whose appointment, Premier Paul Ramadier hopefully declared, would herald a "constructive phase." It was Bollaert's initial task to reopen negotiations with the Vietminh, and he had to do so in the face of intransigence by French generals and colonial officials, who would not admit the military stalemate. The Vietminh, encouraged by its ability to hold off the French, was already determined to insist on an independence that, while it would still guarantee the French certain economic and cultural rights, would not compromise on the inclusion of Cochin China, the colonial stronghold, in the new Republic. As their instrument to deal with the Vietminh, with France directly, or with both, the French now turned to Emperor Bao Dai. Privately, from the outset of this imperial courtship, the French hoped that Bao Dai would be able to rally enough Vietnamese of all parties to support himself as an alternative to Ho Chi Minh. This so-called "Bao Dai formula" was initiated early in 1947, even before the French military situation had deteriorated. In March, they sent their first secret envoys to see the Emperor in Hong Kong, where he had gone after he had resigned as Ho Chi Minh's counselor. In May, after the failure of his mission to Ho, Paul Mus had a talk with Bao Dai, and in June, Bollaert himself traveled to Hong Kong.

Bao Dai was in the unique position at this juncture of being wooed by both sides. The Vietminh had also approached him to propose that he negotiate on *its* behalf with the French. Bao Dai's advisers, notably Dr. Phan Quang Dan, an anti-Communist nationalist who had refused to co-operate with Ho in 1946, persuaded the Emperor to reject these Vietminh overtures. A number of other Vietnamese nationalist leaders, including members of the Dong Minh Hoi and the VNQDD, expressed their readiness to back Bao Dai against the Vietminh; they formed a National Union Front in support of the Emperor, and this was joined by some of the leaders of the Cao Dai and Hoa Hao religious sects. Now began the fragmentation of these political and religious groups, a process that served to aid the French cause. Elements of these different factions sided with the French and/or with Bao Dai against the Vietminh, while others remained pro-Vietminh, and still others stayed neutral, or ended up sporadically opposing both sides. Most acted out of sheer opportunism; some had patriotic motives. One individual patriot with an uncompromising nationalist position was Ngo Dinh Diem, a Catholic leader who had resigned from Bao Dai's government in Annam in the thirties, but who was now willing to co-operate with the Emperor if he stuck to his nationalist guns and didn't knuckle down to the French.

Initially, during the talks with the French in Hong Kong, Bao Dai maintained a strong position. He declared that he would not accept anything less than the French had previously offered Ho Chi Minh, that he would not place himself in direct opposition to the Vietminh and would remain aloof from political quarrels. He would return to

Vietnam, he added, only if he was the clear choice of the Vietnamese people. In the months that followed, Bao Dai weakened his stance and moved gradually closer to the French, and the French, in turn, stiffened their position toward the Vietminh. In the late summer of 1947, High Commissioner Bollaert, after returning from a trip to Paris during which he was admonished not to be as conciliatory as he had been in his statements about possible peace with the Vietminh, offered a truce accompanied by hedged promises of freedom for Vietnam within the French Union; the hedges included continued French control of defense, foreign, and financial relations, and the only concessions concerned the right of the Vietnamese to run their own internal affairs and to decide "for themselves" whether or not Cochin China should join the Republic of Vietnam. In rejecting these terms, knowing full well how the French could still control any Cochin China vote, the Vietminh still kept the door open for negotiations on the basis of earlier and more generous statements Bollaert had made.

It was at this crucial point that Bao Dai climbed down from his "neutral" perch and announced that he was ready to deal with the French by himself for independence; by so doing, he rejected not only the Vietminh but the possibility that he might become the real spokesman for a united nationalist front. It seems likely that the Emperor and his advisers were motivated, at least in part, by discussions Bao Dai had held in Hong Kong with William Bullitt, the American diplomat, whose ties with the French were always close. Bullitt, on a private world tour, had stopped off to see Bao Dai in the British colony, and he later wrote an article for a national magazine in America in which, without mentioning Bao Dai by name, he suggested a solution for "the saddest war," as he called the war in Indochina, that seemed obviously to point to the Emperor as the logical man around whom carefully selected anti-Communist nationalist forces could rally. Whether Bullitt spoke informally for the American government or not wasn't clear—he probably didn't— but his visit and the article led a number of influential French politicians and officials to believe that the United States backed the "Bao Dai formula."

In the period that followed, Bao Dai signed a number of agreements with the French that lent themselves to various interpretations —none of which, as it turned out, gave the Vietnamese the measure of independence they sought. Bao Dai himself, during much of this time, absented himself from Vietnam in order to force the French to implement the agreements more liberally and to make more concessions. These maneuvers by the Emperor proved signally unsuccessful. The sequence of events began on December 7, 1947, when Bao Dai signed his first agreement with High Commissioner Bollaert aboard a French warship in Ha Long Bay. The terms of this brief preliminary statement were vague and unsatisfactory to most of the nationalists supporting Bao Dai, and he himself soon realized his mistake; at the end of the year, he left for Europe, where he saw Bollaert again, as well as a number of other French leaders whose attitude toward the increasingly complex Indochina situation was guided by the equally complex political situation in France, which was undergoing one of its own almost chronic postwar crises. When Bao Dai returned to Hong Kong, he sent Diem to Saigon to try to obtain stronger assurances about Vietnamese independence from Bollaert. Diem failed to move the High Commissioner, who was by now held on leash by Paris; but once more, against the advice of Diem and other nationalists, Bao Dai capitulated to the French, who persuaded him by citing the need for a strong common stand against the Communists in Asia to match the rising anti-Communist position being adopted in Western Europe and in the United States. On June 5, 1948, aboard a ship in Ha Long Bay, Bao Dai signed another agreement with Bollaert, recognizing the independence of an Associated State of Vietnam as part of the French Union. For the first time, the French agreed to the proposition that Cochin China would be part of this new state. Separate protocols were to follow on economic, military, financial, and other matters; this was always a French tactic—a convenient procrastination—and basically the new agreement was just as restrictive as that of the previous December in failing to spell out the terms of independence.

When Diem now refused to head a new government under Bao Dai, General Nguyen Van Xuan, a French-trained officer who had already established a provisional Vietnamese government in Saigon, reorganized it to include representatives from Annam and Tonkin and to give it less of a Cochin China coloration. This new provisional central government—acting in Bao Dai's name—was proclaimed in Hanoi immediately after the signing of the Ha Long Bay agreement in June, and it thus became the first formal opposition to Ho Chi Minh's Republic in the jungle. Ho lost no time in branding Bao Dai and those who formed the new government as quislings. He knew what he was doing. The agreement soon served to stir up more support for the Vietminh than for Bao Dai, especially as the French government took its time in ratifying it and made it clear that the separate protocols would assure continued French control of Vietnam's foreign and defense matters. The French had also seen to it that each of the three new parts of the Associated State—North, Central, and South Vietnam—had separate governors whose loyalty to the new central government was questionable.

Bao Dai remained in Hong Kong and then returned to Europe, thereby beginning his long-term maneuver to get more out of the French. As the Chinese Communists came closer to victory over the Kuomintang, the French, fearing that this would inevitably strengthen the hand of the Vietminh, wanted more than ever to use the Emperor to split the Vietnamese resistance movement. Consequently, on March 8, 1949, President Vincent Auriol of France exchanged letters with Bao Dai at the Elysée Palace, in Paris, and these letters hinted at terms that would be more advantageous for the Vietnamese than those offered in the previous agreements. Vietnam was promised its own army for internal security purposes, though it was stipulated that this force would be advised and equipped by the French and that it had to fight for the French Union if this was demanded by France. Membership in the Union was mandatory and could not be terminated, and in joining it Vietnam automatically had to accept control over its own foreign and defense policies. In economic and financial affairs, the French still controlled the Indochina piastre by tying it to the French franc, even though there would be a single Indochina bank of issue for Vietnam and for the two other new Associated States of Laos and Cambodia. French property remained protected by French laws and regulations, while other matters, such as foreign trade, customs, and immigration, were to be taken up in a subsequent conference attended by Vietnam, Laos, Cambodia, and France. Juridically, French laws were still applicable to all French citizens.

Bao Dai, in commenting upon the "Elysée agreement," as it came to be known, spoke of "profound economic and social reforms" to come and of "the generous support of France on which I know I can count"; but when he finally returned to Vietnam, at the end of April, 1949, he came under the cloud of a contract that, while seemingly better than anything the French had offered before, still imposed many restrictions and did not clearly guarantee the independence of Vietnam. There was one immediate and important benefit: Cochin China had just voted to join itself to the new state, though the limited election that took place had turned into a rather discouraging demonstration of last-ditch efforts by the French *colons* to maintain the colony's separate status. Now, under a new and tougher High Commissioner, Léon Pignon, who had replaced Bollaert, Bao Dai became Chief of State. When Ngo Dinh Diem again refused to become Premier, insisting that the least that Vietnam deserved was a true Dominion status like India and Pakistan, Bao Dai himself took over the Prime Minister's job. The French had won their battle with the Emperor—at least for the moment—but they were now losing the war against the Vietminh, and the Bao Dai government they had managed so painfully to create would prove no defense.

Americans and French at Odds

I had been in and out of Hong Kong and Saigon early in 1947, when the Bao Dai experiment was just starting, and I returned to Saigon in the fall of 1950, when the French were loudly proclaiming the experiment's success. The process of setting up the new arrangement had been terribly slow. Only at the end of December, 1949, nine months after the Elysée letters had been exchanged, had the final agreements between the French and the Vietnamese been signed at a ceremony in Saigon, at which Bao Dai had formally taken over the administration of the new Vietnam Republic. The French National Assembly had ratified the agreements a month later, after a heated debate. No steps had been taken to establish a Vietnamese Army, and the new government had virtually no administrative organs and no money of its own to create them. The French, in fact, had as many or more civil servants in the country than they had had before, because so many Vietnamese functionaries were serving with the French colonial forces and so many others had drifted off, not knowing where they stood professionally or where they dared to stand politically. The much-delayed conference between Vietnam, Cambodia, Laos, and France to work out the details of economic and other relations among them had just begun at Pau, in France, and Bao Dai, who had gone to France to help get the Elysée agreement ratified, had remained there to attend the prolonged and complicated Pau sessions. He was visited in Vichy during the summer by his old friend and supporter, Dr. Dan, who had resigned as Minister of Information during the negotiations for the Elysée pact, because he had felt that the French had not given the Vietnamese enough freedom. Now, in Vichy, Bao Dai seemed to agree with Dr. Dan. "What they call a Bao Dai solution turned out to be just a French solution," he said gloomily. "The situation in Indochina is getting worse every day."

Bao Dai had played a difficult and anomalous role throughout the long period of negotiations with the French, who had understood clearly the man with whom they were dealing. An American diplomat in Vietnam who had come to know the Emperor well, and who admired him, later told me: "Bao Dai, above all, was an intelligent man. Intellectually, he could discuss the complex details of the various agreements and of the whole involved relationship with France as well as or better than anyone I knew. But he was a man who was crippled by his French upbringing. His manner was too impassive. He allowed himself to be sold by the French on an erroneous instead of a valid evolutionary concept, and this suited his own temperament. He was too congenial, and he was almost pathologically shy, which was one reason he always liked to wear dark glasses. He would go through depressive cycles, and when he was depressed, he would dress himself in Vietnamese clothes instead of European ones, and would mince no words about the French. His policy, he said to me on one of these dour occasions, was one of *'grignotage,'* or 'nibbling,' and he was painfully aware of it. The French, of course, were never happy that we Americans had good relations with Bao Dai, and they told him so. Unfortunately, they also had some blackmail on him, about his relationship with gambling enterprises in Saigon and his love of the fleshpots."

The French officials I spoke with in Saigon in 1950 seemed to resent the fact that Bao Dai had spent so much time abroad instead of in Vietnam. "He has concentrated too much on getting what he can from us instead of building up his support among the people of the country," one high-ranking political counselor, a man of liberal background and intentions, told me. "History will judge if he did right in putting so much stress on that." When I asked him how he thought history would judge the French, he smiled and shrugged. The fact remained, as my American diplomatic friend pointed out, that if Bao Dai had not stayed abroad to negotiate with the French, at the time of the Pau discussions and earlier, the Vietnamese would not have obtained even as much as they did. "It wasn't enough, but by simply being there and putting pressure on the French, Bao Dai did better than anyone else could have done," my friend said. "His being a sports-lover, and spending part of his time at Cannes, on the Riviera, or in Paris, had nothing to do with it. Anyone who went through what he did with the French had a right, if not a positive need, to seek some recreation."

In February, less than a week after the French government had belatedly ratified the Elysée agreements, the Americans and the British had together recognized the Associated States of Vietnam, Cambodia, and Laos. While the British bemoaned the fact that the agreements had failed to give the Vietnamese enough independence, the American statement was typically bland. "This recognition is consistent with our fundamental policy of giving support to the peaceful and democratic evolution of democratic peoples toward self-government and independence," a State Department bulletin said. The American position on Bao Dai and the French solution to the Indochina problem were sorely vitiated a few months later, in June, by the outbreak of the

Korean War. About that time, Edmund Gullion had come to Saigon as the American Chargé d'Affaires, pending the arrival of Minister Donald Heath. Gullion, who had Consul General rank and, when the Legation became an Embassy, would become Minister Counselor, was soon to adopt a firm position about the American policy in Vietnam, one that was privately shared by many in the Legation, though not by Minister Heath. As Gullion has since said, he felt at first that the Americans "ought not to rock the boat," but within a few months he became convinced that the United States should be far more firm than it was being in supporting the Vietnamese independently of the French and, at the same time, in persuading the French to grant the Vietnamese a greater degree of freedom. Fifteen years later, in the spring of 1965, by which time he had resigned from the Foreign Service after having served as Ambassador to the Congo under President Kennedy, Gullion said in careful retrospect, "We really should have pushed the French right after the Elysée agreements of March, 1949. We did not consider the exchange of letters carefully enough at the time. It was understandable. We obviously felt it was going to be a continuing process, and we hoped to be able to have some influence over it. But then we got involved in Korea, and since the French were in trouble in Indochina, we pulled our punches."

Soon after Gullion had arrived in Vietnam, in 1950, the United States, responding to French requests for military and economic assistance, had agreed to grant both forms of aid to help restore order and, as Secretary of State Dean Acheson expressed it, encourage "genuine nationalism." The French had mixed feelings about accepting aid from the Americans; they had not forgotten the early support some Americans had given Ho Chi Minh, and they were quick to fear that the Americans might not only regain some of their early pro-nationalist image, tarnished as it might already have become in the eyes of most Vietnamese, but that American businessmen might seek to obtain economic advantages in Vietnam at the expense of the French. General Marcel Carpentier, who had become the French Commander in Chief, made it very clear, even before Acheson's announcement, that he would resign if the Americans gave military aid directly to the Vietnamese. "The Vietnamese have no generals, no colonels, and no military organization that could effectively utilize the equipment," he was quoted by the *New York Times* as saying. "It would be wasted, and in China the United States has had enough of that." The American experience in China was obviously a sore point in Washington, but regardless of this the United States did not yet have any intention, under the circumstances, of giving military aid directly to the Vietnamese. It was too soon to expect the Vietnamese to be able to handle such aid by themselves, and besides the French were running the war. The emerging Korean crisis served to hasten President Truman's decision to give military support to the French. What did set the stage for a great deal of subsequent difficulty, however, was the vagueness of American intentions on the matter of economic aid. The official statement said that such aid would be given directly to the Vietnamese, but this proved to be more easily said than done, and it became an extremely sore subject, not only between the French and the Americans but among some of the Americans themselves. These differences, taken in context with political developments in Vietnam, and with the whole evolving pattern of relations between the United States and France in Europe as well as in Asia, would influence events for a long time to come; their impact is still apparent today in the difficulties that have arisen between the French and the Americans over China and Southeast Asia and over Europe as well.

One of the earliest manifestations of French-American differences occurred in the spring of 1950, when the French forced Bao Dai to dismiss the man he had selected five months before to take his place as Prime Minister of the Associated State of Vietnam. Nguyen Phan Long had made it clear that he wanted the friendship of the Americans and that he wanted American aid, both military and economic, to be given directly to the Vietnamese. His attempt to foster a strong independent nationalist position failed not only because the French wouldn't stand for it but also because he was unable, given the circumstances of the whole Bao Dai experiment, to rally enough popular support. Long, a competent man, had particularly failed to win to Bao Dai's side the growing number of *attentistes*—people who refused to take sides in the political and revolutionary struggle. Many of them had refused to do so ever since 1946, either out of conviction or because of personal reasons; some who might have joined Bao Dai subsequently did not do so because they had relatives in the Vietminh areas or up north, or simply because they did not believe in the Bao Dai effort. They were not ready, as they told me, to join forces with Bao Dai, because they doubted that he could represent the true struggle for independence. Their disinclination to do so became stronger when Bao Dai appointed a wealthy landowner and businessman named Tran Van Huu to become Prime Minister in place of Long. Huu, who had been Governor of South Vietnam, was a plump, suave man who held French citizenship. He was to become known for a remark he made, soon after he took office, to an American acquaintance: "I know that you Americans think I'm a French stooge and that the French have made it possible for me to become rich. This is not true. I married one of the largest fortunes in Indochina, and I fructified it with my own efforts."

It was perhaps no accident that a dozen years after he had become Vietnam's Prime Minister, Tran Van Huu would be living comfortably in Paris, where he would be a member of the small but vocal band of Vietnamese neutralists who, along with President Charles de Gaulle, clamored for peace in Vietnam and for the creation of a new neutral Southeast Asian bloc of nations. In March, 1965, Tran Van Huu left Paris long enough to attend the meeting of neutral Indochina states summoned by Prince Norodom Sihanouk of Cambodia, in Phnom Penh—a meeting that the Communists quickly turned into an anti-American rally. But in Saigon, in the spring of 1950, Huu was singing a different tune. When I saw him at that time, he counseled patience, and insisted that the French would still make good on their promises to give Vietnam full independence. But he did not sound nearly as convincing as Nguyen Huu Tri, who had become a governor of the northernmost sector of the Associated State of Vietnam, and who the Americans hoped would exert more pressure on the French. Tri was firm in demanding complete independence and in insisting that the French stop dragging their feet. "We have had many more promises in the past," he declared. "We now want to see a real transfer of power." Tri pointed out that the ranks of the *attentistes* were increasing because of the common fear that the French would not make good on their Elysée pact promises. Tran van Huu may have taken his cue from Tri when he pleaded in his inaugural address for "the lukewarm and the hesitant," meaning the *attentistes,* to support him. But if anyone was a lukewarm nationalist in 1950, it was Tran Van Huu.

Red Star in the North

It was no accident that Saigon had become a haven for refugees from the Vietminh and that most of them joined the swelling ranks of the fence sitters. Starting in 1949, the Vietminh moved clearly into the world Communist camp, and the Republic in the north was completely taken over by hard-line Communist officials. This development probably got underway early in 1948, when Vietminh representatives attended three important Communist conferences in Calcutta, where decisions were made to begin Communist uprisings in Malaya and Burma. The attitude of the Vietnamese Communists was undoubtedly based on the realities of the international situation: to the north, the Chinese Communists had completed their victory over the Kuomintang, and in December, 1949, their troops reached the Indochina border. By the spring of 1950, at least two Vietminh military training camps were already established in the southern Chinese province of Yünnan. Young Vietnamese conscripts were sent there for political indoctrination and basic training, and veteran fighters went to study modern weapons tactics. After three months, these men rejoined their various units, and by early summer at least four thousand had re-entered North Vietnam. The Chinese now began to send weapons to the Vietminh via roads and trails as well as along the railroad route from Kunming into Tonkin. The supply was limited at first—one typical lot included two thousand rifles, forty machine guns, and seventy-five mortars—but it slowly increased. The Chinese also sent the North Vietnamese some machinery and machine tools, for which they received partial payment in the form of rice, opium, timber, and metals, especially tin.

After the recognition of the Ho Chi Minh regime early in 1950 by both Peking and Moscow, a propaganda campaign was begun to establish Ho as one of the important world Communist leaders. Posters at the Chinese training camps and at Ho's jungle headquarters in Tonkin proclaimed, "Long Live Stalin, Mao Tse-tung, and Ho Chi Minh." The campaign was extended into the south, too, where two top Communist leaders were sent by Ho to reorganize the resistance movement and to make sure trusted Communist political officers were placed in charge. Trappings of the new Ho-Stalin-Mao alliance were quickly distributed in the south; when a company of French Foreign Legion soldiers captured a Vietminh political headquarters northeast of Saigon, they found Chinese Communist and Soviet flags prominently displayed with Vietminh banners alongside three carved wooden busts of Ho, Stalin, and Mao.

As this political drive was mounted, the Communists won a series of stunning military victories over the French in the fall of 1950. Employing a total of about forty battalions, armed with mortars and artillery, the Vietminh attacked a string of French forts on the Chinese border. The most important of these to fall was Caobang, a hundred and ten miles northeast of Hanoi, and within a period of a few months the Vietminh had seized all of these strong points, stretching south from Caobang along Colonial Route 4. The French high command all but panicked and abandoned some other vital strategic bases, including Langson in the east. Bernard Fall, describing the debacle as "the greatest colonial defeat since Montcalm had died at Quebec," said that the French lost six thousand troops, nearly a thousand machine guns, more than a thousand submachine guns, and eight thousand rifles, and that the arms they abandoned were enough to equip a whole Vietminh division. The Vietminh now controlled virtually the whole northern half of North Vietnam. General Giap later wrote, in his *People's War, People's Army*, that these victories at the end of 1950 "marked a new phase in the evolution of our long Resistance," and the Vietminh immediately followed up the border victories with a series of fresh attacks in the Red River Delta. However, they failed to take over the delta, and Giap could not yet sustain a general counter offensive—the third stage of his war plan. He had gone beyond the first stage of retreat and defense, but for the next three years he would shift back and forth between the second stage, a guerrilla war of attrition, and the final one, which would be climaxed by the great victory over the French at Dienbienphu in May, 1954.

The culmination of the Vietminh's political swing into the Communist camp came much earlier, in mid-February, 1951, when an eight-day national Congress attended by two hundred delegates was held somewhere in Vietminh territory. It was here that the Laodang, or Workers, Party was created to succeed the old Indochina Communist Party that had been disbanded in the fall of 1944 and replaced by Marxist Study Groups. The organizer of the Congress, and the man who became General Secretary of the new party, was Dang Xuan Khu, alias Truong Chinh, the pro-Peking extremist and rigid doctrinaire Communist. Although Ho Chi Minh remained the father figure of the Vietminh, and would continue, despite recurrent and false rumors of his death in the jungle, to be its spiritual as well as its practical guide and mentor—adroitly maintaining its position between the Soviet and Peking camps when the split occurred—it was Truong Chinh who now assumed the daily functions of leadership, though he would not remain unchallenged and would suffer his ups and downs. The manifesto and program of the Laodang Party, as issued by the Vietnam News Agency, declared that its theory was "Marxism-Leninism," and added: "The Vietnamese revolution is part of the world-wide movement for national liberation and for the defense of peace and democracy. By fighting for their own independence and freedom, the Vietnamese people contribute to the maintenance of peace in the world and the development of people's democratic regimes in Southeast Asia." Proud references were made to "the gigantic victory of the Chinese people," and Mao, as well as Stalin, Maurice Thorez, the French Communist chief, and Kim Il-sung, the Korean leader, were named to the party's honorary presidium. The "driving forces" of the revolution were described as "workers, peasants, petty bourgeoisie and national bourgeoisie, as well as patriotic and progressive personages and landlords," but the leading class was declared to be the workers. The Republic was to be "A People's Democratic Dictatorship, democratic toward the people, dictatorial toward the imperialist aggressors and reactionaries." Various programs for developing the economy and

carrying out agrarian reform were outlined, and "the progressive culture of the world, especially of the Soviet Union and China was to be
studied and emulated." The Laodang moved quickly to consolidate
its power by announcing the merger of the Vietminh and the old
Lienviet, the popular political front that had been created in 1946,
into a new National Union Front, which adopted the Lienviet name,
and all other separate front organizations were joined to it.

There was no longer any pretext that the Vietminh was a broad nationalist organization in which non-Communists could play a role. All
non-Communists were now dropped from Cabinet, sub-Cabinet and
other administrative posts, and Communist cadres moved swiftly,
under the aegis of the Laodang Party and the Lienviet front, to take
over the direction of peasant, worker, youth, and other groups. Old-
line intellectuals and nationalist leaders who had joined the Vietminh
in 1946 were now cast out. So far as is known, there was no mass
purge, but some were killed and imprisoned, and others simply
dropped from sight. A number made their way south, across the fluid
borders that marked the separation of Vietminh zones from the new
Associated State of Vietnam, often traveling for weeks on foot. Some
had left even before the formation of the Laodang, having seen the
handwriting on the wall, while others came afterward, and the process
continued for many months. Not all these political defectors were
from the Republic in the north; some were ranking officials who had
served the Vietminh in the south, in one or another of the six zones
the Communists had established there. In a sense, because they had
seen the battle between the French and the Vietminh being waged
week by week at close hand in the villages, they were more interesting
revolutionary witnesses than those who came from the far north,
where the Vietminh had been in power for several years: they had
become the fish out of the water that Mao Tse-tung had so often
referred to.

One of them I spoke with, a man named Cau Minh Chien, had
been a prominent official of a special court that had dealt with spies
and saboteurs in a Vietminh zone. His revolutionary life since 1945
had been that of a shuttlecock. He had attended school in Saigon and
become a journalist there when the war ended in 1945. Believing in

the Vietminh cause, he had gone north and had been drafted as a Vietminh propagandist, assigned to an area in Central Vietnam. When the French pushed the Vietminh out of the area during the early phase of the war, he had gone north again and been given a job as a security agent in the Thai country, west of Hanoi, where he helped organize local guerrillas. Chien had known Ho Chi Minh personally and had therefore been accepted, despite his political independence, by the local Vietminh authorities, but he had not been altogether trusted. In 1948, after a number of differences with his immediate superiors over the prosecution of cases, he had resigned and returned to Saigon, where he had started a nationalist newspaper, which lasted a month before the French cracked down on it. He remained in Saigon, hoping to start a business that would earn him a living, but he had been constantly followed by French *sûreté* agents and their Vietnamese counterparts. In desperation, he had gone north again, where once more he was put to work as a propagandist. In the fall of 1950, he had become aware that his non-membership in the Communist Party had brought his usefulness to an end and that his life was in danger, and he once more made his way to Saigon.

When I saw Chien, he was not particularly bitter or even disillusioned, and his faith in Vietnam and the Vietnamese was intact. "We must somehow learn to conquer the hearts and souls of the people," he said fervidly over a glass of wine at a café along the river front. He indicated that he *might* be willing to work as a propagandist for the Bao Dai regime, but he made it clear that he wanted to watch and wait, and that he hadn't yet made up his mind. He was a *nouveau attentiste*. Chien had nothing but disdain for the propaganda program of the south. "None of it appeals to the people in the Vietminh areas," he said. "Propaganda must have a local appeal in order to be successful. Where I was, the leaflets that were dropped by planes were a joke. They had obviously been prepared in Saigon or Hanoi, or maybe in Paris. At any rate, the people laughed at them. Claims of Vietminh terrorism were simply not true, and the fact that the people knew this caused the Saigon government far more damage than good. What the government here must learn is to understand local problems, in every area, and to make its appeal accordingly. Only

D

those who have lived in a certain area can understand it, and these are the people the government must use. You can't use propaganda dropped from the sky in containers to cover every situation. When the army takes over a village or a district, the government should have a squad of propagandists enter with the troops, and they should be people known to the population, not strangers. Now that the Vietminh has increased the people's literacy, the government should take advantage of this and offer something that can be understood and appreciated, not just hollow promises and denunciations of the Vietminh, which the people know aren't true."

Another man I saw was Dr. Pham Van Huyen, a veterinarian and bacteriologist who had come down from Tonkin. Dr. Huyen had studied in France, at the Pasteur Institute. He had joined the Vietminh in 1945 and had become director of agriculture, fisheries, and cattle-raising in the early days in Hanoi. Also a friend of Ho's, he had been asked several times to become Minister of Economics or of Agriculture but had refused when it was made clear that he would have to join the Communist Party. Most recently, he had been in charge of a number of medical services. When he was chosen to join a cultural mission to China, he made his break, because he realized that this was the first step toward purging him; he said that ten of his nationalist and intellectual friends had been in a similar position. "The government still makes a big point of its liberal-mindedness, and appeals to all sorts of groups and individuals, insisting they're welcome in the movement," he said, "but the Communists are now completely running things. The Chinese victory over the Kuomintang and Communist successes in Korea have had a lot to do with it. Even so, popular support for the Vietminh is not what it was in the beginning, but that doesn't mean there is a lot of discontent. And it doesn't mean there is any support for Bao Dai, who is being presented more and more as an American puppet, especially since Korea. Nobody in the north believes that Bao Dai can offer the Vietnamese real independence." As with Cau Minh Chien, Dr. Huyen was potentially willing to work with Bao Dai, but he wanted to wait and see how independent of the French the former Emperor really was. He was particularly anxious to determine for himself the sincerity of the Americans in wanting to help the Vietnamese directly, and not through the French. "The problem is not just to offer money, but to know how to run a country," he said.

Intellectuals such as Chien and Dr. Huyen were willing to talk to American correspondents, though they ran a certain risk in doing so, since the Vietminh assassination squads were still active in Saigon and the Communists did not relish having renegades discuss their problems, such as the food storage, in the north. Ordinary people in Saigon were far less willing to be seen talking to foreigners. With a Vietnamese friend of mine, I spent several mornings wandering around the city trying to engage people in conversation, but without much success. "If you want to know about us, take us to the police station," a fisherman on a boat anchored in the Saigon River snapped, turning his back. The feeling of mistrust was pervasive, and while natural curiosity has always been a healthy Oriental attribute, Vietnamese in these days did not trust each other much more than they trusted the French or any other foreigners. No one could be certain that his neighbor was not secretly a Vietminh agent or sympathizer or one of the two thousand secret security agents or four thousand ordinary police, many of whom wore civilian clothes, who were working for Doc Phu Tam, the tough national police chief. Tam was currently conducting an intensive campaign against Vietminh agents in Saigon and against what he told me was an important fifth column among the five hundred thousand Chinese in the adjacent Chinese city of Cholon. In contrast to the atmosphere of 1946, one felt a sense of fear everywhere. My interpreter took me to visit a friend of his, a wealthy importer-exporter who was purposely living in a shabby flat near Cholon to avoid suspicion, "Of course, I would prefer to live normally," he said, "and to take an active interest in politics, as I once did, but all of us now are waiting. We are fatalists by nature, and we have learned how to keep quiet. If you were a doctor, diagnosing our condition, wouldn't you prescribe silence?"

The Pau Negotiations

The negotiations between the French and the Vietnamese to define the independent privileges of the Associated States of Vietnam, as set forth in the Elysée agreement, dragged on at Pau from the end of

June, 1950, to the end of November. These sessions, which Tran Van Huu attended, were designed to implement the transfer from France to Vietnam, Cambodia, and Laos of the services of immigration, communications, foreign trade, customs, and finances. The negotiations were inevitably complex because they involved two sets of problems and principles that were not easy to mesh—the sovereignty of each of the three states and their association with each other, and their individual and combined relationship to the French Union. Added difficulties involved the administration of the port of Saigon, navigation along the Mekong River, and the role of the Indochina Bank in issuing piastres and conducting foreign exchange transactions. A considerable amount of friction arose as a result of jealousies among the three states as well as between them and France. The states were forced to accept certain limitations on their sovereignty that derived not only from their mandatory membership in the French Union but also from France's insistence that her economic prerogatives be protected. While the French renounced the essential controls they had exercised during the colonial period, they made certain that their "rights of observation" and "intervention" in matters that "concerned the French Union as a whole" were maintained, and this produced a shadowland of French participation in almost all areas. In immigration, for example, the French were accorded access to all files, and they insisted they be allowed to expel anyone whose presence they deemed harmful to the security of the French forces. Similarly, in the areas of economic planning and foreign trade, the French were to participate in all discussions and have a voice in making decisions. When the conference finally ended, Tran Van Huu, who had found it necessary during the negotiations to appeal to England and America to bring pressure on France to be lenient (no pressure was brought), declared that "our independence is now perfect." Not many Vietnamese agreed with him. When the process of implementing the Pau agreements began—the formal date for transferring the various services was April 1, 1951—the French stiffened their position and saw to it that their representation was assured in all deliberations and that their "guidance" was firmly imposed. The right of the Indochina states to exchange diplomatic representatives abroad was still severely limited, and when it came to discussions and negotiations with foreign nations, especially with the United States, the various Indochinese states frequently were not even allowed to participate.

As far as most Vietnamese were concerned, they still felt themselves "second-class citizens," even though the Pau agreements were more liberal than anything the French had offered before, to Ho Chi Minh or to Bao Dai. "The French were still unable to state unequivocally that the Indochina states would be completely independent," Gullion has since commented. "This inability was always reflected in the accords they made. If only they had handled the question of membership in the French Union the way de Gaulle finally handled it in regard to Algeria later on, for example, and not made it obligatory for the Associated States either to join the Union or to stay in it once they joined. While the Elysée agreement and the Pau accords transferred many local powers and agencies to the Associated States, they essentially preserved French control in such key fields as foreign affairs, justice, and finance. Decisions on these matters that affected the interest of more than one of the three states or of France were subject to review by quadripartite bodies in which the French either had a veto or could deadlock action. Existing regulations inherited from almost a century of colonial rule theoretically could not be changed without the assent of the French.

"In a broad sense, the unhappy pattern of Franco-Vietnamese relations exhibited these phases: (a) initial reluctance by the French to make concessions, followed by (b) Vietminh military successes or a stalemate, after which (c) the French grant concessions. For example, the French did not proceed to the March 8, 1949, accords until they failed to defeat the Vietminh in 1948, and the Chinese Communists were well on their way to final victory in China. They did not start to build a Vietnamese national army until after the disasters of Caobang and Langson, in the fall of 1950. And the transfer of local powers got its greatest impetus only after more disappointing military campaigns late in 1951 and early in 1952. This dilatory approach obviously was not calculated to make the Vietnamese peasant believe in the quality of independence being granted. The peasant may not have understood the details of the endless discussions and agreements, but he *did* know that the French still controlled his movements, locally and nationally. He couldn't see independence, feel it, or smell it, or even sense it coming."

Nor was there any evidence visible to the peasant, the "fence sitter" or the average citizen in Saigon that the Bao Dai government, despite the Pau agreements, was making much headway in establishing itself as a truly independent nationalist force. It lacked representative character as well as popular support, and Bao Dai himself did little to rectify the situation. He divided his time between the resort towns of Dalat, Nhatrang and Banmethuout. When his old friend Dr. Dan went to see him at Nhatrang, he was received by the Emperor's mother, who told him that Bao Dai was still asleep. "With tears in her eyes, she said that she and her son were most unhappy, that they did not know whom to trust, that they were heartsick at the atmosphere of hostility that surrounded them," Dr. Dan later wrote. Sailing on the imperial yacht, Bao Dai "complained that his successive governments had been of little use, and added that it would be dangerous to expand the Vietnamese Army because it might defect en masse and go to the Vietminh." This was also the opinion of a good many Frenchmen, but not of most Americans. "I could not inspire the troops with the necessary enthusiasm and fighting spirit, nor could Prime Minister Huu," Bao Dai told Dr. Dan. "Even if we had an able man, the present political conditions would make it impossible for him to convince the people and the troops that they have something worth while to fight for." Dr. Dan agreed that the problem of desertions existed, but he, like other ardent nationalists, felt that the problem had to be met head-on, instead of being postponed, if the Vietnamese were ever going to be able to take over the defense of their own country. "The Vietnamese Army is without responsible Vietnamese leaders, without ideology, without objective, without enthusiasm, without fighting spirit, and without popular backing," he wrote. He pointed out that there were three Vietnamese generals, none of whom had any operational command, and that neither they nor the twenty colonels and lieutenant colonels assigned to administrative jobs could initiate action of any kind.

This whole essential problem of the Vietnamese not being able to initiate anything obviously vitiated their relations with the French. Nationalist groups were still not permitted to meet and talk freely, or to publish their newspapers without censorship. It was apparently Bao Dai's feeling that he had done all he could to move the French and that, in effect, his own role now was that of an *attentiste*—of waiting to see if, perhaps as a result of prodding by the Americans, the French would implement their promises, relinquish the strings they still held, and allow Vietnamese nationalism to burgeon. For that reason, he chose to isolate himself in his resort homes. Furthermore, he did not yet have free access to Norodom Palace, the seat of colonial power in Saigon, and the French were not inclined to give it to him. When I saw Bao Dai, I was impressed with his understanding of the evolving situation, though he was scarcely convincing when, over a glass of champagne, he said, "For the moment, I am devoting all my energies to my country." It was hard to tell where his sit-down tactics left off and his penchant for pleasure began. I kept thinking of another remark he had made, to his private secretary: "To practice politics is like playing a game, and I have always considered life as sport." The day after I spoke with him in Saigon, he was back at Dalat, enjoying his hunting preserves and his other private pursuits. As Gullion had said, he was a difficult man to figure out.

Enter General de Lattre

In mid-December, 1950, General Jean de Lattre de Tassigny was appointed both Commander in Chief of the French Expeditionary Forces in Indochina and High Commissioner—the first and only man to hold both jobs. De Lattre came to Vietnam when French morale was at a low ebb, when the war had begun to be described in Paris as *"la sale guerre"*—the dirty war—and when important political voices were already being raised in favor of French withdrawal. De Lattre was in all respects a remarkable man. He was, above all, a true leader— "No matter what, you will be commanded," he announced when he arrived in Saigon. He made it clear that although it might be the expectation in France that he could do no better than preside over the collapse of the French empire in the Orient in as orderly a way as possible, he had no intention of withdrawing, and the *élan vital* he immediately provided stirred the French forces as nothing else could have done. *Dynamisme* became the order of the day. De Lattre was similar in many respects to General Douglas MacArthur, particularly in the effect his mere presence and manner had on those who dealt with him. "He could influence me against my better judgment," Gullion recalls, "even though I often felt that he didn't really understand the Vietnamese problem. He believed only what he wanted to believe. But he had tremendous courage and a great sense of self-dramatization, and these qualities were necessary for the job he undertook, if he was going to get anywhere."

De Lattre was convinced that he was leading a crusade against Communism. He told me that the French were in Vietnam "to save it from Peking and Moscow," and he predicted victory in fifteen months. He insisted that there was no longer an ounce of colonialism left in French intentions. "We have no more interest here," he said blandly. "We have abandoned all our colonial positions completely. There is little rubber or coal or rice we can any longer obtain. And what does it amount to compared to the blood of our sons we are losing and the three hundred and fifty million francs we spend a day in Indochina? The work we are doing is for the salvation of the Vietnamese people. And the propaganda you Americans make that we are still colonialists is doing us tremendous harm, all of us—the Vietnamese, yourselves, and us." There was a degree of truth to what de Lattre said—the French were partly fighting in the interest of the free world—but his denial that French profits were still a very important reason for the French presence was simply not supportable. The French still owned practically all of the real wealth of Indochina, and their investment was close to two billion dollars; they owned all the rubber plantations, which, despite the war, were still operating— as they are operating today, in 1965—and they owned two-thirds of the rice, all the mines, all the shipping, virtually all the industry, and nearly all the banks. The men who sat behind their desks at the Bank of Indochina could afford to smile at the General's brave words, for French fortunes were being made through the remittance machinery legally established for the transfer of piastres into French francs, falsely pegged at seventeen to the piastre; the franc had remained relatively stable, but the piastre had depreciated more than five times since the end of the Second World War.

Listening to de Lattre, who every now and then closed his eyes and leaned back his long, high-browed, almost ecclesiastic head, I was convinced that he believed implicitly everything he said. His own role in the fight against Communist imperialism was clear. He did, indeed, feel himself a crusader. He was also aware that only the infusion of new blood could save the Bao Dai government and turn it into an independent force to draw popular support away from the Vietminh, and for this reason he, more than other French commanders who came to Indochina, was prepared to create a native Vietnamese Army. In a moving speech he made, entitled "A Call to Vietnamese Youth," he struck out against the *attentistes*—"those miserable persons who want independence without war," as he put it, adding, "This war, whether you like it or not, is the war of Vietnam for Vietnam. And France will carry it on for you only if you carry it on with her. . . . Certain people pretend that Vietnam cannot be independent because it is part of the French Union. Not true! In our universe, and especially in our world of today, there can be no nations absolutely independent. There are only fruitful interdependencies and harmful dependencies. . . . Young men of Vietnam, to whom I feel as close as I do to the youth of my native land, the moment has come for you to defend your country." These were fine, noble words, but their promise remained essentially unfulfilled.

At the time the United States recognized the new Associated State of Vietnam, there were a half-dozen Vietnamese battalions. By the spring of 1953, there were sixty, totaling about 150,000 men, but sixty per cent of these units had been transferred from the French Union Army, and hence were not "volunteers" in the sense that de Lattre meant in his impassioned call to the country's youth. Above all, there was a lack of cadres, and this was due to French mistrust of the Vietnamese. Among the 150,000, there were only some 2,600 officers, and only a handful above the rank of major; the French had to make up the difference, some 7,000, from their own forces. "It remained difficult to inculcate nationalist ardor in a native army whose officers and non-çoms were primarily white Frenchmen," Gullion later pointed out, especially when the so-called "army" lacked any real elements of a high command of its own. "The Vietnamese units that went into action were rarely unsupported by the French. American contact with them was mainly through the French, who retained exclusive responsibility for their training. We felt we needed much more documentation than we had to assess the army's true potential. We needed battalion-by-battalion reports on the performance of the Vietnamese in training as well as in battle and a close contact with intelligence and command echelons, and we never got this. Perhaps the most significant and saddest manifestation of the French failure to create a really independent Vietnamese Army that would fight in the way de Lattre meant was the absence, at Dienbienphu, of any Vietnamese fighting elements. It was a French show."

By that time, de Lattre was dead of cancer. He had almost worked miracles. When he first arrived in Indochina, the Vietminh was on an offensive rampage in the northern part of the Red River Delta and seemed ready to mount a bold offensive to retake Hanoi. A major battle came to a climax at Vinhyen on January 16 and 17, 1950, when the French, using all the firepower they could muster, defeated General Giap's forces and inflicted heavy casualties on them; the Vietminh suffered six thousand dead. In the succeeding months, the French, and the first few Vietnamese units led by Vietnamese officers that de Lattre had been able to create, held off and defeated more Vietminh attacks. By June Giap's move to launch a major counter-offensive had been thoroughly repulsed, and he was forced to retreat to the mountains. He would not again make the mistake of attacking in force in the delta until the war was almost over, although he would thoroughly infiltrate the area. He would concentrate mainly on the highlands, ultimately reaching into Laos, and he would then meet the final French challenge at Dienbienphu. That event was still far off, but by 1952 the Vietminh was well on the road to ultimate victory. De Lattre, whose only son, Bernard, an Army lieutenant, had been killed in one of the first battles just after the General arrived, had himself returned to France in December, 1951, by which time he was so sick that he could hardly move. He died in Paris on January 11, 1952. In summing up de Lattre's role, Bernard Fall has written: "It is un-likely that the Indochina War could have been won by the French, even had de Lattre lived. But there is no doubt that de Lattre would have been able to put a stop to the war on the day he saw that it had become hopeless—as de Gaulle was the man who had the prestige to stop the Algerian War."

United States Aid Poses Problems

Whether de Lattre might or might not have been able to end the costly and futile war before the Dienbienphu debacle remains open to conjecture, though it is probably true that, like de Gaulle, de Lattre would at least have had the courage to try. There were other, more subtle and painful issues involved, and de Lattre's role in Indochina represented only one phase of the essential French predicament, which unfortunately also became the American predicament. It has been argued that if the French had not made the military mistakes they did, before de Lattre arrived and afterward (mistakes that ranged from adopting the wrong kind of strategy and tactics to a reluctance to meet the challenge of creating a true Vietnamese Army sooner and faster), they might have been able to buy enough time for the political situation to improve. But just "buying time" would not have been sufficient; the French would have had to unbend a lot more than they had given any signs of doing. Any amelioration of the situation would naturally have involved the fundamental question of granting the Vietnamese a more meaningful degree of independence, as well as the corollary of per-mitting a bona fide nationalist movement to flourish, unshackled by any sort of restrictions, so that the Vietnamese people would have believed in the anti-Communist crusade de Lattre wished to lead. As it developed, it was solely a French, and not a Vietnamese crusade.

The irony of de Lattre's mission to Indochina was that it served completely to inhibit any trace of an independent American effort there. The Americans, whose interference de Lattre resented, in effect abdicated to the General. Nobody can be blamed for this except the Americans themselves. It may be argued, as some Americans on the scene did, that it no longer would have made any difference anyway, that the time for the United States to be firm had been between 1947 and 1949, when the first tentative Franco-Vietnamese agreements were made and the Bao Dai experiment was starting. This would have required far bolder diplomacy than the United States seemed capable of at that time, since we did not become fully involved in Indochina until 1950; but in view of the disturbing situation in China, and the fact that we had had some experience before that in Indochina, the opportunity must be said to have existed, and to have been totally neglected. There was surely an American awareness of what was happening, and the issue was clearly posed, for example, by Bullitt in his 1947 magazine article; as time went on, it was raised in the reports of some of the American diplomats in Saigon, as well as by numerous correspondents. Certainly after the failure to reach agreement with Ho Chi Minh and the Vietminh in 1945 and 1946 and after the war began, it should have been apparent to anyone with any knowledge of the situation that only a strong nationalist counterforce would have any chance of achieving victory or even containment of the Vietminh.

The basic reason for the reluctance of the United States to take a stronger position on Vietnamese independence was tied to our policy in Europe, and to our earnest desire to bring the French firmly into the structure of the European Defense Community. This concept of an integrated European command had been the natural outgrowth of the wartime collaboration among the Allies. The French, it was clear, could not bear the financial cost of fulfilling their role and meeting their commitments under the proposed E.D.C. plan and at the same time continuing to wage a war across the world in Indochina. Their responsibilities in Africa further complicated the situation. A realistic American policy called for urging the French as strongly as we could to resolve the Indochina crisis as soon and as efficaciously as possible, so that they could play their proper role in Europe. Such a policy, properly executed, would not have meant surrender. It would have meant getting the French to make positive statements about *full* independence for the Vietnamese—to be granted, without strings, at a stated time—and then, and only then, agreeing to support them, economically and, if necessary with military force. "The French could have said unequivocally, as we did with regard to the Philippines, that in such-and-such a number of years Vietnam would be totally free, and that it could thereupon join the French Union or stay out, as it desired," Gullion has pointed out. "An evolutionary solution was the obvious one, and it should have been confronted openly and honestly without all the impossible, protracted preliminary negotiations involving efforts to bring the three Associated States together, to get them to agree among each other, and with France, separately and collectively. The French, in arguing against any kind of bilateral agreements, claimed that their attempt at federation in Indochina was like our effort to build some sort of federated system in Europe. But their involvement and interest in Indochina was obviously different, and they used the formula they devised to avoid any real agreement on Vietnam. The problem grew more complex as the military and political aspects of the situation became unavoidably tied together, and the Korean War, of course, complicated it further. From the outset, the French sought to regard the war in Korea and the war in Indochina as related parts of one big fight against Communism, but it wasn't that simple. Actually, what the Korean War did do was make it more difficult for us to urge an evolutionary settlement in Vietnam. By 1951, it may have been too late for us to do anything about this, but we could still have tried much harder than we did. The trouble was the world by then had begun to close in on us. The E.D.C. formula in Europe was being rejected by the French, just as in 1965 they are rejecting the North Atlantic Treaty Organization concept. Our degree of leverage was being drastically reduced."

Aside from leverage, which is primarily tactical, what was lacking was a persuasive policy of our own in regard to Indochina. No such policy had existed during the war, immediately after the war, in the late nineteen-forties, or in the early fifties; and in many respects, despite our heavy commitment in Vietnam in the sixties, it still does not seem to exist. Some of the reasons for this will be discussed in subsequent chapters, but in the 1948-53 period the confusion of aim and policy was patently apparent in Saigon, as it was also apparent in Washington. There had been a number of Southeast Asia experts in the State Department, and they had held down most of the important country desk jobs in the immediate postwar period. Once the Korean

War started, however, the attitude of the Southeast Asia section became more pro-French than it had been, and this did not help in the formulation of a clear and independent approach toward Vietnam. The consensus was that we should not push the French too hard. In Saigon, a sharp conflict arose over personalities as well as over the origin and application of policy in the field. Donald Heath, the American Minister—later the Ambassador—had previously been Minister in Bulgaria. His background and experience in dealing with Communism had been almost exclusively European, and he had witnessed the cold might of Soviet military expansion into Eastern Europe directly after the Second World War. His natural inclinations were pro-French, and he was sympathetic to the French predicament in Indochina. Heath was a gentle, able man who, in the opinion of most of us who knew him in Saigon, was simply the wrong person for the job—if the job was to accomplish what the United States kept saying it wanted; namely, a true independence for Vietnam. He did not believe in rocking the boat, and when de Lattre arrived, he fell completely under the General's spell. Gullion, as Consul General and then Minister Counselor, had an altogether different approach, and a far more forceful one. The two men clashed, though their personal relations remained cordial on the surface. Gullion could not file cables that contradicted Heath, since the Chief of Mission alone is responsible for those, but he did send dispatches to Washington that, both in quality of reporting and in the recommendations they offered, were in sharp conflict with the policies recommended by Heath and approved by Washington. I discovered that most of the official Americans privately agreed more with Gullion than with Heath. Significantly, Gullion's principal ally was the late Robert Blum, head of the American aid program, to whom the highest compliment had been paid by de Lattre himself when he said, with a disarming smile that did not hide the conviction of his words, "Mr. Blum, you are the most dangerous man in Indochina."

Blum, who had taught at Yale and had worked on the Marshall Plan in Europe, arrived in Indochina in the spring of 1950 as the head of the Special Technical and Economic Mission (STEM). When he left, a year and a half later, for personal reasons of frustration and probably because of pressure that had been brought by de Lattre and had been yielded to by Heath, his gloomy conclusion was that "the situation in Indochina is not satisfactory and shows no substantial prospect of improving, that no decisive military victory can be achieved, that the Bao Dai government gives little promise of developing competence and winning the loyalty of the population, that French policy is uncertain and often ill-advised, and that the attainment of American objectives is remote." Blum had perhaps been in a better position than any other American to make these judgments. The American economic aid program had dealt directly with the Vietnamese at the village level. The emphasis had been on social welfare, on the distribution of cloth and medicines, the building of rural irrigation wells, and the improvement of roads. Blum's information officer and aide, Leo Hochstetter, had made it clear that the United States stood behind the Vietnamese in their fight against Communism. "As I saw my directive, it was to do what we could to help these people, to show them that America was on their side," Hochstetter said. This was why de Latttre was so upset, and this was the basis of his remark to Blum. The French regarded the American economic aid program, totaling $23,500,000 a year for the three Associated States, most of which went to Vietnam, as a direct threat to French economic interests in Indochina, though they hid their objection behind a political smoke screen. De Lattre told me that we were "fanning the flames of extreme nationalism," adding, "French traditionalism is vital here. You cannot, you must not destroy it. No one can simply make a new nation overnight by giving out economic aid and arms alone." It seemed obvious, though not to de Lattre or to any other French official, that no one could make a new nation by refusing to give it enough freedom to act by itself in any of the ways that mattered.

The battle on the distribution of aid had been a long and bitter one. In May, 1950, when the original aid agreements were drawn up for Indochina, with money to be used from the old China fund, the French had wanted a quadrilateral arrangement among the three Associated States and themselves; the United States would have sat in as observer and adviser. We insisted on bilateralism—a direct agreement between ourselves and the Vietnamese, Laos, and the Cambodians—and we got our way. It was one of the rare instances of American firmness. The French, from the very outset, strongly criticized the program, complaining about the manner in which we distributed aid and, above all, about the manner in which we publicized it. By means of leaflets, wall newspapers, sound trucks and radio programs, the program quickly produced an effect in the rural areas. As the French saw it, it was making them lose face. This reaction was predictable. "We recognized from the start that our policy 'to supplement but not supplant' the French would have to be directed simultaneously at two objectives," Blum said shortly before his death in July, 1965. "We wanted to strengthen the ability of the French to protect the area against Communist infiltration and invasion, and we wanted to capture the nationalist movement from the Communists by encouraging the national aspirations of the local populations and increasing popular support of their governments. We knew that the French were unpopular, that the war that had been going on since 1946 was not only a nationalist revolt against them but was an example of the awakening self-consciousness of the peoples of Asia who were trying to break loose from domination by the Western world. We recognized right away that two-pronged policy was beset with great difficulties. Because of the prevailing anti-French feeling, we knew that any bolstering by us of the French position would be resented by the local people. And because of the traditional French position, and French sensitivity at seeing any increase of American influence, we knew they would look with suspicion upon the development of direct American relations with local administrations and peoples. Nevertheless, we were determined that our aid program would not be used as a means of forcing co-ordination upon unwilling governments, and we were equally determined that our emphasis would be on types of aid that would appeal to the masses of the population and not on aid that, while economically more sophisticated, would be less readily understood. Ours was a political program that worked with the people and it would obviously have lost most of its effectiveness if it had been reduced to a role of French-protected anonymity." Blum felt that, despite the nature of his program, it was "greatly handicapped and its beneficial psychological results were largely negated because the United States at the same time was pursuing a program of [military] support to the French," and he was forced to conclude that, "on balance, we came to be looked upon more as a supporter of colonialism than as a friend of the new nation."

The manner in which the French were able to hamstring the American aid program was demonstrated in various ways. For example, despite the principle of bilateralism, they controlled all counterpart funds because they controlled all foreign exchange. Consequently, they retained control over the awarding of all import licenses, through a committee of the Office de Changes, which they dominated despite Vietnamese membership on it. The Vietnamese Committee for Foreign Aid, with which Blum dealt, necessarily had to consult the French on any specific transaction that involved the transfer of foreign funds. The French were also sticklers on legal terminology. In the summer of 1951, negotiations for the first formal agreements were held up for two months by the French, who haggled over a few words in the contract, which, they claimed, gave the Vietnamese too much status. In one place, they objected to the word "high" being placed before "contracting parties." The Vietnamese, they claimed, weren't "high." To take it out, we replied, meant we weren't "high" either, but we gave in. In another place, they objected to the word "automatic" in reference to the use of counterpart funds in Vietnam. This was strictly a legalism, but the French thought it threatened them with further exclusion, and again we gave in to them. In the third case, we compromised. A phrase reading that Indochina should strive for a sound economy "under agreements by the two governments" (meaning us and the Associated States) was objected to; we agreed to take out "by the two governments" but not "under agreements." At one point, early in the battle of cables that went on between Washington and Paris and between Washington and Saigon, the French handed out a communiqué that in effect told the Vietnamese they had been saved from an American trap. The whole argument, so typical of what went on at the time, left a bad taste all around. It was all part of de Lattre's rigid, chauvinistic approach, based on his assumption that the only kind of aid that did the Vietnamese any good was the kind that was co-ordinated with the French military effort, and that anything else, with the possible exception of a few housing and irrigation projects, simply served as an instrument for American publicity and for American undermining of the French. At one point, de Lattre commented to Blum: "As a student of history, I can understand it, but as a Frenchman I don't like it." In the fall of 1951, when de Lattre stopped off in Washington on his way home to Paris, he told our officials, in a somewhat patronizing manner, that there had been some "misunderstandings" on the matter of aid— probably because our aid administration had been "rather new" and had perhaps had too much "missionary zeal." Though the Americans held their ground on the issue of bilateralism, de Lattre sent a cable to Bao Dai in which he claimed he had "persuaded the Americans to see the light."

After Blum—"the dangerous American"—had returned to the United States, he wrote a private memorandum, which aptly summed up the situation at the time, as follows:

The attitude of the French is difficult to define. On the one hand are the repeated official affirmations that France has no selfish interests in Indochina and desires only to promote the independence of the Associated States and be relieved of the terrible drain of France's resources. On the other hand are the numerous examples of the deliberate continuation of French controls, the interference in major policy matters, the profiteering and the constant bickering and ill-feeling over the transfer of powers and the issues of independence. . . . There is unquestionably a contradiction in French actions between the natural desire to be rid of this unpopular, costly and apparently fruitless war and the determination to see it through with honor while satisfying French pride and defending interests in the process. This distinction is typified by the sharp difference between the attitude toward General de Lattre in Indochina, where he is heralded as the political genius and military savior . . . and in France, where he is suspected as a person who for personal glory is drawing off France's resources on a perilous adventure. . . .

It is difficult to measure what have been the results of almost two years of active American participation in the affairs of Indochina. Although we embarked upon a course of uneasy association with the "colonialist"-tainted but indispensable French, on the one hand, and the indigenous, weak and

divided Vietnamese, on the other hand, we have not been able fully to recon-
cile these two allies in the interest of a single-minded fight against Communism. Of the purposes which we hoped to serve by our actions in Indochina, the one that has been most successful has been the strengthening of
the French military position. On the other hand, the Vietnamese, many of
whom thought that magical solutions to their advantage would result from
our appearance on the scene, are chastened but disappointed at the evidence
that America is not omnipotent and not prepared to make an undiluted
effort to support their point of view. . . . Our direct influence on political
and economic matters has not been great. We have been reluctant to become
directly embroiled and, though the degree of our contribution has been
steadily increasing, we have been content, if not eager, to have the French
continue to have primary responsibility, and to give little, if any, advice.

The 1954 Geneva Settlement

The war continued to drag on in what Gullion afterward described as
"the pattern of prediction and disappointment." He added: "It can
be timed almost to the month to coincide with the rainy season and the
campaign season. Thus, in May or June, we usually get French estimates of success in the coming campaign season, based partly on an
assessment of losses the Vietminh are supposed to have suffered in
the preceding fall, which are typically claimed as the bright spot in
an otherwise gloomy fighting season. The new set of estimates soon
proves equally disappointing; by October, French Union troops are
found bottled up in mountain defiles far from their bases. . . . There
are rumblings about late or lacking American aid and lack of American understanding. Some time around the first of the new year,
special high-level United States-French conferences are called. We ask
some questions about the military situation but only a few about the
political situation. There is widespread speculation that the French
may pull out of Indochina if we press them for explanations of their
political and economic program. We promise the French more aid.
The French make a stand: they claim great casualties inflicted on the
enemy. They give us new estimates for the following campaign season
—and the round begins once more."

After the death of de Lattre, Jean Letourneau, who had been Minister of Overseas France and had then become Minister of the Associated States, became High Commissioner in Indochina, retaining his Ministerial post. The combination of jobs gave Letourneau more political power than any previous High Commissioner (including de Lattre) had ever had, and it served further to inhibit the Vietnamese government, which in June, 1952, passed from the hands of Tran Van Huu to Nguyen Van Tam. Tam, like his predecessor, was a French citizen, and he had been Huu's chief of political police. Even Huu was quoted as saying, "Tam is not a Vietnamese patriot, he is a French patriot." In France, there was mounting criticism of the war, and in May, 1953, Letourneau was scathingly attacked by a Parliamentary Mission of Inquiry, which declared that under him a "veritable dictatorship has been established, without limit and without control." The mission, composed of a Socialist, an Independent, a Popular Republican, and a Radical Socialist member of Parliament, referred openly to games of "power and intrigue" being played by "the Norodom Palace clique," to French administrators having become completely isolated from the Vietnamese, and to their "reigning over a country where revolution is smoldering." Prime Minister Tam, with the help of a solidly pro-French Cabinet, was unable to build up any popular support, despite his talk of agrarian and other reforms. In January, 1953, elections for municipal and communal councils in French-controlled areas revealed a surprising amount of openly expressed discontent, especially since the right to vote was restricted to about a million persons out of some thirteen million theoretically eligible: only those in villages regarded as relatively safe from Vietminh infiltration were permitted to cast ballots, and they had to have been registered in a 1951 census conducted as a prelude to possible conscription. Both the mounting criticism in France and the growing discontent in Vietnam were sure signs that the war as conducted by France could not last much longer.

There is no point here to reviewing the course of the war in any detail during 1953 and the spring of 1954—this has been done by Bernard Fall and others. In brief, after Giap and his Vietminh forces had successfully infiltrated the Red River Delta in 1952 and 1953, they pressed their attacks in the Thai highlands in the north and moved toward the Laotian border. Giap refused the French challenge for a head-on battle and infiltrated into additional areas in Central Vietnam, confining the French to a narrow coastal belt. In the spring of 1953, the Vietminh invaded Laos and then retreated, after setting up the nucleus of a Communist government there. In May, 1953, another of the constant crises in the French Cabinet brought Joseph Laniel, an Independent, into the Premiership, replacing René Mayer. Laniel dismissed Letourneau, redivided his two jobs, and sent General Henri Navarre to Indochina as Commander in Chief, replacing General Raoul Salan. Navarre's assignment, though it created a new wave of hope, especially in Washington, was essentially limited to defending Laos if he could, and to protecting the French Expeditionary Corps. He was given to understand that no more French troops would be sent to Indochina and that he was to prepare the way, as best he could in military terms, for negotiation. Mustering what forces he could for a series of mobile stabs at Giap's positions in the Red River Delta, Navarre managed to keep the Vietminh off balance. Giap retaliated by a fresh, bold invasion of Laos in December, 1953, and then Navarre made the big mistake of overreaching himself and deciding, contrary to his basic orders, to draw the Vietminh into a final frontal engagement at Dienbienphu.

The wheels had also been turning politically. Early in July, 1953, Premier Laniel announced that France was now willing to "perfect" the independence of the Associated States of Indochina. By implication, this meant that the various "final" agreements made at Pau in 1951 would be "implemented" further, and that the Vietnamese, the Laos, and the Cambodians would take over the functions that had proved unworkable under the quadripartite control system. (Privately, Bao Dai commented, "What do they mean 'perfect'? What's the matter with the French—they're always giving us our independence. Can't they give it to us once and for all?"). The French, however, remained adamant on the issue of the French Union, and Laniel made it clear that if the Vietnamese decided to quit the Union, the French would no longer have any reason to continue the fight in Indochina; the concept of the union was altered to make it more of "a great fraternal community [of] freely associated, independent, and sovereign states, free and equal in rights and duties." The United States, with the war in Korea over and the danger of Communist Chinese support of the Vietminh stronger than ever, was, if anything, less critical of the French political position in Indochina than it had been before, though a few minority voices were raised. One of them belonged to the newly elected Senator from Massachusetts, John F. Kennedy, who, as a Congressman, had visited Indochina in 1951 and had obtained much of his information from Gullion. On June 30, 1953, in a speech on the Senate floor, Kennedy took note of the fact that "genuine independence as we understand it is lacking in Indochina" and said that "local government is circumscribed in its functions, that the government of Vietnam, the state which is of the greatest importance in this area, lacks popular support, that the degree of military, civil, political, and economic control maintained by the French goes well beyond what is necessary to fight a war," and he added: "It is because we want the war to be brought to a successful conclusion that we should insist on genuine independence. . . . Regardless of our united effort, it is a truism that the war can never be successful unless large numbers of the people of Vietnam are won over from their sullen neutrality and open hostility to it and fully support its successful conclusion. . . . I strongly believe that the French cannot succeed in Indochina without giving concessions necessary to make the native army a reliable and crusading force."

Although some people in the State Department still spoke occasionally of the need to complete the process of Vietnamese independence, the government as a whole—now bearing the main financial brunt of the war in Indochina, spending about $500,000,000 a year—was far more interested in seeing the war prosecuted to a successful conclusion. Secretary of State John Foster Dulles foresaw victory by the end of 1954, and others, including Vice-President Richard Nixon, declared that it was impossible to think of anything but victory. Efforts by the French or by the Vietnamese to start negotiations with the Vietminh were strongly opposed by the United States. One such attempt was made early in 1953 in Rangoon, Burma, by an unofficial Vietnamese-French delegation seeking "clarification" from the Vietminh on the possibilities of peace. But the French had had enough, and the tortuous path to, and from, Geneva was charted in February, 1954, at a conference in Berlin attended by Dulles and the Foreign Ministers of France, Great Britain, and Soviet Russia. The conference failed in its initial aim to resolve the Berlin problem, but it set up a meeting at Geneva for the end of April. Reluctantly, Dulles agreed to the participation of the Communist Chinese, for which he was severely criticized by more conservative Republicans, especially the China lobbyists. His hope was that at Geneva a final settlement of the Korean problem might be achieved, and he was further persuaded to allow the Indochina question to be put on the agenda. The United States no longer considered the two problems to be totally separate, as it once had.

A month before the conference in Geneva began, the outlines of American policy became clear. Dulles suddenly enunciated a policy calling for "united action" reversing a private pledge that had been made earlier to the French General Paul Ely, in Washington, that serious consideration would be given to the dispatch of American bombers for the relief of the beleaguered French at Dienbienphu. Both Dulles and President Eisenhower were desperately afraid that American intervention by itself, particularly with ground forces that might follow an air attack, would place the United States under a permanent stigma of colonialism. Dulles's solution was to create a broad Asian-European alliance, which he hoped would give legal international sanction to intervention in Indochina. This was the genesis of the ineffectual Southeast Asia Treaty Organization. SEATO was the product of Dulles's compulsion to combine the practical tenets of international law, which he had studied and practiced, with the religious fervor of his own anti-Communist crusade—one that, in a political sense, matched de Lattre's military crusade. His mistake lay in trying to shove SEATO down the throats of America's principal allies—particularly Great Britain and France as well as a rather motley and suspicious group of other nations—in such a hurry that they couldn't possibly digest it.

An interesting analysis of what took place before, during, and after Geneva was published in the spring of 1965 by Dr. Victor Bator, a Hungarian-born international lawyer and former diplomat. Dr. Bator's book, entitled *Vietnam, a Diplomatic Tragedy*, is based on a careful examination of government documents and of the personal memoirs of the leading statesmen who were concerned with the Indochina problem at the time. He offers the thesis that Dulles, with the approval of President Eisenhower, and as a result of "partisan pressure of a sectarian faction of Republican politicians," insisted so strenuously on promoting his crusade that he alienated both the French and the British to the point where the United States was placed in the unenviable position of having to go it alone in Indochina after Geneva. By forcing the British and French to commit themselves against their will to discussing the creation of SEATO before a settlement on Indochina was reached, Dulles clashed with Foreign Secretary Anthony Eden and seriously jeopardized the American alliance with Great Britain. As Dr. Bator summarizes it, Dulles and Eisenhower thought that by creating SEATO they could render "American intervention [in Indochina] . . . immune from accusations of being imperialist, colonialist, or paternalistic. They believed that any antagonism to American influence and power was the product of guilt imputed because of British-French association. Their mistaken self-persuasion made out of the anti-colonialist cant the dominating policy-line of the United States, leading it into the maze from which France, by the Geneva settlement, had just succeeded in extricating itself." Then, by refusing to accept the final Geneva draft declarations, though vaguely sanctioning them by separately "taking note" of their terms, including the division of Vietnam at the Seventeenth Parallel, Dulles made unavoidable America's subsequent solitary involvement in Vietnam, particularly as SEATO failed to produce the "united action" he had sought.

The very vagueness and unilateralism of the final Geneva declarations, which South Vietnam also refused to accept, and which *none* of the participants actually signed but simply "took note of" individually, was of course underlined, as Dr. Bator says, by the American refusal to endorse the terms, which Dulles felt represented a surrender. Nevertheless, there were a number of advantages in the refusal of the Americans and the South Vietnamese to sign the agreements, and it is difficult to make a clear-cut case either for or against the American action. For the United States to disassociate itself from the bankruptcy of the French colonial effort made sense, even if Dulles's hastily contrived SEATO formula did not. Dr. Bator believes that the United States made a mistake in forcing "the lockout of the French presence in Indochina" after Geneva. This is highly debatable. It may be argued that there were "many personal and institutional links" between France and Indochina, that these might have been used to "foster friendly relations between the two halves of the truncated country," and that the government of Ho Chi Minh "might have been amenable to diplomatic contacts looking to real stabilization" (though "stabilization" seems too strong a word). American disavowal of the paragraph in the Geneva declarations by which the participating nations agreed to consult each other on measures to insure the cessation of hostilities certainly helped shut the door to further diplomatic enterprise; this was, as Dr. Bator says, "but one item in our general resistance to diplomacy." But the fault did not lie so much in America's tactics as in its larger strategic failure to take imaginative steps of its own after Geneva—if, indeed, some kind of diplomatic contact with the North Vietnamese was even possible. Herein, as Dr. Bator says, Dulles's "innate moral and spiritual strength . . . made his anti-Communist fervor a blinding dogma and deprived him of flexibility when wisdom demanded it." In any case, whatever flexibility might have been demonstrated would not have been wisely exercised in consort with the French, whose role in Indochina by 1954 was far too discredited to make any such further collaboration productive. Some French channels in Hanoi, as represented by the liberal-minded Jean Sainteny, who was back there as the French Delegate General, might have been informally explored, but it seems doubtful that even this would have led to anything constructive. Ho and Sainteny were soon to sign an agreement for the protection of French interests in the north, but it was hedged by as many vague clauses and conditions on Ho's part as earlier French agreements made with both Ho and Bao Dai had been. Even at this early post-Geneva date, the French and the Americans had begun to play separate roles in Vietnam, and their objectives were at variance. While the French maintained that "there are at least eleven cards still to be played in the game"—mostly economic ones—the United States was determined to shore up South Vietnam by itself, à la Dulles. Though it is undeniable that diplomatic channels should always be kept open, bilaterally as well as multilaterally, it seemed doubtful that the possibilities for having a real dialogue with Ho in 1954 were comparable to those in 1946. The exuberant days of the American-Vietnamese Friendship Association in Hanoi were long since gone. And it was surely too much to expect someone as dogmatic and dedicated as Dulles to consider the possibility that Ho, who was pro-Moscow in his orientation, might prove worthwhile cultivating because the Russians and the Chinese might fall out several years later.

Late in October, 1954, in the wake of the Geneva Conference, Ho triumphantly emerged from his forest hide-out, ending rumors that he had died there, and re-entered Hanoi with his victorious Vietminh troops. A film I witnessed at the time showed him to be the same frail, stooped wisp of a man whose classic endurance of body and soul were almost visible aspects of his being, in contrast to the submerged shrewdness and guile that had also marked his long career as one of the cleverest performers on the stage of the world revolution. With typical humility, Ho rejected a gala public ceremony. He arrived in a captured three-quarter-ton French Army truck, shook hands with members of the armistice commission, discussed the Geneva settlement over tea at a long table outdoors, and then made a brief appearance before a gathering of veteran co-workers and friends. Popping almost coyly from behind a curtain in a large reception hall, Ho smiled and reminded his audience, "I am an old guerrilla fighter, you know." On January 1, 1955, as part of a New Year's message to the people of the Democratic Republic of Vietnam, and as the keynote to a five-hour anti-American demonstration in Hanoi, Ho made the following passionate statement: "We must be vigilant and be on our guard against the plans of the imperialistic Americans who are seeking to intervene in Indochina, to incite their lackeys, to sabotage the armistice accords, and to cause war." This, to be sure, was no longer the Ho of 1945-46.

Whatever criticism of the Geneva accords one wants to make, they were the inevitable climax of the Indochina war as it was fought between 1946 and 1954. The compromises that were reached at the conference were probably the best that the West could have obtained under the circumstances. They could only have been avoided by political measures that should have been taken much earlier in the Associated States, and particularly in Vietnam. The offer of the French in 1953 to "perfect" independence for the three states came much too late to do any good, for the war was already lost by then, and there was little or no good feeling left for the French among the people of Vietnam, Cambodia, and Laos. More important, whatever the arguments were about the role that Americans played toward the end of that war—whether they let the French down militarily or whether they were mainly responsible for making the Geneva accords inoperable—there seems little room for debate about the earlier and more crucial American failure of responsibility in Indochina. The whole outcome might have been different had the Americans adopted as firm a position between 1948 and 1952 on the issue of complete independence for Vietnam as they adopted in 1954 on the question of creating new international machinery for dealing with a situation that was already lost. The French alone cannot be blamed for having dragged their feet. The disinclination of the United States to apply pressure when pressure could have been applied—with the threat of withdrawal of financial support if France did not give Vietnam a more definite form of independence—must be considered as important and as destructive a factor as French intransigence, which at least had its roots in the long colonial history of the French. In the final analysis, it was this failure of American policy, and not what happened at Geneva, that created the conditions and circumstances for the subsequent predicament of the United States in Vietnam, a protracted one that has become harder to resolve year after year and that could lead to another Geneva—one that might not even offer the opportunities for partial salvation that existed last time.

CHAPTER IV

❧

The Early Years of Diem

Early in 1951, while I was writing a column from the Far East for fifteen American newspapers, I suggested that the most likely candidate for the Premiership of the Associated State of Vietnam was Ngo Dinh Diem, the long-time nationalist figure who had resigned nearly twenty years before as Minister of Interior in the French colonial regime. There was no particular prescience on my part in predicting the selection of Diem, who was then living in Catholic retreats in New York and New Jersey and making occasional trips to Washington, where he discussed Vietnamese affairs with Senator Mike Mansfield, with Congressman John F. Kennedy, and with several other Senators and members of the House of Representatives. Two years earlier, in 1949, Diem had repeated his earlier refusal to be Premier of what had just become the Associated State of Vietnam, under Bao Dai, and earlier he had turned down offers to serve with the Japanese puppet regime during the war and to join Ho Chi Minh's Vietminh administration in Hanoi after V-J Day. He had remained a respected, if aloof, figure whose reputation was chiefly based on these and other refusals to associate himself with any government he felt did not represent the legitimate nationalist aspirations of the Vietnamese people. Eventually, it seemed to me that Diem would either have to agree to serve on something less than his own terms or he would take over by default; the latter was closer to the mark.

In mid-June, 1954, a month before the signing of the Geneva agreements, Diem finally accepted Bao Dai's repeated invitation to serve as Premier of what was to all intents and purposes a bankrupt government, which few observers gave any chance to survive. The choice of Diem at this juncture was undoubtedly prompted by several factors. The French, who had regarded him as an able enemy, had every expectation that he would fail, and they thought that his failure might lead to the emergence of a more tractable leader who would help them maintain their position, economically at least, in what was about to become South Vietnam. Bao Dai, whose hopes of retaining some semblance of power were by no means dead yet, may have thought that by putting Diem in office under what seemed almost impossible circumstances, he, too, might finish off a political rival and enhance his own chances of being recalled to play a further role, if only as another kind of puppet—a function he had become used to performing. However, Bao Dai still admired Diem, and he was also influenced by the importuning of one of Diem's brothers, Ngo Dinh Luyen, who had worked closely with him when he had been Emperor. There is also reason to believe that Bao Dai acted partly because of pressure brought by some of Diem's American friends, since he realized that the United States was likely to fill the vacuum in Vietnam after the French departure.

Whichever of these reasons was most responsible for the choice of Diem, he arrived in Saigon in the last week of June, 1954, a month and a half after the debacle at Dienbienphu and after discussions were already underway at Geneva. He had been preceded there, on June 1st, by the American who, in the initial period of the Diem regime, was to have the greatest influence on him. This was Colonel Edward G. Lansdale, a remarkable and controversial man, who, though he knows as much about counter-insurgency and the waging of polit-ical-military warfare as anyone in the United States, became a retired Major General in his mid-fifties because of his reputation for being as outspoken as he is earnest and committed. Lansdale, who served with the Office of Strategic Services during the war and afterward as an intelligence office in the Pacific area, had helped rebuild the Philip-pine Army intelligence service and had become an expert in Philippine affairs. When I first met him in 1951 in Manila, he was a Lieutenant Colonel in the Air Force, on special assignment, at the request of President Elpidio Quirino, to help deal with the increasingly serious problem of the Communist-led Hukbalahaps, and he was working with the brilliant, dynamic Ramón Magsaysay, who had been a guerrilla leader against the Japanese and was now Philippine Secretary of Defense. With Lansdale's help and encouragement, Magsaysay mounted a drive that demonstrated almost perfect co-ordination of military, political, and social-psychological strategy and tactics. Magsaysay was a firm believer that a guerrilla war could only be won by positive counter-guerrilla methods, that "one has to learn from one's enemy," and that the way to defeat a rural-based Communist insurrection was to get troops out into the hills and keep them there in pursuit of the enemy while at the same time proving to the people that the duly constituted government had more to offer them in protection and in social and economic benefits. After the Huks had been beaten, at the end of 1952, Magsaysay, again with Lansdale's encouragement, became a candidate for the Presidency of the Philippines, and he won in November, 1953.

Lansdale had made his first visit to Indochina in the summer of that year, having been lent to the French to advise them on matters of "unconventional warfare," including the training and use of Maquis elements, the use of psychological warfare techniques, the gathering of combat intelligence, and the rehabilitation of Vietminh prisoners. He had become acquainted with a number of Vietnamese political leaders in the north, among them Dr. Phan Huy Quat, then a member of the Dai Viet nationalist party, who was to become the Premier of South Vietnam twelve years later. In March, 1954, Secretary of State John Foster Dulles had wanted to send Lansdale back to Saigon on another special mission, but Magsaysay had asked the American government to let Lansdale come back to the Philippines to advise him on certain Presidential matters. Lansdale was in Manila late in May when he received an urgent cable from Dulles instructing him to proceed at once to Saigon. If anything was to be salvaged out of the crisis following the fall of Dienbienphu, Dulles said, quick action was required. The cable ended with a laconic "God bless you."

Lansdale's first task, under the broad secret orders given him by

Dulles, was to learn quickly as much as he could about the chaotic situation in Vietnam, and he spent most of June getting to know members of the two important paramilitary religious sects, the Hoa Hao and Cao Dai; members of the Binh Xuyen, the gangster group that controlled several commercial monopolies in Saigon; leaders of the old nationalist political parties; and military men such as General Nguyen Van Hinh, the Vietnamese Army Chief of Staff, who was also an officer in the French Air Force. On the morning Diem arrived, Lansdale started out in his battered Citroën to join the official American welcoming delegation at the airport, but the huge crowds in the streets deterred him, and he parked his car to join the throng and observe the popular reaction. Although Diem was not supposed to be well known in Vietnam, having been away for four years and never having been a nationalist with a popular following, his return had apparently provoked considerable enthusiasm, primarily, perhaps, as an expression of joy over what seemed to be the end of the long war and as a hope, however forlorn, that the Vietnamese in the south might finally be allowed to go their own way. Since Diem's plane was late, many people in the crowd had been waiting for hours. Finally, the motorcycle escorts swept past, sirens howling, and then, as Lansdale recalls it, "Diem's car, a big black sedan, shot by at about sixty miles an hour and nobody even saw him." The crowd was obviously let down, and so was Lansdale. The next morning, with the approval of Donald Heath, who was still the American Ambassador, he wrote a long memorandum to Diem, based largely on what he had found out in his month of research. Accompanied by George Hellyer, the American public affairs officer, who spoke French, he took the plan to the palace to give it to Diem personally. Everything was in a turmoil there, and Lansdale and Hellyer wandered around for some time; finally they asked a plump man in a white suit, who was sitting alone on a couch, where they might find Premier Diem. "I'm Diem," the man replied. Lansdale promptly told him what had been wrong about the motorcade, that the Premier should have ridden into town slowly in the back of an open car, and Diem agreed. Lansdale then handed him the long memorandum, and Diem, who understood a little English, started to read it with the help of an English-French pocket dictionary. Hellyer volunteered to translate the document, but suddenly realized, to his dismay, that he had forgotten his glasses, whereupon Diem took off *his* glasses and handed them over. Diem listened carefully, frequently nodding his head in agreement. "After that," Lansdale says, "the ice was broken. To me he was a man with a terrible burden to carry and in need of friends, and I tried to be an honest friend of his."

I did not come to know Diem myself until more than seven years later, in the spring of 1962, by which time conversation about him completely dominated Saigon's drawing rooms and dinner parties. There were few men I had known anywhere in public life, I thought then, who seemed to provoke so many strong opinions, pro and con, and yet there was a peculiar impersonal quality to everything that was said about him, as if, despite the urgency of the moment, everyone were talking about a figure in history, already remote and shadowy. The words one heard—"courageous," "proud," "patriotic," "cold," "detached," "uninspiring"—sounded like clichés rather than characteristics of a living, breathing man who held his country's future in his hands. The image was oddly wooden, the portrait unreal, as if there were some doubt as to its authenticity.

When one met Diem, this sense of unreality was borne out. He was a short, broadly built man with a round face and a shock of black hair, who walked and moved jerkily, as if on strings. He always dressed in white and looked as if he were made out of ivory. His self-absorption became apparent as soon as he started to speak, identifying himself and his cause with the nation. He indulged in few amenities of greeting, and since he was a compulsive talker, with whom it was impossible to have an interview—one had an audience; in fact, one *was* an audience—a single question was likely to provoke a dissertation of an hour or more. And as he talked, encompassing his own past with that of history, his dark eyes shone, but they seemed to be looking through his listener, through the walls of his palace, through everything, and one experienced an almost eerie sense of listening to a soliloquy delivered in another time and place by a character in an allegorical play. What emerged out of the torrent of words was strangely incomplete and unsatisfactory—perhaps because it was, more than anything else, an expiation and an apologia, an angry and often impassioned plea for understanding and sympathy, but a plea delivered without much human warmth or empathy.

Some men are destined to be alone all their lives, and Diem, to my mind, was surely one of them. Although he had been an ardent nationalist most of his life, he had spent much of it in spiritual and physical isolation, and this undoubtedly was why he very often found it difficult to establish intimate contact with the people of his country. Diem would never admit the difficulty, and this, too, stemmed from his personality and his background as a mandarin as well as an ascetic. The dynastic name of the family was Ngo, and the Ngos had been privileged mandarins—scholar-courtiers—since the sixteenth century, when they served the Vietnamese emperors who ruled after the Chinese withdrew, in 939 A.D., until the French came in the middle and latter parts of the nineteenth century. In the small village just north of the Seventeenth Parallel in Quang Binh Province, where the Ngo family tombs still stand, the people believed that the proximity of the Ngo ancestors assured good fortune and prosperity, and they used to seek to bury their dead alongside, creeping into the graveyard by night. "They didn't have more than indifferent success," Diem told me. "We planted rows of trees to keep them away."

Sometime in the seventeenth century, the Ngos were converted to Catholicism, and around 1870, during a period of anti-Catholic violence, a pagan mob attacked their home and drove nearly a hundred members of the family into the village church, where they were burned alive. One of the few who was not wiped out was Diem's father, Ngo Dinh Kha, who had left home at the age of eleven to study abroad, first in China and then in Malaya. He was in Penang, Malaya, at the time of the massacre, and returned to Annam when he was twenty-one, when he started a small private school for the children of wealthy families. By the time Diem was born, in the imperial capital of Hué, on January 3, 1901, his father was serving the Emperor Thanh Thai as an adviser at the court, rising to become court chamberlain with the rank of mandarin first class.

Of the six sons and three daughters in Ngo Dinh Kha's family,

E

Diem, the third son, was the most solitary, intense, and dedicated. He went to a French Catholic school in Hué at the age of five, and at six won his first prize for "assiduousness." His older brothers claimed he never missed a day of school, even disobeying his father's orders to stay home on bad monsoonal mornings, when he donned a big coolie hat and teetered for a mile along the bank of a canal to class. He regularly got up before dawn to study by oil lantern, and if any of the other children disturbed him when he was working, he would fly into a rage; in later years, Diem, who rarely displayed any humor, retained his fierce temper, and frequently gave vent to it when anyone under him failed to perform a job satisfactorily. In 1908, after the French had deposed Emperor Thanh Thai because they suspected him of plotting against them, Diem's father, who had been the only one of the court advisers to oppose the move, was also forced out of the palace. "We faced hard times, and for a while we all had to leave school," Diem recalled. "My father owned a little riceland and he rented some more. He had been generous before to the small land-owners and peasants around us, and they now helped him by letting him have the extra land rent-free until a good crop came in. After two or three good ones, we were prosperous again, although not rich. Our family never cared about money." Diem resumed his schooling and at fifteen entered a monastery, intending to study for the priest-hood, but after a short time he gave it up and returned home. He never explained why, but his older brother, Archbishop Ngo Dinh Thuc, who became one of Vietnam's top prelates and also one of Diem's personal advisers, once speculated that his brother found him-self incapable of accepting church discipline because he himself was too strong-willed. Apparently, however, Diem took a personal vow of chastity, and he remained an extremely religious man all his life. His association with women was negligible in all respects, and the only woman he ever saw with any regularity was the attractive, compulsive, and ultimately destructive Mme. Ngo Dinh Nhu, the wife of another Ngo brother who became Diem's closest adviser and ultimately his Rasputin.

A year after his decision to give up becoming a priest, Diem falsified his age and took competitive examinations for the equivalent of a high-school diploma. He did so well that the French offered him a scholarship in Paris, but Diem decided to stay in Annam. He explained that he did so because his father was ill, but there was more to it than that; despite the prestige of obtaining a French education, he wanted to remain a "pure" Vietnamese, and he enrolled at the School of Public Administration and Law at Hanoi. In 1921, he finished at the top of his class and, as a ninth-class mandarin, receiving twelve piastres a month, was appointed to the Royal Library at Hué, where in his spare time he went further into the study of comparative law and the institutions of his country. He was advised by his elders to become less of a bookworm and a recluse and to devote himself more to public affairs, and his next assignment, which represented a promotion in the mandarinal scale and entitled him to a ricksha with two coolies, was as administrative supervisor of a district of seventy villages. Diem was still in his mid-twenties when his responsibilities were widened to include the supervision of nearly three hundred villages in what is now Central Vietnam; his job, in effect, was to act as a combination sheriff and judge in determining disputes between peasants, and as a tax collector and director of public works. Wearing a conical straw hat and a mandarin robe, he rode around the countryside on horseback and dealt more closely with the villagers than he ever would again. He recommended to the French that the villages be given more autonomy and better educational facilities, but the French paid no attention to him. Disheartened, Diem determined to quit his job and go into the mountains to work with the tribal people, but he again took the advice of his elders and stayed where he was. "Although I was very young, they encouraged me by predicting my success," Diem said. "They told me of their confidence in me and predicted I would someday lead my country. This meant I was receiving the blessings of patriots who had already devoted their lives to the cause of freedom, and I was very grateful."

While he was still working in the Hué area around 1925, Diem was one of the first Vietnamese officials to become aware of the Communists and their plots. At Quangtri, sixty miles north of Hué, he discovered some of the earliest underground rings. Typically, he immersed himself in the study of Communism and at the same time sent his own agents to infiltrate the cells. When the Communists began public demonstrations all over the country in 1929, Diem quickly arrested the leaders in his area and sent the French a long report on Communist operations, but the French were more worried about other nationalists, whom they had already begun ruthlessly to suppress. That same year, Diem was made governor of the province of Binh Thuan, in southern Annam—a remarkable promotion, since he was only twenty-nine years old—and he continued his campaign against the Communists, arresting about a hundred of them and attempting to re-educate all but a handful of hard-core party members by turning them over to selected village councils. Diem's success in Binh Thuan became well known, and other provinces requested him as governor, but the French, recognizing his training in public law and administration, appointed him to conduct an inquiry into irregularities among their Vietnamese officials in all of Annam. This led, in 1933, to his being made Minister of the Interior under young Bao Dai, who had just become Emperor. The French had promised to institute a series of reforms designed to liberalize the colonial structure, but they immediately reneged and instead sought to circumscribe Bao Dai's power by appointing a resident official as Prime Minister and by denying the Emperor and his Cabinet control over their own finances. Diem objected strenuously, and he now made his break with the French whom he had served loyally, if sometimes rebelliously, for a decade. When they refused his demand for educational and financial reforms, and for the creation of a Chamber of People's Representatives that would have more than a mere consultative role, he resigned. The French stripped him of his decorations and threatened to arrest or deport him, but Diem refused to back down. "I told myself that I would work more directly for the independence of my country," he told me, in recalling this decision, perhaps the most important of his life. "When the French asked me if I were waging a revolution, I told them we had to transform the country in order to fight Communism. Privately, I was convinced that an alarm had to be sounded to make the people feel the need for daring reforms and to make them respond in an energetic and even violent way. I felt it was my responsibility."

Despite these declarations, Diem for the next ten years led the reflective life of a scholar-revolutionist and mingled with the people far less than he had before. For much of the time he lived in Hué with his mother and younger brother Ngo Dinh Can, who was to become the dominant figure in Central Vietnam. While he was with Can in Hué, Diem went to Mass every day; and when he wasn't reading, he was engaging in one of his three major hobbies of riding and hunting, tending flowers, or taking photographs, developing them himself in a homemade darkroom. From time to time, he traveled south to Saigon and other cities, where he met with other nationalists and intellectuals and discussed a possible revolution. He had no specific plans, no organization, and not much personal support. His chief revolutionary contact abroad was the exiled Prince Cuong De, in Japan, and he had a number of talks in Saigon with the Japanese-oriented nationalist, Phan Boi Chau. On one occasion, he had a long private discussion with Vo Nguyen Giap, who, in his pre-Vietminh days, was a left-wing Socialist flirting with Communism; Giap and Diem tried unsuccessfully to convert each other. The French, during these years, obviously kept Diem under surveillance. They didn't arrest him, because of his past contributions to their colonial administration, but they kept issuing warnings that he was endangering his older brother, Ngo Dinh Khoi, who was governor of Quang Nam Province in the north; Diem occasionally visited Khoi, too, and in 1942 Khoi was forced to resign from the French administration; three years later he was captured and murdered by the Communists.

When the Japanese came to Indochina early in 1942, preserving the French administrative structure and allowing the French to continue operating it, Diem consulted with a number of Japanese officials, but they weren't interested in creating a really free Vietnam. He continued to lie low, traveling occasionally from his brother Can's home to his brother Thuc's in the south. One day in the summer of 1944, in Hué, he was returning home from a walk and noticed a bustle in the neighborhood. He suspected correctly that the French had come to arrest him, so he went to the home of a Japanese friend. The following day, the French declared him a subversive and placed him on a wanted list, and Diem fled south to Saigon, where he lived quietly with some Japanese friends. In March, 1945, when the Japanese interned the French, they belatedly offered Diem the Prime Ministership of an "independent" government under Bao Dai in Hanoi. Diem refused, not because he objected to the Japanese but because he still did not feel he would be able to establish a free government—among other things, the southernmost area of Cochin China was initially to be excluded from it. Furthermore, he now saw the handwriting on the wall and did not want to put himself in the position of being declared a collaborator when the war was over. He returned to Saigon and waited.

He did not wait long. In September, 1945, when Ho Chi Minh seized power in Hanoi, Diem decided, against the advice of his friends, to go back to Hué to warn the people against the new regime. North of the seaport of Nhatrang, he stopped off for the night at the house of some people he knew and was arrested by Communist Vietminh agents who·had followed him. He was taken in slow stages to a Communist camp in the jungles just south of the China border, where he was held in a thatched hut. Dreadfully ill from malaria, dysentery, and influenza, Diem, as he afterward said, would have died had it not been for Tho tribesmen who took care of him. His captors apparently hoped he would either die naturally or be killed by one of the extremists in their midst, but by February, 1946, when Ho was about to sign his agreement with the French and when he wanted the support of as many non-Communists nationalists as possible, he sent word for Diem to be brought to Hanoi. When he confronted Ho, Diem immediately said, "Why did you kill my brother?" Ho said it had been a mistake, that he hadn't known about Khoi. "I told him he was a criminal," Diem said, in repeating this conversation to me. Ho suggested they forget about the past and asked Diem to stay on with him at the palace or in a nearby house and work with him. Diem said that if he remained, he would have to be apprised of everything that went on at all times. Ho gave an evasive answer, and Diem then asked, "Am I free to go?" Ho told him he could, but warned him he would find the countryside hostile. "I'm not a child and will take the risks," Diem replied. The conference ended and, since it was late, Diem remained in the palace that night. The following morning, at six, he simply got up and left, and no one stopped him.

For a number of months after that, he sought to organize some anti-Communist guerrilla bases of his own in the north and debated attempting a coup—he had planted a number of his own agents within some of Ho's defense squads in Hanoi—but he decided he did not have enough arms; in mid-1946, he took refuge in a monastery in Hanoi run by some Canadian priests. When he heard the Vietminh was again looking for him, apparently determined this time to assassinate him, he left the monastery disguised as a monk and moved clandestinely around the countryside, doing what he could to maintain anti-Communist sentiment in the cells he had established, but he made little real headway. When Ho was in Paris to negotiate further with the French, the Communist extremists in Hanoi intensified the search for Diem, and he went into complete hiding. When the war started in December, Diem went south again and spent the next year living with his brother Thuc near Saigon.

Diem's whole career so far had been a series of rejections by him of situations or conditions he felt he could not accept. His principles and his stubbornness had driven him further into both spiritual and political isolation, but in the spring of 1947 he made an effort to start what amounted to a political party called the National Union Front, which declared its main objective to be a mild Dominion status for Vietnam within the French Union—an arrangement that would resemble a British Commonwealth relationship. The party published a newspaper in Saigon and one in Hanoi. The French ultimately shut them both down after a campaign of harassment that led to the arrest of the Hanoi editor for subversion and, afterward, to the assassination by hired gangsters of the editor in Saigon. If Diem's Union was a failure, it had at least brought his name more to the fore in the nationalist movement, and when the French proposed to bring Bao Dai back from exile in Hong Kong and appoint him the head of a new government in the south, Diem for a time became the chief negotiator between them and the exiled Emperor. He made three trips to Hong Kong and back, and did his best to get Bao Dai to stand firm until the French made sufficiently positive commitments for independence, but, to Diem's disgust, Bao Dai backed down and allowed himself to be made a puppet. Once again, Diem returned to the homes of his brothers. When both Bao Dai and the French, realizing the failure of the governments they had attempted so far, made fresh overtures to him, he issued a manifesto that appeared in two Saigon papers, one French and one Vietnamese. It demanded social and economic reforms that went much further than anything the French were willing to grant. "The intellectuals in Saigon did a lot of talking about independence, but few of them were brave enough to rally around my program," Diem said. "They simply went on taking part in puppet Bao Dai governments until the end, engaging in their own petty intrigues." After the French had rejected Diem's conditions, he once again went north to his brother Can's house. In the spring of 1950, when he heard that the Vietminh had sentenced him to death in absentia, he asked the French for protection. They curtly told him they had no police available. Deciding he had done all he could for the moment, Diem applied for permission to go to Rome for the Holy Year, and in August, 1950, with his brother Thuc, he disconsolately sailed.

Diem stopped off briefly in Japan to see Prince Cuong De, and then spent a month in the United States on the way to Europe. He had an audience with the Pope in Rome, and then visited France and Switzerland before he returned, in January, 1951, to the United States, where he stayed two years. Most of that time he lived in seclusion at Maryknoll Seminary in Lakewood, New Jersey, but since he considered himself a political exile whose cause was still a completely independent Vietnam, he sought to obtain support for it by lecturing from time to time at universities, writing a number of articles for serious magazines, and having talks with American political and religious leaders, including, among the latter, Francis Cardinal Spellman. In the face of the continuing American policy of giving the French all-out support, Diem elicited only a limited response in the United States, but during this period he received three more tentative offers from Bao Dai to return as the head of the Vietnamese government, and the third offer, in the summer of 1953, promised him full political powers. The French, however, would not give in to his demand that the Vietnamese be allowed to conduct the war, and negotiations terminated. "If we had been responsible for prosecuting the war, we would have won." Diem insisted when I later saw him.

"The Communists were exhausted, and in many northern provinces the people were not for them, even where the Vietminh had been in control for nine years, and they would have supported a really independent government. The French were defeatist in their evaluations of what the real sentiment of the country was."

Diem Takes Over

Whatever the validity of this assumption, by the time Diem returned to Saigon and formally took over the government, on July 7, 1954, it was too late to prosecute the war any further. The country was falling apart—Diem himself admitted that "Vietnam looked like France at the time of Joan of Arc." He had little left but his pride and a passion for survival. He considered what had happened at Geneva a disgrace, and had wisely ordered Dr. Tran Van Do, his representative there, to disassociate South Vietnam from the agreements that were signed, thereby laying the legal groundwork for his subsequent refusal to abide by them. He considered the division of Vietnam a personal betrayal and echoed Dr. Do's final Geneva declaration that South Vietnam "reserved to itself entire freedom of action to safeguard the sacred right of the Vietnamese people to territorial unity, national independence, and freedom." Despite these strong statements, there is every reason to believe that Diem realized from the start that the division of Vietnam was likely to be permanent—short of another world war—and that he had to set his sights solely on South Vietnam. As he confronted the huge task of creating some order out of chaos, he found that there were very few Vietnamese to help him. Certainly the French, and the Vietnamese who had depended on them for their jobs, were not eager to come forward, particularly since there were still many administrative and financial as well as military matters to be worked out with France, whose troops were still in command of the area and were to remain in Vietnam to protect French citizens and property for another two years. Furthermore, Diem's relationship to Bao Dai, who was still Chief of State, was an inhibiting one, both as to Diem's freedom of action—Bao Dai still exercised the right to make various appointments, for example—and South Vietnam's questionable status as a sovereign government. In order to put up as strong a front as he could, Diem selected a number of independent nationalists as members of his first Cabinet, but they were men who lacked experience in government; practically all those with any experience had served under the French. Diem moved to replace as many of these French or French-oriented people as he could in bureaus and departments in Saigon, and down to the level of the provinces, and he did this with the knowledge that he was sacrificing experience in order to build up a loyal Vietnamese corps of officials who would require time to learn their jobs. Unfortunately, the process of educating them was handicapped by the fact that Diem and his Ministers had no real program of their own.

The sheer administrative problems of running the broken country seemed insurmountable, and they were made more difficult by the two-way movement of large numbers of people: the staged withdrawal, to be carried out over ten months, of Vietminh troops from four specified assembly areas in the south, and the reverse movement of refugees from the north to the south. Some fifty thousand troops and twenty thousand Vietminh sympathizers went north, but as they withdrew from areas they had controlled, it soon became evident that they had left behind a strong network of cadres to carry on covert political, psychological and, ultimately, paramilitary operations. The movement from north to south was at first expected to amount to no more than sixty or seventy thousand, but the figure eventually reached 860,000. The new government had to contend with this influx on an emergency basis when the French, a few days after Diem's arrival, announced that their forces would immediately evacuate the southern part of the Red River Delta, thereby leaving many people, including the bulk of the north's two million Catholic population, at the mercy of the Vietminh. There were those who thought this precipitate French action was calculated to embarrass Diem. In meeting the crisis, the United States Seventh Fleet and the China Air Transport, a private airline, helped transfer the refugees, and the French also contributed some planes. The cut-off date for the evacuation was May 18, 1955, and though Diem claimed later that twice as many as 860,000 would have fled the north if they had been allowed to, realistic estimates put the number of those who wanted to leave but couldn't at no more than 400,000. There were problems enough in resettling those who did come down, and the plight of the northern Catholics, who were initially herded into slum-like transit camps before they were able to build their own farming and fishing villages, was personally agonizing for Diem. He made a special effort to help these refugees establish themselves in their new communities, and the government's efficient handling of this crisis was commendable, in contrast to the manner in which similar refugee crises were handled elsewhere in the world.

Any subsequent critical assessment of Diem, of his stubbornness, of his refusal to delegate authority and to take advice from anyone but his family, and of his imperious habits and ways, must be made not only on the basis of his complicated personality but also on that of his first twelve or fifteen months as Premier, during which, except for his family and a few Vietnamese friends and his American supporters, he literally stood alone. As the French hastily withdrew most of their public servants, there was scarcely any administrative talent left, and disorder, abetted by banditry, mounted in the countryside. Communications everywhere were in a state of collapse, the Vietminh having sabotaged the railroads and set up obstacles on the roads and in the rivers and canals. Vietnamese soldiers were deserting by the thousands, and for a time Diem's actual authority scarcely extended beyond Saigon itself, where he had only a single battalion of loyal troops upon which he could completely depend.

With virtual anarchy prevailing, it was only natural that plots against Diem arose. They involved the French, the various sects, and General Hinh, the Army chief. The first of these crises concerned a blunt effort on Hinh's part, with the subtle backing of the French, to get rid of Diem, although it was never quite clear just how much Hinh was bluffing or how far he really intended to go; he was certainly deterred by the threat of the Americans to cut off all assistance to Vietnam if he did move against Diem. In September, Hinh refused to obey Diem's order to leave the country. A few weeks later, when it looked as if Hinh were getting ready to mount a coup, Lansdale took advantage of his old friendship with Magsaysay, who was much admired by Hinh and his staff, to spirit most of Hinh's top officers off to Manila in response to what he told them was "a special invitation" from Magsaysay. Hinh later pretended to have been duped, but he didn't sound very angry, and this, among other things, indicated that the General wasn't really serious in his coup maneuvers.

The problem of the sects and its solution furnished one of the more exciting and, as it developed, ironic chapters in Vietnam's postwar history. Of the three of them, the Binh Xuyen, led by a colorful brigand named Le Van (Bay) Vien, provided the most formidable challenge initially, although Vien had only twenty-five hundred men under arms, as compared to an estimated twenty thousand in the Cao Dai and fifteen thousand in the Hoa Hao. The Binh Xuyen had simply graduated from sheer banditry in the Saigon River Delta area to racketeering protected by Bao Dai—who was said to have received forty million piastres for selling Bay Vien the control of gambling and prostitution in Cholon, the Chinese city adjacent to Saigon, and control of the Saigon-Cholon police. The other two sects, however, were odd amalgams of politics and religion. Both the Cao Dai and the Hoa Hao, which are still in existence in Vietnam, hold their own elaborate religious ceremonies. Though they are Buddhist offshoots, they blend the practices and forms of various other religions and rituals of secret societies into their worship; the Cao Dai, which is headed by a Pope, conducts these in lavishly decorated temples. In 1954, the Cao Dai was said to have two million followers in the area northwest of Saigon toward the Cambodian border, while the Hoa Hao was credited with a million and a half supporters in the southwestern provinces below Saigon, but both these estimates may have been high. Neither sect has ever been completely cohesive; prior to 1954 the various factions of each had followed an opportunistic line, co-operating first with the Japanese during the war, in an anti-colonial drive against the French, then with the Vietminh against the French, and finally, again for opportunistic reasons, siding with the French in order to obtain arms to maintain themselves in their respective areas, where many of their troops sporadically fought both the Vietminh and the French. In effect, the two sects had created their own states, collecting their own taxes and running their own villages in a semifeudal sort of way.

By 1954, they also constituted a considerable political threat, both as separatist groups and as quasi-nationalist elements that Saigon politicians sought to use to further their own ends. As such, they presented an obvious danger to the shaky new Diem regime, and one that had to be dealt with cautiously. Diem's initial tactic was the classic one of divide and conquer, and in September, 1954, by bringing four Hoa Hao and four Cao Dai leaders into his Cabinet, he hoped to isolate the Binh Xuyen. Militarily, with the help of the Americans, Diem sought to integrate the sect forces into the regular Army.

Lansdale personally rallied the support of one of the most important Cao Dai commanders, Trinh Minh Thé. Thé, who had been consistently anti-French since 1951, was still fighting them in the fall of 1954 when Lansdale visited his headquarters, on Black Lady Mountain in Tay Ninh Province, near Cambodia. Though the two men were under a linguistic handicap, they got along well. Thé, a small, trim young man, seemed a legitimate nationalist patriot to Lansdale, though many Vietnamese simply considered him a bandit. Lansdale was struck by Thé's natural qualities of leadership, which reminded him of Magsaysay's, as well as by his compassionate hopes for the people; and the affection he had for them was obviously returned. Thé had several thousand troops who were being well supplied with arms from a mountain arsenal run by Chinese deserters from the Kuomintang. Within a matter of weeks, Thé moved a portion of his troops to Saigon and came there himself to command them. Reports later circulated by the French and their Vietnamese agents that Lansdale bribed Thé to support Diem have been vehemently denied by Lansdale. "Thé rallied for purely patriotic reasons," Lansdale maintained. "The most I ever paid him was a cup of coffee or a meal when he visited me, and this was scant repayment for the hospitality he had shown me up in the mountains. All he finally got was a month's pay for his troops when they were integrated with the Vietnamese Army."

As the issue with the sects was mounting to a crisis in Saigon, the wheels were also turning fast in Washington. In September, the French sent a mission to the United States ostensibly to regulate matters of rendering assistance to the three new states of South

Vietnam, Laos, and Cambodia; the Americans had already made clear their desire to give aid directly to the Vietnamese instead of funneling it through the French, as before. But what the French were really after was a secret agreement with the State Department to get rid of Diem. In his place, they wanted a more pliable man, like General Hinh or former Premier Tran Van Huu, and their essential objective was to build a bridge to the government in Hanoi that would enable them to protect their economic and cultural interests in the south as well as, hopefully, in the north. This was contrary to the aims of the Americans, as expressed at the highest level by President Eisenhower and Secretary of State Dulles and by a special interdepartmental task force on Vietnam headed by Kenneth Young. With Diem as a nationalist fulcrum, the Americans wanted to build up a single army that would be trained by American officers and could serve as the instrument for pacification in the countryside, where a land redistribution program and other social-economic reforms would be introduced. "We realized we had to proceed carefully with the French," Young has recalled, "so when they made clear their position on Diem, we sent a cable to Senator Mansfield, of the Foreign Relations Committee, who was abroad, asking him what he thought of Diem as Premier. Mansfield was an old friend of Diem's and we knew what the answer would be in advance, of course, but it stunned the French. While they then dropped their open campaign to dump Diem, it became apparent that they were still maneuvering behind the scenes toward the same objective, and we realized that while we still had to work with the French in Vietnam, we would have to adopt a more independent position."

Reluctantly, after the Washington meeting, the French signed a joint communiqué that backed Diem, and on October 23rd a letter drafted by Young was sent by President Eisenhower to Diem, in answer to Diem's request for American aid. This is the letter that has frequently been quoted in recent years, by Presidents Kennedy and Johnson, to justify the American presence in Vietnam. The following month, President Eisenhower selected General J. Lawton Collins to go to Vietnam as his personal envoy to help establish security, get the military training program started, and pave the way for the planned agrarian reforms. Originally, Collins' mission was to last ninety days. His friendship with General Paul Ely, the French Commander in Vietnam, would be an asset, it was thought, and, in fact, fairly successful tripartite teams of Americans, Frenchmen, and Vietnamese were established to deal with the problem of the sects (whose financial support the French ostensibly now cut off) and to bring them into the regular military structure. Collins and Ely also reached a key agreement for training the Vietnamese forces. A Training Relations Instruction Mission (TRIM) was established, headed by General John (Iron Mike) O'Daniel, who was also the head of the Military Assistance and Advisory Mission that had been helping the French during the Indochina war and was still in existence. O'Daniel had a French chief of staff and an American deputy chief of staff, and each of the four divisions—Army, Navy, Air Force, and National Security—had alternate American chiefs and French deputies. The National Security division, which was the only one actually advising the Vietnamese on operations, was headed by Lansdale, and this was how the Americans began advising and training the Vietnamese forces. TRIM was one of the rare instances of effective Franco-American co-operation in what was otherwise a tenuous and difficult relationship.

The first political problem to be solved after Collins arrived concerned General Hinh. Following the discussions in Washington with the French, and Diem's momentary success in having isolated the Binh Xuyen, it was possible to bring the Hinh matter to a head. When Bao Dai realized that the Americans meant business with their threat to cut off aid unless Hinh stopped his plotting or would-be plotting, he ordered him to go to France, where he has remained ever since. (Today he is a high-ranking officer in the French Air Force.)

Victory over the Sects

There now began one of the strangest and most obscure chapters in the early history of Ngo Dinh Diem's rule, of which some of the facts have only recently come to light. In January, 1955, Diem shut down the Binh Xuyen gambling casinos in Cholon, depriving the gangster group of its prime source of revenue and throwing down the gauntlet to it. There is reason to believe, however, that the French secretly continued to back the Binh Xuyen, and that even though they formally withdrew their financial support of the Hoa Hao and Cao Dai private armies, they continued to give them funds, too. While the French publicly joined the Americans in urging Diem to broaden his political base and co-operate further with the sects— and while Diem refused to accept the demands of the sect leaders for more political power, and, under the inspiration of his brother Ngo Dinh Nhu, moved further toward a showdown with the various sect factions—certain French elements privately continued to work with the sects for the removal of Diem. On the surface, the French withdrawal of financial support for the sects looked like a move in Diem's favor, but it was probably calculated to cause Diem trouble by stirring the sects' resentment. What the French envisaged was the creation of a new coalition, consisting of some of the sect leaders and some pro-French Vietnamese politicians, and they hoped that such a coalition would enable them to build the bridge to Hanoi that they still desired. In the back of their minds was the not unwarranted expectation that the plebiscite scheduled, according to the Geneva declaration, for 1956 would, if it was held, probably result in a victory for Ho Chi Minh. Looking ahead, they undoubtedly figured that their chances of maintaining their economic and cultural position in South Vietnam would be enhanced if they could promote a more malleable administration than Diem's. Certainly any individual who was an ardent exponent of Vietnamese nationalism in the south would not help the French cause. Since, under the Geneva terms, the French remained partly responsible for the execution of the plebiscite, they foresaw a way of using it to help them appease the new power structure in North Vietnam; and in Jean Sainteny, once again the chief French representative in Hanoi, they had a man who could be depended upon to maintain as close an association as possible with Ho Chi Minh. The whole American program for South Vietnam, based on the introduction of three hundred million dollars' worth of aid and the slogan of "Security and Reform," was obviously antipathetic to the French plan; and though Generals Collins and Ely continued to work amicably together on such matters as building the technical machinery for the Americans to take over the training of the new Vietnamese Army, ~~~~ er Frenchmen in Saigon, notably the old colonial elements, did ything they could to impede unity.

By February, 1955, the covert French campaign had helped convince General Collins and others at the American Embassy that Diem was a hopeless proposition. Diem himself certainly contributed to Collins' disillusion. Almost from the start, the two men did not get along. Unlike Lansdale, whom Diem regarded as a friend, Collins, as far as Diem was concerned, was a General who liked to give orders and to lecture, which was also ironic, for if anyone ever liked to lecture, it was Ngo Dinh Diem. A great mimic, Diem used to demonstrate to friends how Collins talked to him, brandishing a finger in his face. This is the sort of thing mandarins do not take to, and Ngo Dinh Diem was, above all, a mandarin. The facts remained that Diem was not an especially likable or persuasive figure in the eyes of most Americans in Saigon and that dissatisfaction with him, as a result of his stubborn ways, was also growing back in Washington, where his only staunch supporters were Secretary Dulles and his brother Allen Dulles, the head of the Central Intelligence Agency; Walter Robertson, Assistant Secretary of State for the Far East; and Kenneth Young, who was still head of the Southeast Asia section of the State Department and head of the Vietnam task force.

In the third week of March, 1955, when Diem refused to agree to an outright demand of the sects that he reorganize his government, the Cao Dai and Hoa Hao Ministers withdrew from the Cabinet, and the two sects, plus the Binh Xuyen, re-formed themselves into the United Front of Nationalist Forces. On March 29th, fighting—led by the forces of the Binh Xuyen—started in the city. Diem's palace was attacked and various sections of the city were burned. General Collins, who by this time had turned strongly against Diem, gave him some military advice about how to fight back; Diem ignored it, and that, as far as Collins was concerned, was the last straw. A tentative truce was arranged by General Ely and the French command, which had failed to help the government troops repulse the assault, but Collins, who had been called back to Washington, had made up his mind: Diem had to go. Before he left, in mid-April, he instructed Lansdale, with whom he had had some pointed disagreements, to continue the liaison with Diem but to ease up on giving him any further advice on any substantive matters. Lansdale later remarked that Collins assured him the United States would continue its support of Diem, but Diem himself told Lansdale that he knew Collins had decided against him.

When Collins returned to Washington, he went directly to the White House to see President Eisenhower, who promised to support him in whatever he recommended. Then Collins went to the State Department and told the Vietnam task force what he had told the President, and what Eisenhower had said. "We seemed to be confronted with a *fait accompli*," Young has recalled. "It appeared to be a Presidential decision that Diem had to go. By this time, even those of us who had continued to support Diem were beginning to have serious doubts about the validity of the Diem formula. He might be a nationalist symbol, we thought, but was he the real substance of nationalism? Could he mobilize his people and carry out what we hoped to achieve with our security and reform program?"

In spite of what the President had told Collins, Young began searching for a compromise formula, and he and his associates on the task force came up with one that they thought would be feasible: Diem would become the President of Vietnam, the symbolic nationalist leader; but the functioning "general manager," perhaps as Premier, would be Dr. Phan Huy Quat, the former Dai Viet Party man from the north, whom Lansdale, among others, had cultivated, and whose own nationalist credentials were honorable. Secretary of State Dulles was against the compromise formula at first, but his brother Allen supported it, as did Senator Mansfield and Assistant Secretary of State Robertson. General Collins, too, finally accepted it. On April 28th, when Collins left to return to Vietnam, a cablegram was prepared for dispatch to the Saigon Embassy, explaining what had been decided and why, and setting forth the terms under which the American program, still solidly based on the security-plus-reform principle, was to be developed.

"At six o'clock on the afternoon of the 28th, I took the cable into

Secretary Dulles's office," Young recalls. "The Secretary signed it. After all the long discussions and all the headaches they had provoked, we were once again hopeful that a solution could be reached—we even thought we had a new Magna Carta. We were sending the cable in advance of Collins' arrival in Saigon so that certain necessary arrangements could be made there and the machinery set in motion to get the new program going. Then, shortly after Dulles signed the cable, I got a call from him. He had just received a cable from Lansdale. Fighting had broken out again in Saigon, between the Binh Xuyen and the government forces."

The scene now shifts back to Saigon. The fighting that had started with a Binh Xuyen mortar attack on the Presidential palace had led Diem to order immediate counterbattery fire, and by midafternoon a key fight was raging for the National Police Headquarters. Lansdale had been riding through the streets and was convinced that the government forces, with the support of his friend Trinh Minh Thế's Cao Dai elements, would be able to defeat the Binh Xuyen. At the Embassy, however, he found a mood of confusion and despair, partly reflecting what the French had been feeding Collins and the rest of the staff all along—that the Vietnamese Army still wouldn't and couldn't fight and that Diem was through.

"I knew this wasn't so, and while the Embassy staff was debating what kind of report to send to Washington, I challenged some of the attachés and the others to go out and see for themselves how angry the Army troops now were, and what their real mood of resistance was," Lansdale has said. "In fact, I begged them to go look. But the only man who would go was Iron Mike O'Daniel. He rode past the Vietnamese troops in his sedan, flying the American flag, and though he wasn't supposed to take sides, he leaned out and gave them the thumbs-up sign, shouting, 'Give 'em hell, boys!' He was a real fighting man."

At one point during this final Binh Xuyen crisis, Bay Vien had tried to kidnap Lansdale, who continued to ride around the city to find out what was happening so he could report further to Washington. The situation, chaotic enough in its own right, had been further complicated by a cablegram Diem had received from Bao Dai, excoriating him for being responsible for the bloodletting and ordering him to return to France. Bay Vien's radio station had somehow got hold of the cablegram before Diem did and was broadcasting it. When Lansdale went to see Diem, Diem was in a state of virtual shock. The message had come as a last blow, and had hurt him deeply. "Shall I obey?" he asked Lansdale. Lansdale reminded him of the basic principles that were at stake, and Diem himself agreed that, despite what Bao Dai had said, he was on sound moral ground in battling against a group of gangsters who were trying to grab control of the city's forces of law and order and upset the legal government. No answer was sent to Bao Dai; it is unlikely that Diem, at this juncture, would have obeyed the cable anyway. He had been determined to put down the Binh Xuyen ever since he had revoked its gambling concession, but Lansdale's support, in the face of Collins' opposition, had helped bolster his confidence.

Back in Washington, there was total consternation when Lansdale's wire was received indicating that the Binh Xuyen attack was being repulsed. Secretary Dulles immediately telephoned his brother Allen at C.I.A. Then urgent instructions were cabled to Saigon to disregard the previous long cable containing the new policy statement, including the decision to kick Diem upstairs and install Quat as the chief administrator. On the basis of the new urgent wire, the first one was burned. By the time Collins' plane arrived back in Saigon, the whole American policy had again been reversed. At first Collins was angry, and he pointedly accused Lansdale of inciting a mutiny, but when he discovered what had happened, and saw that the whole Embassy staff had swung around in favor of Diem, he was satisfied that the turn of events had justified the switch.

There was little doubt that Ngo Dinh Diem was saved, at the end of April, 1955, by the chronological accident of the Binh Xuyen crisis coming to a climax when it did. Diem probably realized that he was about to lose the support of the Americans and was ready to join the issue with the Binh Xuyen on his own, but the option had not been entirely his, since the Binh Xuyen had itself chosen the moment to make its final stand. At any rate, this was another important turning point in the relations of the United States with

Vietnam. The fact that certain French elements had encouraged the Binh Xuyen, expecting Diem to capitulate, added a note of irony to the showdown. In the light of what happened afterward—the trouble the Americans had with Diem and the events that ultimately led to the coup of November, 1963, which overthrew him—the irony of the 1955 events is further apparent.

For Lansdale, though he had helped save Diem, the victory over the Binh Xuyen was tinged with tragedy. Shortly before the Binh Xuyen troops were driven out of Cholon and Saigon, in the first days of May, Trinh Minh Thé's troops, which had taken part in the battle, were caught in a trap. Thé had sought to cross the Canal de Dérivation without artillery support. "I went to see Diem," Lansdale has recalled. "He and his military commanders were together, jubilant about their success so far. I told them about Thé's guerrilla forces trying a formal assault across a bridge defended by gunboats and against a fort on the other side—a suicidal assignment and a misuse of guerrilla elements, especially without artillery support. I was angry, and I guess I sounded it. Anyway, Diem's commanders left to arrange for some artillery, and Diem asked me to sit down. He started chiding me for my strong feelings about Thé, claiming that Thé was only a peasant and presumably not as worthy as other leaders in Vietnam, by which he meant himself and his brother. I was pretty sharp in my reply. Thé was a staunch patriot in my book, and he had supported Diem in the darkest hours, obeying orders and risking his troops. My own feelings went even further than that. I had felt from the start that we shouldn't put all our eggs in one basket, that it was always important to look for alternatives. As a matter of fact, if worse came to worse and if the whole thing collapsed and the Binh Xuyen or someone else took over, I felt we ought to get ready to fight back from the hills, like guerrillas, and I had even made some preliminary surveys, with the help of Thé and others, about where we would withdraw to, and what mountains would be our sanctuary, and so on. I didn't tell all this to Diem, of course, but while he was remonstrating with me about Thé, Nhu came in, with a long face. He said he had just received a report that Trinh Minh Thé had been shot in the head and killed. Diem's face worked and tears came into his eyes. He asked me to forgive him for what he had just said. It was the only time I ever saw him give in to his emotions. Impulsively, I put my hand on his shoulder."

During this final Binh Xuyen battle, there had been still a further complicating factor. General Nguyen Van Vy, regarded by some Americans as another possible alternative to take over in case Diem lost out, was named by Bao Dai to be Chief of Staff. Though Vy was also a Vietnamese patriot, Diem didn't trust him, suspecting he was pro-French as well as pro-Bao Dai. "Actually, Vy was the only one who could con the French out of some howitzers we wanted that we had given them for the Vietnamese Army," according to Lansdale. "As soon as he got hold of the weapons, he turned them over to the Vietnamese commanders with a big grin, and they were used at once, to great advantage, against the Binh Xuyen. There were so many wheels within wheels at the moment that Diem never believed Vy was on his side. Vy was briefly arrested by Diem, and then was released by another Vietnamese general. After that, he fled the city and eventually the country, and went to France."

Whatever Diem had believed, he had proved himself correct in accepting the challenge of the Binh Xuyen and of the other sects against the predominant advice of the Americans to temporize. By mid-May, 1955, the Binh Xuyen had been driven into the swamps east of Saigon, where the remnant of its forces gradually disintegrated and were finally wiped out in September, though Bay Vien managed to escape to Paris. In the Mekong Delta area, government forces then went to work against the dissident Hoa Hao elements, headed by another colorful figure named Ba Cut. Ba Cut had volunteered to stop fighting if he was made a lieutenant general in the government army; while negotiations were being conducted for his surrender, a government patrol captured him and he was eventually executed. Another Hoa Hao leader, Tran Van Soai, did surrender and was given asylum. The few Cao Dai forces that had not already come over to the government side also gave up, though some of the leaders, notably the sect's Pope, Pham Cong Tac, fled to Cambodia, where they remained in opposition to Diem.

In May, 1955, shortly after Diem's decisive victory over the Binh Xuyen, a meeting of the North Atlantic Treaty Organization was held in Paris, where it was inevitable that the Vietnam issue would once more be deliberated between the French and the Americans. In a series of heated conversations, the French again made no effort to hide the fact that they still were against Diem. The confrontation was a dramatic one. The French called Diem an American puppet and threatened that unless Diem was removed they would pull out their troops and cancel other forms of assistance they were still rendering Vietnam. Dulles called their bluff and told them to go ahead, and at one point threatened that if the French did leave, the Americans would get out, too. This upset the French so much that they subsided. Meanwhile, from his villa in Cannes, Bao Dai was still doing all he could to wangle Diem's ousting. Dulles refused to talk to him, but Kenneth Young kept in touch with him almost daily through an intermediary since the Americans felt they had to keep the lines open to Bao Dai. At a crucial moment during the discussions with the French, a cable came in from Malcolm Macdonald, the chief British representative in southeast Asia, suggesting that nothing more be done in Vietnam to rock the boat, and that took the rest of the wind out of the French sails. At a final session, they remained silent as Dulles gave one of his most effective speeches, admitting Diem's drawbacks but stressing his honesty and incorruptibility and denying that, in any sense, he was a puppet. "Dulles handled the whole affair with magnificent subtlety and dexterity," Young has recalled, "and he won the day. If he hadn't stuck to his guns, and if Diem hadn't stayed on at that time, the chances are there would have been total chaos in Vietnam, to the benefit of the Communists. Yet, in retrospect, perhaps Collins was correct in his essential judgment of Diem. Maybe we should have remembered, later on, what he said, when we were having such a hard time getting our programs of assistance introduced and implemented, and getting the Vietnamese to fight the war in the right way. In the context of 1955, however, I think we were right in what we did, but there were straws in the wind, lessons to learn, which we tended to forget afterward. The whole Diem affair, down to its final dénouement in 1963, is a haunting one, and I don't imagine that any of us who were involved in any phase of it will ever forget it."

Diem Consolidates Himself

After the events of the spring of 1955, despite the fact that the United States had in effect recommitted itself to Diem, there remained considerable skepticism about him among many of the Americans in Saigon. They felt he had won his battle with the sects primarily because of the vacillation and divisiveness of the sect leaders, an opinion that did not give Diem sufficient credit for having brought the sect issue to a head himself. The difficulties of dealing with Diem were still apparent, and they led to increasing impatience and annoyance. Collins, who stayed on for a short time as Ambassador after his return from Washington, continued to treat Diem in military fashion, talking to him bluntly and in a manner that invariably caused him to react by withdrawing further into himself. Diem was obviously shocked by the cold, superior attitude of Collins; this was something he had not experienced during his earlier sojourn in the United States, though he had not been altogether well treated then either. "Sometimes I think Asians are too reserved, that they talk too much by nuance," he once remarked. "We ought to be as rude in our talk as Americans, and get things done." As time went on, the Americans would have been glad to settle for that. Diem tended to speak in grandiose terms about his country's future, but to the Americans he seemed desperately slow in putting into practice what he preached, as well as in implementing what he promulgated. For his part, Diem grew increasingly tired of an endless procession of Americans, who didn't know the Vietnamese situation as well as they thought they did, but kept telling him what to do and making it plain that they controlled money and material. Frequently he bored them by trying to explain himself and his reasons for doing things as he did, and the more he talked, the more impatient the Americans grew. As he was criticized for procrastinating, his resentment grew in direct proportion to the degree he was prodded. His habit of wanting to do everything himself, of being unable to delegate authority, which had become noticeable early in his administration, gradually reached ridiculous extremes, and ultimately he insisted on doing such things as individually approving all exit visas for Vietnamese traveling abroad and determining the position of newly planted trees in public gardens. And as his innate remoteness and his mistrust of people, which had been largely justified during the first few months of his regime, tended to drive him further into himself, he was led to depend almost solely on the members of his family, and particularly on his brothers Nhu and Thuc.

Lansdale, who remained in Vietnam until the end of 1956, continued to be the American who was closest to Diem, but despite, or perhaps because of, his support of the Premier, he was among the first to note the deleterious influence of Nhu. "It was Nhu, more than anyone else, who kept Diem suspicious of people," Lansdale recalls. "Diem had to act like the real leader of his country and get around as much as possible. Even if he didn't like people or trust them, he had to get used to working with all kinds of Vietnamese in order to build up a sense of mutual trust. But Nhu seemed to go out of his way to get derogatory information about people. He would come in and say he had proof that so-and-so, who had just been proposed for a new job, was no good. He was like an old lady spilling gossip over the back fence. At the outset, Thuc was a better influence on Diem, and so was the younger brother, Luyen, but Nhu, who regarded Luyen as a rival, got him out of the country and back to Europe as soon as he could."

It was Nhu who, in October, 1955, organized and manipulated the election whereby Diem overcame his last apparent hurdle—Bao Dai. Diem unseated him as Chief of State in a referendum, winning by the overwhelming margin of 5,722,000 votes for himself, with only 63,000 for his opponent. Diem thereupon became South Vietnam's first President—and virtual dictator. The Americans felt that Diem's public image was hurt by the fact that Nhu had rigged the huge vote for his brother, and that Diem would have won easily anyway without any manipulation. But a more important development —and one that must be ranked high on the list of what went wrong with the Diem regime—came in 1956, when Nhu set in motion his most important private political organization, the Personalist Labor Revolutionary Party, called the Can Lao Nhan Vi Cach Mang Dang, the nucleus of which he had formed during the Indochina war with the help of a small group of intellectuals and labor leaders. Both the Can Lao and the official government party, the National Revolutionary Movement, which had come into being in October, 1954, had as their credo the pseudo-philosophic theory known as personalism. Personalism, as espoused by Nhu, was a peculiar mixture of Western and Eastern thought that pretended to stress the development of individual character as the basis of community democracy in Vietnam. It sought to mesh the individual's spiritual growth with the community's social needs, and together these would stimulate the nation's emerging political life. At first glance, personalism seemed, more than anything else, to be a convenient mixture of thoughts that was all things to all men. It embraced elements of French Catholic *personnalisme* as expressed by the late Emmanuel Mounier, who sought to blend Marxism with certain concepts of Christianity, and several other philosophies and religions that ran the gamut from Confucianism to Existentialism and Moral Rearmament.

What the Can Lao actually amounted to, though, was a personal rather than a personalist organization that served primarily as a political intelligence agency for Nhu; he used it to detect Communists or anyone he suspected of Communist or other oppositionist tendencies, and it was thus a powerful weapon in obtaining and maintaining loyalty to the Ngo family. The Can Lao was dominated and run by Nhu's henchmen in Saigon and in the provincial administrations, and while its structure and organization were weak, and it never held any big meetings, the awe it created, and ultimately the sense of fear it imposed, became key factors in the evolving Diem-Nhu dictatorship. The Can Lao's membership was never disclosed— estimates ran from five to fifty thousand—but it was known to include many members of the National Assembly, a completely controlled body chosen in elections in 1956 and again in 1959, as well as individuals, carefully selected by Nhu, who moved anonymously through all the echelons of government, down to the level of villages and hamlets, factories, schools, and small military units, tracking down cases of malfeasance and corruption and disloyalty to the regime. On the recommendation of any of the seven Can Lao bureau chiefs, a suspected person could be arrested and brought to trial. Nhu, who blandly admitted the party's structure was not unlike that of the Communists, and who used the organization slowly to build up his paramilitary control of the countryside, to stifle any opposition, and to inhibit the formation and operation of any independent political parties, once described personalism in the Can Lao image to me as follows: "The personalist conception holds that freedom in an underdeveloped society is not something that is simply given or bestowed. It can only be achieved through militancy and vigilance, by doing away with all pretensions and pretexts for not realistically applying ourselves to our goals. In a situation of underdevelopment, and during a bleeding war of internal division, it may be argued that there is reason enough not to seek to develop democracy, but our personalist approach is precisely militant in denying this. Human rights and human dignity are not static phenomenons. They are only possibilities which men must actively seek and deserve, not just beg for. In this sense, of believing in the process of constant perfecting of oneself in moral as well as practical ways, our personalist approach is similar to Confucianism. Personalism stresses hard work, and it is the working class, the peasants, who are better able to understand the concept than the intellectuals. We must use personalist methods to realize democracy at the level where people are fighting and working, and in our new scale of values it is those who participate physically and selflessly in the fight against Communism who are the most privileged, then those who courageously serve the interest of the villages without profit, and finally those who engage diligently in productive labor for their own as well as for their villages' benefit." This sort of semipractical, semimystical talk was typical of Nhu, and it often left his listeners bewildered. A number of Americans, including some visiting scholars, spent considerable time trying to understand and explain personalism, but they usually gave up because it seemed such a hodgepodge, and because whatever it was, it was only a theory, while in practice it was what Nhu wanted it to be.

The Can Lao had the unofficial approval of a number of Americans, including some members of the C.I.A. Their feeling was that Diem needed a political party of his own, which he had never had, if he was going to develop his image in Vietnam. Lansdale, among others, had tried to persuade Diem to allow the old Vietnamese political parties to function again and then to build up his own front in cooperation with them. The Can Lao was obviously the wrong instrument for such co-operation. It quickly grew apparent that it would become Nhu's personal machine for running the country under what amounted to *kempetai* (Japanese secret police) methods, which he had carefully observed during the Japanese occupation. It now seems clear that the time to stop Nhu was in 1956, when the Can Lao was created. As the years went by, there was less and less chance of curbing Nhu, or of separating him from Diem, but in those early days there was at least some chance.

Organizing the Countryside

Nhu's ability, from an early date on, to subvert the structure and forms of the Vietnamese government after 1954 was undoubtedly facilitated by the fact that the system created was an extremely strong Presidential one that gave Ngo Dinh Diem more powers to control the whole country administratively and politically than had been held by the French Governors General, who had shared their control with various other officials within Indochina itself, as well as back home in Paris. In many respects, despite the fact that the earlier Vietnamese Emperors ruled by divine right, the Presidential powers as prescribed in the Constitution of the Republic of Vietnam, which was promulgated in October, 1956, were broader and more all-encompassing than those the Emperors wielded in practice. This had been due largely to the historic tradition of village autonomy in Vietnam and to the fact that before the modern era it had been physically impossible for a central authority to control remote rural areas. In the colonial era, the French purposely retained the system of decentralization, since it enabled them to impose their rule from the top, down through their own administrative echelons, and kept any cohesive national force from developing. But when Diem took over the fragmented southern half of Vietnam, he and his advisers felt, with considerable justification, that a strong central authority had to be established if the new nation was to have any chance of surviving. Although on paper the Constitution provided for the separation of powers, the position of the executive was far stronger than that of the legislative or the judicial arms; in fact, the President could rule by decree in any emergency—a condition he could more or less define himself—and suspend any laws. In place of the colonial regional system of government, whereby the central and southern parts of the country had been administered more or less separately, forty-one provinces were created, with a chief in each directly responsible to the President; in theory the province chief controlled district and village officials below him, but in practice, especially under the watchful eye of Nhu, the central government dominated them, too, and sent direct orders down to them on virtually all matters.

At the top, the administrative structure, consisting of the various ministries, directorates, and bureaus, was based on the long-established French system; the civil service proved to be just as paternalistic as it had been under the French, which was not surprising in view of the fact that for so many years the French had never inculcated any sense of independence or authority among the Vietnamese civil servants, and had made sure that very few of them ever rose to positions in which they were called upon to make decisions on their own. Diem had been more or less forced to create a National Assembly as a result of the promises he had made during the early political crises, but its functions were restricted in the Constitution, and it immediately became what Nhu had undoubtedly anticipated—a rubber-stamp body that grew to be disparagingly referred to in Saigon as "the government's garage." Diem made his greatest mistake, in the opinion of a number of his advisers, in abolishing elections for village chiefs and for municipal councils in June and August of 1956. Henceforth, the village heads were appointed by the province chiefs. Diem made this decision ostensibly on grounds of security; he felt that if the elections were allowed to take place, the Vietminh, already established clandestinely in many areas, would win a large number of them. Dang Duc Khoi, a young nationalist who later became Diem's press officer and eventually turned against him, was among those who thought Diem's decision unwise and afterward came to regard it as a vital error of judgment. "Even if the Vietminh had won some elections," Khoi said, "the danger in doing away with the traditional system of village elections was greater. This was something that was part of the Vietnamese way of life, and the concept could have been retained without interfering with Diem's legitimate desire—indeed, his need—for a strong central government. The security problem existed, but it wouldn't have made much difference if the Vietminh had elected some village chiefs—they soon established their own underground governments anyway. Diem's mistake was in paralyzing himself. He should have adopted a more intelligent and persuasive policy and concentrated at the outset on obtaining the support of the people. In that way, he could have properly challenged the Vietminh." Certainly, the system of government that evolved in Vietnam in 1955–56 was scarcely "revolutionary," either in form or in substance, and while this was probably not intentional on the part of the men who helped frame the Constitution, the document proved to have few safeguards against one-party rule and dictatorship. As time went on, Diem and Nhu came to ignore the Constitution completely and acted by decrees and by personal—and often private—orders to underlings all the way down to the village level.

The creation of the legal machinery of government was only one of the problems Diem had to face after he had managed to destroy the sects. More important was the physical task of taking over the countryside, particularly the areas that had been held by the Vietminh during the eight long years of the Indochina war, where bridges and highways had been destroyed, railway lines had been sabotaged, and the economy was at a standstill, with the population suffering from hunger and disease. The only agency that could properly do this was the Vietnamese Army, which totaled about 250,000 after Geneva. There were immediate handicaps to the use of the army as a means of pacification: its equipment was poor, its officer corps had been decimated, and morale was generally bad throughout the ranks as a result of desertions. In addition, there was a considerable amount of suspicion and mistrust among officers and between them and civilian officials, as a result of the plotting and counterplotting and the jockeying for power that had been going on. Some of these problems were ironed out in a series of informal conferences, and several rather shaky military-civilian teams were created. A second series of conferences led to tentative agreements for the Americans to participate with the French, whose forces were still in the country, in giving advice to the Vietnamese in the take-over period. In view of the Vietnamese suspicion of the French, this was an especially sensitive matter, and the Americans, as best they could, had to act like honest brokers, though their sympathies most often were with the Vietnamese. Diem, who had already abrogated the 1950 agreement that Vietnam, along with Laos and Cambodia, had made for the establishment of an economic and customs union with France, wanted the French troops to leave as soon as possible, though the Americans advised him to move slowly and at least wait until he had an efficient army of his own.

The first take-over action started in the Camau Peninsula, in the southernmost part of Vietnam, early in 1955. It ran into many problems because of the unavoidable use of inexperienced troops. Propaganda was also largely experimental. Twenty-man propaganda teams initially came in with the troops and then operated in the villages on their own. These teams, which were armed, carried portable transmitters, leaflets, booklets, and posters and did the best they could to engender enthusiasm for the new government. Among other things, they hopefully distributed shiny new pictures of Diem to replace the old frayed ones of Ho Chi Minh that many peasants had pasted on their cottage walls. Operation Brotherhood, a voluntary Filipino organization, sent doctors and nurses to work among the people in the villages, compensating somewhat for many of the difficulties that arose from poor follow-up action by the Vietnamese forces.

After the Camau operation, and with its faults in mind, another take-over was carried out on a large scale in the crucial Quang Ngai and Binh Dinh area in Central Vietnam, which traditionally had been a cradle of revolution and had remained a Vietminh stronghold throughout the colonial war. This operation went off more smoothly.

Indoctrination and training of troops showed considerable improvement over those of the troops in Camau, and the propaganda program was also more successful. Vietnamese soldiers behaved much better, helped the people rebuild their communities, and were enthusiastically received almost everywhere; in fact, despite the long stay of the Vietminh, when their last contingents boarded ships for the north, they were jeered. A week after their departure, President Diem made a surprise visit to the Binh Dinh region and was accorded a genuine and spontaneous welcome. In the months that followed, Diem made numerous trips around Vietnam, and at the outset many of these were successful, even though he could never completely drop his mandarin aloofness. Soon afterward, however, when tight controls began to be imposed and the image of dictatorship began to take shape, these trips became carefully organized,. contrived efforts to force the acceptance of Diem on an uncaring and even morose population, which by then had begun to lose faith in the new government—the abolition of the village elections being one important reason.

Once the take-overs were accomplished, the Vietnamese, assisted by the Americans, organized the first civic action programs. Since three-fourths of the civil servants in the country lived and worked in Saigon, there was a problem of getting people out to the countryside; nobody wanted to go. A plan sponsored by the Defense Ministry to have civilian workers, dressed in black calico like the peasants, go into the villages to work alongside the people was bitterly fought by old-line *fonctionnaires*. President Diem had to intervene to get a pilot program started. When a training center was finally set up in Saigon and its director, Kieu Cong Cung, asked for volunteers, no one came forward. Cung then selected a number of carefully screened men from among the 860,000 refugees who had come down from the north. After being trained, they were formed into four-man teams, and, wearing native black pajamas and blouses, they went out into the provinces, moving from one village to another. When they first arrived in a village, they would call a meeting to explain their presence and announce their plans, and then they would set to work. First they built village halls, schools, and dispensaries, and then roads. Invariably, in these early days, before the Vietcong started its campaign of assassination of such government workers, the co-operation of villagers was obtained, although the province and district chiefs often disapproved of what they claimed was the usurpation of their authority. This early civic action at the grass-roots level may have been the high point of successful people-to-people accomplishment under the Diem regime. It was followed by the creation of village Self-Defense Corps units, which the Defense Ministry sponsored, with American co-operation. Villagers were trained, given weapons, and formed into village guards under regular Army commanders in each region. These original Self-Defense Corps units represented a true armed citizenry, which Diem envisaged as a popular force to combat Communism, and their *esprit* at first was remarkable. Later, when the influence of the Can Lao began to be felt and the whole temper of the regime changed, military as well as popular morale sagged, and the efficiency of these local units diminished.

The Self-Defense Corps and a parallel military organization called the Civil Guard, created as a regional force under the direction of each province chief, were the first government military units to suffer from the renewal of Communist activities in South Vietnam. It became apparent as early as August, 1955, that such activities would be renewed. At that time, though the Americans advised caution and suggested he explore the technicalities further in the north, Diem made it clear that he would not agree to holding the national plebiscite for reunification stipulated in the Geneva agreements; he cited the existence of a Vietminh underground in South Vietnam and the impossibility of having a free election "as long as the Communist regime in North Vietnam does not allow each Vietnamese citizen to enjoy the democratic freedoms and fundamental rights of man." The Vietminh undoubtedly was fully prepared for Diem's decision, despite the sense of pretended outrage with which it was greeted in Hanoi. In fact, according to P. J. Honey, an outstanding British student of North Vietnam, the Communists, while attending the Geneva Conference, privately expressed the opinion that the plebiscite would never be held. Nevertheless, soon after the vote deadline passed in July, 1956, without any disturbances, Vietminh propaganda in areas where the Communists had held sway began to be subtly directed

F

against, among other things, "the sabotage of the Geneva agreements." The Vietminh also attacked the alleged reforms of the Diem administration, particularly the plan for redistributing land to the peasants, and began to criticize the Diem government as an American puppet regime. By 1958, the Vietminh had fully resumed its campaign of terror in the countryside, kidnaping government officials and threatening villagers who in any way co-operated with the government. By then, too, many peasants had begun to be caught in the middle on the issue of taxation; the Vietminh, where it felt itself in control, had started to collect its own taxes—usually rice—from the villagers, and the government, sometimes in the same places, sought to maintain its tax collections. Military incidents in the countryside were rising, and in an average month the local and regional units were becoming involved in a score of engagements. Usually, these were hit-and-run Communist attacks on Self-Defense Corps or Civil Guard headquarters, the purpose of which was both to seize weapons and to heighten the atmosphere of terror.

After the spring of 1956, the Americans had taken over responsiblity for reorganizing and retraining the Vietnamese Army. Several hundred American officers of the Military Assistance Advisory Group (MAAG), under Lieutenant General Samuel Williams, who had replaced General O'Daniel, were sent to Vietnam to supervise this process. The Americans were to reduce the Vietnamese Army by about 100,000 and build the remaining 150,000 troops into a force able to withstand a possible attack from the north—at least long enough to enable the Allied powers to send help under the banner of SEATO. In this context, the new Vietnamese Army was primarily rebuilt along conventional lines, which many military and non-military observers felt was a mistake in view of the kind of conflict that was likely to develop in South Vietnam. These critics maintained that by sending the most able Vietnamese junior and senior officers to be trained at bases and camps in the United States and in Okinawa, MAAG was creating a Vietnamese officer corps that was not educated to handle a guerrilla war situation. As the war later unfolded, most of these officers demonstrated their incapacity to confront a fluid guerrilla type of action, and they insisted on meeting the Vietminh (by then the Vietcong) challenge with a conventional response that brought about defeat after defeat. There were some early efforts to develop Ranger-type forces trained in guerrilla tactics; but the opportunity to build a real rural-based army, modeled on the early success of the village Self-Defense Corps, was neglected in the main effort to recreate the regular army as a defensive holding force. This defensive psychology proved hard to overcome; and by the time an attempt was made to overcome it, it was very late. The Vietcong was riding high.

CHAPTER V

The Last Years of Diem

By the end of 1958, the Vietcong had increased its political and military offensive in South Vietnam to the point where security in the countryside had become a serious problem and the government was in trouble. In their campaign to isolate villages, particularly in the delta, the Communists had begun to smuggle in armed guerrillas from the north. These were southerners who had gone north in 1954 and been retrained as the vanguard of the new revolutionary army to "liberate" South Vietnam; they now joined the stay-behinds who for four years had been organizing militant village cells and were engaging in widespread terrorism, including assassination of hamlet and village chiefs, teachers, local security heads, and other government officials. By this time, too, the Vietcong had begun to set up their own administrations in the villages, run by political cadres who were in charge of indoctrinating the population and collecting taxes—both money and rice—and creating new espionage nets. The hard core of guerrillas numbered four or five thousand by the end of 1959, but the figure was to double during 1960; and the substantial build-up of regional, or provincial, elements and of local forces—peasants who worked in their fields by day and joined in the attacks on government outposts at night—was also underway. The Vietcong had definitely moved into the phase in which the armed struggle against the South Vietnamese government was considered to be as important as political warfare. By the end of 1959, the Communists controlled about a third of the countryside, and they had already managed to create important bases in secluded forest areas in the delta and in the highlands. Within a year, they were claiming half the country, and the government troops everywhere were on the defensive. Although Diem's forces outnumbered the guerrillas by a large margin, estimated at seven or eight to one, the guerrillas clearly held the initiative, and the quality of the government troops was poor. Steps were taken late in 1959 to retrain and re-equip the rather motley Civil Guard, and to make the regular Army more of a flexible fighting force by adding units trained in the manner of American Rangers; but these measures took time, and there was little or no cohesion among the various government military troops—the Army and the regional and local contingents. A new force, the Republican Youth—Nhu's idea—was created early in 1960 to help in the defense of hamlets and villages. The shortage of weapons, however, was still severe and most of these units were armed first with homemade knives and clubs. As the United States began sending in more weapons, the older guns were passed down the line, from the Civil Guard to the Self-Defense Corps and ultimately to the Republican Youth.

The popularity of the Diem regime had begun to wane seriously as early as 1957. In February of that year, in fact, an unknown would-be assassin narrowly missed killing Diem while he was visiting a provincial fair in the low plateau area north of Saigon. By 1960, the ruling family (and particularly Nhu) had become aware that its hold was precarious and that it had to depend more than ever on the loyalty of a handful of men. This was true not only in a political sense but also, more significantly, in a military one; Diem and Nhu could no longer afford to select military commanders on the basis of ability, but solely by virtue of their loyalty. This naturally tended to inhibit the efficiency of the Army, but the wisdom of such moves, as far as Diem and Nhu were concerned, was borne out in late 1960, by a major attempt to overthrow the Diem regime.

On the morning of November 11th, three paratroop battalions on duty in Saigon seized most of the key government centers in the capital and then prepared to attack Diem's palace. The Americans had known in advance that the coup was coming and while they did not assist it, they did nothing to stop it; apparently they did not even warn Diem. The leaders of the coup, a small group of military men and civilians, made the mistake of bargaining with Diem instead of following up on their attack. On the evening of the eleventh, Diem announced he would step down and allow the formation of a new government of "national union," initially to be chosen by the rebels and a group of generals. But the next morning, when the coup leaders were broadcasting their "victory," troops loyal to Diem moved quietly into the city from points just to the north and the south and recaptured the important installations. The coup collapsed, and its leaders, including Colonel Nguyen Chanh Thi, fled to Cambodia.

It was difficult to gauge the amount of support behind this first major coup attempt. Most citizens in Saigon were probably neutral; but a surprising number, including government workers and businessmen, later told me they had secretly hoped the coup would be successful, even though they were not prepared to take part in it. The attitude toward Diem and his family had begun to change from disinterest or contempt to animosity, chiefly because of the economic and political regimentation imposed by the government by this time. In the countryside, where there was less political awareness or even knowledge of what was going on in Saigon, many peasants had begun to formulate their own opposition to the government; this was also due to increasing regimentation. Beginning in mid-1959, the government had started a plan to regroup the rural population into so-called *agrovilles* in order to cut them off from Communist penetration. Though the government described them as part of its "social revolution," the *agrovilles* were purely defensive. They coincided with the building of more defensive forts throughout the country, small bamboo and sometimes concrete structures manned by the Civil Guard or by Self-Defense Corps units. Both measures clearly showed the lingering influence of French military thinking on the Vietnamese (the French had similarly sought to regroup parts of the population during the last stages of the Indochina war and had regularly engaged in fixed positional warfare). Originally, the government planned to build a hundred large *agrovilles*, each of which would hold about four thousand persons, and about four hundred smaller communities. In some respects, they were similar in concept to Soviet collective farms or Chinese communes; Nhu may have been inspired by those examples. They were to be self-sustaining, and each was to have a residential and a business area, as well as an official center. They would be popular, the government hoped, because they would afford the peasants the security they no longer could enjoy in the Vietcong-infested areas, but things didn't work out that way. Almost all the peasants who were moved to the *agrovilles* deeply resented having to leave their old homes, where in many cases their families had lived for generations, and the assistance the government gave them was negligible—about five dollars and a small loan to help pay for the acre and a half of new land each farmer got. Furthermore, each peasant was supposed to build his own house after tearing down his old one and lugging the materials with him to the *agroville*. After a year and a half, by which time only a score or so of the *agrovilles* had been built, the government gave up the program.

Land Reform Attempted

The lack of security in the countryside, coupled with poor administration, had severely hampered the government's land reform program, and had further served to diminish the peasants' support of the Diem government. The Communists, naturally, were quick to capitalize on this dissatisfaction. When Diem came to power in 1954, one of his first declared aims, which the Americans encouraged, was to introduce agrarian reform. At that time, forty per cent of the nation's 2,300,000 hectares of riceland was owned by a quarter of one per cent of the rural population; about a fourth of the large landholdings were French, and the rest were owned by wealthy Vietnamese or by the Catholic Church. Almost a third of this riceland had been abandoned as a result of the war and of the migration of peasants to more secure areas. Traditionally, in Vietnam most of the land not owned by individuals or by the Church was communally owned, and each year, or every two years, the individual farmer was allotted two or three hectares on the basis of bids, a practice that led to many abuses. In the case of privately owned land, the rent rates forced upon the peasants often amounted to fifty per cent of the crop, and the tenant had no security, his presence on the land depending only on a landlord's willingness to rent it. Early in 1955, the Diem government introduced a program for rent reduction and security of tenure. Rents were limited to a maximum of twenty-five per cent of the total yield, and a tenant was assured of being able to farm his land for a period of three to five years, after which he had the option to renew his contract unless the owner himself wanted to farm the land. Any increase of yield resulting from a farmer's investment or use of improved technique belonged to the tenant without any increase of rent. While some peasants benefited from this part of the land reform program, it was hindered by bad administration and lack of proper enforcement. Peasants were frequently in arrears on their rents, and the system of agrarian courts established to settle landlord-tenant disputes soon came to be dominated by the landlords and by officials friendly to them, to the obvious disadvantage of the peasants. Furthermore, the peasants objected to paying rents for land that had been unoccupied because of the war—almost a third of the total riceland.

In October, 1956, the government introduced the second and more significant phase of its land reform program, which involved transfer of ownership of riceland not communally owned. Under the terms of the law, no person was allowed to own more than a hundred hectares of riceland, and any amount above that was to be bought by the government. Landlords received ten per cent of the purchase price in cash and the rest in government bonds, bearing three per cent interest and maturing in twelve years. The average price per hectare amounted to about seven thousand piastres, which was about two hundred dollars at the official rate at the time, and half that at the free-market rate. Peasants were to buy the land at the same rate, payable in six annual installments without interest, and it was estimated that this would amount to about twenty-five per cent of the annual gross yield from their crops. The six-year period was considered by many experts to be much too short, and they felt the pay-off time should have been at least fifteen or twenty years. Some seven hundred thousand hectares belonging to twenty-five hundred owners were declared subject to transfer. The French government financed the transfer of French land to the Vietnamese government, while American funds helped buy the Vietnamese-owned land.

By the end of 1962, only about a third of the land that was supposed to have changed hands actually had, and only about ten per cent of the total of more than a million tenant households had obtained any of it. In the first place, the amount of transferable land came to only about twenty per cent of the total riceland in the country because landowners were allowed to retain anything under a hundred hectares, and the fact that land not used for rice was not made available was another restricting factor. The Americans had fought vainly against both these limitations. Land owned by absentee landlords was not distributed free, and this was a further drawback. Perhaps the most disturbing aspect of the land redistribution program was the manner in which influential politicians and members of Diem's family obtained huge amounts of land that had been taken over by the government from French or Vietnamese landlords but had not been distributed to the peasants. Among these individuals, for example, were Vice-President Nguyen Ngoc Tho, whose capacity for survival has been greater than that of most Vietnamese leaders. (After Diem was overthrown, he headed the new provisional government for a time, and after that he "retired," an extremely wealthy man.) Truong Van Chuong, Mme. Nhu's father, who resigned as Ambassador to the United States shortly before Diem's overthrow, was another of the successful "land grabbers"; when he quit as Ambassador, Mme. Nhu let the cat out of the bag by declaring, after her father's property had been confiscated, that he had quit because he opposed Diem's agrarian reform measures. Probably the biggest fault of the land redistribution program was its failure to recognize the fact that the Vietcong had turned over land to the peasants for nothing in the areas they controlled; in view of this, the price the peasants had to pay to buy land from the government was undoubtedly too high. In fact, in order to win the peasants over, the government might have footed the whole bill and distributed the land gratis. The Vietcong had considerable success in propagandizing against the government program for these reasons, even though they followed up their own free land distribution by collecting taxes that were often higher than those the old private landlords had levied.

When the government started to implement the 1956 land redistribution scheme, it sought the help of the Confederation of Vietnamese Labor, which was then one of the few free labor bodies in Asia and the only one successfully to begin organizing tenant farmers. The head of the union, Tran Quoc Buu, has always denied any political ambition, though he has often operated behind the scenes politically. Buu, a close friend of Ngo Dinh Nhu since the early fifties, had been consulted about the land reform program. Nhu thought that Buu's cadres in the tenant farmer's union, with their intimate knowledge of rural problems, would be able to help put the program across to the peasants. What happened was a tragic example of the compulsive fear Nhu and Diem had of any organization that could become a threat to their power. Their inclination always was to destroy or undermine the influence of any such group, and the fact that Buu was Nhu's friend, and that his union might have developed into the spearhead of real agrarian reform in South Vietnam, did not deter Nhu from almost wrecking it. The union's cadres, urging acceptance of the new land reform scheme by the peasants, frequently found themselves in a hostile atmosphere because of the alliance that had grown up between the landlords and many government officials against the plan. In numerous places, union representatives were arrested; in one area, south of Saigon, where many of the farmers were union members, Buu later told me that the wife of the province chief had originally owned three-quarters of the land and that the chief had tossed all the union cadres into prison.

Another stumbling block to the success of the program was the so-called system of Farmers Associations. These were originally established, with the support of Buu and the Americans, to help the peasants get credit facilities and other forms of assistance, but too quickly they came to be dominated by local officials and landlords, and consequently were more paternalistic than progressive. "The effect of these associations on our cadres in the country also became disastrous," one of Buu's officials told me. "Some of our people were kept in jail for two or three years, and, to save others from arrest, we had to withdraw because of the opposition to us. The failure of the government to give us the support we needed prevented us from convincing the farmers that the Vietcong propaganda they were subjected to was false." The unfortunate conclusion was not that the Diem government purposely spoiled its own program (though in effect it allowed that to happen) but that it foolishly and willfully eliminated its best enforcement workers. Naturally, a considerable coolness developed between Buu and Nhu. Union representatives and Americans who were aware of the situation privately expressed the opinion that Nhu was not at all unhappy about the weakening of his old friend's role among the peasantry. Buu, in fact, came close to being arrested himself. "I don't think the government wanted to destroy the union completely, but it wanted to make sure it wasn't going to get anywhere as a popular force," one American official said. Although the unfortunate result was the weakening of a top-flight Asian democratic labor organization and the loss of another opportunity to rally the peasants to the government cause, no remonstrances were ever made by the American Embassy to the Diem government about the suppression of the farmers' union. "We just haven't got around to talking about it," I was told at the Embassy. "There's so much else to do."

Kennedy Tackles the Problem

By 1961, both in Washington and among the Americans in Saigon, there was a growing debate about the Diem government and what could or should be done about it. The discussion ranged from metaphysical abstractions concerning Diem's complicated personality, including his masochistic relationship with his family, to the harsh realities of the way in which Diem and Nhu were conducting the war as a kind of private operation. This soon became the subject of violent argument in the American press, especially as reflected in the stories sent home by correspondents from Vietnam. Many of these correspondents felt that the United States was temporizing with the Diem regime, that it should be firmer in its supporting role, and that at the very least it should insist on a more active voice in the allocation of aid and in the direction of the military campaign against the Vietcong.

In January, 1961, an episode took place that had it turned out dif-

ferently, might have made all the difference in the world in our relations with Vietnam and in the prosecution of the war. President
Kennedy had just taken office, and one of the first things he did was
to send for Lansdale, then a Brigadier General, who had gone to Vietnam under prior orders to write a report on the situation. Lansdale's
paper, on the basis of his earlier experience in Vietnam, dealt with
what he regarded as the American failures to use political power for
what it was worth in backing the cause of real nationalism and in conducting the war in ways that would counter the increasingly successful
guerrilla effort of the Vietcong. As a man who understood the nature
of guerrilla warfare, and who at the time was recognized as the Pentagon's leading expert on the subject, Lansdale felt that the Vietnamese
military structure and military methods of operation (which the
Americans, in their pale advisory role, were countenancing) were all
wrong. He felt that if the bitter conflict stood any chance of being won,
we would have to be firm in insisting on a complete reorganization of
the government's fighting machine; we would have to make it a force
capable of dealing with Communist subversion in a meaningful and
imaginative way, much as Magsaysay had done in the Philippines in
1951–52.

When Lansdale returned to Washington—after he had submitted
his report to his own superiors—he was suddenly summoned one
afternoon to the White House and, much to his surprise, ushered
into a conference room where the President was presiding over a
mixed group of high Pentagon, State Department, and National
Security Council officials. To his further surprise, President Kennedy,
after commending his report, indicated that Lansdale would be
sent back to Vietnam in a high capacity. Kennedy's declaration at the
meeting obviously raised the hackles of many officials whose agencies
had been criticized by Lansdale. The upshot was that nothing further
happened about Lansdale's appointment. It is now known that objections to it were raised in the highest levels of the Kennedy administration; in fact, there were threats of resignation. In the sense
that some drastic action in Vietnam should have been taken at this
time, whether it involved Lansdale or not, this was another vital turning point in the long and tortuous history of America's Vietnamese involvement. There was still a chance to do something to save the Diem

regime, depending largely on getting Nhu out of the country. Difficult as it would have been to achieve at this late date, Lansdale might have been able to persuade Diem to do it, because he had remained one of the few Americans Diem had ever trusted. More important, some feasible ideas about how to fight a guerrilla war might have been set in motion, and the miscalculation of what had always been essentially a revolutionary situation might thereupon have been altered.

In March, 1961, Frederick E. Nolting was chosen as the new Ambassador to Vietnam, to replace Elbridge Durbrow, who had been in Saigon since 1957. Durbrow had urged reforms on Diem, but he had not been backed up forcefully enough by Washington, and the result was that Diem had come to resent what he regarded as Durbrow's nagging. Relations between the two men became particularly difficult after the November, 1960, coup, when Durbrow had been noticeably silent, though he undoubtedly knew what was taking place. Nolting, a quiet-spoken Virginian gentleman, was sent out to mend fences and re-establish a smooth relationship. He managed to do this, but as things turned out, of all the postwar American Ambassadors in Vietnam, Nolting was probably most miscast in trying to deal with the peculiar mandarin psychology of Diem and the pathological nature of Nhu. Trying to persuade Diem and Nhu to do things in a more polite way was simply a further lesson in futility. In a day and age when most Ambassadors are simply glorified messenger boys for the State Department and the White House, Nolting was not really to blame. He was simply doing what Washington wanted him to do; and what Washington wanted was to coax the South Vietnamese into taking a number of "corrective steps"—we now tried to stay away from the nasty word "reform"—in order to give the government a broader social and political base. If Diem and Nhu relaxed the hold they and a few trusted associates maintained, we felt that the government would present a more popular and winning face to the people. The theory was fine, but it was obviously totally unrealistic in practice, and the proof that Nolting's polite tactics were getting nowhere was attested in a remark Nhu made privately, in May, 1962, that "Mr. Nolting is the only intelligent Ambassador the Americans have ever sent to Vietnam."

Aside from Diem's and Nhu's fundamental mistrust of people,

their ideas—espeçially Nhu's—about introducing democracy in an underdeveloped country differed totally from ours, and they were therefore completely disinclined to accept any of our suggestions. Both Nolting and General Paul D. Harkins, when he succeeded to the direction of American military effort in Vietnam, grew increasingly loath to push Diem and Nhu too hard. Harkins, a conventionally minded military man deemed it his duty to remain optimistic in the face of an ever-growing volume of evidence that the war was going badly; and he did all he could to deny the growing negative reports of the American press, which were based not only on its own observations but on hard facts obtained from American military advisers in the field. Eventually, Harkins' relationship with a number of the American correspondents on the scene assumed the characteristics of a vendetta, a situation that did credit to neither side, no matter how one might evaluate the rights and wrongs of it.

While we continued to temporize with the Diem regime, we moved closer to the decision that the Vietnamese war was also our war; Vietnam, we felt, was the place where a line ought to be drawn, beyond which we should not permit the Communists to advance. We were already footing a large bill for the war, and had begun, under President Kennedy, to commit an increasing amount of manpower. We had tied ourselves, through geography and circumstance, to the Vietnamese struggle; and the question of how far we should go in bringing about certain changes in the conduct of the war—which involved the need for some substantive changes of procedure and personnel in the Diem regime—paradoxically became more important in direct ratio to our reluctance to do anything about it. What took place between the middle and the end of 1961 established the full outlines of our commitment, and placed us on the horns of a dilemma that we never afterward seemed able to escape.

The prosecution of any war, especially one as deeply complicated as the Vietnamese, involves many matters that cut deeply across military, economic, social, and political lines. It was obviously difficult to disentangle these lines in Vietnam in 1961 and 1962, but one way to delay, or avoid, disentangling them was to fall victim, as we did, to the bureaucratic process, whereby endless discussions were held but little or nothing was accomplished or sustained. In this sense, the peculiar cycle of American engagement in Vietnam at the time repeated itself. Though the circumstances were different from those of ten years earlier, when we were dealing with the French, our relations with Diem revealed many similar aspects of uncertainty and indecision about how we really wished to play our part as the declared leaders of the free world. In the most basic sense, as during the French time, we proved ourselves incapable of defining what we meant by the word "intervention," either in moral or practical terms. We seemed unwilling to confront the harsh and unpalatable fact that in today's world not only is war a continuation of politics by other means, but the reverse is also true: that subtle but firm political involvement in the affairs of other countries with whom we are engaged in a common enterprise is often the only way to get results and avoid military as well as political disasters.

By the fall of 1961, the Americans in Saigon were convinced that Diem was moving much too slowly in combating the Vietcong, and that this was principally due to his insistence on doing almost everything himself or with the advice of his brother Nhu and a few others. "I think he holds back deliberately on many things, so as to make it appear an idea is his and not ours," one American diplomat told me. "It takes constant persuasion on our part to get even the smallest suggestion accepted, and until he gives the signal to go ahead, nothing gets done because everyone is afraid to move. Then there's the problem of establishing the mechanism to implement a decision, which can take more weeks or even months." The relationship that had grown up over the years between the Vietnamese and the Americans had by now produced a great deal of friction and mixed emotions. "We always felt that you Americans wanted to test us too much," Mme. Nhu once told me. "We have our whole lives and experience behind us in Vietnam. Why do you keep asking us to prove ourselves?" There was a certain truth to this, though it was a remark made out of context; what it did express was the almost total lack of mutual understanding, and in this respect the Americans were probably as much to blame as the Vietnamese. Over and above the emergence of a family oligarchy, there was virtually no meeting of minds among the Americans and the Vietnamese. There were some friendships, some mutual admirations, and, on occasion, some spontaneous examples of co-operation and accomplishment (these invariably took place at the lower levels), but there was little realization of the fundamental fact that a war was going on, and already being lost, which would affect the lives of everyone concerned for a long time. What was lacking was a proper dialogue, and in this sense Mme. Nhu's comment was germane. What was taking place was a contest between the Americans and the Vietnamese, one in which each side was convinced that the other wasn't doing enough to "prove" its loyalty and perseverance. Beyond mistrust was the whole tragic overlay of history, of colonialism and "neo-colonialism," of white men versus yellow men, and of the sort of deep miscomprehension that could only be resolved—perhaps—in time of peace, but surely not in time of war.

The truth of the matter was that had it not been for the big Communist offensives that began in 1960, the alliance between the Americans and the Vietnamese would have been even less effectual than it was. Our role in Vietnam evolved less on the basis of what we believed in than on what we felt had become unavoidable; by regarding what we were doing as basically a holding operation, we drifted almost automatically into a negative psychological position and appeared to have lost whatever revolutionary appeal we might have had earlier. It was therefore inevitable that individual Vietnamese nationalists, and the Vietnamese people as a whole, lost faith in us as revolutionary mentors. The French had been respected although ultimately hated; the Americans had come to be accepted but unappreciated. The increasingly important role played by the American press both clarified and aggravated this situation. Ambassador Nolting once pensively commented that he wished the American traditions of a free press were not being so thoroughly demonstrated in Vietnam, because "it makes my job of persuasion [vis-à-vis Diem] so much harder." Nolting's efforts at persuasion, however moderate, were not made easier by the fact that Washington had let it be known, rather flat-footedly, that "Diem is all we have, and there just aren't any alternatives." In the first place, this was not true, and in the second place, it was sadly reminiscent of the sort of talk that had gone on in China in 1946, when we used to say that "Chiang Kai-shek may be a son of a bitch, but he's *our* son of a bitch." Naturally, Washington's feelings about Diem reached the palace in Saigon and served further to raise the ire of a ruling family that had come to power with a well-developed persecution complex and had subsequently developed a positive mania for survival. Under the circumstances, the problems of American policymakers were admittedly difficult. Having created the dilemma with Diem, we now *compulsively* kept our firm grip on it. The suspicion persisted that we could not win with him, while at the same time we were frightened by the risks of fostering a change in the midst of a growingly brutal war.

In this kind of atmosphere, procrastination and delay became inevitable and served to breed more confusion. As conflicting American views were expressed both in Vietnam and in the United States, the Vietnamese were quick to turn them to their advantage. In the spring of 1961, Vice-President Lyndon B. Johnson paid a visit to Vietnam and made it clear that American support would be continued —and, in fact, increased—and that we had full confidence in Diem. The effect of Johnson's visit was to stiffen the resistance of the Vietnamese to carrying out a number of things we wanted them to do— things which the American Embassy had thought they were on the verge of doing as a result of patient pressure. This included the devaluation of the piastre and relinquishing of full Vietnamese control over income from American economic aid imports. After Johnson left, the Vietnamese would no longer even discuss these matters. In the summer of 1961, Professor Eugene Staley, of Stanford University, was sent to Vietnam to direct an all-embracing economic study on the basis of which a new American aid program would be formulated. The Staley report was never made public, but it was known to recommend a number of changes in the administration of aid, as well as certain reforms of a political nature. In October, 1961, General Maxwell D. Taylor headed another mission to Vietnam, which in effect was a follow-up to the Staley mission. Taylor was dismayed by a number of things he thought were wrong with the Diem regime and he recommended a tougher American approach. He drew up a list of some thirty subjects on which he suggested the Americans should act forcefully in its relations with the Diem regime. They included, among other things, recommendations that we stand firm on our demand that Diem and Nhu decentralize their administration, both in its civilian and its military aspects, and that we insist on a revamping of the muddled system of collecting and interpreting intelligence about the Vietcong. Taylor also felt strongly that certain political reforms should be instituted and that bona fide nationalist leaders who were in jail should be freed.

The calculated response of the Vietnamese, as engineered by Nhu, was to start a violent newspaper campaign against American attempts to "infringe on Vietnamese sovereignty." The question was raised as to whether Vietnam ought not to reconsider its relations with the United States. What followed over a period of several weeks was a game of bluff, which the Vietnamese won hands down. Instead of standing firm at this crucial point, the Americans backed off and accepted Diem's vague promise that he would co-operate with us in gradually putting into effect some of the reforms we wanted. By January, 1962, after prolonged discussions, a communiqué was issued, and it became apparent that Diem and Nhu had obtained everything they had sought in the way of additional military and economic support without any clear indication that they would really carry out any reform measures. This was the final turning point in our long and painful relationship with Diem. For those of us who had been in China in 1946 and followed the efforts of the Americans to get Chiang Kai-shek to adopt certain reforms, the comparison was marked. Every time we had thought we were getting somewhere with Chiang and giving more leeway to the more liberal members of the Kuomintang, we did certain things (such as selling China huge amounts of surplus war property at a crucial moment) that enabled the more reactionary elements around Chiang to convince him that he didn't have to execute any of the reforms the Americans desired because we had made clear our determination to go on helping him in the war against the Communists anyway. In Saigon, during the 1961-62 period of negotiations, Nhu played a role similar to that of the Kuomintang reactionaries. It was obvious, he told Diem, that the United States would not abandon the regime, and therefore there was no need to give in to the

American demands. As a result of giving Diem the upper hand again, the Americans in Saigon were once more restricted to polite persuasion and exhortation, but our fundamental position was now permanently weakened, and the slow descent into chaos became inevitable. "We've now conditioned the Vietnamese to shout about 'sovereignty,' " one disgusted American said. On the surface, the Embassy pretended that progress was being made. "It needs time, and we aren't prepared to throw the baby out with the bath," another ranking officer told me a few months later. "I'm impressed from week to week with how much the baby will eat." Privately, however, almost all officials made clear their dissatisfaction with how the weaning process was going. "In spite of our having over-committed ourselves to Diem, we ought to have kept some leverage," a third Embassy officer said forlornly. "There are a lot of ways to apply pressure. Among other things, we could do just as much stalling as they do and keep back certain things they want. Tell them point-blank, 'You don't want to do this— O.K., then we'll stop doing that.' You might call it passive resistance. It's an old Oriental game and it's about time we learned how to play it."

Diem did a few things we recommended, such as establishing a National Economic Council of fifty-five members to advise him on all sorts of economic matters and appointing provincial councils designed to help democratize the provinces; nevertheless his administrative machinery, despite some revamping, remained ponderous and almost archaic in its structure. The biggest bind, as far as the Americans were concerned, was the lack of flexibility in mounting the new counterinsurgency program against the Vietcong. On both the military and the economic-financial fronts, there was not nearly enough quick reaction, offensively or defensively, to Communist moves and to situations that were generally critical. The United States was trying to obtain permission to use more of its aid funds directly to help province, district, and village chiefs fight the Vietcong. While Diem had agreed in principle, he was afraid to give us too free a hand or to place too much confidence in local administrators who could become too cozy with the Americans and establish their own little empires. American military advisers in the field constantly complained that promised financial and material assistance of all kinds did not reach their areas soon enough or at all. The reason was that the government simply sat on a lot of it; counterpart funds for use in the war were primarily under its control, and material help, once it was unloaded at the dock, was completely under its supervision. The American economic aid mission had belatedly recommended that these goods be put in warehouses under our supervision and that we give them out as we saw fit, a degree of control we should never have relinquished in the first place on the basis of our earlier experience in China.

Anti-Diem Opposition Fizzles

On the political front, despite the rebuffs they had received after the Taylor mission, the Americans kept hoping that a loosening of some of the reins of the Diem regime would serve to inspire greater support of the central government in Saigon and, at the same time, provoke a more imaginative thrust in the countryside. Repeatedly, the Americans suggested that Diem either establish a coalition-type regime or permit a political opposition to function freely. It was proposed, for example, that Diem invite into his government some of the opposition or *attentiste* elements in Vietnam or abroad and some of the younger people whose lack of enthusiasm and growing malaise were due to their dismay over the repressive aspects of a regime that had almost totally inhibited freedom of action and expression. Naturally, any such political move on Diem's part would have had to be accompanied by a relaxation of these formal strings of control, but unfortunately they seemed to be increasing constantly. Although the Americans vainly urged him to reconsider, he passed and promulgated a law that forbade all kinds of meetings unless they were authorized by the government. Public meetings required seven days' advance notice, and, of course, could be disapproved, as they usually were. Even private meetings of associations and unions not held during working hours required forty-eight hours' notice. Weddings and funerals could not be held without twenty-four hours' prior notice. Penalties for violations ranged from fines to six months in jail. There were many Assemblymen who disapproved of the Public Meetings Law and the more widely discussed Bill for the Protection of Morality—Mme. Nhu's pet piece of legislation, which, among other things, banned all forms of public dancing. Afraid to speak their minds, these Assemblymen went around privately admitting their shame but declaring that they "could not go against the wishes of the ruling family." They suggested abjectly that the Americans should test the dance ban, for example, by purposefully violating it. (One Embassy girl who did, at a private party in her home, was arrested and the intervention of the Embassy was required to keep her out of jail.) Oddly enough, Diem would probably have abided by the Assembly's decision to postpone or even turn down the two laws, but such was the mysterious impact of his dominating personality, and that of Nhu and his wife, that not a single voice was raised in public protest. All this was in keeping with other harsh strictures. For example, no book—fact, fiction, or poetry—could be published in Vietnam unless it was first submitted to censorship. The local press, Vietnamese and Chinese, was completely controlled by means of government publication permits that could at any time be revoked, and the French and English-language papers in Saigon had to submit all their copy to censors; the English-language paper, the *Times of Vietnam,* became Mme. Nhu's mouthpiece and often brazenly attacked American policy.

Simultaneously opposing Diem and keeping one's freedom in South Vietnam was never easy, and by 1962 there were some thirty thousand prisoners in about fifty jails throughout the country, about two-thirds of whom were classified as political prisoners. Many were captured Vietcong insurgents, but there were also a lot of "suspects" who had languished in jails for months or even years. Among the prisoners were some three hundred non-Communist liberals arrested solely for having expressed anti-Diem views or for being suspected of having spoken out in favor of the abortive 1960 coup. *Habeas corpus* was something that was just talked about, and although the government gave lip service to a pledge to bring prisoners to trial systematically, many of them never were accorded even a rudimentary hearing. One of the most prominent was Dr. Phan Quang Dan, the leader of the Free Democratic Party, whose analyses of earlier events have already been quoted. Dr. Dan, who had fought the French, the

Communists, and then Diem, had won a seat in the National Assembly elections of 1959. He was not allowed to take it, however, because he was accused of having violated election regulations, which he may have done, as others certainly did; the fact remains he was the obvious choice of his constituents. Perhaps because he was so embittered, he had made the grievous error of jumping on the coup band wagon when it was apparent that the coup had already failed. Under the circumstances, Dr. Dan's arrest was probably justified, but after an inconclusive military trial he remained in jail, where he was tortured, until after the end of the Diem regime.

Some months after the 1960 coup, an effort was made by the Diem regime to foster a controlled political opposition. The idea, later attributed to Nhu, was actually that of Dr. Tran Kim Tuyen, the brilliant director of Social and Political Studies, and in effect it turned out to be tantamount to the establishment of a national intelligence service. Dr. Tuyen came from Phat Diem, one of the Catholic enclaves up north, and he had been responsible, in 1954, for persuading a considerable number of Catholics to give up their homes and property in the north and move south. Subsequently, Dr. Tuyen had been among those who had tried unsuccessfuly to get Diem to maintain some contact with individual northerners, including members of the Hanoi government, in the hope that even a few might eventually be persuaded to defect. When the idea of creating a mild opposition first came up, Dr. Tuyen was aware that he would have to move cautiously, especially since he was operating under Nhu's surveillance. The group that was created was called the Committee on National Union. Tuyen's top assistant was one of the ten members named to it, so that the government could be kept fully informed of what all the Committee members were doing, publicly and privately. This scarcely could be described as political freedom, but the Committee did manage to hold a few meetings. Its popular impact, however, was virtually nil, and it didn't last very long.

Two opposition political leaders I knew in 1962 were Dr. Dan Van Sung, the head of the Front for Democracy, and Dr. Phan Huy Quat, whom the Americans had come so close to backing for Premier in 1955, ten years before he finally got the job. Early in 1962, Dr.

Quat sent an open letter to Ambassador Nolting asking his help in getting the government to initiate "large scale and sincere" reforms in order to build popular support. Dr. Quat also suggested that non-Communist political prisoners be released and that really free elections for the National Assembly be held. Nolting had made an earlier appeal for antigovernment leaders to get together and try to improve the government from within instead of carping from without. This prompted Dr. Quat to inform Nolting that he had written to Diem proposing "a direct exchange of viewpoints in an unofficial and relaxed atmosphere," in order to encourage the national unity movement. He had received no reply from Diem, nor did he get an answer to a second letter he sent the President suggesting how rural reforms might be better implemented. Now, in his letter to Nolting, Dr. Quat concluded that "the political structure does not seem to provide favorable opportunities for sincere and constructive nationalists to participate in national affairs." Nolting sent Dr. Quat a polite reply, which Dr. Quat and his friends considered essentially meaningless, as far as any real support for them was concerned. It was apparent more than ever that Nolting was not supposed to rock the boat.

Dr. Sung, who was operating more clandestinely than Dr. Quat, had also unavailingly sought Diem's permission for opposition political parties to exist freely and to be allowed to contribute to the democratic process. In a long talk I had with him, he emphasized that "there are no political leaders here, there is no political class as such." In 1960, Dr. Sung had been permitted to publish an open letter in which he asked for the liberalization of the Diem regime, for the release of political prisoners, and for the right of his party to run candidates for the National Assembly. Since he had evoked no response from the government, he had decided not to risk running anyone, but when a by-election took place near Saigon late in 1961 to replace an Assemblyman who had died, Dr. Sung put up a candidate. The government held back some necessary technical papers concerning the man's military status until three days after the election, so he would not get on the ballot.

On February 27, 1962, two dissident pilots bombed the Presidential palace in another attempt to kill Diem or some members of his family.

No one was killed, though Mme. Nhu was hurt. This attempt, however, did succeed in killing off the halfhearted efforts that had been made to create any kind of open political opposition. "We don't even talk about freedom of the press or ask for other liberties any more," Dr. Sung told me when I spoke with him afterward. "Of course, we would like to see some checks and balances established in the government—for example, a National Political Council that might have some supervision over the various government departments, if not over the executive—but Diem has now completely surrounded himself in a protective oligarchy."

Whenever Diem or Nhu were approached about their reaction to men such as Dr. Quat and Dr. Sung, the reply was that they could play governmental roles "if they subject themselves to national discipline, but they have no more right than anyone else to demand to be taken into the government." As Nhu once put it to me, "There's always going to be an opposition. If we take these people in, there will be another opposition springing up, because they are controversial men. Perhaps in three years, when the situation has been stabilized, we can talk of the right of political parties to function." Mme. Nhu expressed it even more simply. "You open a window to let in light and air, not bullets," she said. "We want freedom, but we don't want to be exploited by it." Another of Diem's right-hand men, who preferred to be anonymous, said, "We don't need more politicians, we need more good administrators. Just to broaden our base politically, sharing power with some others, won't bring democracy. We're faced with a highly dangerous situation and we can't tolerate dissension. In America, as in England, there exists a true opposition. Here it's a matter of others wanting to take our place, and their criticism is negative, not constructive." These answers seemed to be less than persuasive, especially in view of Dr. Sung's modest hopes for creating a freer political climate and his suggestion of some modest mechanisms that might have been adopted. The inability of the opposition elements to get together and present a united front admittedly had hurt their chances, but by the middle of 1962 there was no longer any point in even trying.

An Uneasy Partnership

In the spring of 1962, when I returned to Saigon, which I had always regarded as the loveliest of Southeast Asian capitals, there were few outward signs that the city was living on borrowed time. It had retained its sense of buoyancy and well-being, despite the fact that the dance halls were being closed down and that everyone was complaining about the morality bill, which contained a number of other restrictions, too. It imposed penalties for taking part in beauty contests, for adolescent drinking or smoking, for prostitution (a prostitute "surprised" three times with three different men was subject to arrest), and for contraception ("We're underpopulated," Mme. Nhu told me). The government insisted that the clean-up campaign was inspired not only by its own moral fervor, which it seemed forever to proclaim, but by the complaints, according to Mme. Nhu, of the Vietnamese soldiers in the field that they were "dancing with death" while their more fortunate companions in the cities were "dancing with girls." Four or five hundred government troops were being killed and almost a thousand were being wounded or taken prisoner each month. The soldiers, therefore, many of whom had been on duty for a year or more, may justifiably have resented the gaiety in Saigon, but it seemed to me that the government was going too far in its proscriptions. Saigon itself was not far removed from the violent fratricidal revolution that was raging throughout the countryside, including areas a scant dozen miles from the city. Manifestations of the war were visible the moment the visitor arrived at Tan Son Nhut, the city's noisy, no longer drowsy airport. American helicopters carrying Vietnamese to and from battle were dropping in and out like beetles, while fighters and bombers buzzed overhead and large transport planes shuttled north and south with supplies. The Saigon River was full of ships bringing in materials of war, and the city's streets teemed with uniformed Vietnamese and Americans.

It was not long before I realized that the fiction of American non-involvement in Vietnam was bothering American soldiers in the field as much as, if not more than, it had disturbed the Republicans in Washington a few months earlier, when they had accused President Kennedy of a lack of forthrightness on the subject. The feeling among the six thousand Americans in the country—particularly since the arrival a short time before of the first batch of a hundred helicopters, which were noticeably stepping up the pace of the war—was that the public at home ought to be told the whole truth. The truth was, they felt, that we were now involved in the war "up to our necks," as several put it, that American men and planes were beginning to be shot at regularly, and that it was impossible to obey the admonition to fire a gun only if fired at first. The formal explanation—that we were in Vietnam solely to train and advise the Vietnamese—had been persisted in for legalistic reasons, as everyone admitted. It was obvious, though, that this was no longer fooling anybody, least of all the Russians, the Chinese, and the North Vietnamese—or the Polish, Canadian, and Indian members of the International Control Commission established at Geneva in 1954. (The latter had dwelt for several years in their own Cloud-Cuckoo-Land of ignoring, through the convenient excuse of lack of unanimity, the specific accusations of armed intervention and build-up repeatedly made both in Hanoi and in Saigon.)

It was also not long before I realized that the relationship between the Americans and the Vietnamese was not an easy one for either side. Though the caliber of our officers was extremely high, the Americans, by nature impatient, were anxious to get on with the job; the Vietnamese, proud and stubborn, didn't relish taking advice, especially from Occidentals. They had done that long enough, and the fact that the Occidentals were friends this time didn't altogether alter the situation. After all, this was still their country and their war, even though, in the larger sense, we had now chosen to make it ours as well. There were other things, such as formally training the regional Civil Guard to supplement the regular (170,000) Vietnamese Army. The Vietnamese had wanted to do it years before, but we were afraid. (We had wanted the Guard kept to limited constabulary duty and didn't want to arm men with rifles that might be lost or surrendered to the Vietcong in combat.) The Vietnamese had been proved right, for the 70,000 members of the Guard, and the equal number of Self-Defense Corps soldiers beneath it at the village level, were now carrying the war to the Vietcong as much as the Vietnamese Army was. There were some other things involving military strategy and tactics, about which the Americans seemed to be right and which the Vietnamese were still objecting to, for their own reasons. These included the creation of an organized, cohesive intelligence system and a smooth-functioning military administration (there was still no proper line of command in the Army and no functioning staff in Saigon). Operations were mounted in the field by President Diem, or by his immediate staff, more often by whim and hunch than by planning and co-ordination with the various corps commanders. Some of President Diem's favorite division commanders or province chiefs were able to persuade him to approve of actions that simply suited their particular needs or their egos.

Despite many annoyances of red tape and delay that came to a climax in Saigon, and that undoubtedly hurt the over-all war effort, I found encouraging the patience and patriotism and the will to fight of the individual Vietnamese soldiers in the field. Many of them were sons of men who fought before them in a nation that had been in steady rebellion for more than two decades—against the Japanese, against the predatory Chinese occupation troops in the north, against the French, and against itself in civil conflict. (One high Vietnamese officer, a Buddhist, who had lived through it all, having fought with the French against the Vietminh, told me that he kept having a recurrent dream in which he had a Japanese wife, a French mistress, a Chinese cook, and was reincarnated as an American military adviser.) The big problem now, everyone agreed, was how to go about creating more zeal among the average apolitical farmer, who in many respects had to be regarded as a premature neutralist, wishing only to be left alone to tend his fields. It was admittedly hard to rally distrustful peasants by trying to get some economic and social assistance to them and at the same time trying to improve the condition of military security. What made the task even more difficult was that there were actually three different wars going on simultaneously, and all three, because of geographical and ethnic considerations, required different, if related, approaches. One war was taking place in the flat, watery delta of the south; a second in the high plateau and coastal areas of Central Vietnam; and a third in the high mountains and jungles of the north.

The Delta

"There are those who cannot imagine how guerrillas could survive for long in the rear of the enemy. But they do not understand the relationship between the people and the army. The people are like water and the army is like the fish. How can it be difficult for the fish to survive where there is water?" Nowhere does this well-known dictum of Mao Tse-tung's apply more literally than in the vast delta of South Vietnam formed principally by the Mekong River and its many tributaries. And no guerrilla army has applied it more to the letter than the Communist forces of Vo Nguyen Giap, the supreme commander of the Vietcong, who masterminded the victory over the fort-bound, road-bound French and then applied his grand strategy to join South Vietnam to the Communist north. A large proportion of the provinces south of Saigon, bounded by the South China Sea and the Gulf of Siam, is a seeping mass of rich rice paddies and swampland, interlaced by some twenty-five hundred miles of natural and artificial canals. The majority of the villages in the area are strung out along the sides of the canals, and the chief mode of transportation is the river boat and the sampan. It was here, in the delta, that the Communists in 1962 were concentrating their main offensive. In every sense, this was a war of the water and the fish. More often than not the Vietcong was managing (and still is managing, in 1965) to elude the government troops because of the efficacy of the Mao doctrine—using the people to hide among and to depend upon, either through the threat of reprisals for failure to co-operate or because the Vietcong is trusted, especially in areas it has controlled for a long time. In many cases, whole peasant families have belonged to the Vietcong, the father and eldest son as full or part-time fighters, the mother as a provider of food, and youngsters of fourteen or fifteen as spies on government troops or as couriers.

This kind of fluid opposition moves swiftly, usually by night, from place to place, attacking government outposts in the dark, setting ambushes by day, and assassinating or kidnapping government officials wherever and whenever possible; and it can only be fought through the tactic of rapid retaliation, based upon intelligence of the Vietcong's whereabouts. The problem is also tied to the fundamental need for establishing security in the villages and to the gradual evolution of some new form of village democracy. To achieve this, the Diem government, late in 1961, having abandoned the earlier *agroville* program, adopted a bold new scheme to build so-called "strategic hamlets" throughout the country. In time, all of South Vietnam's sixteen thousand hamlets (an average village is composed of three to seven hamlets) were to become "strategic"; i.e., militarily secure.

The concept of strategic communities, still being employed in Vietnam today, was not new, as Diem once pointed out to me. It was adopted centuries ago by Vietnamese villages seeking to defend themselves against Chinese bandits. But in 1962 the idea was adopted with revolutionary fervor as a positive ideological answer to Communism. Like so many other things, the idea was generally credited to Nhu, who, in fact, originally opposed it. It was introduced, in its modern version, by British veterans of the campaign in Malaya, notably Robert Thompson, who in 1950 helped create the concept in that beleaguered country. There, the Chinese population, among which the Communist guerrillas thrived, was gathered together in newly built villages and offered government protection, thus cutting the guerrillas off from their popular base of support. When Thompson's plan was first offered to the Vietnamese, Nhu dismissed it. It was only when he saw that the Americans were ready to back it with considerable funds that he suddenly swung around in its favor, thereafter adopting the plan as his own. As with everything Nhu did, he applied it to his own peculiar purposes, using it to promote his concept of personalism and to shore up his own system of loyalties.

First, with the help of government-trained civic action teams of twenty or thirty men, each hamlet was supposed to establish its own security by surrounding itself with barbed wire, mud walls, and double rows of spiked bamboo sticks arranged in and along ditches and in the bottom of moats. Then it was to create small defense units from among the younger citizens; this hamlet militia was akin to the Republican Youth already established by Nhu. The idea was for the government to lend this militia a sufficient number of weapons for six months; after that, it was hoped enough guns would be captured from the Vietcong so that the original weapons could be turned back to other government units, particularly to the Self-Defense Corps. Once the security of the strategic communities was established, the social and economic phase of the operation would begin. The civic action team members were to introduce such things as agricultural co-operatives, and were to help the villagers build schools and medical clinics, while also "educating" them to a new understanding of the benefits the government could give them once they became immune to the threats or blandishments of the Vietcong. Separate groups were to be formed—of men from forty-five to sixty and from eighteen to forty-five, women from eighteen to forty-five, and youngsters from fourteen to eighteen—and each member of each group was to be assigned a special task to help keep the community secure and to improve it in various ways. These groups, and the hamlets and villages as entities, were also supposed to elect their own leaders and councils, but the government was extremely careful about how this modest reversion to local elections was to be carried out. A secret document prepared for Nhu was made available to me; it declared that while freedom and democracy were to be considered "end objectives," democratic liberties "out of season" would only give the Communists an opportunity to sabotage the village organizations. This was the same old argument Diem had used in 1956 to do away with the whole idea of village elections. Consequently, the document added, although some sort of voting was to be permitted, the civic action cadres and, in particular, the district chiefs, who had never been regarded as exemplars of democracy, were to be "clever," seeing to it that the "right" people were always chosen; if necessary, a veto was to be applied. Actually, very few elections of any kind were ever held.

While Diem and Nhu gave lip service to this concept of creating a new democracy "from the bottom up," the peasants—at least in the villages I visited in the delta—did not seem overly impressed with the whole idea of the strategic hamlets. They were aware of the possible benefits of being surrounded by bamboo spikes and moats, and having some local militia defend them, and perhaps having a few new roads built to help them move about more readily; but there was not much evidence that they were benefiting from any social or other essential economic improvements. In some cases, where security had been improved, the villagers seemed less afraid than they had been before. There was even evidence of their being more willing to render intelligence about the Vietcong to the government troops. By and large, however, the improvement seemed negligible. The chief reason became apparent as the plan was introduced: the government tried to push it too far and too fast. In the interest of projecting itself into as many places as possible, it vastly overextended itself and insisted on creating strategic hamlets, replete with barbed wire, moats, and so on, where no real security existed. As a result, the Vietcong invariably moved in quickly and wrecked or burned out the hamlets, or applied the old Communist tactic of boring from within and sowing dissension. Even where the strategic hamlets were somewhat better protected by the proximity of Civil Guard, Self-Defense Corps, or regular Army units, the peasants appeared to have scant knowledge of what the propaganda handed out to them was all about. If anything, they retained their skepticism about the traditionally remote central government, particuarly since the cadres in their midst were usually strangers, brought in from Saigon or from other parts of the country. As one Vietnamese with a keen understanding of the peasant problem said to me (and the same is as true in 1965 as it was in 1962), "To the peasants, the government is not what it says it is. Words are not enough. It's the people who represent the government in the peasants' daily life who count—the soldier, the village or district chief, the tax collector. They are the image of the government, as they always have been, and unfortunately most of them continue to put the government in a bad light. Because official pay is so low, corruption is customary and is accepted. Each man, all the way to the province chief, owes his job and influence to someone else, and favors and kickbacks are paid all the way along the line."

If Diem and Nhu were aware of this, they did little to attack the problem at the point where it should have been attacked first—at the level of personal favoritism and corruption. It was also true that there were simply not enough good trained administrators to deal with the complicated mechanism of the strategic hamlet scheme. Since 1962, the strategic hamlet idea has undergone many alterations. In only a few places has it been applied with any degree of success. One such area was the region around Saigon, where secure communities were built up gradually and zones of security extended in accordance with more realistic appraisals of how much territory could actually be defended. Recently, however, as the Vietcong has taken over larger and larger chunks of South Vietnam even these hamlets around Saigon have been lost.

The Communists have their own plan for creating what they call "combatant villages." In many respects, it is a far more forceful program than the government's, and it demonstrates the great difficulties in the battle to win over the peasants. A captured Vietcong document that I read gave a graphic account of how a village in Kien Phong Province, west of Saigon, was successfully turned into a combatant village in 1961. Starting in 1959, high-level Vietcong cadres began the task of re-establishing the party's position in the village, which had "deteriorated" in the previous years of relative peace. The village, which has a population of six thousand, was more or less under government control—both Army and Civil Guard units were stationed nearby—so at first the Communists had to work under conditions of extreme secrecy, hiding in the swamps and fields by day and entering the village only at night. From the outset, they kept stressing one vital point—that the land the peasants had come to control during the long war against the French, when the landlords were absent, had now been unfairly reclaimed by the landlords, who were using government soldiers to collect back rents. Such land rightfully belongs to the peasants, the Vietcong said, and its cadres cleverly concentrated on undermining the influence of the village elders and the government administrators. According to the document, they pointed out to the peasants that if these elements retained control of the village, the task of the "cruel landlords" would be made easier.

These arguments made headway, and the population soon started to turn against the government, disbanded the old village council, and no longer paid any attention to the government's spokesmen.

The Vietcong then established their own security force in the place; they got the population to take part in self-defense activities, including the laying down of nail-studded boards to hamper the advance of government troops and the building of eleven bamboo barricades at the entrances to the village. A school and a first-aid clinic were built by the party. Homemade weapons, including guns and grenades, were fashioned, and when six hundred government soldiers attacked the village, in the fall of 1961, they were defeated and withdrew. "The experiences at this village clearly show that if one fails to base propaganda on the practical interests of the people, one cannot expect the people to stand up and face the struggle," the document declared. It emphasized the fact that constant self-criticism by cadre members had much to do with the success of the Vietcong's program and that a revolutionary spirit had to be maintained because "once the people are satisfied about getting land, the movement tends to degenerate. . . . We must therefore increase our spirit of dedication, and be determined to carry out party policy, always serving the people's needs. We need to develop better methods. We must rid ourselves of any strong desire for peace, eliminate our fear of the enemy. We must avoid becoming too optimistic. We must eliminate bureaucratic attitudes. We must remain always vigilant."

The ability of the Communists to create and sustain such villages depended, of course, on their ability to maintain complete, or at least sufficient, control of an area. Throughout the delta, the Vietcong was able to move around almost at will, slithering eel-like from zone to zone. It used as its bases the all but impenetrable mangrove swamps, a number of large isolated sections of forest, and the wild and desolate sections along or near the China Sea. Many of the swamps were close to cities and villages. At Mytho, for example, a city of fifty thousand in Dinh Tuong Province, an hour's drive south of Saigon, the Vietcong brazenly ran up their flag, a yellow star on a red background, atop a palm tree across a narrow canal from the American military headquarters, and regularly poured in rifle fire.

G

There was no evidence that the Vietcong were suffering from a lack of supplies or weapons; in fact, even at this time a variety of automatic guns of Chinese, Russian, or Czechoslovak manufacture were already being used by the Communist forces. Men and material were both flowing in regularly from the north. The material, mostly rifles and ammunition, was being distributed through secret staging and supply areas. At least one such major Vietcong base, surrounded by barbed wire and complete with an auditorium full of pictures of Ho Chi Minh and other Communist leaders, lay in a swamp area thirty miles east of Mytho. The government attacked this base once in 1962 and dispersed the Communists, but they were back in a month. Keeping after the Vietcong—even trying to find them—was like trying to identify tears in a bucket of water.

In 1962, I watched two operations that had varying degrees of success and that were typical of the way the war in the south was then being waged. The first was a combined operation involving the use of both American Army and Marine helicopters to lift elements of the Vietnamese 7th Division from field headquarters in Dinh Tuong Province to areas in the adjacent province of Kien Hoa, where about a hundred Vietcong were reportedly located. The idea of the division commander, Colonel Huynh Van Cao, was to have the two task units conduct a wide sweep to surround the Vietcong and then, when the enemy was flushed, to drop a third blocking force, thereby driving the Communists toward a large canal being guarded by another river force. Colonel Cao was one of President Diem's pet division commanders—he had been chiefly instrumental in saving Diem during the 1960 coup, when he had rushed his troops north to Saigon. When I saw him, he still had a direct telephone line to Diem's office. Cao's senior American adviser was Lieutenant Colonel Frank B. Clay, the son of General Lucius D. Clay. Clay and Cao seemed to have established a good working military relationship—Clay, in fact, had managed to persuade Cao to create a joint chiefs of staff board with the Americans. On this occasion, however, as before, he had been unable to get Cao to cut down the unrealistically large size of the area to be covered by the big sweep and to operate in a narrower sphere. As a result, the Vietcong elements managed to get away before the troops on the ground could reach them. They dispersed through the villages or immersed themselves in the canals, using bamboo tubes to breathe through. An air strike later killed a few, but the forty helicopters could have been employed far more wisely, Clay and the helicopter pilots agreed, if they had been used to hedgehop troops from one place to another in rapid pursuit of the enemy. When this was pointed out to Colonel Cao, he seemed to agree, though not strongly enough to change his tactics once the operation had begun.

Early the following morning, I flew on another operation to lift and drop some troops in Phong Dinh Province, just to the north of Soctrang, the Marine helicopter base. The objective this time was more limited—to trap a Vietcong battalion between some small canals near two villages—but the results were only slightly more effective. Most of the Vietcong battalion fled before we arrived, but six of the enemy were killed, some ammunition and propaganda documents were seized, and the government forces rounded up more than a hundred Vietcong "suspects." An increasing number of such suspects were being taken into custody in the delta for "rehabilitation."

If they were believed to have been aiding the Vietcong in any way, they were imprisoned. Squatting and roped together in a field, they ranged from boys of fifteen to old men of sixty. As I looked them over, I wondered about the dangers of such large-scale roundups in the campaign to win over the confidence of the villagers. "Political prisoners" of this sort were often shackled together in small cells for months. Under American supervision, seven million new laminated identification cards were being issued to all Vietnamese over eighteen to replace the old flimsy sheets of paper that went back to when the French were still in charge. These cards, bearing special provincial identification marks and other matter that could not be faked, including each owner's fingerprints, were expected to eliminate some of the risk of imprisoning innocent people.

American Army advisers were also being assigned at this time to each of the country's province chiefs—mostly Vietnamese Army officers who held operational control over the Civil Guard and Self-Defense Corps in their areas. Within Colonel Cao's division area, Major Dean Hagen, an enterprising adviser from Lawton, Oklahoma, and Major Nguyen Nhoc Thang, the chief of Ba Xuyen Province, were having some success with Civil Guard units against local Vietcong forces. Major Thang, an unusually burly Vietnamese, was one of the relatively rare officials I met at this time who seemed aware of the need to fight the war against the Communists on broad social and economic fronts as well as on a military one. He was hopeful that the people in his area were beginning to support the government, citing his experience of a few days earlier. He had gone to a village where the Vietcong had been active, and upon learning that the Communists had cut the road in hopes of ambushing him on the way back to his headquarters in Soctrang, the villagers had voluntarily offered him a boat to go home via the canals. Major Thang was also working closely with another American element, a Special Forces team that had just set itself up near a Vietcong-infested mangrove swamp south of Soctrang. The team, at the time one of nine like it in South Vietnam, was training the first of four hundred Vietnamese especially selected by Major Thang as a kind of private force. Each volunteer had had at least one member of his family killed by the Vietcong—and the group, to be equipped with guns by the Americans, was to operate secretly in the area.

Among other forces operating in the delta were a dozen Catholic priests—who, with informal American assistance, were creating their own small home-guard units to protect their villages—and a strengthened river patrol under the Vietnamese Navy that was convoying troops and supplies up and down the main canals. All in all, there seemed to be a chance for the government to make life miserable for the Vietcong throughout the rainy season, from May to November. In a talk I had one afternoon with Colonel Clay at his Mytho headquarters, he had an anticipatory gleam in his eye as we watched the clouds gather for the usual afternoon shower. "Mobility remains the key to improvement, of course," Clay said, "and with better maps and any kind of visibility the helicopters will still be able to operate part of the time during the rainy months down here. They can land on small patches of ground and they can drop troops into rice paddies where the water isn't too deep. We've got some new plastic boats that are unsinkable, and some armored personnel carriers on tracks that can get around in this terrain. I can visualize all sorts of delightful operations, like a mobile water force supported and resupplied by helicopters, sweeping through the swamps. I'm going home in a month, but I almost wish I were starting my year of duty in Vietnam now." If Clay had come back a year later, he would have been highly disappointed. Few of the operations he was hopeful about ever materialized, and the military situation in the delta continued to deteriorate as the Vietcong stepped up their offensives and the government seemed unable to maintain any momentum of its own.

Central Vietnam—the Plateau and the Coastal Zones

In the area a hundred and fifty miles north of Saigon, stretching from the Cambodian and Laotian borders eastward to the sea, the war against the Vietcong is comparable to the guerrilla struggles that were waged in the mountains of Yugoslavia and Greece during and after the Second World War. "To seize and control the highlands is to solve the whole problem of South Vietnam," General Giap once said, and most American and Vietnamese military experts agree with him. In 1961-62, the Communists were infiltrating troops from Laos along a series of jungle trails into the Truong Son chain of mountains that runs down Central Vietnam. These troops filtered off in all directions, into other mountainous areas near the coast, into dense growths of forest land, and south along the Vietnamese-Cambodian border toward the delta. Some of these well-armed hard-core fighters remained in the central region, most of which is mountainous jungle and the rest of which is flat red dirt farmland bounded by scrub. After increasing their ranks by drafting members of mountain tribes as well as Vietnamese in the lowlands, the Vietcong had started an offensive on the central plateau. Even then, in the summer of 1962, it was apparent that the Communists' aim was to interdict the government routes of communication in the highlands, to establish for themselves an interlocking series of bases, liaison stations, training centers, workshops, supply and ammunition depots, and rest camps, and to get ready for an effort to cut South Vietnam in two, from the western borders to the coast.

The key factor in sustaining the government was the assistance rendered by the Americans in planning counteroffensives, with air support, and in mapping psychological warfare campaigns among the backward tribes and lowlanders caught in the Vietcong vise. However, the Vietcong's capacity for constant replenishment and resupply of forces across the Lao border emphasized the difficulties the government faced in maintaining a counteroffensive. Seven Vietcong battalions were reported to be in the border zone, and there were mysterious radar indications of mountain airdrops, possibly from Russian or Chinese transport planes, which were known to be operating in and out of the nearby Laotian airport of Tchepone, held by the Communist Pathet Lao. For the government, the most encouraging sign was the continued improvement of the American-trained Civil Guard and Self-Defense Corps, and the Vietcong's concern was being demonstrated by attempted ambushes of both. What was already shaping up on the plateau was, in effect, a battle for survival. Here, as elsewhere, the Vietcong had to live off the country, the richest parts of which are the coastal provinces. The government's aim was to put enough pressure on the Communists to drive them back into the hills, where they would have trouble foraging for food and obtaining re-enforcements.

An ambitious corollary effort was being pressed to rally more of the tribesmen to the government's side. In the area around Kontum, one of the most critical in the highlands, Major Dam Van Quy, a regimental commander in the 22nd Division, who had received Special Forces training in the United States, had successfully used guerrilla tactics, including night patrols and counterambushes, to keep the Vietcong on the run. Quy's troops had managed to establish safe zones of four or five miles on both sides of Route 14, one of the main arterial highways, and into these zones his men had moved several thousand *montagnards,* or mountain people, of the Sedang tribe. Coaxed out of the hills, the Sedang families had been relocated in fifty new villages, and the tribesmen had been issued six hundred old American and French rifles, which they were being taught to use so they could help protect their villages. Vietnamese teams were also teaching them the rudiments of sanitation and dispensing some medical aid. With Major Quy, I visited one of the villages, where some four hundred tribesmen had been resettled. They had come down with their livestock and personal belongings, burning their old homes so the Vietcong couldn't use them, and had built new long houses in the valley. A peaked-roof "happy house" for bachelors stood in the center of the village, and a church and school were being planned. Surrounding the village was a spiked bamboo fence, and beyond, in the new fields the Sedang had been given to cultivate, tribesmen with rifles were guarding the workers. The men within the village, clad in loincloths and carrying spears, seemed impassive but content in their new surroundings. They kept grinning at us and offering us rice wine, a fermented homemade beverage that the *montagnards* drink like water and that tastes awful.

The Sedang experiment in Major Quy's area was one of several being made among the *montagnards* of the high plateau in a general effort to remove them from Communist domination and prevent the Vietcong from using them as a source of food and intelligence and, in some cases, as conscripts. The Communists began wooing the tribes during the war against the French, and after the partition of Vietnam in 1954 they stepped up their activities. They promised the *montagnards* autonomy and exploited the fact that the Saigon government settled thousands of refugees from the north in areas the French had reserved for the mountain folk. There are more than half a million tribesmen on the low and high plateaus of South Vietnam, and they are divided into some two dozen tribal nations, each of which has its own language and a variety of dialects. Ethnically, these highlanders are considered by anthropologists to be the most confusing mixture of races and cultures in the world. The peninsula of Indochina was originally inhabited by Australian aborigines and Negroid Papuans of Melanesia. Then came an influx from China and Tibet into Indonesia and Malaya, and this was followed by a reversal of migrations that brought a predominantly Indonesian strain back north. A Mongolian element moved in, and after the Cham-Khmer wars, the defeated Chams sought the highlands as a place of refuge and mixed with the tribes. The bewildering assortment of racial, linguistic, and cultural groups that developed, ranging from tribes that don't even use fire to others that are fairly sophisticated, has never been fully catalogued. Some of the more primitive strains are still antagonistic to all outsiders. Some are patriarchal, and some are matriarchal. Intertribal association has been essentially friendly, and although the pigmentation of their dark skins varies from one group to the next, it is difficult for foreigners to tell the tribesmen apart. Their ornaments are different, but as one observer wrote, "They are all clothed in evangelical poverty, by a ray of sunlight, a rag, and a knife or an axe." Except for a handful whom the missionaries have won over to Catholicism or Protestantism, they are all animists who worship spirits of the soil, the forest, the streams, and the mountains around them. They propitiate these spirits on the basis of dreams and superstitions that deal with such matters as the movements and sounds of small deer and birds, the color of fish, and even the quality and timing of a man's sneeze. Their lives are dominated by their sorcerers, and their tradition of law, handed down by custom and often surprisingly modern in dealing with such matters as adultery and stealing, is exercised by magic rites, at which pigs, chickens, and water buffaloes are sacrificed in elaborate blood ceremonies. The tribes tend to make demands of each other for the slightest affront, but they are also lazy and love feasts, and will put aside their passion for justice and revenge in favor of a good drunken party; their gorging and heavy drinking has contributed notably to their high rate of mortality. They live by hunting and fishing and by raising small crops of rice and corn, and when they exhaust one forest area, they simply move on to another. Most of them have made occasional sorties into the lowlands, where they offer ironwork, pottery, bamboo, and other forest products in return for salt, jars, gongs, and cloth, but their relationship with the Vietnamese has always been marked by the traditional mistrust lowlanders and highlanders have for each other. The French periodically sought to explore the mountain country and colonize the tribes, but the efforts of a few enlightened Frenchmen to teach improved methods of agriculture and offer some education seldom went beyond an elementary paternalism that found little support in Paris and was invalidated in many cases by the land grabs of rubber planters. The *montagnards* were too slothful to want to work on the plantations or on the roads the French put in, so, for the most part, they simply retired farther back into the hills and continued their isolated way of life. In 1962, the most successful attempt by Americans and Vietnamese to win over the highlanders was being conducted among the hundred thousand members of the Rhade tribe, who are the third largest group, after the Koho and Jarai, and most of whom live in Darlac Province, south of Pleiku. Four miles northeast of the city of Banmethuout, a Special Forces team of twelve Army men and two civilians was teaching the Rhade, who are considered the élite of the mountain tribes but whose political sympathies had been some-what in doubt, how to fire weapons, watch trails, conduct counter-ambushes, and adapt themselves to their new lowland villages. Sixty such villages had been created in 1962, and a roving protective force of four hundred Rhade soldiers was patrolling the general area. The Communists had tried to infiltrate them with secret Rhade agents, but they had usually been spotted and captured. The most encouraging aspect of the American Vietnamese program was the increasing num-ber of Rhade appearing voluntarily at the Special Forces camp, often with their families, asking to be taken in. The Vietnamese govern-ment, originally loath to start the Rhade program because of past tribal antipathy, seemed to be all for it now, and the Ameri-cans were going out of their way to impress upon the Rhade that it was the Vietnamese who were responsible for authorizing the use of guns and who were supplying medical and other facilities.

In the intensified effort to wean the various tribes away from the influence of the Vietcong, one American was conducting an unusual private campaign of friendship and aid in a mixed village of Jarai and Sedang just outside of Pleiku, south of Kontum. He was an Air Force liaison captain named Ray Hibbs, from Gurdon, Arkansas, and he admitted that his sympathy for backward Ozark mountaineers at home might have had something to do with inspiring him. Two or three times a week, Hibbs went out to the tribal village laden with medicines he had scrounged through Air Force friends in Saigon, Manila, and even the United States, and he distributed them to the villagers, who were suffering, as most of the tribespeople were, from all sorts of maladies and diseases. Hibbs had been in the Air Force sixteen years and had always been interested in medicine, and there was nothing that he wouldn't try curing. He had managed to obtain vials of penicillin, which he kept in an icebox in his room at the American Army Headquarters in Pleiku, and he had injected scores of villagers for respiratory and other ailments. He had also got hold of some antibiotics for the treatment of intestinal worms and other stomach disorders common among the tribesmen, and he had ointments for their many skin diseases. He had used pliers to pull teeth, which wasn't easy, since the tribesmen liked to file their teeth down to narrow points that were hard to grasp. Part of his regular routine was to bring pots and pans to the villagers and to teach them how to keep clean so their wounds wouldn't fester. "It's taken awhile for me to gain their confidence," Hibbs said, "but now they come running out and asking for more medicine. They're a lot healthier than they were a couple of months ago."

This early effort of the Americans and the Vietnamese to win the support of the tribes was among the most hopeful developments in Vietnam in 1962, but unhappily, as so often occurred, the original impetus was not maintained. The Americans were never able to persuade the Vietnamese to foster really good relations with the tribal people and thus finally eliminate the tribes' distrust of the government. So long as the Americans stayed on the scene, working with the Vietnamese in the tribal camps, things seemed to go all right; but as soon as the Americans left to start a new camp somewhere else, the old animosities between the *montagnards* and the Vietnamese re-arose, and the camps fell apart. The *montagnards* would struggle back to their old homes, or the Vietcong would wean them back. Bit by bit, the *montagnard* program collapsed, and within a year of my 1962 visit there were only half as many tribesmen who could safely be counted on the government side—no more than two hundred thousand, if that, out of a total of some seven hundred thousand. The situation grew gradually worse until, in 1964, a tribal rebellion took place, led by Rhade elements. Thousands of *montagnards,* reacting against what they claimed was discrimination by the Vietnamese, took to the hills, where the Vietcong, which may have been instrumental in encouraging the revolt, put them back to work growing food and, in effect, serving as supply and transportation units. The Communists made the most out of the government's failure to keep its promises to the tribesmen and reiterated their own earlier pledges to establish autonomous tribal areas after the Vietcong won the war. In sum, the collapse of the *montagnard* program, so promising at the outset, must stand as one of the major setbacks in Vietnam. It seemed doubtful in 1965 that it could be recovered, though some efforts were being made.

Another significant government failure in this period was called Operation Sunrise. This was the first comprehensive plan for pacification of the central region. The operation took place in the province of Binh Duong, thirty miles north of Saigon. Binh Duong was chosen because the Vietcong had strong concentrations to the west and controlled a large forest area known as Zone D to the east. In the first phase of Operation Sunrise, the government forces moved in close to the forest and, with the help of propaganda leaflets, tried to persuade the farmers to leave voluntarily and to come live in the first of several new strategic villages near the town of Bencat. A letter dropped to the peasants from the air included the following plea from Brigadier General Van Thanh Cao, who was in charge of the strategic community program in a belt of ten provinces stretching through the center of the country:

No matter where you are, on the edge of the jungle, along a river or in some far away and isolated place, I hope that my heartfelt words will reach you and bring you hope and belief in a brighter future. Because you have lived a traditional way of life, you have attached yourself to the land to make a living. Your ancestral home, the old roads and lanes, all this is familiar to you. It is not easy for you to leave. You know you are in an area under the domination of the Communist bandits and must resign yourselves to their violent acts. One day they threaten you, another day they collect money and rice. At night they force you to beat drums, dig ditches and roads, destroy bridges. From time to time they force you to work for them as porters, carrying their supplies, serving as targets to receive bullets in their stead during ambushes or in attacks on military posts. Now the time has come to distinguish clearly between black and white. President Ngo Dinh Diem understands profoundly your sufferings. He has ordered me to find means to bring you back to places where you can have a prosperous and secure life. . . . Think hard about yourselves, your villages, your families. . . . Let us be courageous in looking for a new future. . . .

In spite of General Cao's words, and the promise of new schools, new hospitals, and agricultural assistance—including new land as well as fifteen hundred piastres (twenty-one dollars) in cash for each relocated family to build a new house and have a little money left over—Operation Sunrise started badly when many of the first eight hundred and sixty-six persons were forced to leave their old homes, which the government burned, and to forsake their old farmland at the start of the planting season. Their new village of Bentuong had not been properly prepared, and looked like a refugee camp. The fact that only a seventh of the group included men of military age was proof that others either hadn't wanted to leave their homes or were afraid of Communist reprisals if they did. The civic action program, for which the Americans accepted both moral and financial responsibility, was slow in getting started. For the first few weeks little enthusiasm was engendered for the whole operation, after which it began to pick up some support. A few more towns were created and a growing number of young men began emerging from the forest, but it could not be said that Operation Sunrise had succeeded in motivating the people of the area to adopt the new life prescribed for them by the government.

Partly on the basis of the lessons learned from Operation Sunrise, the government shortly thereafter launched another broad plan to create strategic communities in the province of Phu Yen, on the coast of the China Sea. Phu Yen and the provinces that border it to the north and south were prime objects of the Communists in their grand plan to sweep across from Laos and Cambodia and establish bases on the coast. The combined Vietnamese and American plan was called Operation Sea Swallow, and it had as its ultimate objective the creation of two hundred and seventy-four strategic villages in the province, making at least a third of it totally secure. Sea Swallow got off to a good start. In the first phase, government troops blocked off the properous rice and fishing areas near the town of Tuyhoa, on the coast. A triple row of bamboo and cactus fences was erected along a ten-mile stretch, and within this zone the first few villages were made secure and their inhabitants were indoctrinated by civic action teams. In the second phase of the operation, the security plan was to be extended farther inland into the prosperous river valley toward the base of the low mountains; in the third phase, the Vietcong were to be pursued into the hills. The Americans, who helped plan the operation militarily and who supported it financially, tried to obtain permission from the government in Saigon to make agreements directly with the province chief of Phu Yen, so that immediate needs for help could be met in the villages. The Diem government fought against this for many months, and finally, with considerable reluctance, granted limited approval, still insisting on its right to countersign any agreements. This dispute over freedom for the Americans to operate in Phu Yen slowed down the operation, and it was not long before the Vietcong struck back; in fact, Sea Swallow never did get much beyond its first phase. What looked like a successful venture turned sour within a matter of months. Today, in 1965, the Vietcong control practically all of Phu Yen province, the government being confined to a few towns, such as Tuyhoa. In the summer of 1965, I rode over the area in a small plane, flying low so that I could observe what had happened. Many of the strategic hamlets built in the coastal valley during the first phase of Sea Swallow lay in ruins, having been burned out by the Communists, and the whole area was desolate and deserted.

The Mountainous Jungles of the North

Below the Seventeenth Parallel, in upper South Vietnam, a deadly game of blindman's buff was being played in a precipitous jungle that combines the worst features of Korea's backbreaking ridges and Panama's thick rain forest. Jungle warfare experts agree that there is no more difficult terrain in the world than this, and that to survive here, let alone fight, is a full-time job. The Vietcong, as a roving guerrilla army inured to hardship, had adapted itself better than the government to this kind of war, but with American aid, particularly helicopters for mobility and bombers for attack, the Vietnamese troops of Major General Tran Van Don's I Corps were moving into the Communists' mountain redoubts and applying pressure against them while guarding against further infiltration from the north. This was primarily an interdicting operation, but one that was vital in bottling up the Vietcong and keeping the enemy from using its hidden bases and supply centers as springboards for attack into the coastal zones and for the establishment of "liberation areas" there.

Seventy-eight outposts of the Vietnamese armed forces were spotted among the peaks that rise to eight thousand feet and are interspersed with rushing streams. One of these isolated posts, called Bengiang, was built on an almost perpendicular slope only twenty miles from the Lao border. It could be reached by Route 14, which up here was a narrow dirt road along a twisting river. In the dry season, it could be traveled in convoy, but not very safely even then. The jungle on either side was so thick that a man crouched by the roadside could drop a grenade into a passing car without being seen simply by sticking out his hand. Bengiang was far more satisfactorily approached by helicopter, which is the way I went there in the summer of 1962 with a party of American advisers headed by Brigadier General Howard K. Eggleston, who commanded the Army section of the Millitary Assistance Advisory Group, and their Vietnamese counterparts. The outpost was the regimental headquarters of the 4th Regiment of the Vietnamese 2nd Army Division. The men who were occupying it—and, with the help of some Civil Guard detachments, patrolling the nearby area—were stationed there for two years. They were living primarily on fish and rice, but every now and then they got some live chickens, ducks, and pigs dropped by parachute in baskets from helicopters.

As we climbed up the mud steps of Bengiang toward the ridgeline on top, we had the uncomfortable feeling that the Vietcong must be watching us. Though we were assured that mines and traps had been laid on the ridges around us, it was, I think, the consensus of the Americans, who didn't say so out loud, that Bengiang, built a year before they got there, was a miniature Dienbienphu that could be devastated by mortar and enfiladed machine-gun fire from all sides. Less than a battalion of a Vietnamese regiment was on duty in the shallow bunkers and trenches. The rest of the regiment, along with Civil Guard units, was distributed over an area of two or three square miles, patrolling by day and establishing counterambush positions by night. The night before our arrival, elements of one of four Vietcong companies in the area, half of them composed of *montagnards* of the aggressive Katu tribe, had attacked one of the advance Army posts with explosive charges at three o'clock in the morning. Only five men were manning the post at the time—others were out on ambush duty —and one of them was killed before regimental headquarters could be reached by telephone and a mortar barrage could be called down to force the Communists to withdraw. This, I was told, was a typical action in the mountains. The Vietcong, we learned, were building machine-gun emplacements and trenches all through the area for their rainy season offensive. In answer to General Eggleston's sharp questions, the regimental briefing officers suggested they could best be helped by improved air reconnaissance, which would facilitate quicker air support when the Vietcong attacked. A large white metal arrow mounted on a swinging wooden stanchion, with small cans of sand fastened on it containing gasoline flares for use at night, stood ready to show the pilots where the enemy was headed. More grenades and more barbed wire were also requested by the Vietnamese and by the regimental American adviser, Major Richard Shaw, of Lawton, Oklahoma, who was spending half his time at Bengiang. "After I'm out here for two weeks," he said, "headquarters back at Danang looks like New York City."

Danang, which the French called Tourane, at this time was a sleepy, run-down port that served as headquarters for the Second Corps and for the 93rd Army Helicopter Company. Every week, the helicopter pilots flew more than a hundred missions, most of them carrying troops or supplies to the mountain outposts and bringing out casualties; the planes were frequently shot at by the Vietcong. The Communists were slowly building up their strength in the mountains, and General Don, with the help of the helicopters and other planes provided by the Americans, was trying to anticipate the enemy's moves. In the rich coastal province of Quang Ngai, where the Vietcong were trying to carve out their first "liberated zone," Don had effectively blocked the guerrillas by pressing against them in two high areas in the north and south along the coast and simultaneously infiltrating behind them along a center ridgeline farther inland. His long-range plan was to squeeze the Vietcong forces and make them break through into the lowlands, where he hoped to meet them in the open and outnumber them.

Despite government pressure, the Vietcong were still strong throughout the mountain regions. They dominated the tribal peoples and frightened or coerced thousands of them farther back into the hills. American missionaries of the Worldwide Evangelical Crusade, which had been active in the area, told me that many of their tribal preachers had been murdered, some of them buried alive. "I know a hillside where there are a hundred graves of tribesmen who were against the Communists," Gordon Smith, the head of the Crusade in the area, said. "Unfortunately, the Vietcong are stronger than the government in the hills, so the tribal people follow them. The government hasn't come down to the people's level, and the people still believe what the Communists tell them, in spite of the terror. In the high mountains, the tribesmen are destitute. We've lost contact with them. They've fled their villages and run off, and they're hiding under trees and living off bits of rice and an occasional trapped animal. The Vietnamese don't know how to handle them. They have no anthropology to guide them."

Near Danang, the American Special Forces and some Vietnamese cadres were doing their best to skip anthropology and leap all the way up to the present. They were teaching groups of volunteer Sedang and Katu tribesmen how to shoot guns, lay explosive chains of fire for ambush, and use walkie-talkie radios, so they could go back and defend their villages. The camp, at Hoacam, was probably the biggest melting pot in Vietnam. In addition to the Sedang and the Katu, a company of Nung tribesmen were there, half of them to provide security and the other half to be retrained. The Nungs, who fought for the French and the Chinese Nationalists, were said to be as good soldiers as the famed Indian Gurkhas. While the various tribes were put through their paces, Vietnamese Rangers were getting advance unit training, and recruits of the Republican Youth were being given a basic five-week paramilitary course under the government's civic action program for the strategic villages.

Off the coast of Danang, northward beyond the old city of Hué to the Seventeenth Parallel and from there eastward out to sea, the Vietnamese Navy of some three dozen small patrol vessels and amphibious craft and ships, aided by units of the United States Seventh Fleet, were watching the waters for Vietcong junks heading south with agents and supplies. The patrol was concentrated in the north, but it also was doing what it could to check the fifteen hundred remaining miles of South Vietnamese coastline, along which the Communists were landing reinforcements and supplies at isolated spots from oceangoing junks. The junks would start out to sea from North Vietnam, beyond the picket lines at the Parallel, and skirt the island of Hainan before heading south. This sort of sea-borne infiltration, like that on land, could be cut down, but was impossible to stop completely.

By 1965, the whole picture in the north had changed. Many, if not most, of the mountain outposts had been abandoned, and the Communists controlled practically all of Quang Ngai Province and huge portions of the other provinces to the north and west of Danang. Danang had become a huge American-Vietnamese base, and most of the fifteen thousand American Marines sent into the country were guarding it and the new airbase being built to the south at Chulai. Though the Marines had initially been brought in solely to serve in this defensive role, thus releasing Vietnamese Army troops for offensive actions, it was not long before they were being sent out on patrols outside of Danang, where they suffered their baptism of fire. Danang, in effect, had become a powerful enclave supported and protected by the Americans. Hundreds of planes flew into and out of the airfield on attacking missions in North Vietnam, as well as in South Vietnam. Some sixty miles off the coast, where a few American destroyers had previously patrolled to help spot the Vietcong junks moving south, aircraft carriers of the Seventh Fleet now provided planes for what had become almost daily massive attacks against the north. I visited one of these carriers, the *Ranger,* and was deeply impressed by the modern efficiency of this floating factory of war. All day scores of planes, of seven or eight different types, were catapulted off the deck and brought back, and there was no doubt that the powerful bombs they carried were doing great damage in North

Vietnam, destroying bridges and highways and wrecking vital installations such as radar stations. A correspondent who had only recently come out to Vietnam remarked, "They just ought to show this ship to the Vietcong—that would make them give up." It was a typical American remark, said not out of pride, but simply out of awe. Mostly, through no fault of the young man who said it, since he had just arrived, it was said out of ignorance.

When I saw Danang itself again, it was hard to believe that this was the same place I had visited in 1962. The whole atmosphere had changed. Where the Special Forces camp had once been engaged in one of the last efforts to weld some of the tribal elements into a broadly based force to fight the war among the people of the back country, there was now a camp full of nineteen- and twenty-year-old Marines. They had little or no understanding of the kind of war they had suddenly been thrust into, and were scarcely qualified, either in military counter-guerrilla terms or in their political indoctrination, to take part in it. Their Vietnamese counterparts, the government troops under the leadership of the aggressive Brigadier General Nguyen Chanh Thi, were conducting operations and maintaining a tenuous control of some areas, but the Vietcong were moving into more valleys and more villages, and growing more daring. The main topic of conversation in Danang, among the Vietnamese and the Americans alike, concerned the likelihood of a major Communist attack against the big base. The consensus was that the only thing holding it off was American air power and the Marine guards.

After my 1962 trip, which had ended up in Danang, I wrote the following final paragraph in an article for *The New Yorker*: "The Vietnamese and the Americans agree that, on all fronts, the coming year will be a crucial one that will go a long way toward determining the outcome of this war. American military aid has perhaps bought enough time for the government to rally itself from what appears to have been near defeat last fall. But socially and psychologically, the outcome is still in doubt. The government must still prove itself, at the level of the people who live on the land. It has begun to do so in some areas, but it has not yet won over the bulk of the population. To deprive the Vietcong of bases is one thing, but to fill the void in the minds of the people is something else. In the long run, the Communists believe that time and space are in their favor. No matter what happens, the government cannot *patrol* a whole nation. Its ability to *control* it by winning the support of the citizenry will depend on whether or not it can come of age politically, as well as socially and economically."

What was soon to happen in Vietnam, as everyone now knows, was to prove, beyond any reasonable doubt, that the Vietnamese government of Ngo Dinh Diem did not have the capacity either to win the support of its people or to confront its political challenges.

CHAPTER VI

❦

The Untold Story of the 1963 Coup

The grim events that occurred within a month of each other in South Vietnam and the United States in the fall of 1963—the brutal murders of the leaders of both nations—underlined the strange historical association that had developed between the two countries during the previous decade and demonstrated that, in their capacity for violence, Americans were not so different from Vietnamese, whose lives had been dominated by violence for many years. The news of the terrible assassination of President Kennedy was received in Saigon in a profoundly personal way; one newspaper typically said, "We would like to bury the late President with all the flowers of Vietnam and all the tears we can shed." The slaying of President Diem and his brother Nhu, though—deplored by most Americans as a cruel and unnecessary climax to an otherwise carefully executed *coup d'état*—did not especially upset most Vietnamese, whose resentment against the two brothers, particularly against the mystical and tyrannical Nhu, had become deep. A sense of relief over their removal was expressed everywhere, and the tension and repressive atmosphere that had tangibly been building up in the months before the coup on November 1st and 2nd gave way to an almost anticlimactic mood of relaxation.

The improbable circumstances of the coup—including its complex planning and the considerably more than tacit approval given to it by the United States—can now be related, in its entirety, for the first time. The story is a classic one of a regime plunging headlong to disaster against a background of plots within plots, of duplicity and counter-duplicity. All of this must, in the first instance, be related to the seemingly paranoid condition of Nhu, and to the machinations of his ambitious wife. Together they worked on Diem's vanity and suspicion of others, and were increasingly able to dominate him and, through him, the entire government in the final year of its existence. During this period, according to Vietnamese friends of mine who were in a position to know, Nhu's fundamental contempt for all people, Vietnamese as well as American, led him to dwell increasingly in a megalomaniac world of his own. He reveled in playing off individuals and groups against each other and allowed himself to deny all reality as he moved inexorably toward the tragedy that pulled everyone around him into the abyss. "We knew that Nhu was smoking opium in the last year and maybe taking heroin, too, and that this helped create his moods of extremism," Nguyen Dinh Thuan, who had been Secretary of State, told me. "You could begin to see madness in his face, a sort of somnambulistic stare, always with that cold smile. I was reminded of the Latin proverb *'Quos deus vult perdere dementat* —Whom God wishes to destroy he makes mad.' It was as if a devil had taken possession of him. The atmosphere was like the last days of Hitler. Nhu believed only what he wanted to believe and fitted all facts to his concepts. If we tried to tell him what the situation actually was—that a certain Army division wasn't where he thought it was, or that if American aid were cut off we could not continue financing the war without serious inflation—he simply told us we were fools and defeatists."

What made the situation worse was that Nhu had gathered round him a group of sycophants who kept feeding his swelling pride. In earlier days, he had had some efficient young brain trusters who had acquired valuable political experience in other countries, but after the abortive coup of 1960 he had replaced them with men like Colonel Le Quang Tung, the head of Vietnamese Special Forces, who was also murdered in the 1963 coup. Tung, a former servant in the Ngo family in Central Vietnam, was a noncom with the French expeditionary troops during the Indochina war. After the war he received an appointment from the Ngos as a lieutenant in the intelligence section, in which job he squeezed money out of wealthy businessmen, especially Chinese, for the Can Lao Party. Late in 1960, Tung received a nonstop promotion from lieutenant to colonel and was put in charge of the newly created Special Forces, which was in effect a private army for Nhu and Diem and was responsible for, among other things, the final crackdown on the Buddhists in August, 1963, which helped precipitate the coup. "People like Tung encouraged Nhu's bitterness and charlatan conceit," another Vietnamese close to the scene said, "and Nhu's supposed perspicacity and reputation for long-range thinking, which was always exaggerated anyway and was essentially composed of copying bits and pieces from others, vanished altogether. As signs of his mental illness seemed to increase, he kept more and more isolated and, when he saw anyone, gave vent to outbursts of anger or bravado. One day, he said to me quite seriously, 'The Americans should take George Washington's statue down and put up mine. I saved Vietnam for them.' "

As Nhu withdrew further into himself, he refused even to see Cabinet Ministers any longer, because they presented arguments contrary to his thinking and tried to get him to shift his course. When several despairing Ministers finally tried to resign, they were persuaded to stay in office by Nguyen Ngoc Tho, the Buddhist Vice-President. Tho was doing his best to act as a moderating influence; then he himself found the situation increasingly intolerable and wanted to quit in his turn, but the coup plotters, knowing that action was imminent, urged him to remain so as not to arouse suspicion. As the Buddhist crisis mounted, Nhu's chief ally in encouraging him to bring it to a head was his wife, who had developed her own power obsession, and with increasing hysteria threw herself into political matters and collected her own handful of female sycophants.

"At first, Nhu simply let his wife go her own way," Secretary of State Thuan said afterward, "but then he began taking more of her advice, and in time he began vying with her to see who could be more extremist. The two of them, and Archbishop Ngo Dinh Thuc, who was running things in Central Vietnam, worked close together, and at length Diem listened only to them. Those of us who knew the situation from inside were always aware of the utter futility of the Americans' efforts to separate Diem from Nhu. Diem would never have removed Nhu. His own personal weakness on top of his natural mandarin bent led him to go along with the Nhus and with Thuc in their crazy destructive schemes. Whenever some of us tried to show him the gravity of the Buddhist situation, and momentarily felt that perhaps we had begun to bring him around, Nhu would brainwash him all over again."

The Buddhist Revolt Erupts

The Buddhist rebellion of 1963 was undoubtedly as much politically as religiously motivated. It must properly be considered against the background of the long Vietnamese social crisis that began when the Diem regime was established in 1954 and nearly a million northern Catholic refugees streamed across the Seventeenth Parallel to become the most ardent supporters of Diem's government. Since they were destitute, they chose, only naturally, to stay together, and, led by their priests, they started new villages, often bearing the names of old ones they had forsaken in North Vietnam. In short order, they ceased being squatters and became a "new class." Because Diem could rely on them, and because their priests had ready access to the Presidential palace, Catholics came to dominate a significant proportion of the country, especially in Central Vietnam. Many of the district and province chiefs as well as many village leaders were Catholics, as were many of the important military leaders. Catholic villages, through the influence of this burgeoning hierarchy, benefited most from relief and aid programs. They got the most land grants to build schools and hospitals with the help of assigned soldiers, were given priority for loans under the government's agricultural credit system, received official permission to cut and sell lumber from carefully protected national reserves, and obtained export and import monopolies, including exclusive rights to deal in such new and profitable products as kapok and kenaf.

While various members of the Ngo family in one way or another were reaping their own financial rewards as a result of their manipulations with Catholic henchmen, it cannot be said that—until the end—the ruling family was engaging in conscious religious persecution of the Buddhists. Buddhists constitute about eleven million of the country's fifteen million persons, but only some four million of them are practicing followers of the Buddha, the rest being primarily ancestor-worshiping peasants. However, favoritism toward the Catholics, which the palace in Saigon not only condoned but encouraged, led to increasing discriminatory and repressive social measures against the Buddhists on the part of the priests and officials in the countryside, who were the real leaders of the nation's million and a half Catholics. (Discrimination against the remaining portion of the population, the animist hill-bound tribes, took a different form, as has already been noted.) As the military situation grew more serious in 1960, so did the position of the Buddhists. For example, in the building of strategic hamlets, the Catholic population was often exempted from the necessary physical labor as a result of the intervention of the priests, and outside soldiers or specially assigned work brigades did the work instead. In other land development schemes, Catholics were given the best and safest areas near the coast to cultivate, while Buddhists were sent farther inland, where land was not only inferior but life was also a lot more dangerous under the shadow of the Vietcong. Moved perhaps as much by the instinct of self-preservation as by pure opportunism, hundreds of non-religious people—in some cases, whole villages at a time—sought conversion to Catholicism, a process not all priests encouraged, even though the ones who didn't sometimes found themselves in trouble. A number of local officials were given government funds for distribution to zealous priests, enabling them to conduct propaganda campaigns to counter mounting criticism of the government, and in some cases Catholic villagers were given weapons and told to protect themselves and their families against a possible Buddhist revolt. Sometime around mid-1962, as the Saigon regime grew more and more frightened, the campaign against the Buddhists did take on the aspect of persecution, religious as well as social and political. And where there had been only a smoldering discontent and a growing malaise, by the spring of 1963 a burning anger against the authoritarian actions and attitudes of the government had begun to roll across the countryside.

The Buddhist rebellion erupted in early May at Hué, the old capital on the northern coast and a traditional center of Buddhist learning. Nine worshipers were shot and killed in consequence of an argument over the right of Buddhists to fly their flags, hold mass meetings, and make radio broadcasts during the commemoration of the 2,507th anniversary of the Buddha's birth. The celebration overlapped with a Catholic one commemorating the twenty-fifth anniversary of Archbishop Thuc's consecration as bishop—Thuc's see was also in Hué. When Thich Tri Quang, the Buddhist leader of Central Vietnam, refused to send Thuc a congratulatory telegram, the government gave orders for strict enforcement of a two-year-old ban against flying religious flags, despite the fact that during Thuc's celebration the Vatican flag was displayed along with the national flag and Thuc's pictures were all over Hué. The Buddhists defiantly began to show their flags and banners three days before the Buddha's birthday, on May 8th, while the Catholic flags and pictures were still up. When the provincial administration backed down on its order against the Buddhist display, further agreeing to allow Buddhist altars and lanterns, as well as flags, to remain on the streets, the Buddhists were emboldened, and they determined to go through with plans they had made for a mass meeting on May 8th against religious persecution. That morning, at Thuc's behest, Buddhist crowds, gathered at the Hué radio station, were ordered to disperse, but fire hoses, blank shells, and tear gas failed to move them. Major Dang Sy, the Catholic deputy province chief, then ordered his troops to use live ammunition and grenades, and the killings took place. The government claimed that the murders were caused by Communist plastic grenades, but all neutral observers agreed that Major Sy's men were responsible.

Five weeks later, following negotiations, Diem and the Buddhist leaders issued a joint communiqué that gave in to some Buddhist demands, including their right to display flags regularly, but the government still refused to admit guilt over the Hué incident. Privately, Nhu issued orders to the cadres of his Republican Youth organization to "protest" to the government over its having signed the communiqué. By this time, the first of seven Buddhists who eventually committed sacrificial suicide had been soaked in gasoline by his adherents and had set fire to himself at a Saigon street crossing. World opinion, shocked by the man's death, became increasingly critical of the government's handling of the Buddhist matter. American efforts to persuade Diem to settle the problem peacefully simply served to arouse Nhu and his wife to make wilder claims that the Buddhists were nothing but publicity seekers dominated by Communists. The Nhus also maintained that the Americans were just trying to blackmail them with the threat of curtailing aid. If the Buddhists, for their part, were by now obviously determined to press the issue in every possible way, including staging dramatic suicides and holding additional protest meetings throughout the country, the Nhus were equally determined to suppress them with force and protect the regime at any cost. By early August—goaded by Mme. Nhu, who had called Diem a "coward" for having made concessions to the Buddhists and had castigated Nhu, too—Nhu was talking vaguely to a number of generals about the possibilities of a coup that would be directed against the "weakness of the government" and would be anti-American as well as anti-Buddhist.

Nhu was not making idle threats. "If a government is not capable of enforcing the law, it should fall," he told one high-ranking American official, who had maintained regular contact with him. The Buddhists had been handled far too gingerly, he added, and now enjoyed more privileges than other religious groups did, as a result of which there had been "serious repercussions" in the ranks of the Army, the Republican Youth, and Mme. Nhu's Women's Solidarity Group. Nhu, who liked to use quotations, cited Oscar Wilde's remark that "dying for a cause does not make it just," applying it to the Buddhist bonzes who had burned themselves—"barbecues," Mme. Nhu had called the suicides. As Nhu rambled on, he became increasingly vehement, and finally he declared that he was "fed up" with his brother's way of handling the Buddhist problem and that he was ready to take over himself as the head of a new government that could deal with the matter in a better fashion. He made it clear that family ties would no longer stand in his way if he felt that he had to "save" Vietnam, not only from an internal rebellion but also from "foreign domination," by which he implied American rather than Communist domination.

His chief responsibility, he added, was to his Republican Youth organization, whose members were "shedding blood." He indicated his belief that in the National Assembly elections scheduled for August —which would never be held—he could get enough of his Republican Youth candidates elected to "take over" the government by peaceful means, if possible, and then push through his strategic hamlet program. The more Nhu talked, the more his American listener became convinced that he was emotionally distraught but completely serious about what he was saying and that if he was unable to achieve his aims peacefully, he was quite ready to conduct a coup to oust his brother.

On August 21st, Nhu conducted what in effect was a "half coup" against the legal government, designed to keep Diem as a front but to place himself in full control. Following a declaration of nationwide martial law, Buddhist pagodas were raided all over Vietnam. In Saigon, Colonel Tung's white-uniformed Special Forces used teargas bombs and grenades in storming the Xa Loi and three other pagodas, arresting several hundred Buddhist priests in their saffron robes and hauling them away, screaming, in trucks; three took refuge in the American Embassy, where they were given asylum, and one of them, the chief strategist of the Buddhist rebellion, Thich Tri Quang, remained there. Similar violent raids took place in Hué, where a number of persons were reported killed or injured. It developed afterward that Nhu, in an attempt to implicate the Army generals in his anti-Buddhist action, had forced them to sign a predated memorandum implying that they had known about the raid (all but one or two of them had not known) and this accounted for the fact that the first reports of the raids sent abroad indicated that the Army had conducted them. Nhu had also fooled the top echelon of the American Embassy by pretending he was prepared to deal with the Buddhists, though a number of junior Embassy officials had warned of what was likely to happen. The day after the raids in Saigon, Henry Cabot Lodge arrived to take over as Ambassador, having been rushed out ahead of schedule on the personal order of President Kennedy.

If Nhu thought he had "taught the Buddhists and the Americans a lesson," as he bragged, his plan quickly boomeranged. Among other miscalculations, he had failed to anticipate the reaction of high-school and college students. Students in Vietnam, though politically conscious, traditionally had not played as active a role in politics as their counterparts had in China and other Asian nations; but this time they did. Unrest among the student bodies in Saigon and Hué quickly followed in the wake of the pagoda raids, and as high schools and colleges were closed, several thousand students were arrested for demonstrating; the arrests created a serious morale problem in the Army, since the brothers and sisters of many soldiers were jailed. A number of leading professional people and some military officers, whose loyalty Nhu doubted, were also imprisoned, and although most of the prisoners, including the majority of students, were released when martial law was lifted on September 16th, several hundred were held and, as they subsequently described in detail, were subjected to torture by electric shock and by having water poured into their noses and down their throats.

As the terror mounted, the United States, under Ambassador Lodge's tough leadership, moved belatedly toward a showdown with the Diem regime. After the pagoda raids, Washington suspended the twelve-million-dollar monthly allotment it was giving Vietnam in the form of imported foods and manufactured products, which the government sold to help balance its budget and pay for the war. At this, Nhu stubbornly refused to allow his Ministers to dip into Vietnam's own reserve funds, insisting that funds could be obtained "somewhere else" by raising new crops or levying new taxes, both of which had previously been tried unsuccessfully and neither of which could be done overnight, anyway. At bottom, Nhu probably still thought he could bluff Washington, but when he finally saw he couldn't, he publicly accused America of having caused the "process of disintegration in Vietnam." Individual Americans in Saigon were now threatened, and the atmosphere was no longer merely tense but positively dangerous.

Another important factor at this point was Nhu's flirtation with the Communist government of Ho Chi Minh. Sometime in September, Nhu conferred with the French delegate general in Hanoi, who visited Saigon with a Polish member of the International Control

Commission. These talks followed General de Gaulle's statement implying that peace between north and south was possible and that a neutral Vietnam would receive France's help. At first, Nhu probably thought he could use the threat of negotiations as another means of bringing the Americans back into line, but as the situation deteriorated further, he really began to believe that he might make a deal. Vietnamese friends later told me of a prophetic remark made in 1959 by a French priest who knew Nhu very well: "Nhu is perfectly capable of making an arrangement with the Communists, and he will do so when he sees himself cornered. He is a man totally committed to the policy *'Après moi, le déluge.'* " As the weird events that unfolded were afterward put together, it seems likely that Nhu largely sealed his doom by carrying on the Hanoi talks, because they helped harden his opposition and created a solid front among the officers who conducted the coup.

The Machinery of the Coup

The plot for a coup began as far back as mid-1962. The chief original plotter was Dr. Tran Kim Tuyen, the tiny physician who had turned to politics and who had worked for several years as director of Social and Political Studies. On two occasions—after the abortive coup attempt in November, 1960, and after the second abortive effort in February, 1962, when the Presidential palace had been bombed—Dr. Tuyen had written to Diem to protest Mme. Nhu's increasing meddling in politics. When Nhu was shown the first letter, he ignored it, but he took offense at the second, and thereafter Dr. Tuyen was out of favor. However, he kept his job until mid-1963, mainly because Nhu thought he could use the doctor to keep tabs on plotters against the regime. There are those who later insisted that Dr. Tuyen was all along an *agent provocateur,* lending himself to Nhu's purposes and going so far as to lure Cabinet members into corrupt financial transactions so Nhu would have something on them. This may have been part of Dr. Tuyen's ploy, but he was playing a far deeper double game and was seriously plotting against the regime. The fact that in September Dr. Tuyen was in effect "exiled" to Cairo as Consul

General, a minor post, seemed to prove that Nhu himself had grown scared of him and wanted him out of the way.

By the time he left, Dr. Tuyen had laid his plot quite thoroughly. His principal instruments were Colonel Do Mau, chief of military security; a number of senior Army colonels occupying key military positions around the country; the commanding officers of several marine and paratroop battalions stationed near Saigon; and some contingents of the 5th Division that were operating north of the capital. Dr. Tuyen also had his men distributed in Nhu's Special Forces and in elements of Nhu's palace guard, and he had the support of some Cao Dai and Hoa Hao elements, of some important civilian leaders, and of some government officials. But what was even more significant was that Dr. Tuyen had access to an elaborate undercover network stretching far into Army combat units in the field, which he had originally established as a sort of pro-Nhu anti-subversive corps. As these various elements were welded together,ᐟ Dr. Tuyen had some trouble maintaining liaison among them, particularly as some of the military contingents wanted to turn dissidents, but he managed to restrain them. His first projected date for a coup was July 15, 1963, but he found himself unable to rally sufficient support among the top generals, who, because of his past record of working primarily for Nhu, didn't particularly trust Dr. Tuyen.

After Dr. Tuyen left the country—Nhu carefully kept the doctor's family in Saigon as hostages—the essential elements of his plot were inherited by his accomplice Do Mau. Do Mau was now able to enlist General Tran Thien Khiem, the executive officer of the Joint Chiefs of Staff, who had the most direct control over troops in the field, and these two men continued to plan the coup in detail. Their principal instruments were the contingents initially lined up by Dr. Tuyen, plus an independent group of young officers, mostly Signal Corps, plus some Transportation Corps and Air Force men, making common cause with some students' and workers' groups, which, under the name of the Military and Civilian Front for the Revolution in Vietnam, had begun plotting on their own early in August. Their leader was a cousin of Do Mau's, so it wasn't difficult to establish liaison at the crucial moment. The fact was that young officers throughout the military were becoming increasingly disillusioned with the regime, and this feeling was strengthened when they saw that people everywhere were still willing to flock to the pagodas, even in the face of gun muzzles.

The reluctance of the top-ranking generals in the Army to attach themselves to the plot that had been formulated by Dr. Tuyen and Do Mau was not due entirely to their suspicion of the doctor. Almost from the start of the Buddhist crisis, the generals had begun to mount their own plot against the regime, and the Americans had soon become aware of it. The principal organizer among the general officers was General Tran Van Don, the former commander of the First Corps in the north. He had become acting chief of the Joint Chiefs of Staff but did not have as much control over field forces as his executive, General Khiem, who had not yet been brought into the Tuyen-Do Mau scheme and was initially suspected by the other generals of being too pro-Diem. Two others were with General Don—General Duong Van Minh, deprived of his field command by Diem and now occupying an innocuous palace role as a military adviser, and General Le Van Kim, the former commandant of the National Military Academy, who had been out of favor with Diem for a long time and had no job at all. In view of the fact that the three generals had been effectively put on the shelf by Diem, they lacked the direct contact with combat troops and regimental and division commanders that Dr. Tuyen and Do Mau had established, but they did succeed in obtaining promises of co-operation from the commanders of the two corps north of Saigon, General Do Cao Tri in the First Corps and General Nguyen Khanh in the Second Corps. The Don group wanted to stage a coup as early as July 8th but decided to hold off because it had not mustered sufficient strength. On July 11th, having got wind of what was going on, Nhu summoned most of the country's general officers to the palace and issued a veiled warning to them. While this served to confuse and divide them, the plotting continued on a more subdued level. The generals by now had become aware that Nhu might be plotting his own coup, or phony coup, which would place him above Diem in actual power, and for that reason they had to be doubly careful. After Nhu made his move with the attack on the pagodas on August 21st (and especially as Nhu tried to involve the generals in the attack) Don and his group almost decided to move at once, despite the fact that they were not yet prepared and did not have enough strength to take over the palace. They again held back, fearing that a blood bath would result if they failed and that Nhu would emerge on top. They were also worried because, through another leak in security, Nhu had again learned what they were up to and because they felt that too many Americans knew what was going on. These worries were borne out when, on September 1st, the *Times of Vietnam,* the English-language paper that was the Nhus' mouthpiece, printed a long "exposé" headlined "C.I.A. FINANCING PLANNED COUP D'ETAT."

Officially, the attitude of the United States was still to work with Diem and try to get him to accept the major political and military reforms that had been urged upon him for so long. Washington's hope of achieving some measure of success when it withdrew part of its financial support to the Saigon regime after the pagoda raids had not been rewarded, and a new period of jockeying had begun. In the growing confrontation between the regime and the Americans, Nhu and his wife chastised the Americans with increasing bluntness, and when Mme. Nhu went on a world tour and made a number of speeches in Europe and the United States, the conflict was fully publicized in the world press. With few exceptions, the reaction was against the Diem-Nhu regime, which was now widely held to be a dictatorship engaged in an inexcusable form of religious oppression, and the Americans were criticized for condoning it as much as they had and for not doing more to restrain it.

A considerable amount of confusion and difference of opinion had by now arisen among American officials in Washington who were dealing with the subject of Vietnam, and the political aspects of the problem had become inextricably intertwined with the military. Defense Secretary Robert McNamara and Admiral Harry Felt, the Pacific Fleet commander, had made repeated visits to Vietnam and had consistently come away convinced that the war was going well and could be won, and that consequently any change in government would be detrimental. The fact of the matter was, as any correspondent in Vietnam knew, the war was going badly and the process of disintegration in Saigon was having a distinct effect on the morale of troops in the field. A small improvement in the administrative relationship between the Americans and the Vietnamese, as a result of which the rural civic action program, for example, was making headway, was not enough to alter the basically deteriorating situation caused by the increasing number of Vietcong attacks—frequently entrapments— which were grabbing more of the countryside from the government. A number of American officials—among them Roger Hilsman, the Assistant Secretary of State for Far Eastern Affairs, who had also made two visits to Vietnam—were far less optimistic than McNamara and the top-ranking American generals on the scene. Hilsman urged a much stronger stand to force Diem to make changes. His estimate of the situation was that there was "a forty-per-cent chance that Diem would change and get rid of Nhu, preferably by getting him out of the country; a forty-per-cent chance that Diem would do nothing about Nhu and that the generals plotting against him would take action; and a twenty-per-cent chance that nothing would happen, that things would just go along as they had, in which event we would lose Vietnam in a year."

The conflicting reports and estimates reaching the White House did little to help President Kennedy reach a judgment. On one occasion, when he received in person the reports of a Pentagon general and a State Department officer who had both returned from Saigon, the President smilingly asked, "Did you two guys visit the same place?" By early October, however, the President had reached the point where he publicly declared that "a change of policy and perhaps personnel" was required in the Saigon government. By this time, actually, things had moved a lot further, and the machinery for the coup, with the knowledge and approval of a handful of Americans on the scene, was being well prepared.

The Plotters Strike

On October 2nd, an American representative who had been informed of the plotting going on, and who knew most of the plotters personally, met with General Don at the seaport of Nhatrang. General

H

Don brought him up to date on the progress of the planned coup. The principal problem the generals had was the same as before—to rally enough support behind them before they struck, and to restrain the other coup group of plotters, the Tuyen-Do Mau faction, from striking too soon. The most difficult task General Don still faced had to do with enlisting the support of, or neutralizing, the commanders of the other two corps in the country. These were General Ton That Dinh, who was military governor of Saigon as well as commander of the Third Corps, and General Huynh Van Cao, who commanded the Fourth Corps, south of Saigon. Both these generals had maintained their loyalty to Diem and Nhu, and it had been no accident that they had been given control of the troops surrounding Saigon. Cao, it will be recalled, had saved Diem during the 1960 coup. During the August pagoda raids, though he had used only Special Forces troops, Nhu had given over-all charge of the anti-Buddhist operation to General Dinh, an unconscionable braggart and a man of consummate ambition. A few days after the anti-Buddhist raids, Dinh had begun boasting privately and publicly that it was primarily he who had saved the country from the Buddhists and the Communists and from "foreign adventurers"—meaning Ambassador Lodge and certain elements of the C.I.A. As Don now explained it to his American friend, he and his co-plotters had decided to play upon Dinh's vanity and to utilize him for their own ends.

At first, Don had egged Dinh on to ask Diem and Nhu to make him Minister of Interior. The reaction was just what Don and the other generals had expected; Diem and Nhu had become furious, and had told Dinh he was too big for his breeches and should stop meddling in politics. Dinh then had accepted Nhu's suggestion that he take a brief leave, thinking he would be considered too valuable to be let go. While Dinh was resting in Dalat, Don had consoled him and had continued to play on his vanity, promising to suggest to Diem and Nhu that the interests of the country would best be served if Dinh *were* given the Interior job and Don himself be made Secretary of Defense. As Don outlined the story to his American friend at the Nhatrang meeting, he had actually made such a suggestion to Diem and Nhu, but in such a way that it had been impossible for them to consider it seriously. As Dinh had continued to fume, Don and his partners felt they had won him over to their side, though they still didn't trust him. When Dinh returned to Saigon to resume his old job, the plotters had him carefully watched twenty-four hours a day. "We had sufficiently compromised him so we could eliminate him, if necessary," Don said, "but because of his command position he was the key to our plot and we needed him." Though Dinh still seemed to be wavering, which in fact he was, he agreed to dispatch his deputy, Colonel Nguyen Huu Co, who was fully in on the plot, to set in motion an elaborate subplot to neutralize General Cao, in the Fourth Corps to the south.

In the fortnight that followed, General Don's American friend, with the knowledge of American officials in Washington and Saigon, kept in close touch with the plotters. A few days after his Nhatrang talk with Don, he met General Minh in Saigon. Minh, it appeared, was to be the official leader of the coup, though Don was doing the essential planning. He disclosed that there were three possible approaches being considered, which were not mutually exclusive: key military units were to go into insurgency and encircle Saigon; direct military action was to be taken against units·loyal to the government in the capital itself; and Nhu and another Ngo brother, Ngo Dinh Can, who ruled in Hué and had been involved in the Buddhist crisis there with his brother Thuc, were to be assassinated, while Diem would be sent abroad (Archbishop Thuc, as well as Mme. Nhu, were already abroad).

Minh stressed the fact that his group must move fast because the other group of plotters—the military leader of which had become Colonel Pham Ngoc Thao, the inspector in charge of the strategic hamlet program—was preparing to strike, and if they failed it would be catastrophic. What Minh chiefly wanted to know was whether the Americans would go along with the coup, at least to the extent of not thwarting it, and would the United States continue to give aid to Vietnam if a new government took over? On October 10th, the American go-between informed Minh that the United States would not stand in the way of a coup if it took place, and that if it was successful and if a new regime could improve military morale and effectiveness, could obtain popular support, and could deal on a practical basis with the American government, it would receive aid. Between October 10th and 26th, further meetings took place between the American representative and the plotters. Generals Don and Minh had made one effort to talk to Ambassador Lodge directly—at a reception in Saigon —but they had refrained when they saw government security agents watching them. Besides, Lodge was in an extremely difficult position since he was still friendly with Diem and officially accredited to the Diem government, and though he knew what was going on, he did not wish to be directly involved in the proposed coup in any way. The plotters, however, had satisfied themselves that they could count on the Americans' support, and, according to Don, General Harkins, the chief of the American military advisory group, had told him personally the United States would not intervene to stop a coup. The troops to take part in it were primed, Don told his American contact; they included elements of the 5th, 7th, 9th, 21st, and 23rd Divisions, as well as Air Force, armored, paratroop, Marine, and Navy contingents. The date, Don added, would be sometime between October 26th and November 2nd.

But a serious hitch had developed, and the whole plot now became bizarre. In the plan to neutralize General Cao in the Fourth Corps, Colonel Co, the man designated to do the job, had succeeded in bringing the various corps unit commanders into the coup scheme, but he had overplayed his hand, and an officer who was loyal to Diem had reported Co's activities to the palace. General Dinh, Co's boss, was called in to see Diem and Nhu. After saying that he was at fault for not detecting Co's disloyalty, Dinh suggested that Co be shot. Nhu refused, saying he wanted to use Co to find out more about the plot. More important, Nhu wanted to use the vacillating Dinh in a remarkable counterplot of his own. According to Nhu's scheme, a few days after October 26th, Vietnam's national holiday, General Dinh, along with Colonel Tung and his Special Forces and loyal elements of the palace guard, was to conduct the first stage of a weird pseudo-coup to which Nhu gave the name Bravo 1. To fool the Americans as well as the plotting generals, Colonel Tung would send some of his units out of Saigon on alleged combat duty. Meanwhile other loyal troops and tank units would secretly take up positions around the city. Then, suddenly, supposedly anti-Diem police units and goon squads would stage a fake revolt in Saigon. Diem and Nhu, at the first sign of action, were to go to Cap St. Jacques, a resort southeast of Saigon, where they had a command post with full communications prepared. It would look, they thought, as if they had fled a bona fide uprising. The phony revolutionary government in Saigon would proclaim a fuzzy new program, and some well-known political prisoners would be let out of jail. Other hired gangster squads would then go into action, and there would be a blood bath, during which, it was planned, some Americans as well as some Vietnamese would be killed. Within forty-eight hours, to "restore order," Generals Dinh and Cao, using the troops they had stationed around Saigon, would attack the city and take over. This second stage of the coup, to be called Bravo 2, would culminate in Diem and Nhu returning from Cap St. Jacques as vindicated heroes.

It was all very craftily laid out. However, the original group of plotters organized by Dr. Tuyen and Do Mau, and now being directed by Colonel Thao, learned of the first stage of Nhu's fantastic scheme. This group had already made plans to carry out *its* coup on October 24th, but General Don, with the assistance of General Khiem, and also with the help of the American who had all along been aware of the plotting, persuaded Colonel Thao to hold off, convincing him that, among other things, he lacked sufficient transportation facilities. Nhu, in turn, had got wind of this postponement, and thereupon decided to advance *his* schedule, skipping the first stage of his counter-coup, Bravo 1, and going right into Bravo 2, the second stage, in which, after signs of an uprising, General Dinh's troops would seize control of the city. General Dinh, caught up in all this duplicity and counter-duplicity, had his own doubts about whether Nhu's plan would work. Most observers, however, as they went over the whole plot and subplot afterward, are inclined to believe that at this stage Dinh was inclined to be more loyal to Nhu than to the coup generals with whom he had made a tenuous contract.

The role of General Khiem, who was in charge of over-all troop dispositions, now became vital. Up to now, Khiem had been cautious, which was why Generals Don and Minh had not altogether trusted him. The moment he was given full proof of what Nhu was up to, however, he agreed that the plotters had to act quickly, and he was spurred on by the proof that was submitted to him of Nhu's behind-the-scenes talks with the French and Polish representatives from Hanoi. Another important factor was the fact that Khiem had been working with both coup groups—the generals' group and the Tuyen-Do Mau-Thao group. At this juncture, Generals Khiem and Don and Colonels Do Mau and Thao worked out details of the planned attack, and for the first time the two separate but complementary groups of plotters were together. But now came the climax—more Graustarkian than Shakespearean. Toward the last week of October, General Dinh, who had been told, at least in part, of what General Don and his partners were planning to do and had been promised an important role if he went along with them, apparently reported to Nhu what was about to happen. The coup was set for November 4th, and Nhu, scheming up to the end, suggested that Dinh get the date advanced to November 1st, thinking to throw the plotters off schedule, so that he could proceed with his Bravo 2 countermeasure. The plotters, still suspicious of Dinh and immediately making new plans of their own, agreed to the new date. Then, quietly alerting units whose participation Dinh did not know about, they outsmarted Dinh, boxing in his troops, which Nhu had counted on for carrying out his own plan.

On the evening of October 28th, by prearrangement, General Don and the American go-between met at a dentist's office in downtown Saigon. Don asked that all American military officers and political officials be admonished not to discuss any possible coup action with any Vietnamese, because there was a grave danger of further leaks, and he also suggested that Lodge stick to his planned schedule, which included a trip to Washington on October 31st. As for Dinh, Don said the generals had him under complete surveillance and there would be no problem about him. The next day, Dinh gave orders for Special Forces units to move out of the capital. Whether he did this in compliance with Nhu's orders for the phony coup or in behalf of the real coup is not clear, but it was probably the former. In the meantime, Colonel Do Mau, in his job as military security chief, issued false intelligence reports to Diem and Nhu, purporting to alert them to a Vietcong build-up outside of Saigon. This was designed to get units loyal to the government diverted while coup units could quietly be brought into the capital area.

The coup was to start at 1:30 P.M. on November 1st, in the middle of the siesta period, which Diem had just ordered cut down to one hour. At seven-thirty that morning, orders were sent to the coup elements to start moving into town. General Don and Colonel Do Mau called a meeting between eleven o'clock and noon at joint military headquarters on the outskirts of Saigon, near the airport, to be attended by all the top officers in the country. The only one who wasn't alerted to be there was General Dinh, who was told to remain at his own Third Corps headquarters, near the capital. Everyone else who was supposed to be at the meeting showed up in time except for the pro-Diem commander of the Vietnamese Navy, who was shot and killed by a trigger-happy escort while being brought in under guard. Four other pro-Diem officers were placed under immediate arrest. The American contact man, summoned by General Don, went to the meeting after alerting the Embassy that the coup was in progress; he was the only American present. General Minh brought out a tape recorder and read a prepared proclamation in which the plotters set forth their aims. Then he asked each officer who agreed to go along with the coup to announce himself and his support. Several copies of this tape were made and distributed to various local coup headquarters around the city, so that if the coup failed none of those present at the meeting would be able to say that he had not joined the conspiracy voluntarily. In this fashion, a number of reluctant officers joined up. Shortly after the coup got underway— fifteen minutes early, because elements of the 7th Division had jumped the gun—Colonel Tung, the Special Forces commander, was brought in under guard and was forced at gun point to order his troops around the headquarters area to lay down their arms. Once that was accomplished, thirty-five armored personnel carriers filled with coup troops headed for downtown Saigon and the palace.

From the moment the coup started, it was carried out with complete precision. Two marine battalions, two airborne battalions, and two battalions of the 5th Division under General Dinh, who had now finally opted for the coup because he no longer had any choice, were hurriedly brought into the city, along with the three dozen tanks, and they were all deployed at crucial points. In less than an hour, the central police headquarters, the post office, the radio station, the Ministry of the Interior, and the Ministry of National Defense were seized and placed under guard. The palace was surrounded and the Presidential guard barracks were placed under attack by tank and mortar. By three-thirty in the afternoon, heavy fighting was going on around the palace itself. From the beginning, Diem and Nhu had been completely fooled. When a member of Nhu's security police telephoned the palace to report these various military actions, Nhu assured him that they were part of a careful palace scheme. Only after Nhu learned that all the key points had been taken by the rebel task forces did he begin to suspect what had happened. He thereupon tried to telephone General Dinh to tell him to counterattack, and when Dinh could not be reached, it became clear to Nhu that he had been out-foxed. When the two brothers were asked over the telephone to surrender, they brazenly demanded that the generals come to the palace for "consultations"; this was reminiscent of the 1960 coup, when the plotters had been inveigled to hold talks just long enough to enable Diem and Nhu to regain the upper hand. This time, the rebels refused to dicker. When Diem telephoned Ambassador Lodge (who had canceled his trip to Washington at the last moment), Lodge expressed anxiety about Diem's safety and recommended that he and his brother surrender themselves. Diem and Nhu again rejected the idea, and also brushed aside a suggestion that they take refuge in the Embassy. The call ended with Lodge saying he would try to protect Diem and his family from personal harm.

At 4:45 P.M., one of the coup generals once more reached Nhu at the palace. Colonel Tung was put on the phone, and he told Nhu he had surrendered; shortly afterward, Tung was taken out and shot in the yard of the headquarters compound. Nhu was told that unless he and Diem resigned and surrendered, the palace would be bombed. At five-fifteen, General Minh called the palace again, and spoke to Diem, who hung up. With Nhu at his side, Diem frantically started telephoning all the divisional and provincial headquarters he could reach, asking for help, but none was forthcoming. One supposedly loyal division of General Cao's Fourth Corps had been commandeered by Colonel Co; and General Cao, who had believed to the very end that Nhu had arranged the coup, was being held prisoner. Final, frenzied calls by Nhu to his paramilitary units, including the Republican Youth Corps, were also futile. By dusk, leaflets prepared by the plotters were being dropped from transport planes, and bombers were circling the city. Truckloads of Vietnamese students, some of them just released from jail, were careening through the city, proclaiming the success of the revolution. However, the battle wasn't over. Some Presidential guards who had barricaded themselves in the zoo, near the palace, were firing mortars at the coup forces, and when Diem and Nhu refused two more demands to surrender, it was apparent that there would be a fight to take the palace and the palace grounds, where some tanks and some other Diemist guard units were still entrenched. Starting at nine o'clock in the evening, small-arms fire and artillery began to be poured into the palace, and demolition specialists were summoned. By midnight, about two dozen tanks under the command of Colonel Thao had gathered in the streets outside the palace, and a full-scale attack began at 3:30 A.M. on November 2nd.

Long before that, probably by eight o'clock the previous evening, Diem and Nhu had sneaked out of the palace through a tunnel and had gone in a British Land-Rover to a spot near the water front, from where they had taken a French Citroën to the many-roomed house of a rich Chinese friend in Cholon, the Chinese section of the city. Direct communication had long before been set up between this house and the palace for just such an emergency. During the attack on the palace early on the morning of the 2nd, the insurgents repeatedly telephoned a military aide of Diem's, who had remained in the palace, and put individual unit commanders on the phone to prove to him that the place was surrounded, that all key points in town had been secured, and that all "loyal" troops had joined the rebels. The aide relayed the information to Diem and Nhu in the Cholon house. At 6:50 A.M., on November 2nd, Diem telephoned General Don from his Cholon hideout and finally agreed to surrender. He didn't say where he was, but about the same time Colonel

Thao and his forces, having entered the palace, discovered that Diem and Nhu were not there. Thao found out from a captured officer where the brothers were, and after telephoning General Khiem, his immediate superior, he was told to go get them.

At seven in the morning, Colonel Thao arrived at the house in Cholon. After he had entered it, he picked up a telephone to call the palace and report his whereabouts to the rebel officers now in control there. Diem and Nhu, apparently listening over another extension in the house and recognizing a strange voice, managed to flee to a small Catholic church nearby, where they hid. Around nine, Diem got to a phone and called General Khiem, again agreeing to surrender. An armored personnel carrier was sent to get him and Nhu. The first man the brothers saw get out of the carrier was Colonel Duong Ngoc Lam, the head of the Civil Guard, who had joined the coup only after it had started and whom they trusted. However, behind the Colonel in another vehicle was General Mai Huu Xuan, one of the original plotters, who had been ordered to follow Colonel Lam. According to one subsequent report, it was Xuan who gave orders for the brothers to be killed. Another, more recent account indicates that the order came directly from General Minh. In any event, the brothers were murdered in the personnel carrier by a police major. He shot Diem in the head, then Nhu, who was then repeatedly stabbed by other escorting officers.

About 11 A. M., the bodies of Diem and Nhu, which had been brought to coup headquarters, were claimed and taken by a relative to a Catholic hospital, where a French doctor simply made a formal statement of death but did not conduct an autopsy. Some of the generals, especially Dinh, who were opposed to any murder and had been shocked by it, were trying to make it appear that the brothers had committed suicide, but no one believed these stories. The original death certificates described Diem not as the head of state but as "Chief of Province," one of the earliest jobs he had held in his career during the French colonial period, and described Nhu as "Chief of Library Service," one of *his* early posts. This was said to be a Vietnamese way of expressing contempt for the two oligarchic rulers. No one has ever found out for sure where they are buried, but the best guess is that several days after the coup the bodies were quietly placed in unmarked graves in the military headquarters compound.

One of the first to rush back to Saigon was Dr. Tran Kim Tuyen, who was and still is considered by many to have been the mastermind of the coup, and who surely laid the early groundwork for it. He returned within a few hours of Diem's and Nhu's demise, and it proved to be his biggest mistake. He and four of his top aides and some of the other men he had worked with were arrested a few days later. Dr. Tuyen is still in jail today, though his aides have been released, and he has not been summoned to trial. Whatever happens to him, it has become obvious that no matter who plans a coup or carries it out, there can be only one set of victors.

The coup, despite the weird events and circumstances that almost defeated it several times, succeeded in the end primarily because it was a genuine home-grown plot that expressed real grievances against a regime that had become totally corrupt and oppressive. The broad final plan, as conceived by General Don, had been carefully executed over several months, and particular care had been taken in establishing the loyalties of those who took part in it and in neutralizing or eliminating the officers who remained loyal to the old regime. The most brilliant part of the scheme had been General Don's maneuver to obtain the necessary support from the erratic General Dinh, and then to turn Dinh's double-dealing into an asset. The co-operation of important civilians, including some members of Diem's inner circle, proved another significant factor. In spite of the constant danger of security leaks, they were held to a minimum in the latter phases of the plot, when the plan was made known to only one American in Saigon, who relayed it to a few superiors, who in turn kept in touch with Washington. Although the Americans were not happy about the murder of Diem—they had less qualms about Nhu—the coup was executed with their full knowledge and with their consent. The approval given by Washington to go ahead, in the first place, and the carefully guarded role then played by Ambassador Lodge, acting through the American go-between, were crucial. For the record, when Lodge returned, he said, in a long interview with the *New York Times:* "The United States was not involved in the overthrow of the Diem regime. The United States was trying to change—bring about a change in the behavior of the Diem regime. . . . We were trying to bring about this by thoroughly legitimate political means. The overthrow—of the Diem regime—was a purely Vietnamese affair. We never participated in the planning. We never gave any advice. We had nothing whatever to do with it. I—there were opportunities to participate in the planning and to give advice, and we never did. We were punctilious in drawing that line." Under the circumstances, this was what Lodge had to say, but it must be remembered that President Kennedy had himself spoken of the possible need for "a change in personnel' and that the United States' withdrawal of financial support for the Diem regime had in itself certainly helped encourage the plotters of the coup. It may not be too much to suggest that—especially since Lodge was already somewhat concerned with Republican Party plans for the 1964 Presidential election, and it had become apparent that he worked directly for the President of the opposite party rather than for the State Department—Lodge felt compelled to issue his discreet statement. But in Saigon the reports of the Americans' advance knowledge of the coup were immediately spread, and Vietnamese subsequently substantiated these reports. To be "involved" in the coup did not require direct participation in its execution or the utilization of a large number of Americans; in this case, one man on the scene had been able to accomplish all that was necessary. And it may be assumed that what took place in Saigon between the time the coup was planned and mounted and the date of its successful conclusion would not have occurred without the prior approval of one man in Washington, President John F. Kennedy. It seems particularly ironic and tragic that Kennedy and the handful of Americans who knew that the coup was about to occur should have taken particular pains to secure the safety of Ngo Dinh Diem (he was supposed to have been flown out of the country) and that the precipitate murder of Diem by the extremist officers who conducted the coup should have preceded by less than three weeks the assassination of John F. Kennedy himself.

CHAPTER VII

❧

The Revolution Manqué

The most significant fact about the *coup d'état* of November 1 and 2, 1963, was that it was just that—a *coup d'état* and nothing more. It was certainly not a revolution. In Saigon, immediately afterward, there was, in fact, a notably unrevolutionary air—a mood of repair and convalescence that was perhaps inevitable after several years of increasingly brutal dictatorial methods. On the surface, the city was in the process of rejuvenation; the lid was off and fresh zest and hope were welling up. Unfortunately, the gay atmosphere proved to be more frenetic than real. The old, easygoing way of life in Saigon was finished, although some of its surface manifestations—the open-air flower market, the slender silken-clad women floating past the bright shops—lingered. It soon became apparent that fresh tensions were building up, and as the Vietcong took advantage of the period of transition to step up its offensives throughout the country, the city became filled with new rumors of conspiracies.

It would be wrong to say that the junta of twelve general officers headed by Duong Van Minh and calling itself the Military Revolutionary Council, which sat on top of the provisional government headed by Premier Nguyen Ngoc Tho, was totally inactive and inept. It quickly became apparent, however, that the junta lacked both a policy and a plan, and that the generals, particularly the five who formed a kind of inner council, had little or no knowledge of how to

213

run a government. Nevertheless, they insisted on trying to run it, and thereby set the stage for a two-year period of military domination that completely inhibited the development of civilian rule and unavoidably led to more coups and attempted coups. In this atmosphere of experimentation and random plotting, the United States did little to stabilize the situation, and once again it may be said that an opportunity in Vietnam was lost. Having helped stage a coup by, at the very least, encouraging it from the sidelines, we sat back and resumed our role of paternalistic and wealthy overseers, pouring more aid into the country, and eventually more troops, but we made no effort to guide the inexperienced and frustrated Vietnamese into political maturity. It may be said, as some still say, that we had no proper role of this kind to play, and that it would have been "interference," that Puritanical scare-word behind which the United States hides so much of its customary political inaction and which it then abandons in sudden moves—as in Santo Domingo in 1965—in favor of emergency military thrusts that are given a last-minute political explanation or motivation. After all our years of experience in Indochina, a disinclination to interfere hardly seems to have been an excuse for our failure in Vietnam after November, 1963, to provide the sort of discerning counsel backed up by persuasive and, if necessary, forceful measures to help the Vietnamese, politically fragmented as they were, establish a workable government. The fact is that many responsible Vietnamese leaders were asking that we do just this, and that we also make clear our own aims in Vietnam. Instead, we dealt repeatedly in tired shibboleths, in continued bland expressions of optimism; and in consequence our policy, if indeed we had one, was obscured in a welter of words that unfortunately soon became involved in a Presidential political campaign. The admission must be made that we had no more of a post-coup plan than the Vietnamese had.

The magnitude of the task facing the victorious leaders of the 1963 *coup d'état* was undeniable, and the fact that they confronted it with no understanding of the phenomenon of the national revolution made it all but insurmountable. Overnight, they had replaced what had started out in 1954 as an authoritarian but national regime and had then drifted into whimsical and absolute dictatorship, in which everything was done incestuously and capriciously. Despite what has subsequently been said (with the peculiar type of political nostalgia to which Americans are so addicted—that "at least Diem got things done") that regime obviously had outlived itself. It is true that for the first two or three years, despite the weight of his family and his sense of isolation, Diem had attempted to create a national revolution; but he very quickly lost his cause when he disassociated himself from the people of the country, who were willing to make sacrifices but who instinctively refused to accept the violation of human rights, the mounting oppression, and the corruption and greed. After the November coup, these same people were still waiting to be reached and stirred, but they were left in a void.

Almost at once, a mood of self-preservation on the part of the nation's new rulers set in. One of the first things the junta did was protect itself by shunting to unimportant posts a large number of junior and senior officers, as well as private individuals, who had been involved in one way or another in planning and helping carry out the coup. Dr. Tuyen, of course, received the harshest treatment; it was apparent that though charges of corruption were leveled against him, there could be no proof that he had done anything but plot an extremely delicate and dangerous course with the view to overthrowing the oligarchy—particularly Nhu—for whom he worked. There were others, mostly men who had belonged to or co-operated with the Tuyen-Do Mau-Thao group of plotters, who claimed, with justification, that they had prepared the way for the coup and taken the greatest risks, and whom the generals now wanted to eliminate for fear they would become the spearhead of a fresh opposition. The generals were undoubtedly motivated by their own lack of trust in one another. They were a group of men of varying backgrounds and degrees of ambition brought together, mainly by Don, in order to do a job that had to be done. But once the job was finished, they were totallly insecure in their individual and collective political orientation, and they lacked any sense of dynamic enterprise, let alone revolutionary fervor. It is here that the United States, with its experience as a onetime revolutionary nation and with its supposed administrative talents, could and should have played a much more active role than it did. It may be granted that this would not have been easy, for there were qualities of pride, patriotism, chauvinism, and even xenophobia and emerging "anti-whiteism" among many Vietnamese, but there were just as many who thought otherwise, and who all but begged us for help. Since we made it clear that the fight against Communism in Vietnam was "our fight," too, our obligation to become involved, to avert a further catastrophe, such as was threatened by the burgeoning new conflict between the Buddhists and the Catholics, should have been apparent and accepted.

Beyond getting rid of those coup elements they considered a potential opposition, the junta generals replaced, or more often switched, many officials of the old regime in the provincial administrations as well as in the central government. Not all these replacements were applauded locally—especially where individuals clearly associated with the former regime were simply moved from one province or district to another. The sad truth was that Vietnam was faced with a grave shortage of men who possessed proper qualifications and had completely clean pasts. This shifting around of officials was inevitably accompanied by a certain amount of "head-hunting" (some of the more notorious pro-Diem officials and Can Lao Party members were summarily dismissed from the Saigon and provincial administrations), but the results satisfied no one. Almost from the outset, the Buddhists argued that the new broom was not sweeping clean enough, and that the Can Lao and other oppressive elements remained influential. The Catholics, meanwhile, claimed that they were the ones now being discriminated against and that the new government was motivated by a policy of revenge. In this atmosphere, it was difficult, if not impossible, to create a functioning administrative machinery and to prosecute the war against the Vietcong effectively.

The Communists had always linked Diem with the Americans and demanded that he must go. Once the new government took over, the Hanoi regime and its South Vietnamese shadow, the National Liberation Front, immediately sought to smear it as having been stage-managed to power by the United States and being just as much an American puppet as its predecessor. It was difficult to judge the effect of this propaganda, just as it was difficult to gauge the full impact of the fall of Diem and Nhu in the countryside, where the government for so long, under French and earlier Vietnamese administrations as well as Diem's, had stood for little that was positive and in varying degrees had always been accepted by the peasants as a necessary evil. What largely enabled the Vietcong to continue making inroads in the villages was the local impact of oppression in the shape of the small-time officials who collected provincial taxes, forced peasants to buy lottery tickets, indulged in petty forms of graft and corruption, and so on. Most of these minor bureaucrats remained where they were. The junta never seemed to realize that the political and social programs of the war were as important as its military aspects, and that unless meaningful improvements were quickly introduced into the villages along with security measures, and people could be made to believe in the fight they were being asked to continue waging against their fellow Vietnamese, then the enemy could never be beaten or even contained, and some sort of accommodation with the Communists would become unavoidable.

It was in this sense, above all others, that neither the Vietnamese nor their American supporters seemed able to cope with the revolutionary challenge confronting them. As one knowledgeable Vietnamese friend of mine summed it up: "During the last year of the Diem regime, there was a small group of civilian and military leaders who were genuinely concerned about the destiny of the country and secretly worked hard on a plan to save it from the errors that had been compounded during the Diem period. When the coup took place and these people were shunted aside, the generals who took over seemed to consider their principal aim to be the preservation of unity in the armed forces. They were, in essence, 'twenty-fifth hour revolutionaries,' and this accounted not only for the policy of revenge that was instituted but also created the circumstances for a whole new climate of favoritism and corruption. Once again, personal loyalty took precedence over ethics. Nothing was done to apply the old time-proven Vietnamese motto: *'On Co Tri Tan*—Review the past in order to shape the future.' No declarations were issued that might have served to put the revolution into focus—the long struggle against colonialism that the Vietcong was seeking to subvert. There seemed to be no strategy and no tactics for implementing the very basic changes that were necessary after the years of repression under Diem. Some very fundamental reorganization of the government was required, but it never took place. The purpose and function of a number of agencies needed sharp redefinition in view of their long period of subversion by Nhu. But from the administrative standpoint the situation simply became more confusing than ever. Instead of streamlining the bureaucracy, the government added several agencies. Province chiefs had more Saigon bosses than they had had before and as little freedom to maneuver as they had under Diem and Nhu. A new code was required to restimulate political parties, and a redefinition of civil rights was needed. In the absence of a working constitution, some sort of body should have been created with adequate powers and means to check on the constitutionality of government actions in the period before a new constitution was adopted. Some instrumentality was needed to help explain the implementation of new national policies to the people. Not one substantial issue was forced. A period of drift simply set in. Furthermore, the economic condition of the country grew worse. Prices of rice and other essentials rose, and as the inflation mounted, it was no wonder that pressure groups took advantage of the growing discontent for their own purposes, and that the Vietcong was able to capitalize, militarily and psychologically, on the confusion and chaos."

Troubles Face the New Rulers

In the month immediately following the coup, government troops suffered their heaviest casualties of the year, especially in the delta area south of Saigon—in the provinces of Long An, Kien Hoa, Ding Tuong, and Vinh Binh—where the Vietcong moved swiftly to take over most of the countryside, confining the government forces to major towns and highways. Much of the blame for what happened belonged to the old regime, which had vastly exaggerated the progress made in the development of the strategic hamlet program and the general consolidation of the rural areas, and which had constantly concealed the seriousness of the military situation. In became obvious that the Diem government had overextended itself, spread its forces too thin, and that, coup or no coup, the Vietcong would have profited from its planned major offensive. But when it took place, the new junta was almost totally unable to cope with it, and as a result, the morale of the regular Army, as well as of the Civil Guard and Self-Defense Corps, sank lower and lower. Some top officers were hurriedly dispatched to key areas to stem the tide, but the process of disintegration had advanced so far that little could be done except to face up to reality and admit that most of the delta was now in Communist hands. For the first time, the upper-echelon Americans, notably, Secretary of Defense McNamara, who soon after Diem's overthrow made one of his periodic trips to Vietnam, ceased issuing over-optimistic statements about the war; they demanded more careful reporting from American officers in the provinces in place of summary government statistics of the sort that had for so long been taken at face value. The true picture had, in fact, been reported for many months by correspondents, on the basis of extended tours into the delta and other areas, but they had been accused of being "hypercritical." And the military advisers in the field they had quoted had been criticized at American military headquarters in Saigon for "indulging in pessimism."

Much of the trouble had stemmed from the fact that Diem and Nhu, as noted, had kept on building strategic hamlets in places where they could not feasibly be protected. Most of the province chiefs, afraid to challenge the regime in Saigon, had either built these hamlets according to orders, with the result that the Vietcong had quickly overrun them, or had not built them at all, merely issuing false construction claims in order to satisfy their Saigon bosses. In one of the delta provinces, an American adviser summed it up by saying, "There was a combination of lying and trying to go too far too fast. In many places, hamlet militia units were totally untrained and incapable of protecting their homes even if they had been motivated to do so. Peasants who had been relocated in new hamlets never received the relocation allowances due them from the government, and frequently had to pay for materials to construct their new homes when they were supposed to have been paid by the government, out of American aid funds." American advisers readily admitted the fault had been theirs, too. "We just didn't do enough checking up," one of them told me. "We were victimized by Diem and Nhu just as much as the Vietnamese were."

One of the few important decisions the new government did make, in consequence of the declining military situation, was to put a halt to the building of new strategic hamlets, to abandon those that could not be safeguarded, and to consolidate those that were considered salvable. Premier Nguyen Ngoc Tho admitted to me that when his government took over, only twenty per cent of the 8,600 strategic hamlets the old regime claimed to have built could in any sense be regarded as usable. "Nhu had tried to make the strategic hamlet program the basis of his whole anti-guerrilla policy," Tho said, "and he had received strong support from the Americans. He demanded that the province and district chiefs order villagers to build strategic hamlets by the dozen, without any compensation—in fact, the peasants were told to make financial contributions to the program. The natural result was to create a tremendous discontent in the rural areas, and when Diem and Nhu were overthrown, most of the people wanted to abandon the strategic hamlet program. But that would have been extremely dangerous, we felt, particularly as we had to reorganize the local and provincial administrations and get new officials to take over. Total chaos would have resulted if we had given up the strategic communities completely, and the Vietcong would have benefited even more than they did. So we decided to pull in our horns as carefully as we could, to see to it that the people would be paid what was owed them, and that they would henceforth be relieved from the pressure of corruption imposed by the former Diemist officials."

This was a rather negative approach, and it epitomized the quandary in which the new government found itself; namely, how to get rid of the influences of the former regime and at the same time maintain some kind of functioning operation in the midst of a war that was going much worse than anyone had imagined or admitted. On the one hand, the government was accused of being too revengeful and of concentrating too much on "bringing to justice" those who had been guilty of past sins, either of corruption or cruelty; there were, in fact, quite a number of indiscriminate arrests made at first, without charges being made, although most of these individuals were set free after a few days. Two of the generals on the new junta —Mai Huu Xuan, the new police chief, and Ton That Dinh, who was rewarded for having "joined" the coup by being given the Ministry of Interior—were reported to be competing with each other in arresting people and then releasing them in return for pledges of loyalty or cash payments. On the other hand, notwithstanding the fact that not everyone who worked for Diem was necessarily "pro-Diem," and that it was impossible to fire every provincial or district official, the government found itself under growing attack for allowing too many of the known members of the old guard, especially Can Lao Party men, to remain in office. Some of this criticism was justified. For example, the junta was extremely slow in dismissing or shifting a number of top officers who had played a known role in the anti-Buddhist campaign, and among these was General Do Cao Tri, commander of the First Corps. After weeks of jockeying, Tri was not released from active duty, as many thought he should have been, but was moved from the First Corps to the command of the Second Corps, where he set up a new private power complex.

This fundamental inability to come to grips with administrative and personnel problems was largely due to the nature of the junta's structure. The Saigon *Daily News,* the more outspoken of two new English-language newspapers that appeared after the coup, aptly summed up the situation as follows: "Since November 1st, the power once vested in the hands of Mr. Diem has been split, not so much between General Minh and Premier Tho as between General Minh and his fellow generals of the Military Revolutionary Council. Mr. Tho's powers are only delegated powers, which he received from General Minh under the terms of the provisional Constitution. But in regard to other generals in the M.R.C., General Minh is only *primus inter pares,* the first among equals. In the M.R.C. no one lays down the law. There are twelve generals in that body, and unanimity being the rule if we are not mistaken, there are potentially twelve Molotovs in it, as in the Security Council, each of them able to say

'Nyet!' and block any decision he does not approve of. Theoretically, a government by twelve equals is a government by none—which is to say that Vietnam has no real government at present. But, practically, in any human organization, some members wield more influence than others. How many are they? How much ascendancy do they have over the rest? We do not know, because the meetings of the M.R.C. take place behind closed doors."

If anyone was supposed to be a single leader, it was General Minh, chairman of the M.R.C., but he proved sadly incapable of the task. As the same newspaper wrote in another editorial, entitled "Between the Devil and the Deep Blue Sea," "General Minh's scruples are understandable. After having helped bring down a dictatorship, he does not want to set up a new one in its place. This is a laudable attitude, but no one asks him to become a new dictator. Far from it. This country wants no more dictatorship." What was desperately needed was a dose of dynamism, the sort of directing fervor that Magsaysay had demonstrated so successfully years before in leading the battle against the Huks in the Philippines. A number of Americans who had known Magsaysay kept urging Minh to assume a Magsaysay-like role, to move around the countryside wherever possible, dropping into places unexpectedly as Magsaysay had, rallying peasants as co-operative sources of intelligence, and exhorting soldiers to get out and really probe for the enemy, so that the rate of contact with the Vietcong would be increased. (Only six per cent of an average thirty-five hundred small unit government operations a week were making any contact when the junta took over.) But Minh, though he announced his good intentions—"Our job is to illuminate the people and conquer their hearts," he told me—did very little illuminating. He made a few trips around the country, but in most of his speeches—and he was not a good speaker—he adopted a defensive posture, spending his time defending the new government against the criticism that it might adopt a policy of "neutralism," as was being urged by the French. "To fall into the neutralist trap would mean to surrender unconditionally, because neutralization of Vietnam would simply allow the Communists to expand," Minh declared. This was well and good, but the government was begging the question. It seemed to be caught in dead center, unable to move in any direction, and this increased the criticism directed against it. "It is too early to draw up a balance sheet," Minh said at a press conference, where he and his fellow officers were subjected to a barrage of questions from the aroused Vietnamese press. The posture remained defensive, however. Much of the criticism resulted from the fact that so many newspapers had appeared after the coup—there were suddenly almost fifty of them—and many were fly-by-night journals that had only their own axes to grind or were seeking to be sensational. Here again the government failed to meet the challenge of permitting freedom of the press and, at the same time, of issuing a new press code that would make clear at once the necessary limits to irrational attacks that simply served to confuse and arouse the public.

One of those in particular who was subjected to attacks by the press was Premier Tho, an able administrator with a somewhat suspect past. Tho, as Vice-President under Diem, had played a passive but nevertheless useful role while the coup was being prepared. As indicated, he had known it was coming and had kept a number of Cabinet Ministers from resigning and thereby precipitating a crisis too soon, which Nhu might have taken advantage of to create his own dictatorship. Five weeks after the coup, Minh went out of his way to answer the attacks on Tho by declaring that the M.R.C. had appointed Tho as provisional Premier because he had, "from the very outset," taken part in the planning of the coup and therefore enjoyed the "full confidence" of the M.R.C. In a tempestuous press conference, Tho lashed back at his critics and defended himself from charges that he had countenanced the attacks against the Buddhists by Diem and Nhu, citing proof that he had opposed the pagoda raids bitterly and that he would have resigned himself had not General Minh asked him to remain. The fact that Tho was a holdover from the old regime and that he was known to have derived considerable benefits from it, such as in the purchase of lands under the land reform program already referred to, was only one basis of the attacks brought against him. Essentially, he and his Cabinet were accused of being "tools" of the junta generals, and while this criticism was in many respects unfair, it crystallized a growing feeling of discontent against the continuation of a military form of government.

The problem of the Army's role in Vietnam since the fall of Diem

—what it has been and what it should be—has been much debated and never resolved. It has been argued, with considerable justification, that under the circumstances of a violent war being waged in the countryside (a revolutionary struggle that, from the enemy's standpoint, combined all the attributes of military, political, and psychological warfare), an indefinite period of military leadership was both unavoidable and necessary after the Diem dictatorship was overthrown. It has also been maintained that while the Army had to conduct the war, and while the conduct of it demanded political as well as military action, much more could and should have been done in the immediate post-Diem period to create a climate for the development of political life. (There will be more about this later.) For the moment, in reviewing the short and unhappy life of the military junta under Duong Van Minh's ineffectual leadership, it need only be pointed out that the junta fell between the two stools of *neither* providing leadership *nor* taking sufficient steps to create the conditions whereby a civilian administration could acquire and assume leadership and the national political life could be stimulated. The question may again be raised—could the United States have done more to avoid the impasse that was so obviously emerging and, in a more positive sense, could it have stimulated and perhaps even guided a more rational political development?

After the coup occurred, Colonel Pham Ngoc Thao—the ultimate military leader of the old Tuyen-Do Mau coup group, and a man from whom much more would be heard—was assigned two important tasks prior to being "banished" to take a course at Fort Leavenworth, in the United States. Thao's first task was to create the nucleus and then project the membership of a Council of Notables, which was to serve as a sort of interim advisory body of leading citizens during the period while the junta still held sway. His second job was to encourage the formation of two or three but not more than four political parties, around which the new political life of the nation might hopefully be organized. Thao succeeded in his first assignment; the Council of Notables, consisting of fifty-eight men and two women, held its first meeting on January 1, 1964, at Dien Hong Palace in Saigon. General Minh appeared before it and said: "No one can be more earnest than we [the military] in wishing that the time will very soon come when the essential democratic institutions are established on solid foundations, so that we may turn power over to a civilian government elected by the people. . . . With the assistance of the Notables, we shall proceed to reform the Constitution; we shall seek, in particular, a clear-cut separation of powers, an effective protection of individual liberties, and the promotion of a legal and constructive opposition. On the last-mentioned point, we wish to avoid the evil current in nascent democracies; namely, the confusion resulting from proliferating political parties." A few days later, Premier Tho told the new Council that he expected "a rational attitude" and "impartial and realistic judgments" from its members. He added that the government was seeking "to clear the way for a permanent regime, which our people are longing for," and he asked the Council's help in making suggestions "which can be easily implemented, proposals not exceeding our means at present, and measures inspired by the quest for the common good rather than the interests of one group or one locality."

The Council consisted almost exclusively of well-known professional and academic leaders, and of a number of men who had been politically active in the pre-Diem period. It included no representatives of the peasantry or of the labor movement and, as such, was scarcely a representative national body. It was, rather, a traditional group of "notables" in the old colonial sense, and though it was composed of many citizens who had the best interests of the nation at heart, it was limited both in its orientation and its approach. It soon became involved in endless discussion and debate, and it never did get around to performing what should have been firmly assigned to it as its initial task—the drafting of a new constitution. Tho, when I saw him later, confessed that the Council of Notables was not nearly as representative as it should have been, and said, "We have asked the Notables to work on the Constitution, but they're more ambitious—they want to let off steam. They don't want to be a rubber stamp, like the old Diem Assembly." It was healthy, to be sure, "to let off steam," but that was about all the Notables did.

Colonel Thao had to admit defeat in his second task. He found it impossible to persuade the various political groups and factions that had sprung up, many of which consisted of only a few individuals, to get together and form no more than four so-called political "fronts," which then might become the basis of subsequent parties. Within a month and a half of the coup, there were no less than sixty-two political parties in Vietnam. Some had been formed from the nucleus of old ones, and had then split up; others had been set up by political exiles returning from France or Cambodia; still others started from scratch. The majority of these political fragments were also, in one sense, a healthy manifestation of relief from long years of oppression. But unfortunately they did little but criticize the government and each other, and they soon added only more confusion to an already chaotic situation. As the Saigon News editorialized: "Democracy without political parties is absurd. Are we to think that, to our political parties and our politicians, democracy means only the right to criticize and not the obligation of accepting responsibilities and incurring criticism? If that is so, then Nhu and Diem were right, because they held that Vietnam was not ripe for democracy. Are our parties and politicians prepared to accept that view? And by what right have they criticized Mr. Nguyen Ngoc Tho for having conceived his government as only a government of technicians?"

About all the Military Revolutionary Council did to guide the nation's political development was to forbid all officers to engage in any political activity and to sever all ties with political parties. This was designed chiefly to avoid the sort of political favoritism that had grown up in the Army during the Diem days and to make the Army concentrate on its principal task—fighting the war. A separate order went out for all military men to avoid all forms of corruption; any soldier or officer found guilty of engaging in corrupt practices would be severely punished, the warning said. This was another noble bit of action that combined *mea culpa* for past sins with implied support of future civilian responsibility for conducting the government. However, corruption, both in the Army and out, continued as before, and so did politicking, which increased as the new military struggle for power took shape. During December, 1963, and January, 1964, the generals of the junta showed alarming signs of developing their own new power blocs. The Tho government of "technicians" did what it could to stem the tide of inflation and provide some financial and economic order, but it lacked any real power of enforcement. The Council of Notables fussed and fumed and produced nothing but clichés and its own cliques. And the Vietcong continued to win battles and to widen the scope of their control of the countryside by combining, as they had adroitly learned to do, blandishment and terror. It was unclear what the United States was doing, beyond extending more aid and encouragement to the bogged-down government. Certainly there were no signs that it was offering the sort of down-to-earth, realistic guidance that was so desperately needed by a nation struggling to survive in the midst of a violent war and at the same time trying to make itself overnight into what it had never been—a fledgling democracy. Ambassador Lodge told me that he regarded the military effort as far more important for the moment than the development of political parties or the writing of a new Constitution. Lodge, in many respects, gave the impression of having lost interest; he had done his job in Vietnam, and done it well, probably better than any other Ambassador since 1945, and now he seemed anxious to take a rest. Furthermore, his wife was not well and he wanted to get her home. And the Republican campaign beckoned.

One thing the Americans could always do well, whether they were Embassy people, rural affairs advisers, or military advisers, and that was make apt observations about the Vietnamese. There were many Americans who were fully aware of the new government's lack of direction and purpose, and of the fact that there was little time left if the tide of the war could be turned. One of the more observant Embassy men made this comment: "General Minh is playing much the same popular role as General Naguib did in the Egyptian revolt. But he does not yet have a South Vietnamese Nasser behind him."

A New Leader Appears

He was wrong. A Nasser was present, and he was only biding his time to strike. He was General Nguyen Khanh, the new commander of the northernmost First Corps, and the idea that he might someday be master of South Vietnam had been in Khanh's mind for several years. Even before the November coup, he had conceived a scheme of his own to grab power. Of all the generals in the Vietnamese Army, Khanh, considered one of the ablest, was also one of the most un-gregarious. His reputation as a lone wolf was one that he had culti-vated, though there was much in his background that was obscure and that had served naturally to create in him not only a sense of isolation but also a desire to assert his authority. Khanh's mother had run a bar in Dalat that was frequented by roistering Frenchmen. Soon after her son was born—at Travinh, in 1927—she sent him to live with his father, a Vietnamese landowner, and with the woman his father was living with, a well-known Vietnamese actress and singer of the day, who brought Khanh up, playing the role of a stepmother. For much of the time, the family lived in Cambodia, where Khanh first went to school. Afterward, he attended school in Saigon while living with French-Vietnamese relatives. At the age of eighteen, Khanh says, he was one of a group of twenty high-school graduates who fled Saigon to join the Vietminh in the countryside. They were away for fifteen months, mostly working with small Vietminh bands in the delta region; when a larger, better organized, and more thoroughly indoctrinated group of a hundred or so Vietminh guerrillas took over, Khanh and his companions were told that they were "too tired" and lacked "proper discipline." Upon being disarmed, they returned to Saigon. Soon afterward, Khanh entered the first special Vietnamese military training class ever established by the French, and as it happened, most of the coplotters in his coup of January 30, 1964, were members of that class, which numbered seventeen. Only eleven—including Khanh—passed the course and were graduated, in 1947, and eight of them, plus the six who didn't graduate, soon went out to join the Vietminh. Khanh maintains that he tried to dissuade his classmates from leaving by ex-plaining what he had already learned about how the Communists dominated the Vietminh, but in fact it appears that he himself was persuaded to try the Vietminh again. In any event, after a few months the whole group had become thoroughly disillusioned and returned to the government side, and thereafter, despite their anti-colonial views, they fought with the French against the Vietminh.

By 1952, when Khanh was a top officer of one of the French-directed mobile groups in the plateau area of Central Vietnam, he had become convinced that the French had no intention of granting any real freedom to the puppet Vietnamese government in Saigon, and he thought seriously of deserting with his troops and fighting both sides from the jungle. He hung on because the war was almost over anyway, but then came the settlement at Geneva, which disillusioned him further. When Diem succeeded in establishing a government in the south, Khanh took heart, and for a number of years he supported the new government, eventually becoming Diem's Deputy Army Chief of Staff. By 1960, however, when the opposition to Diem had started to mount, Khanh seems to have begun to look upon himself as the potential leader of his country. During the abortive military coup of November, 1960, it was Khanh who defended Diem in the palace by consulting with the opposition just long enough for Diem to bring up loyal troops from the provinces; but the truth of the matter is that Khanh simply thought the coup would fail anyway, and besides it wasn't the kind of coup he wanted. A year or so later, at the instigation of Nhu, whom he had come to detest, Khanh was transferred to a corps command in the plateau area and now he began to plot in earnest. He established lines of communication with the conspiracy against Diem being mapped by Dr. Tuyen, but he also formed a plan of his own, which some Americans knew about. He was ready to move in August, 1963, when the Buddhist crisis that helped bring Diem down reached its peak with Nhu's attack on the pagodas, but at that moment someone betrayed Khanh to Nhu. In the chaotic weeks that followed, during which several groups of plotters were working separately and Nhu was preparing his counterplot, Khanh remained more or less in the background, but some parts of his August scheme were incorporated into the final plot that overthrew the Ngo family.

For a time after the new junta had established itself under General Minh, Khanh retained his old corps command in the plateau. Then, in mid-December, he was shifted to the northernmost corps, which had its headquarters in the cities of Hué and Danang. Since he had requested a command in the delta, where most of the fighting was going on, he was perfectly well aware that his transfer north was the result of military politics and represented the desire of the other generals, who regarded his lone-wolf characteristics as dangerous, to keep him as far away from the capital as possible. I saw Khanh at that time in Hué, and he made no attempt to hide his annoyance over not having been given a more important job. When I asked him to tell me the details of the November coup, he replied cryptically, "It is too soon yet to tell the whole story, but someday I will tell it to you."

As it developed, the second coup, like the first, involved a typical Vietnamese cabal on the part of a disgruntled group of generals and colonels, who were as much annoyed as Khanh at having been put on the sidelines by the junta. Other motives played their part, though, including Khanh's by no means unjustified feeling that the junta was simply too big and too divided within itself to carry on the war. In the weeks before Khanh's coup, the customary flow of rumors in Saigon was swelled by the impact of bad economic conditions—the price of rice and other commodities had kept rising—and there were strikes, accompanied by some violence, and student demonstrations. The press was maintaining its campaign of recrimination and attack against Premier Tho's provisional government, and the Council of Notables was engaged in a particularly inconclusive debate about politics. A serious cholera epidemic increased apprehension among the city's population, and the final disruptive factor was the imminence of Tet, the Vietnamese New Year, when everyone traditionally seeks to settle affairs—not only his own, but those of his neighbors and of the nation itself—and when a desire to clean slates builds up an attitude of recklessness over a period of weeks.

At this point, about a month before the junta was overthrown, Khanh was approached by the enigmatic man who had been one of the principal tacticians behind the November coup. This was General Do Mau—he had been promoted from Colonel—a silent, saturnine officer who was once a bus boy, briefly attended a French military school, and in time had become head of military security under Diem. While he had never commanded any troops of his own, Do Mau's thorough knowledge of the backgrounds of most of the officers in the Army, including their personal weaknesses, had enabled him initially to bring together many of the elements that overthrew Diem in November. The members of the new junta respected but feared him, too, and after the November coup they had gradually isolated him, eventually placing him in the relatively innocuous post of Minister of Information and transferring his closest friends to new posts a safe distance away. Casting about for "replacements," Do Mau soon found them among officers who had been exiled in Cambodia or France and had returned to Vietnam after the fall of Diem. The most important of these in Do Mau's scheme was Colonel Nguyen Chanh Thi, the tough, opportunistic former paratroop commander, who had fled to Cambodia after the unsuccessful 1960 coup against Diem. Do Mau persuaded the junta to send Thi up north as Khanh's deputy, pointing out that Khanh had been largely responsible for crushing the 1960 revolt, and that Thi would therefore be a good choice to keep *him* in check. What Do Mau really had in mind, though, was to use Thi as a means of building a firm bridge between himself, in Saigon, and Khanh, in the north; he correctly figured that whatever old enmities may have existed between the two would be forgotten under the new circumstances. Having made one move, Do Mau quickly made a second; General Tran Thien Khiem, who had been one of Khanh's old fellow cadets and who had worked closely with Do Mau in the November coup, had just been demoted from Executive Chief of Staff to commander of the Third Corps, around Saigon, so Do Mau had no trouble gaining his co-operation for the new plot. Khiem controlled the 5th and 7th Divisions, and he brought the commanders of both these outfits into the plan, thereby giving the plotters the backing of vital troop elements close to the city. Khiem and Do Mau and Khanh, who were now keeping in regular touch surreptitiously, built up their group by gaining the support of some Marine, Air Force, and Special Forces officers, and a miscellaneous group of other officers. Two additional important men were brought into the plot—General Duong Ngoc Lam, the chief of the Civil Guard, who had also been promoted from Colonel and whose willingness to co-operate was easy to obtain because his name had been mentioned in connection with an alleged swindle of military funds being investigated by the junta; and General Duong Van Duc, who had just returned from exile in Paris and was acting as assistant to General Le Van Kim, the chief of the junta's general staff and its most able officer.

The organization for the new coup was now more or less completed. It remained for President Charles de Gaulle of France to trigger it by going ahead with his plan to recognize Communist China and publicly proposing the neutralization of the former Indochina states. In late December and early January, as student demonstrations against neutralism and de Gaulle mounted in Saigon, the Council of Notables not only accused the provisional government of lacking a firm policy on the neutralist issue but went as far as to recommend that relations with France be broken off. The crisis came to a head when a reputed French agent, Lieutenant Colonel Tran Dinh Lan, who had served in both the French Army and the Vietnamese Army, suddenly returned to Saigon after several years in France, reportedly bringing with him several million dollars' worth of Vietnamese piastres. Lan moved into the home of one of General Kim's top aides, and reports got around that other French agents were secretly arriving in town. These rumors, whether they were true or simply planted by the conspirators, served to spread the belief that a French-sponsored neutralist deal was in the offing, and thus furnished an excuse for the new conspirators to act.

General Duc, whose years of experience in France had given him a good idea of what the French might be up to and what their relations with pro-French members of the Vietnamese Army were, had prepared some incriminating documents for General Do Mau. They purported to show that three prominent members of the junta—Generals Kim, Don, and Xuan—had been bought by French agents and were about to declare that Vietnam would go neutralist and sign an agreement to end the war with the north. Certain Americans got wind of these documents, and there is no doubt that some of the high-ranking Americans in town knew what was going on. A number of meetings between Khanh and American officers in the north took place in Hué during the first two weeks in January, and while they may have dealt partly with routine military matters, it is very likely that they also dealt partly with the new coup. However, it cannot be said that the Americans played any role in the Khanh coup. A number of secret meetings of the plotters were also held in Saigon during January, too, and Khanh flew down to attend most of them. They usually took place in the secluded house of a colonel, who was a nearby province chief. On January 25th, a few days before the coup, Khanh flew to Saigon for a final meeting, and then returned north. On January 28th, he came back to the capital in a civilian plane, wearing civilian clothes. He still retained a small beard, which he has sporadically worn whenever he has set out to do something; he refuses to take it off until he considers the job at hand finished. The next day, January 29th, Khanh's deputy, Colonel Thi, followed him to the capital. Elaborate precautions were taken by the plotters to have their agents around town meet each other in out-of-the-way spots to exchange information and orders. There were no betrayals. On Wednesday night, the 29th, the troops that General Do Mau and General Khiem had alerted quietly took their positions around the city. They ultimately included many of the same forces that had been used in the first coup: armored cars and tanks and some elements from the 5th and 7th Divisions, two airborne battalions and one Marine battalion, and some scattered Special Forces, Ranger, and Civil Guard units. The homes of the generals of the junta were surrounded, and a number of American officers and Embassy officials were alerted to be in their offices at two o'clock on the morning of Thursday, January 30th, to be kept in touch with events. At about three o'clock that morning, General Khanh took over the general staff headquarters on the outskirts of town. Ambassador Lodge was informed of this and of eveything else that was going on during the night, including the arrest of the top junta leaders. By daybreak, it was all over, without a shot having been fired, and the city was going about its business. Yet if there was no opposition, there was little popular enthusiasm, either, and the general apathy was in sharp contrast to the open expressions of joy and relief when Diem and Nhu were overthrown.

While General Khanh was trying to persuade General Minh to

stay on in some capacity, the three junta generals implicated in the alleged French plot—Generals Kim, Don, and Xuan—were flown to Danang, up north, and placed in private custody. Also arrested and flown north was the volatile General Dinh, the Minister of Security, who was not suspected of being pro-French so much as just a dangerous plotter willing to join the other three out of expediency. Lieutenant Colonel Lan, the returned "French agent," was imprisoned, too.

General Khanh lost little time in establishing his full authority. In an immediate broadcast to the nation, he explained why he had conducted his "purge," decrying the fact that the junta had made no progress in its three months in power. "The political, economic, and social situation in the countryside still offers no promising prospect," he said. "There has not been one single compensation worthy of the sacrifices accepted daily by the soldiers." This much was sadly true. Whether Vietnam would be better off with one man at the helm was debatable. In any event, the United States was about to be faced with another challenge.

CHAPTER VIII

❧

Khanh's Rise to Power

The year in which General Nguyen Khanh ruled Vietnam, for the most part singlehandedly, was perhaps the most frustrating and turbulent in the experience of the Americans since they had become deeply involved in Vietnamese affairs in 1954. It was a year in which the United States commitment to participate in the war was clearly spelled out, by such measures as the naval and air bombardment of North Vietnamese bases early in August, 1964, in retaliation for attacks against American warships in the Gulf of Tonkin by Communist motor patrol boats; and by the gradual dispatch of more planes and more American troops to South Vietnam.

This greater American commitment in the Vietnamese conflict was partly predicated on the hope that it would encourage the South Vietnamese to fight more effectively against the Vietcong, whose support from North Vietnam had steadily been increasing, not only in numbers of hard-core troops, including some North Vietnamese regulars infiltrated into South Vietnam, but also in the quality and quantity of weapons smuggled into the south along various land and sea routes. However, the hope of rallying the South Vietnamese proved essentially futile, and the war continued to go badly, for political as much as for military reasons. It seemed impossible for the leaders of South Vietnam—under General Khanh, as before under the junta—to create a popular government, to overcome their natural tendency to engage in constant power struggles in which the military continued to play the leading part, or to establish harmony among the fractious and embittered religious and civilian elements. In this continuing condition of chaos, the United States made some sporadic efforts to bring the various contending groups together, but these attempts were mostly "fire-fighting" maneuvers prompted by specific day-to-day or week-by-week crises, and did not demonstrate a willingness to come to grips with the more complicated and fundamental political problems of the disturbed and fragmented nation. The basic American disposition seemed to be that these were Vietnamese problems, which the Vietnamese should settle by themselves. As the crises mounted, the degree of power held by the United States seemed to diminish. More and more Americans were in Vietnam, but they seemed, in ratio, to be accomplishing less and less, and they also found themselves the object of increasing antipathy.

At the outset of General Khanh's rule, there were various plus and minus factors. He moved swiftly and boldly to consolidate his take-over. First he announced himself as Chief of State and as Chairman of the Military Revolutionary Council, supplanting General Minh, but then he managed to persuade Minh, who was still a popular figure and had not been accused in the alleged French neutralist plot of the former junta, to remain as nominal Chief of State. This was partly the result of pressure brought by the Americans, who felt that Minh would be a stabilizing and unifying factor in the new regime, and that by co-operating with Khanh he would insure some degree of continuity. This theory of amelioration and harmony would soon be totally disproved. With Minh relegated to a kind of limbo, Khanh became the sole ruler of the M.R.C. It became apparent at once that he was far more politically oriented and motivated than any of his junta predecessors, and initially he sought the help of veteran Vietnamese politicians and technicians to create a new governmental machine that would be efficient and would have a popular appeal. A week after the coup, he summoned from a decade of exile in Paris Dr. Nguyen Ton Hoan, a Catholic and one of the former leaders of the southern branch of the old Dai Viet right-wing nationalist party. Dr. Hoan, although he had been out of the country for a long time, had been among the most active of the

Paris exile group, publishing a magazine there and keeping up his contacts with the underground members of the Dai Viet in Vietnam during the period of the Diem regime. However, as one of the rather typical Vietnamese intellectuals of the forties and fifties who never had much popular following, Dr. Hoan was unable to form a government when he returned to Saigon, as General Khanh had hoped. Khanh thereupon decided to act jointly as Premier and as Chairman of a reorganized Military Revolutionary Council, which was enlarged to include seventeen generals and thirty-two other officers. Dr. Hoan was appointed the top Vice-Premier in charge of the program of rural pacification, and as such he was given supervision over five Ministries, among them the key ones of Interior, National Defense, and Rural Affairs, and two special commissions, all of which were primarily engaged in consolidating the strategic hamlets in South Vietnam, renamed New Rural Life Hamlets. A second Vice-Premiership was given to a Harvard-trained Vietnamese banker-economist named Nguyen Xuan Oanh, who was not a Dai Viet member but had some ties to the party. Oanh was put in charge of the nation's finances and economy. A third Vice-Premier was General Do Mau, who took over social and cultural affairs.

In selecting his Cabinet of thirteen Ministers and two Secretaries of State at the Cabinet level, and in choosing new province and district chiefs (a fresh reshuffle that caused more delays in the administrative procedure), General Khanh originally tried to include members of various political and religious groups, among them representatives of the Cao Dai and the Hoa Hao sects, which still had some military strength in the western sections of the country and in the delta. Considerable progress was made by Khanh in bringing these armed elements, defeated by Diem in 1955 and since engaged in fighting both the Vietcong and the government, back into the government fold. However, although Khanh emphasized that he had no party affiliation, the basic orientation of his government at the start was clearly Dai Viet, and Dai Viet members held many of the secondary as well as top posts in the government. This soon provoked criticism from other anti-Communist nationalist parties and groups that were banned or were quiescent during the Diem period and now wanted a larger share of the pie, and from individual intellectuals who felt that what the country most needed was new young political leaders and parties capable of appealing to the population without the heritage of failure and the divisiveness from which the old nationalist organizations generally suffered.

From the beginning, General Khanh and his Cabinet faced the monumental task of altering the outlook of a tired and disillusioned people, many, if not most, of whom were already convinced that the war was lost, and of the futility of waging an uphill battle against what very likely had become the best guerrilla army in history. General Khanh frankly acknowledged the difficulties in the opening paragraph of his new "Program of Action," proclaimed in mid-March, 1964, when he declared that the combination of Diem oppression and Vietcong pressure had brought things to a point where "the people kept more and more away from the government, were no longer interested in fighting for survival, and were gradually approaching annihilation." Khanh's plan to save Vietnam revolved around two basic principles: the mobilization of able-bodied citizens, especially younger ones, to perform tasks that would directly aid in prosecuting the war—either in its paramilitary aspects or in the promotion of social and civic action in the countryside—and a continued reorganization of the New Rural Life Hamlets, eliminating the isolated and overextended ones, as the junta had only begun to do, and giving equal stress in those retained to improvement of security and of local living standards. As the hamlets became safe and gained economic and social strength, they were to be re-extended carefully on the "oil slick" theory, gradually being moved from the more populated areas outward. Decentralization of government power, Khanh said, was his principal aim. "We shall place full confidence in the anti-Communist patriotic elements in the various localities in establishing their own substructure, because only local people can exterminate the Communist traitors from their localities," he declared. He stated the perennial hope that village elections would be held as soon as feasible and that a new National Assembly would be elected within a year. In order to get this election scheme started, General Khanh abolished the Council of Notables. Many observers, Vietnamese as well as

Americans, considered this an unwise and premature step in view of
the fact that election promises had been broken so many times before
during the last ten years and that the Council, despite its inconclusive
bickering, had at least afforded prominent citizens a chance to express
their views. Before an election could be held, the Vietnamese Constitution, promulgated and largely ignored by the Diem regime, had
to be revamped or modified, and there were those who felt that the
Council, or a smaller adjunct body, should still have been given this
task.

In its more specific aspects, Khanh's national survival program,
which he began explaining to the people in weekly broadcasts, included plans to simplify the military and paramilitary structure by
assimilating the Civil Guard—the provincial or regional force—
into the regular Army, and by joining the village Self-Defense Corps
with the Combat Youth, which had operated mostly within hamlets.
A new law was promulgated to bring the local and provincial forces
up to strength (the Civil Guard was about twenty per cent under
its authorized strength of eighty thousand, and the Self-Defense
Corps had been thirty per cent under its allotted strength of seventy-
two thousand men). Through the beefed-up American military aid
program, an added fifty million dollars a year, over and above the
five hundred million Vietnam was already receiving annually, was to
help finance the increase in local forces and be used to pay these
troops, as well as the regular Army soldiers, a bit more each month.
A new training program was started to prepare young Army officers
to take over as chiefs of two hundred and thirty-seven districts in the
country, and these freshly indoctrinated leaders were to be in charge
of the holding part of the "clear and hold" military plan. As the
Vietcong was cleared out, they were to maintain security in the districts, get political activity started, and supervise social development
programs. The last, according to Khanh's blueprint, included a reappraisal of agricultural reform schemes never implemented by Diem
and Nhu; peasants who had been "illegally" occupying land formally
expropriated by the Diem regime from wealthy Vietnamese and
French landlords, but not yet reapportioned, were to be allowed to go
on tilling it free for five more years; then they could buy and pay

for it over twelve years, instead of the six-year period previously stipulated. In addition, as part of the effort to increase cultivation, the land tax was to be abolished for poor peasants, and farmers who couldn't afford to buy fertilizer would be helped. The development of small rural industries was to be encouraged, and industrialization in the cities was to be stimulated. In the area of public health, dispensaries were to be built by the government in all hamlets and villages, and medical centers and surgical wards, as well as mobile health units, were to be established in all provinces. In alleviating slum conditions in the cities, especially in Saigon, nurseries, orphanages, and low-cost cafeterias were to be constructed, and in the countryside a low-cost housing scheme was to be instituted in areas where the Vietcong had destroyed the homes of peasants or ordered the peasants to destroy them, usually by removing the roofs and burning them, preparatory to moving the people into new Vietcong villages.

General Khanh's bold program was received with more of a shrug than enthusiasm; so many promises had been made before and never kept. There was a lot of confusion over exactly what he meant by national mobilization of all able-bodied citizens; the younger generation, especially college students, became panicky over the possibility of being drafted, while administrators in all echelons were frightened by the harshness of Khanh's threats to crack down on anyone he felt was not working hard enough in the war effort. (Khanh quickly showed himself to be much tougher than the members of the junta, and in some respects as tough as Diem and Mme. Nhu, in combating pleasure and profligacy; he condemned "feasting" and denounced "intellectuals who sit around in teahouses and talk and don't support us"; and though dancing was now allowed on weekends in cafés, the twist, which Mme. Nhu had outlawed but which had reappeared after the first coup, was again forbidden.) It was not until April, nearly a month after the announcement of Khanh's mobilization plan, that a new draft law was promulgated to clarify the situation. Under the plan, the draft age was broadened to include both younger and older men—between the ages of twenty and forty-five—but younger ones, particularly single men, and widowers without dependents would be called up first, while full-time college students would be exempt until they completed their studies, although some would be expected to work in rural areas during their vacation periods as a kind of Peace Corps. A Civil Defense Corps was also to be mobilized, beginning with a goal of seventy-five hundred by the end of 1964 and ultimately to total forty thousand. It was to include men and women to be assigned to the hamlets, and those called for service would receive some military training and be taught how to maintain order in a period of disaster as well as how to take over many of the administrative tasks previously performed by local guard units, which were to be released for military duties.

Under the broad new pacification plan, half the country's provinces (forty-three at this time) were held to be "critical" and fourteen, practically all in the delta, were designated as "supercritical." It was mostly in the delta that the government began the strategic withdrawals that were considered necessary in order to eliminate outposts and fortified hamlets that could not be defended against the Vietcong. Some American military and non-military advisers felt that these withdrawals were too hurried, especially since they enabled the Communists to walk into abandoned areas with much fanfare. Both psychologically and militarily, the Vietcong capitalized on these "cheap successes" and coupled them with well-timed attacks on district capitals and other towns, which on occasion were captured and held briefly, as a sort of object lesson to show the people what the Communists could do. During the government's withdrawal and consolidation period, half or more of the hamlets in the worst provinces were sacrificed, but their surrender amounted to a formality in many cases, since the Vietcong had controlled the surrounding countryside all along. As the stress was placed on shoring up the hamlets and villages that were retained and actively protected, it was hoped that the people, seeing that security could really be established on a permanent basis in these places, would be more willing to volunteer much-needed intelligence on Vietcong troop movements. There was also the hope that as security increased, many of the younger men who joined the Vietcong irregulars (the so-called "territorial" troops and local guerrillas) would return to their homes under the government's "open-arms" program and take part in the national effort without any more fear of Vietcong reprisals.

The manner in which General Khanh assumed power and promulgated his program in South Vietnam seemed, in many respects, to impress the Americans far more than it impressed the Vietnamese— at least the visiting Americans from Washington. The United States decision to step up its aid to Vietnam—following the belated awareness in Washington that the picture was truly grave, which everyone familiar with the military facts on the ground had known all along —came after another one of Secretary of Defense McNamara's periodic visits to Saigon. More than ever, this had become "McNamara's war," and the appointment of one of his former chief assistants, William Bundy, as Assistant Secretary of State for Far Eastern Affairs underlined the fact. The role of Ambassador Henry Cabot Lodge, who was at this time a leading contender for the Republican nomination for the Presidency, became more and more that of a pro tem proconsul. This fitted in with the McNamara concept of operating in the most direct possible way, through his own lines to the White House (which Lodge himself had always represented more than the State Department), and with the least amount of interference from other American agencies. It was hardly noticed, for instance, that there had not been a Vietnamese Ambassador in Washington for months, and the significance of this was that McNamara, Lodge, and Khanh operated as a team and that the State Department, despite a quick stopover in Saigon by Secretary Rusk, came to occupy a secondary position as an observer and reporter of the situation. McNamara soon made it clear that Khanh had all the American, and particularly all *his,* support. Once again, the United States was putting all its eggs in one basket.

Gropings and Embarrassments

Two months after Khanh staged his coup, it was apparent that the new regime was still groping. There had not been a significant military victory, nor had the government managed to make the impact that Khanh had sought on the civilian population. There were signs that serious differences existed among the politicians and the military men in Saigon, and there were stirrings of more religious trouble. Inevitably, with Khanh's assumption of power more changes were

made in the ranks of the province chiefs and in the command structure of the Army. This served to lower the morale of troops in the
field and to make the average citizen wonder whether the constant
shifts of personalities would ever cease. Khanh was obviously caught
in the dilemma of wanting to make himself a more popular figure—
he went on a number of barnstorming trips—and of not being willing, or able, to risk relinquishing his tight hold on the government.
His sources of power in the Army had never been very strong, since
he had been a lone wolf, and even those generals who were momentarily supporting him loomed as potential rivals. Khanh sought to
bolster himself by giving promotions and key assignments to officers
he thought would most likely stand by him; but some of the men he
chose, including a few in important command posts, failed to
demonstrate any particular competence, while others could at best be
described as erratic opportunists.

I had left Saigon shortly before Khanh grabbed power, and when
I returned, shortly afterward, rumors of more coups or of Khanh's
possible assassination were already being heard. It seemed to me that
even within a matter of months there was a new air of stridency in the
city, and one could almost feel the internal stresses and conflicts. The
face of the town showed it. The prostitutes were more brazen, the
beggars, including hordes of tattered youngsters with automatically
outstretched hands, were more professional, and there was a sudden
appearance of Vietnamese "Teddy boys," who went out of their way
to pick fights with American servicemen. The teen-age sons of American dependents had started a Honda motorcycle club and roared
wildly, among the thousands of other motorbikes and small taxis,
through the once quiet, now raucous streets. On the surface, the
city still had the rich and diverse pattern of life that had always made
it a unique blend of the Orient and the Occident, but no one seemed
to enjoy the place any more. Beyond the ominous feeling that the
Vietcong were slowly encircling the town, and that their men were
increasingly in it in spite of an effective counter-intelligence squad,
there was a deep fatigue and uneasiness, and a foreboding that more
changes to come might not be for the better. More than ever before in
all the years I had known it, Saigon seemed raw at the edges, as if

the sores and strains it had so long endured might at any moment prove too much to bear, and the whole city would fall apart.

As Khanh tried to get his reform program started, and to establish his *bona fides* as the ruler of South Vietnam, he increasingly gave the impression of a man being forced to extemporize, with no dependable support other than that given him by the Americans. At the end of March, in an obvious attempt to make it appear that he held the reins of power firmly in his hands and that the Army was solidly behind him, he summoned a meeting of the Military Revolutionary Council—it was the Council's first meeting since Khanh's coup—and managed to obtain a 53–0 vote of confidence for himself. The support was more apparent than real, for the Army was becoming more and more divided within itself and new cliques were developing. There was a growing resentment over the manner in which Khanh had seized control of the government, and of his attempt to make what was essentially a power play of disgruntled officers, led by himself, appear to be a heroic operation to rescue the country from a neutralist plot. Khanh never did prove the charge that Generals Don, Kim, and Xuan had been planning to make a deal with North Vietnam, as advocated by the French, and he consequently was never able to persuade General Minh to cooperate with him as Chief of State. Aside from resenting the fact that he had been deposed by a younger man whom he regarded as an upstart, Minh deeply resented the fact that, in addition to his fellow generals of the first junta, some of the junior officers of the Army had been falsely accused; about thirty had been arrested by Khanh and then set free when Minh demanded it as a condition of his joining the new government. Khanh tried to duck the issue of the alleged plot as long as he could, and then tried to bolster it by making a fresh charge that French agents wanted to assassinate him and renew the attempt at a neutralist solution. He offered no evidence to prove this, other than his own statement that the French had paid a terrorist $1,300 to kill him during one of his barnstorming trips; later he said the price on his head "was much more than that." American intelligence agents said they knew nothing about it, though they admitted it was conceivable that, in view of France's new policy of recognizing China and favoring a neutralist solution in South Vietnam, some irresponsible Frenchmen might have pretended to hatch such a scheme. Late in May, having been quietly advised by the Americans for some time to do something about the generals he had been holding under arrest, Khanh suddenly summoned a rather weird "trial" of the arrested officers, which went on for twenty-four hours in Dalat. The upshot was a vaguely worded communiqué that accused them of having lacked a proper "revolutionary policy" and "a clear-cut political attitude," and of having been inadequately aware of "their heavy responsibilities," and of letting "their subordinates take advantage of their positions." They were officially reprimanded, deprived of any command posts for various periods, and allowed to remain in Dalat with their families under surveillance. The solution satisfied no one, least of all General Minh, who was perfunctorily accused of misusing some piastres before being allowed to sit in as an adviser on the trial panel, and he went into a fresh sulk. The danger of permitting the generals, even if purportedly watched, to sit around loose without anything to do but plot seemed obvious. It was suggested that they be sent to the United States on military study assignments, and some tentative arrangements were even made to accomplish this, but they were never acted upon. All in all, the case of the accused generals continued to be one of Khanh's biggest embarrassments.

Khanh soon suffered other embarrassments, too. His romance with the Dai Viet Party did not last long. In April, Ha Thuc Ky, one of the Dai Viet leaders, resigned as Minister of Interior because he felt he was not being given enough freedom to run his Ministry. Ky was particularly upset because he was not allowed to name the director general of police and security, an important sub-Cabinet post, nor was he permitted to select new province chiefs, which Khanh was also doing himself; he was afraid that Ky would place too many Dai Viet men in the provinces. Vice-Premier Hoan, the other Dai Viet leader in the government, also ran into trouble with Khanh. Dr. Hoan, whose ambitions to have another chance at the Premiership were clear, never did get to take charge of the new rural pacification program, because the generals of the Military Revolutionary Council quietly assumed control of it instead. As Dr. Hoan's position became weaker and more untenable, he charged that he was being ignored by both Khanh and the Americans, and when a Catholic demonstration, in reply to a Buddhist one, took place in mid-June, he gave his quiet endorsement to a militant minority element among the demonstrators who denounced both the government and Ambassador Lodge for "fomenting religious discrimination" by supporting the Buddhist revival in the country and condoning the alleged persecution of Catholics. Even the speakers among the more numerous "official" demonstrators, who had the sanction if not the full approval of the local Catholic hierarchy, claimed the Catholics were being "victimized in an unjust and ruthless way" and accused the Khanh government of "demagogy instead of genuine democracy." To a considerable extent, the worm had turned, and the Catholics were now on the political defensive. The Buddhists continued to claim that they, too, were still being persecuted in some Central Vietnam areas, where the crisis of 1963 began and where, they asserted, local Diemist holdovers in provincial and district jobs were continuing to seek revenge for Diem's overthrow. Five Buddhist laymen in two provinces were said to have been killed in the months since the first coup, and others to have been arrested. It was apparent that while the immediate religious issue was overblown, the whole religious question between the predominant Buddhists and the minority Catholics, who comprised a fifth of South Vietnam's fourteen and a half million population and who still held many key Army and official posts, could again explode. In this atmosphere, the most important figure was that cryptic personality, Thich Tri Quang.

Tri Quang, a highly intense and nervous man in his early forties, had from the outset of the Buddhist revolt of 1963 proved its inspirational leader and the most militant and politically active of the monks in Vietnam. When he emerged from the American Embassy after his period of asylum in the wake of the November coup, he immediately set about seeking to unify the country's two chief Buddhist branches, the Greater Wheel and the Smaller Wheel, and various lay groups and factions. The history of Vietnamese Buddhism dates from the third century, but, unlike other Asian nations, it was always an amorphous and loosely constructed religious movement that contained elements of Confucianism, Taoism, animism, and ancestor worship, and most of the so-called Buddhist population traditionally crossed lines and worshiped several things at once, depending as much as anything else on the schedule of family, village, and national holidays. The predominant Greater Wheel (Mahayana) branch, whose followers believe that anyone can attain enlightenment, or Buddhahood, were active in the central and nothern parts of the country. The Smaller Wheel (Hinayana) groups, whose followers believe that many can reach sainthood but only one among millions can become the personification of the Buddha, were gathered in the south. Tri Quang, whose headquarters were in Hué but who came to Saigon regularly, was seeking to organize a general Buddhist revival. While he denied that he wanted to see Buddhism become a state religion, as it had once been, he apparently was out to build up a Buddhist mass base in the villages and make it something more than just a religious force. Early in 1964, before Khanh seized power, the two main wheels and some of the other Buddhist groups did join together in a unified Buddhist association, headed by a High Clerical Council in charge of doctrinal and spiritual affairs, of which Tri Quang became secretary general, and an Institute for the Propagation of the Buddhist Faith, a secular body headed by the less militant Thich Tam Chau. Despite the outward manifestations of unity, however, the Buddhists remained divided on numerous spiritual and practical matters. Tri Quang and Tam Chau also disagreed about tactics of organization, and they soon became engaged in an undeclared competition to capture the allegiance of the southern Buddhists.

Tri Quang's real motives were the source of much speculation, among both Vietnamese and Americans. While he formally eschewed politics, his methods and strategy, as he had first demonstrated them so successfully in Hué in 1963, revealed a keen political sense and bore considerable resemblance to those of the Communists, especially in such matters as manipulating crowds and dispersing progaganda. At one time, Tri Quang had been in the Vietminh movement, but he had broken with it in the early fifties and had since expressed staunch anti-Communist and more guarded anti-neutralist views. "The Buddhists are simply citizens of Vietnam, and we should not involve ourselves in politics," he told me, "but we must make better moral and judicious use of our talents, and it is our responsibility to serve the nation in a positive and concrete way, because the defense of Buddhism and the defense of the nation go together." A revivified Buddhism in the villages, with Buddhist cadres helping to create social as well as religious consciousness among the people, could certainly have become a positive factor in the war effort. Tri Quang and his followers, however, who started a weekly magazine in Hué in the spring of 1964, tended, like the Catholics, to be increasingly critical of the Khanh government and of America's unrestrained support of Khanh. Despite their anti-Communist posture, there were increasing intimations that, under certain circumstances, they might make an accommodation with neutralism. It was significant that Tri Quang's younger brother, a Buddhist monk in North Vietnam, paid a secret visit to him in Saigon in May, 1964, reportedly accompanied by one of the political spokesmen of the Vietcong's southern political arm, the National Liberation Front. If one wished to assume that Tri Quang meant what he said about having no political ambitions— Buddhist precepts actually forbid it—it seemed increasingly apparent that he might play the role of a Vietnamese *éminence grise*.

Taylor Replaces Lodge

At the end of June, 1964, Ambassador Lodge did what everyone had been expecting him to do for some time: he resigned to go home and take part in the Republican political campaign in the United States. He was replaced by General Maxwell Taylor, who had been acting as Chairman of the Joint Chiefs of Staff, and, as General Taylor's Deputy Ambassador (a new post), President Johnson appointed America's top-ranking career diplomat, U. Alexis Johnson. In his farewell statement, Lodge declared, "Vietnam is on the right track, and, with persistence, its freedom and independence will surely be achieved." Lodge, far more than previous American Ambassadors, had been realistic in his appraisals, and he was saying nothing less than he could under the circumstances. Privately he did not feel so optimistic, and he reflected what, at the time, was the prevailing mood in Saigon—cynicism among the Vietnamese and growing frustration among the Americans. The designation of a topflight team like Taylor and Johnson created a momentary sense of excitement that helped dispel the sense of defeatism, but, despite a small flurry of government victories, the military situation was regarded as far too serious to warrant anything more than cautious hope that the government's ability to retaliate to the expected Vietcong offensive in the months ahead, and to sustain a counteroffensive, would be manifest. General Taylor, notwithstanding his qualifications as a man who knew Vietnam and who understood the nature of guerrilla warfare, was faced with some of the most complicated and perplexing problems any soldier-statesman had ever dealt with, problems that cut far deeper than military strategy and tactics alone and that concerned the whole social and political fabric of a tired and stricken nation. Some of these basic questions were brought out in the open at a remarkable American briefing conducted by a departing senior military adviser, and in the light of the Taylor appointment this may have been a carefully calculated device to prepare the way for a supposed new line of American toughness. In his long denunciation, the officer, a colonel with three years' experience in the field and famous for his frankness, condemned the whole Vietnamese military and administrative structure as being riddled with "second-raters" who, he said, had no ability for "management of the war" and who went about their business in the manner of "the blind leading the blind." In decrying "politics, corruption, and nepotism" at the top, and sheer incompetence or laziness at the middle and lower levels, the colonel reminded the Vietnamese that their Vietcong antagonists had become stronger and better in the last three years not only because they had better weapons, including such new things as electrically detonated anti-personnel and vehicular mines, but also because they went about their work of winning the war with dedicated ardor "twenty-four hours a day, seven days a week, convinced that their cause is right." The most significant thing the colonel said, in view of Taylor's impending arrival, was that "we must develop a technique to put the squeeze on these little guys to get results" and "influence decisions at the top level." This was what Taylor had unavailingly recommended in 1961, when he suggested that Washington put some "squeeze" on the Diem government. Presumably, that is what he was being sent out to do again. To work with him, in addition to Ambassador Johnson on the political side, he had a new tough head military deputy in General William C. Westmoreland, a capable military officer sent out to replace General Harkins, who had simply refused to face facts and had believed that by being eternally optimistic he could somehow engender a response from the Vietnamese.

For a few weeks, it looked as though the Americans were finally facing the facts—that they were willing to stop being half in and half out of the war in Vietnam and to assume a more active and directive role. An increasing number of specialists in various fields were said to have been assigned to function in effect as a sort of brain trust at a high administrative level—in economics and finance, foreign relations, public affairs, and psychological warfare. It was said that more of these civilian experts (eventually to total several hundred) would be sent out in the months ahead to perform co-ordinating roles at the four military corps headquarters, and on down through the echelons of the country's forty-three provinces. Short of further military involvement, it appeared that the United States was making available the best American military brains to stimulate the Vietnamese Army effort and at the same time quietly creating a shadow government of non-military advisers. Whether this would do the trick and, as the colonel at the briefing put it, permit Washington to formulate and implement "a national campaign plan that is beyond the competence of the Vietnamese government," and really turn the tide of the war, remained to be seen. As things turned out, unfortunately, the test was never made, for the brain-trust plan was never accepted by the Vietnamese, in principle or in fact, and the United States, as it had so often done before, simply backed down and didn't insist upon its implementation. Only one of the top brain trusters, Howard Simpson, an expert in psychological warfare and public affairs, was actually appointed, and, in spite of his considerable knowledge of Vietnam (he had been there during the early Diem days), he quickly became frustrated by the endless amounts of red tape in which he found himself enmeshed and by the uncertain political situation he had to deal with.

The first problem General Taylor faced when he arrived early in July was the touchy relationship between General Khanh and General Minh, whose position as titular Chief of State had become more and more meaningless and whose relations with Khanh had gone from bad to worse. It had become apparent that Minh, though less capable, was considerably more popular than Khanh, both with the common people and with the younger officers and troops. More important, he was a particular friend of General Taylor's, with whom he had played tennis and exchanged confidences in the past. The expectation was that General Taylor would try to get Minh to co-operate more actively and fully with the Khanh government, at least temporarily. Even if Minh agreed, he now represented a fresh threat in Khanh's eyes, as well as in the eyes of a number of other "second-coup" generals, who felt their positions weakened by Taylor's arrival. Consequently, while the news of Taylor's appointment was publicly acclaimed because of his stature, the effect was to set the town further on edge and to engender a whole new series of rumors and conjectures about realignments and power plays. Professional fortune tellers, always popular in Vietnam and at the time enjoying a boom among all ranks of people, were predicting dire events.

Whatever happened next in a country that had become inured to change, Khanh, until and unless he could solidify his position with the military, was not likely to respond to the mounting pressure to "civilianize" his government. This had now become the most troubling aspect of his five-month-old regime. Much was expected of the new role of the Americans in this regard, particularly of Deputy Ambassador Johnson, who, as a political expert, was looked upon as a man who might be able to persuade Khanh to broaden the base of his government. Vietnamese pressure was being brought on Khanh to create a more democratic atmosphere as a prelude to the local elections that he had promised would soon be held preliminary to the selection of a provisional Constitutional Assembly in the fall. There was considerable doubt that the war would permit the holding of more than scattered elections in the countryside, and if they were pushed too fast, the inevitable result would be an effort by the Vietcong either to disrupt and make a mockery of them or to infiltrate further the ranks of the peasants in the villages, and guide the results to their liking. However, there had been so much talk about "reaching the people" and obtaining their support for a more concerted war effort that Khanh made a tentative move to establish a political framework for the country. His own wariness was amply demonstrated at a meeting of representatives of a score of political parties and numerous independent leaders who were called together to create a new code for the existence of parties and to make a fresh attempt to form either a single bloc, like the Indian Congress Party, or two or three strong groups. Referring obliquely to the parties' past incapacities, Khanh told the politicians, "we have to do our best to avoid these shortcomings in order not to find ourselves in the tragic situation of the French Fourth Republic, which was for a time divided because of the quarrels between the political parties, thus weakening the national forces. This painful experience should give us some food for thought." Politicians and parties, Khanh added, are "only a means to an end and not the end itself," and he urged the hundred or so leaders present to put a stop to their long history of bickering among themselves and accept their responsibility "of establishing a bridge of understanding between the people and the government."

Khanh was applauded for his sentiments, and the politicians immediately started huddling, but many of those who were at the meeting remained as skeptical of his true intentions as he was of theirs, and of their ability to get together. With the recollection of the last years of Diem and Nhu still firmly in their minds, the intellectuals (which is what the more serious politicians in Vietnam like to be called) spoke constantly in private of Khanh's own dictatorial tendencies and capacities. Beyond that, they evinced a profound contempt for most generals and for the military as a whole. What they particularly objected to was the low personal and professional qualities of many of the military leaders, especially those who had for so long been more interested in feathering their nests than in winning the war. There were plenty of civilians, too, including some politicians, who had shown the same inclination to reap profits and rewards, and who had succeeded, frequently in cahoots with one general or another. For their part, the generals looked upon the intellectuals as having frittered away their time talking in teahouses and as lacking a national conscience and purpose. The sad part about all this was that what each group said about the other was largely true. In a fundamental sense, this was what was ailing South Vietnam. This was what also had spurred the sharper and more purposeful northerners, initially guided by a more driving nationalist spirit and by now completely molded in a disciplined Communist doctrine, to create a more functioning if frugal and rigidly controlled state, and to lend direction and zeal to their Vietcong cadres fighting among the rural people of the South.

The jockeying that went on among the politicians, and between them and Khanh, at this crucial time must be considered against the special political background of South Vietnam. The situation in the country had become so chaotic because parties and their leaders had been rent by many years of the sheer struggle to survive, first under the French and then under the Diem regime. As a result, the anti-Communist movement remained deeply fragmented, and it had had little if any social and psychological impact on the peasants, who comprised eighty-five per cent of the population. In the past, revolutionary activity had always been concerned with overthrowing the Chinese invaders from the north, who ruled the country sporadically for nearly a thousand years, or other invading racial groups, like the Khmers, or unpopular local tyrants. During the first half of the century, the French colonists had proved harder to fight than previous oppressors because they were more firmly entrenched and because they combined cruel military and police methods with gloved-hand treatment for a few chosen Vietnamese who were reared and educated according to the needs and desires of French officialdom. The south was the center of both French culture and French strength. Among the individual nationalists and their scattered supporters, who between 1930 and 1945 had to operate clandestinely, mostly in Central Vietnam and in the north, there had developed a heroic sense of martyrdom but little else. In 1945, in the north, a well-organized, tough-minded native internal enemy had appeared for the first time in the form of the Vietminh, and the Vietminh front effectively took over the anti-colonial struggle. At first, as we noted earlier, it had attracted many non-Communist nationalists but none of them ever carried much voice. The older nationalist parties, like the Dai Viet and the VNQDD, in effect surrendered the nationalist cause to the revolutionary strategy and tactics of the Vietminh. As expressed to me by my previously quoted friend Dr. Dan Van Sung, one of the most astute of the Dai Viet leaders who went underground during the Diem regime and who, in mid-1964, was seeking a fresh approach with a mixed group of intellectuals, "Out of sheer irresolution, the anti- and non-Communists allowed the Vietminh to seize the initiative and take command of the resistance movement, and this proved to be the Communists' greatest victory." After the French were defeated and Diem took over, there had been no political movement in South Vietnam that had not been destroyed or disintegrated, in sharp contrast to the dynamism of Ho Chi Minh's regime in the north. Diem's most effective aides were isolated young nationalists who either had been with the Vietminh in the early years or had gone abroad to study in exile, mostly in France but also in England and the United States. These young men, essentially part of a French-trained élite, suffered a *crise de conscience* after Dienbienphu, and overnight, as individuals, they had matured politically and begun for the first time to acquire a governmental responsibility. As one of them once told me, "All our background, based on fifty years of disillusioning nationalist history, had now been telescoped, and all at once we had to do a lot of practical things we never dreamed of before. Within a few months, for example, I found myself acting as chargé d'affaires in an Asian Embassy and representing my country at Afro-Asian conferences and at the United Nations in New York."

Such contributions, while commendable, were not enough. A national purpose and goal were still lacking. As we have also seen, the Diem government, like the Kuomintang in China, gave little more than lip service to land reform and other measures for the improvement of the farmers' lives. The urban-rural cleavage in South Vietnam, which had always been great, had grown worse as the regime came under the increasing domination of Ngo Dinh Nhu.

Nhu's gravest fault, as the intellectual theoretician of the family, had probably been his mistaken conviction that he understood the countryside, and this had been demonstrated by the social and administrative failure of his strategic hamlet program and by the use of his own satraps and paramilitary units to run the villages. There had never been an effort to build up democratic and libertarian institutions or social consciousness among the people. The Vietcong had actively stepped into this void in 1958, although it can be said to have begun filling the void as early as 1956. The result, as Dr. Sung pointed out, was that the Communists had as much an open road to success in the southern rural areas after 1958 as they had had in the north ever since 1945. "We remained unprepared," Dr. Sung says. "Our fight against the Vietcong was and is a fight against a national delinquency. We have to change the social and psychological conditions that have so long been neglected and that helped the spread of Communism in the countryside."

Whether the intellectuals and politicians actually had a chance to achieve this in mid-1964 by getting away from their parlor discussions and down to the grass roots was conjectural. Fundamentally, though politics as such was less important than the creation of military security, supplemented by material measures to improve the lot of the peasants, a free political atmosphere and less military control over all phases of life seemed to be essential to the creation of confidence. During the conference Khanh summoned, there was an effort by some of the old-line party leaders, especially the Dai Viet ones, to recreate the former party groups in their old images, but there was also a healthier, fresh tendency on the part of Dr. Sung and a dozen or so other prominent intellectuals and professional men to reach a new approach, and this seemed to be the most encouraging political development in many years. "The past party groupings are no longer useful," Dr. Sung emphasized. "They were part of the clandestine revolutionary underground, but things are different now. We need something more appropriate to build toward a proper democracy, and to get away from the old-fashioned ideas. Above all, we need dedicated young cadres who are willing to work actively among the peasants and workers, and we need a political regrouping on this basis. We older people can give some guidance, and in that sense we can still be useful, but it's the young men who must carry the burden and do the hard work." The immediate objective of the new front that was being formed by Dr. Sung and his friends was to help draft a new constitution, to work toward limiting the number of political parties to a few instead of two dozen, and then to draft a platform for the front's practical political participation in the war at the village level. If the front could be formed, it was hoped that it would take an active part in the coming elections for village councils and would thus enter the political arena from the bottom instead of from the top as a new popular force in Vietnam.

Several members of the same group of intellectuals also presented a manifesto to Khanh, proposing a full-scale reorganization of the government so that a separate civilian Cabinet, functioning under the direction of the Chief of State, could relieve the Military Revolutionary Council, and Khanh as its head, of many governmental burdens, allowing it to concentrate on military matters. Though he continued to meet with representatives of the group, Khanh showed little inclination that he was willing to go anywhere nearly as far as they wanted him to go in altering the structure of the government. He seemed reluctant to turn over anything more than limited administrative responsibility to the civilians, and it is here that his ambition and his appreciation of his chances for survival came into play. In a speech to a group of officers, he reiterated his belief that the Army is still "the only organized and disciplined force capable of leading the country," and he did little to endear himself to the politicians by saying they were still engaged in "a mere scramble for individual interests." In an interview I had with him, he put it more politely. "We can only provide the formula for democracy now" he said. "We can create a foundation, the institutions for a state, but we cannot achieve full democracy for some time, perhaps for another generation or two." This was not unlike what Nhu had said.

It was typical of Khanh to take a step forward and then move back. What he had done, it soon became apparent, was open the door to the politicians out of some sense of desperation and an awareness of the need to improve his public image, but he had no intention of really stimulating free political discussion. After the conference that he addressed, a governmental inter-Ministerial committee held a few meetings with a selected number of politicians to draw up the new political code that had been the ostensible purpose of the conference, but the sessions quickly broke down into mutual recriminations of insincerity, and they were postponed indefinitely. It looked very much as though Khanh had planned it that way. Though he was more of a political animal than any of the other generals, he had no coherent political philosophy of his own, and he was operating out of pure expediency, on the basis of his private intuition. The Americans, who were later to insist strenuously that a civilian government be created, sat by during these critical political discussions and did nothing to help keep them going or to project a formula that might have led to the setting up of two or three main parties. In fact, I was astonished to discover that there was no one at the Embassy who knew any of the politicians at the meeting Khanh had called, except on a casual basis. Dr. Sung, for example, whom I had known since his underground days of the Diem regime, and who was regarded as one of the best-informed men around, asked me one day if I would introduce him "to someone at the Embassy." He had never met anyone there, he said, either since Diem's overthrow or before. No one had ever sought him out.

John Mecklin, who was the head of the United States Information Service in the period before and shortly after the coup against Diem, has commented that he was amazed that none of the American correspondents who were in Vietnam during those days made an effort to get to know top-ranking Embassy officers well, by asking them out to lunch or dinner. In the first place, despite the extremely bad relations between the American mission and the correspondents at that time, this was not quite so; in the second place, the lack of close association between correspondents and Embassy personnel was just as much the fault, and the loss, of the latter as of the former. But far more significant, it seems to me, was the failure of American officials to get to know important Vietnamese, on a private and informal basis, and the request Dr. Sung made to me emphasized this. It was a simple matter to arrange to have him meet a top man at the Embassy, but to the best of my knowledge, until he subsequently came to hold an important position in the government, I do not believe the opening meeting was ever followed up. Nor was Dr. Sung the only one I introduced to the Embassy. There were at least half a dozen other political friends of mine, who, one would have thought, would have been sought out by the Americans themselves in the normal conduct of official reporting. None was, and all of them were eager to meet Embassy people. The failure of the Americans to play a possibly important role behind the scenes during the political conference Khanh staged, for his own ulterior motives, must thus be ascribed to ignorance of the situation and, above all, to lack of personal contacts. American diplomats always seemed to want to deal only with the top men of the country, and they consequently missed a great deal of what was going on below the surface. Under the circumstances, it was no wonder that the United States always seemed to act out of expediency, meeting each crisis as it arose. Its officials on the scene, with one or two rare exceptions, didn't know the people who could have told them what was brewing.

Reforms in the Provinces

With both the internal political and the religious situations so uncertain, the military one so fluid, and the diplomatic one involving the Americans subject to constant re-evaluation, it was difficult to make a fair appraisal of the ability of the Khanh regime to deal with the vital program of pacification of the countryside. Some of the new reforms being introduced by the Vietnamese in co-operation with the Americans were beginning to show results, but they had to be measured against the discouraging fact of the long erosion in the rural areas and the added fact that good leadership among the Vietnamese remained scarce; district chiefs as well as province chiefs were still being regularly shifted, and there was little or no continuity of administration anywhere in the countryside.

One of the most insecure provinces was Long An, just south of the capital district, which I visited early in the summer of 1964. Out of Long An's population of 382,000, only 67,000, including 22,000 in the capital of Tanan and about as many in the six district capitals, could be said to be in pacified territory. Out of two hundred and sixty hamlets, only about thirty in the province had been made partly or wholly secure, and of the twelve that had allegedly been made safe since the end of January, only three had not been re-infiltrated by Vietcong agents. Usually these agents appeared in the evening or at night, cut the barbed-wire fence that had been erected all around the hamlet (or made the villagers do it), passed out propaganda, and intimidated the villagers into leaving. Two-thirds of the ninety thousand people "relocated" under the Diem regime in Long An—that is, brought in from outlying areas to new hamlets closer to the main highway of that province or in a circle around Tanan—had gone back to their former homes. Many of them went because they had better land there, and, despite the increasing demands of the Vietcong for higher taxes (an average of a sixth of a farmer's annual income and sometimes as much as a half), they preferred to live in their old surroundings. Others returned simply because the government had failed to give them the promised relocation payment of two thousand piastres. Some of this was now being rectified, and there were a few other hopeful signs. The hamlets that were more or less secure were getting much-needed fertilizer at controlled prices, free bags of rice and corn seed, and piglets to raise.

Of the six hamlets I went into, all of them no more than three kilometers off the highway—which could be safely traveled only by day—three were considered wholly pacified and three partly safe; one of the latter was attacked by the Vietcong two nights later. According to surveys made by local government teams of sixteen men engaged in psychological warfare and propaganda work, in police control, in health reform, and in training of local militia, from a third to a half of the population in these "safe" hamlets could be considered pro-government. The rest were primarily neutral, and ten or fifteen per cent of the inhabitants were pro-Vietcong. In one of the hamlets, for instance, twenty-two out of about a hundred families were known to have young men serving in the Vietcong regional or guerrilla forces, and the government agents had not yet been able to get these families to persuade any of the youths to *"chieu hoi"*—accept the government's plea to be amnestied and be received with "open arms." 'The *chieu hoi* program was one of the most important in combating the Vietcong, both to weaken the enemy's morale and to obtain much-needed intelligence, but at this time, throughout the country, only about fifteen thousand had come over to the government side, while there had been as many, if not more, desertions from the government, mostly by local Self-Defense Corps troops who were in the process of being amalgamated with the hamlet militia into a new Popular Force to protect and hold a hamlet or village area once the Army had cleared it of Vietcong. The deserters had mostly just gone back to their homes, while the soldiers remaining displayed little willingness to do their job as they were supposed to, that of maintaining twenty-four-hour patrols around the villages they were protecting instead of just staying in their blockhouses at night. One of the Self-Defense Corps posts I visited had just been attacked and obliterated by two Vietcong companies a few hours before, at two o'clock in the morning, with a loss of eleven lives, and the whole complement of twenty-eight men had been asleep inside the post when the Vietcong, in two heavily armed companies, struck across the rice paddies. As a result, two hamlets a bit farther down the dirt road off the main highway, which the Self-Defense Corps detachment was supposedly protecting, automatically lost their alleged pacified status.

None of the people my interpreter and I spoke with in the six hamlets seemed particularly enthusiastic about what the government was giving them in the way of food or relocation payments, and the reason was obvious—the Vietcong were too close by and the government's presence was still too remote and inconstant. The best they would say was that the government troops no longer made them work for nothing on village fortifications, as used to be the case, and that the soldiers now did most of the work themselves or paid the people to do it. The essential work in the new pacification program, the so-called basic civic action and consolidation work, was supposed to be carried out by various sets of teams and cadres. In each province, there were three-man teams in charge of the program: the Vietnamese province chief; the American military sector adviser, who worked primarily with the Vietnamese Army but also with the province chief on co-ordinating local military operations; and the rural affairs officer of the United States Operations Mission. Assigned to work under these teams were American and Vietnamese specialists in the fields of health, agriculture, psychological warfare, and so on, who moved around the provinces helping support the holding operations that were supposed to follow up the Army's clearing function. Until recently, this whole program had lacked direction and cohesion, and there had been a lack of understanding and motivation on the part of the Vietnamese—the failure to realize, for example, how vital good police work was in the hamlets in first rooting out and then keeping out Vietcong agents, and how important it was to establish a system of priorities in introducing practical social and economic improvements and conducting meaningful propaganda activities. Invariably, it had taken weeks, if not months, for the Ministries in Saigon to act on requests funneled up equally slowly through provincial channels. One of the most salutary of the recent reforms the Americans had been able to introduce after much persuasion now enabled each province to conduct its operation under independent budgetary control; that is, money was allotted by the U.S. Operations Mission (USOM) and by the Vietnamese government, and the province spent it according to its needs and then made an audit afterward, instead of, as before, having to apply for each request and waiting indefinitely for it first to be approved by Saigon, and then finally getting the money or materials weeks or months later. This new process of decentralization, with contracts drawn between USOM and each province and funds then spent locally for needed materials and projects under the supervision of each three-man province team, seemed to be far more efficient, but there remained a desperate need for trained personnel. The government had just begun to train the cadre teams that were to perform the basic civic action groundwork in the villages as they were made safe, first assessing needs and then seeking to have the required men and supplies brought in. These cadres were to be local people, working in their own and nearby hamlets and villages, and the hope was that there would be seven thousand of them by the end of the year, and eventually forty thousand. In addition, fifteen thousand non-government cadres were to be chosen from among various local political and religious groups to work chiefly as propagandists and psychological-war experts, trying to undo what Vietcong agents had done in the villages and projecting the government's image.

In some areas that were less insecure than Long An, the new pacification program was beginning to take hold, but it had really only begun. As one American rural adviser told me, "The big problem remains bodies—Vietnamese bodies that will do the work when they are shown how, and you have to show them. Morale is the key, and unless we can stimulate them, overcome the spiritual and bone fatigue that exists way down, then the whole show will continue to lag. The big thing is to follow through with quick concerted action on government promises and obligations. Never underestimate the political significance of fertilizer."

The Vietcong Grows Stronger

Whatever degree of success the new pacification plan might have, no one expected the Vietcong to sit idly by and not subject the government troops and the civic action workers to constant harassment and counterpressures. In organizing the countryside and running it with a combination of blandishment and terror, the Communists were continuing to show far greater administrative ability and imagination, and in several of the delta provinces, in particular, their own "shadow governments," composed of parallel military and political structures, by this time ran all the way down from the province level to the lowest hamlet.

The basic organization of the Vietcong in South Vietnam was, and still is, built around five regions, numbered five through nine and stretching down from the Seventeenth Parallel dividing the north and the south to the delta; there are also four separate tactical jungle zones, all north of Saigon. Over-all military strategy is undoubtedly formulated in Hanoi and radioed or sent by cadre couriers down to these regions and zones, which operate under the general direction of the Central Office of South Vietnam, but the various regional commanders are given considerable leeway in determining the kind of activity they want to engage in at a specific time—whether to concentrate, that is, on small or large unit actions, terrorism, sabotage, or propaganda. Political action is under the direction of the Central Committee of the National Liberation Front, which was founded in December, 1960, as an ostensible all-party movement to embrace "all patriotic South Vietnamese, irrespective of age, sex, social class, religion, or political alignment." The Front, which pretends to be a purely South Vietnamese organization, with the objective of creating a neutral coalition government in the south as a prelude to reunification with the north, has held two major congresses, one in February, 1961, and one in January, 1964, in one of the special jungle zones near the Laos border. At the one in 1964, under the chairmanship of Nguyen Huu Tho, a former Saigon lawyer, a hundred and fifty delegates—representing all sorts of vaguely defined groups and associations of peasants, students, soldiers, artists and writers, women, professional people, mountain tribes, and religious factions—heard some thirty reports about the progress the Front had been making, and the general tone was one of complete confidence that the war was being won. Subsequent military developments, certainly, have done little to diminish this tone.

As well as the Vietcong were doing militarily, they were having problems of recruitment by mid-1964. At that time, the official American estimate of hard-core Communist troops in South Vietnam was twenty-five thousand, though unofficial estimates, which I obtained from my Vietnamese friends, set the figure considerably higher, at thirty-five thousand or even fifty thousand. Regional and local forces were said to total about a hundred thousand. The latter had been badly depleted by battle injuries, for which there had been a lack of sufficient antibiotics and other drugs. The Vietcong rest camps in Laos and Cambodia were reportedly crowded, and in some villages of the delta it was said that in order to obtain replacements Communist cadres were enlisting youths of fourteen. There was no doubt that the Vietcong had just about exhausted the supply of retrained southerners—that is, of elements that had gone back north after 1954 and then been re-infiltrated into the south when the "second revolution" started in 1958. Consequently, it became necessary to strengthen the hard core by infiltrating more and more North Vietnamese into the south, and this process had already begun in the summer of 1964. By then, too, the weaponry of the Vietcong had become considerably stronger, and the regular forces were using heavy mortars and heavy machine guns, 57- and 75-millimeter recoilless rifles, as well as some new-type anti-aircraft guns. The newer weapons were being smuggled in from outside, but the bulk of ordinary guns was still being captured from the government. There was a severe ammunition shortage, however, especially for the newer, heavier weapons, and to bring in fresh amounts along the Mekong River tributaries and canals from Cambodia, or down through the long trails from Laos, was a tortuous task. Technicians were also in short supply. All this undoubtedly accounted for the fact that the early monsoonal lull had lasted longer than usual, and had only begun to be broken, in late June, by the Vietcong's first major attacks. At first, the government forces held their own surprisingly well, and in four successive battles, in the delta and in central and northern Vietnam, they won significant battles. By July, however, the pattern of Vietcong ambushes had been re-established, and the government troops were again on the defensive in most areas.

Most observers already agreed that the major battles to come would be waged in the highlands, where the Vietcong would seek to cut South Vietnam in two across its narrow belt, and that the ability of the government to meet this challenge would probably determine the outcome of the war. There was some talk at this time of making an effort to seal the border between South Vietnam and Laos in a line running across from Quang Tri, on the South Vietnamese coast, to Tchepone, a large Communist base just across the border in Laos, and then farther across to the Laos-Thailand border at Savannakhet; if this could be done, it was argued, it would be much harder for the Communists to filter down men and supplies from North Vietnam. One plan that was discussed, in Taipeh and in Saigon, involved using Chinese Nationalist troops for this operation, but nothing ever came of the idea. It was decided that, much as outside help was desired, the reappearance of Chinese troops in Vietnam would bring back too many memories of the bad manner in which Chinese occupation troops had behaved in 1945 and 1946, and that, furthermore, the Kuomintang would regard the move as an opening wedge in its long-thwarted campaign to "reinvade" the mainland.

As for North Vietnam, its capacity to go on giving assistance to the Vietcong was regarded as not diminished, despite reports of an increased tightening of belts in the north. According to officials —mostly Indians and Canadians of the International Control Commission—who were permitted to travel between Saigon and Hanoi, the city was gray and austere, compared to French times. It had been tidied up and painted, however, people were better-dressed, and, if their lives were still regimented fourteen or more hours a day, they seemed to have enough to eat. In parts of the country there were reports of some undernourishment but no famine. However, the population, estimated at eighteen million, was said to be rising to the point where, in two or three years, the annual rice output, already apparently at its peak in point of land utilization and application of fertilizer, would no longer be sufficient. Some supplementary crops, such as home-grown manioc and a little imported wheat and maize, couldn't fill the gap. At the moment, though, as a friend of mine who had just come back commented, "The fact that they talk publicly and in the press about food shortages shows that things can't be that bad yet. Naturally, they need the south's rice, but their diet is not that restricted. They have some meat and fish, and the stalls in Hanoi almost always have fresh vegetables and fish for sale. The soldiers are well fed and there is certainly no attitude of despair. I shook hands with Ho Chi Minh the other day, and I've never seen him look so pudgy and pink."

K

CHAPTER IX

❧

Seeds of Chaos

The series of political crises that began in South Vietnam in the summer of 1964 clearly demonstrated the country's inability to create a strong and vital government that could unite the many divisive elements and provide the desperately needed inspirational leadership in the war. This crucial period also revealed the growing inability of the Americans to deal with the ever more complex Vietnamese situation and, either through persuasion or a more direct application of diplomatic leverage, to avoid the catastrophes that helped push South Vietnam further toward collapse and defeat. Neither the South Vietnamese leaders nor the American policymakers, in Saigon or in Washington, seemed to comprehend sufficiently the nature of the impending disaster; nor did they know how to come to grips with the fact that the war, in the deepest sense, was a political one, requiring techniques and solutions that had to be superimposed on the military conflict, or joined with it in a way that would be more than complementary—that would, in fact, provide a conscious, driving motivation to combat the zealous, highly organized, and effective methods devised and being executed successfully by the Vietcong.

It may be questioned whether South Vietnam was capable, in view of its recent past, of establishing a central government that could cope with the situation. There were by now many factors and arguments that could be cited to support a negative answer. Perhaps, as some of the most experienced and thoughtful Vietnamese maintained, what was needed was not more, but less government, at least at the top. They suggested that it would be more efficacious to approach the whole problem from a regional point of view. In this context, the country might be divided not into forty or fifty provinces, which almost everyone agreed was too many, but into ten or twelve or at most twenty. These larger provincial areas, headed by chiefs with the full confidence of a functioning but not overweaning or cabalistic central government in Saigon, could then become the real nuclei of the war effort. In such a scheme, the four cumbersome military corps would be eliminated, and the largest Army units would be divisions or brigades, working in conjunction with the newly organized Regional and Popular Forces (the successors to the Civil Guard and to the Self-Defense Corps and hamlet militia) under the direction of the province chiefs, who would be qualified military men with political deputies. Such a plan of organization would be closer to what the Vietcong themselves had achieved, and in many respects would appear to be a more satisfactory way of combating a guerrilla enemy.

In lieu of the adoption of such a plan—it was discussed and even considered officially, though it was mostly favored by Vietnamese in Saigon and Americans in Washington who were among the "outs" and not the "ins"—the idea that there *had* to be a strong central government in Saigon persisted. Certainly if there was to be any kind of consistent war effort, it was important to obtain a government that could maintain power long enough to put some kind of plan into effect without being subjected to constant harassment and the danger of repeated coups. Here again, given the divisive elements that existed in South Vietnam and the increasing number of Vietcong agents in key places, nothing short of a miracle would have improved the situation, even *if* the United States had shown a firmer hand. In tracing the background and build-up of the crises that took place in 1964, one must first go back to the November revolution of 1963, when a whole set of inchoate and contesting forces was released. As we have seen, during the nine years of the Diem regime, and during the long period of the French before that, there had been no freedom of expression, no democratic forms of any sort. When Diem fell, the dam burst. The desire to say what one wanted and to play a role in the new emerging society was all but obsessive, and found expression more in clichés than in reasoned, constructive terms. This was true of political parties, of the religious movements, of student organizations, and of the press. Democracy was a new game which everyone wanted to play without understanding the rules. Moreover, at a time when the nation was in peril, the rules would have to be limited. But the military men who had taken power knew little about political theory or methods, and had no idea of how to design limited freedoms. The newly emancipated elements who were demanding more freedom had no idea how to temper these demands in view of the problems of a nation at war. On top of all that, there was a deep bitterness, the heritage of long years of oppression, and out of this grew a desire for personal and group vengeance. In such an atmosphere, chaos was all but inevitable.

The November junta, as noted, did practically nothing to meet the social and political challenge. General Khanh, when he took over, began to move in the direction of establishing democratic forms but soon recoiled, as in his quickly abandoned "experiment" to open the door for the political parties to get together. As the issue between the Buddhists and the Catholics mounted, with each side making exaggerated claims of persecution, the students began stirring again. In Saigon and Hué, they conducted rallies against neutralism, for more political freedom, and so on, indicating more clearly than anything else that they didn't really know what they wanted. In attempting to deal with these essentially political matters, General Khanh found himself in deep water. In mid-July, with discontent still rising, he tried to counter it by rallying the nation in favor of an attack on North Vietnam. This was not yet American policy, however, and it brought him into sharp conflict with Ambassador Taylor, doing little to strengthen the rather tenuous relationship that had quickly grown up between them because of the ties between Taylor and General Minh. At this time, too, Khanh was suddenly faced with his first threat of a coup. The instigator of the plot was Dr. Hoan, Khanh's disgruntled Vice-Premier. Hoan had the backing of his Dai Viet aides and sympathizers, who included a number of top military leaders; the only thing that made the plotters hesitate, apparently, was a fear that even if they captured the government, they would be unable to win the support of the Americans. It had become an accepted "coup rule" in Saigon by now that no coup could succeed if the Americans didn't support or at least countenance it.

As a result of admonitions from General Taylor, Khanh, a bit sheepishly, toned down his demands for attacks against the north, though he still maintained his right, as the head of an independent nation, to go on making them. Just then, when his position was most shaky, Khanh got what he wanted—on a small scale. On August 2nd, in an action considerably short of a Pearl Harbor, three North Vietnamese motor patrol boats, part of what was aptly called its "mosquito fleet," ineffectively attacked the American destroyer *Maddox* about thirty miles off the North Vietnam coast. On July 30th, three days earlier, the North Vietnamese claimed that American warships had shelled two of their islands, and though Washington officially denied it, it later became known that two islands harboring radar installations *had* been attacked by gunfire—not by warships, in the usual sense, but by motor patrol boats mostly manned by American-trained Vietnamese and some other nationals. Similar commando- and sabotage-type raids had previously been admitted by the South Vietnamese, but not by the Americans, to have taken place in the north. The attack on the *Maddox,* and another one on August 4th against the *Maddox* and a second American destroyer about sixty miles off the coast, may have been the result of these island attacks, or they may have been decided on by Hanoi for the twofold purpose of seeing how the United States would react and how serious the Chinese were in their promises of giving assistance. At any rate, American carrier-based planes, on August 4th and 5th, attacked and destroyed about two dozen North Vietnamese patrol boats and supporting facilities, including an oil depot, along a hundred-mile stretch of North Vietnamese coast. The sharp American response was undoubtedly designed to prove to Peking and Hanoi that we were really not "paper tigers" and that we meant what we had been saying all along about using all means at our disposal to protect and support South Vietnam.

As far as General Khanh was concerned, the most salutary effect of the raids was to shore up his government at the very moment when he needed it most, and in view of his earlier demands for raids there was some irony in their taking place when they did. In Saigon, where any chicanery is believed possible, there were even those who at first suspected that Khanh had somehow contrived to arrange the initial attack on the *Maddox* in order to obtain the response he wanted. If this was obviously untrue, it was held possible that the United States had goaded the North Vietnamese into firing at the *Maddox* by venturing at some point into the twelve-mile offshore limit set by Hanoi, and that we did so not only to test the mettle of the North Vietnamese but to help Khanh over his political crisis. At any rate, the American retaliation was welcomed by Khanh— not like a man who may just have won a reprieve from collapse, but with the poised assurance of a truly vindicated prophet. In a radio address, he solemnly called on the Vietnamese "to keep calm so as to clearly see your responsibilities in the face of events, brush aside private differences, and willingly submit yourself to the national discipline." What he did not do (which many Vietnamese, though not General Taylor or anyone at the Embassy officially, told him he should have done) was arrest the leaders of the plot against him, including the dissident military elements, and he thereby allowed the seeds of his opposition to grow. Instead, on August 7th Khanh placed the country under a state of emergency, which included a number of proscriptions and restrictions on the movements and liberties of the Vietnamese population; full censorship was reimposed and, among other things, the distribution of food was placed under government control.

Nine days later, on August 16th, Khanh made his biggest blunder. Acting precipitously, he ignored various drafts for a new constitution submitted to him by political groups and by independent jurists, and issued a new, hastily drawn, and badly conceived constitutional charter of his own that gave him virtually complete powers. The Americans, taken by surprise, were dismayed, although they were not against Khanh solidifying his leadership. Khanh had shown the draft to Ambassador Taylor and to Deputy Ambassador Johnson, and they persuaded him to tone down certain passages and insert a bill of rights, but they had not advised him to hold off altogether, as would have seemed the wise course. Khanh got the Military Revolutionary Council to approve his new charter at a special session and to elect him President of South Vietnam. As such, he was able to get rid of a thorn in his side—one that many felt the Americans should have helped him remove sooner. This was General Minh, the inactive and sulky Chief of State, whose post the new charter abolished. Relations between Khanh and Minh had completely deteriorated, though Ambassador Taylor was still trying to patch them up, which was just about as impossible as the American attempt in 1963 to separate Diem from his brother Ngo Dinh Nhu. Taylor's efforts only led Khanh to become more suspicious of the Ambassador, even though Taylor kept reassuring him of American support. Had the Americans acted differently and dealt more resolutely with the Minh problem, the critics afterward said, Minh could have been prevailed upon to leave the country, at least temporarily, and the air would have been cleared much sooner.

Khanh Temporizes

The week between the 16th and the 23rd of August was probably the most critical. Had Khanh, during this brief time, made some effort to follow through on his pledge to establish a more broadly based civilian government to work under his new authority, the students and the Buddhists might not have reacted as strongly as they did against the new charter, and the troubles that followed might have been avoided. But Khanh did nothing, and by now it was apparent that his behavior pattern showed him to be an odd mixture of a brave and daring man with a surface sophistication that did not altogether hide a deep unsureness of himself. This unsureness, and his response to it, revealed a basic character flaw: he kept veering from absolute immobility—the incapacity either to take strong measures when he should or to make concessions when they seemed advisable—to a condition of panic, which invariably led him to do one thing or the other at the wrong time and in the wrong way, thereby playing into the hands of his enemies. At this critical moment, the Americans also did nothing. In fact, during that week,

Ambassador Taylor did not even see Khanh. Privately, several top Vietnamese, including some members of Khanh's Cabinet, warned their American friends that disaster was coming if Khanh was not pressured to take some steps to placate the civilian and religious elements, but the advice, though passed on to the proper Embassy authorities, was not acted upon.

By August 21st, when the lid began to blow off with the first serious student demonstration, it was already too late, though political action by Khanh within a few hours might still have avoided the worst. At this point, however, Khanh began to temporize. He met with a group of students, agreed to some of their demands for a liberalizing of restrictions, and drew diagrams on a blackboard in his office to show them that the new constitution really contained a proper balance of powers, which was scarcely true. The students remained dissatisfied and continued to hold disorderly rallies, and in the two days that followed, they attacked the radio station and the Information Ministry for allegedly having distorted their views. As early as August 21st, too, Buddhist dissatisfaction with Khanh had become openly manifest. On that day, Thich Tam Chau, as President of the Buddhist Institute for Secular Affairs, declared that "our stand is getting tougher now," and it was made clear that the Buddhists were going to use "pressure as well as diplomacy" to get Khanh to take action against their alleged oppressors—namely, the former Diemist Can Lao Party members. Already, Buddhist cadres were beginning to move in on the student demonstrations, while Vietcong agents in the city acted quietly on the fringes of the student mobs to incite disorder. The roles of the Buddhist extremists and of the Communists were separate but parallel, and they had a joint destructive effect. The Communist position, of course, was an obvious one. The Vietcong not only clearly helped provoke the critical situation by working among certain elements, especially the various student factions and the random mobs of hoodlums, but also, once the violence began, Communist agents brought into the city from nearby areas fanned it and benefited from it as much and as long as they could. During this period, they concentrated almost totally on a political rather than a military offensive.

The situation involving the Buddhists was more complicated. The militant Buddhists had been largely responsible for provoking the government crisis in the first place, forcing it to come to a head in the streets. Their leading strategist was still Thich Tri Quang, who the Americans were now willing to concede might be "a dangerous man," whose long-term aim was to make Vietnam a Buddhist neutralist nation, on the order of Ceylon or Burma, and whose short-term aim, it was apparent in the August crisis, was to guide events in such a way that his own position among the Buddhist masses would be enhanced, enabling him to emerge as something of an autonomous "religious war lord" in the central and perhaps in the lower part of South Vietnam. While his trained organizers worked to gain a hold on the student demonstrators on August 21st, it became obvious that whether the Buddhists and the Communists were working together or not, they had the same objectives, and that the victims of this subversion were the bona fide student leaders and their ranks. Student leaders completely lost control of their own people as the Buddhist cadres kept going back to the pagodas for orders and then returning to the scene of the demonstrations. The Buddhists, at this time, also injected themselves into the broader political situation by demanding that the government cease its continued acts of repression against them, and Tri Quang cleverly kept the ball rolling by alternating a moderate line and a tough one. The moderate line was expressed by Thich Tam Chau, who, despite having greater influence in the south than Tri Quang, in this case had to go along with him in self-defense if he wanted to maintain his position as a symbolic leader among the Buddhist people in the countryside. Complicating the matter further was the effort of the Catholics to provide a kind of buffer force between the Vietcong and the Buddhists. This was tactically sound, but the Vietcong-directed hoodlums infiltrated the Catholic columns, too, inciting clashes with the Buddhists. Throughout, the Communists worked hard to set one religious group against the other, and the hoodlums, including a large number of delinquents who had recently been dismissed from a coal mine labor camp, were their chief instruments.

By August 23rd, with the formation of a new Movement for the

Salvation of Buddhism in Danger, similar to the League for the Salvation of Buddhism that had led the attack against Diem, the Buddhists were moving in high gear. As the student demonstrations continued, bombs were set off at various places in town, probably by the Vietcong, and by now Buddhist and student demonstrations had also spread to other cities, notably to Hué and Danang. The position of the government was still that "the use of force on our side could give our enemies reason to overthrow us." The enemies, including the old Dai Viet crowd, were certainly active, and on the night of August 24th there was another coup rumor; I found out later that the Dai Viet generals had indeed been ready to move that evening, but that General Khiem, the Minister of Defense, who had been wavering all along between supporting the Dai Viet and sticking with Khanh, whom he had helped bring to power, advised the Dai Viet leaders to wait.

General Khanh, whenever faced with a severe crisis, had tended to withdraw into a kind of ivory tower. He was now commuting almost nightly between Saigon and his retreat and private base of operations at Cap St. Jacques, on the coast about forty miles southeast of the capital. He was there on the evening of August 24th when he asked the three top Buddhist bonzes, Thich Tri Quang, Thich Thien Minh (Tri Quang's chief aide), and Thich Tam Chau to come down for consultation. They peremptorily refused, so Khanh rushed up to Saigon. They met that evening and the Buddhists handed Khanh a list of eight demands, including the elimination of all Can Lao influences, the abolition of the August 16th charter, the establishment of government councils to assure the full freedom of religion and expression, and the holding of free elections by the first of November, 1965. Instead of patiently discussing each point with the three Buddhist leaders, Khanh made the revealing mistake of telling them he wanted to consult the Americans. At one o'clock on the morning of August 25th, an unusual conference took place between Ambassadors Taylor and Johnson and Khanh, during which Taylor "unofficially" advised Khanh to accept the Buddhist demands in principle but to be tougher than he had been and not to buckle down to any minority. The conference lasted until three in the morning, and by five Khanh issued a communiqué in which he promised to "revise" the new constitution, diminish press censorship, rectify local abuses by arranging trials by "field courts" for alleged guilty elements, and permit continued demonstrations with the proviso that anyone responsible for acts of disorder would be punished. This was not enough to satisfy the students or the Buddhists, and later that morning an angry crowd of twenty-five thousand gathered in front of the Prime Minister's office near the center of town. Calmly and bravely, Khanh faced the mob, denying that he wanted to be a dictator. He made no further promises to meet the crowd's demands, especially for the total abrogation of the August 16th charter and for the establishment of a civilian government, and he made no effort, as he had indicated he was prepared to do when he had spoken with Taylor, to have the unruly mob dispersed. He withdrew as suddenly as he had appeared, and then, in midafternoon, came the stunning announcement from military headquarters that he was quitting, that the August 16th charter would be withdrawn, and that the Military Revolutionary Council would meet the next day to choose a new Chief of State and would then dissolve itself.

On the twenty-sixth and twenty-seventh of August, the Military Revolutionary Council met in the spacious headquarters compound. From what I learned afterward it was a highly histrionic session, during which a dozen or so of the generals openly wept and engaged in a mass *mea culpa* performance, blaming themselves for various failures of the past several months. Apparently, this was chiefly for the benefit of the colonels on the Council, to whom the general officers wanted to justify themselves, if only because the colonels now held the balance of power and were in the position not only of making decisions but also of taking decisive action of their own to alter the course of events. Khanh had hurt his cause by bringing to the meeting the three generals of the first junta who had been accused of the pro-French plot and had remained under house surveillance in Dalat. Now Khanh hoped to forestall a new bid for power by General Minh by raising the specter of the return of the three generals to office, since they presumably would be reinstalled with Minh. His plan backfired when the Council refused to seat the generals, and

after spending most of August 26th in a private house in the headquarters compound they were whisked back to Dalat. The maneuver
helped Khanh's other chief competitor for power, Defense Minister
General Khiem, whom a minority in the Council supported for leadership. The Council was also annoyed at the manner in which Khanh
had announced it would be dissolved without having its entire membership consulted.

Anarchy Grips the Streets

The moment of this agonizing period I shall remember most vividly
came about nine o'clock on the evening of Thursday, August 27th,
while I was having dinner with some friends on the veranda of the
Continental Hotel. It had been a day of horror that had its inception
shortly after noon, when the customary quiet of the siesta hour had
been broken by hundreds of bicyclists, mostly young men and women
in their twenties and thirties, suddenly appearing all over town,
heading in every direction. This, as it turned out, was the beginning of the huge predominantly Catholic demonstrations, in response to the mass Buddhist and student turnouts of the previous
five days, and the bicyclists were heading for some twenty designated
gathering points in the city. In midafternoon, at the biggest of these
demonstrations, in front of military headquarters, six in the crowd
had been killed when Army troops, lined up inside the gates behind
coils of barbed wire, had sent shots ricocheting down off the cement
ceiling of the entrance structure and up from the street in front of
the surging mob. At dusk, I had had occasion to visit a Vietnamese
friend along one of the city's busiest thoroughfares, and, riding in a
small taxi through a dusty traffic jam that was even worse than usual
for that time of day, I had counted a score of young men with
bloodied, bandaged heads or wounded arms and legs—the result of
battles with knives and clubs that had raged in front of the radio station, in the market area, and at other isolated spots, and that had left
a total of thirteen dead, including the six at military headquarters, and
at least forty seriously injured. Now, at 9 P.M., the city seemed to have
calmed down, but as we sipped our coffee, we heard fresh shouts

from up the street (Tu Do, the main street that runs alongside the hotel). The shouts grew louder and then, running pell-mell by us in the street and on the sidewalks, came some three hundred bare-footed youngsters, dressed in torn shirts and shorts. They ranged in age from eight to seventeen; the big ones carried large sticks, about four feet long, while the small ones, in keeping with their size, brandished shorter clubs, a foot or so in length. As they swept past, heading for a nearby statue commemorating the death of a young girl killed by police a year earlier during the Buddhist disorders, the piercing shrieks of the small boys sounded like weird bird cries above the raucous voice-changing shouts of the older ones. We quickly deter-mined that these were not simply Buddhist youths but predominantly "Teddy boys" and rag-tailed kids. It was apparent that someone—later fairly well established to be an agent, or agents, of the Vietcong —had collected them, paid them, and furnished them with their sticks. They had obviously been whipped into a frenzy, and as I watched them swing into the broad square in front of the hotel, I was reminded of William Golding's novel *Lord of the Flies*. I had never imagined how real his story, of malevolence and murder taking hold of a group of youngsters, could be, and these stampeding club-wielding boys, I thought, were the saddest manifestation so far of what looked like Vietnam's impending disintegration.

The histrionics that took place during the youthful procession downtown were only slightly less emotional than those that had gone on during the second day of the Military Revolutionary Council meet-ing. After two days of weeping and bickering, and after the failure of General Khiem to name General Minh Prime Minister and himself Chief of State, General Khanh was renamed Prime Minister, but he refused to accept the post with either of his two rivals as President. When the Council then voted to reinstall him alone, he again refused, because he felt that he had lost face and that the minority vote against him, while relatively small, was an affront. At this juncture, what appeared to be the totally unworkable triumvirate of Khanh, Minh, and Khiem was chosen, as a last resort, and Khanh appeared alone before the Catholic crowd at the gates, to apologize for the deaths of the six who had been shot down and to plead for unity and patience. Thereupon, Khanh, in a state of total fatigue, had taken off to rest in Dalat. As we sat around the hotel, after the departure of the hoodlum teen-age mob, no one professed to understand what really had happened during the day of deliberations at military headquarters. The new "troika" of generals was supposed to guide the nation for two months, during which time an attempt would be made to form a new government, though there still was a caretaker one theoretically headed by General Khanh as Prime Minister; he had definitely resigned as President. Actually, no one knew just what Khanh's status really was, or what kind of interim government, if any, was in control, and the situation looked hopeless in the light of the lack of leadership and prevailing anarchy.

The anarchy continued the next day. On the morning of Friday, August 28th, the hooligans were back, rampaging through Saigon, and on that day four more persons, including at least one member of the youthful mob, were killed as street battles between Buddhists and Catholics and mixed bands of hooligans spread throughout the city. Unarmed police and unarmed troops stood by and watched as the mobs roved at will, commandeering trucks and buses. It was not until the following day that law and order were re-established and the police, with the help of paratroopers brought into town, were told to keep the demonstrators in check, with guns and bayonets, if necessary. By then the disintegration had become so great that I had grave doubts as to Vietnam's ability to recover and survive. As the government foundered, and General Khanh remained in Dalat in a state of exhaustion, pondering his future and the future of his country, the capital sank into a vacuum. The so-called "troika" that had been formed never even met officially, and Nguyen Xuan Oanh, one of the three Vice-Premiers previously under Khanh, was designated to be acting Prime Minister while Khanh was resting and thinking. But Oanh was not taken seriously because of his pretense of importance and because he spoke English better than Vietnamese.

There were repeated rumors of a new coup, and the moment seemed ripe for one. On the one hand, the Dai Viet was again threatening to take action, and a second threat was now posed by the so-called "colonels' group," composed of commanding officers of certain divisions and regiments and of junior officers below them who had all played a decisive role in the Diem coup. Having felt cheated out of the spoils of victory at that time, they had become even more discontented with the manner in which the bickering generals had been running the country. On the night of September 2nd, dissident troops, most of them aligned with the Dai Viet leaders, began to move on the city, and only the quick response of some of the colonels' forces that had got wind of the plot stopped the advance by midnight. For the time being, it appeared, the colonels decided to string along with General Khanh and give him a chance to resurrect himself. Both the Buddhists and the students, however, were continuing to add to the political turmoil by issuing veiled threats of further action, while in Central Vietnam, in Hué, a burgeoning movement with distinct overtones of separatism was attacking the temporary government.

The tactics of the Hué group, called the People's Revolutionary Committee, bore the trademark of Thich Tri Quang—of saying one thing and meaning another. Tri Quang himself, his leading lay lieutenant, Dr. Le Khac Quyen (the medical dean at the University of Hué, who was the official head of the new committee), and Sub-General Nguyen Chanh Thi, the highly emotional commander of the 1st Division who had upheld the students' right to demonstrate, all publicly denied that they sought to establish an autonomous government. Although the leaders of the group professed to be anti-Communist and anti-neutralist, the language and most of the political and economic aims of the committee sounded very much, both in tone and content, like those of the Communists. Dr. Quyen, a thickset man with whom I had previously had a long conversation, seemed a strange mixture of fuzzy ideologist (talking about wanting to establish syndicates of workers and professional people à la Mussolini or some early European Socialists) and of impractical politician; and he obviously had a lot of opportunist in his make-up. It was apparent that he had no love for the Saigon government. He had now indicated his committee's intention to call a national convention, possibly on its own, "to establish a revolutionary and clean government," and to summon a series of smaller provincial assemblies to achieve the same aim. To all appearances, these would be "rump parliaments," at a time when the government faced the difficult, if not impossible, task of selecting a new National Legislature to represent all elements in the country. In sum, the Central Vietnamese leaders, while still pledging a guarded loyalty to Saigon, gave every indication of being ready to go their own way, if and when they decided it was desirable. Their awareness that Central Vietnam was a poor region economically, without much rice, which would have trouble going it alone, was probably a deterrent, but the big danger lay in their deciding to risk it, in which event a large chunk of Vietnam would undoubtedly go neutralist and would soon succumb to the Communists.

On September 4th, General Khanh finally returned to Saigon from his Dalat retreat and announced a tentative formula for getting the country back on its feet and for establishing an administrative machinery for two months, after which a new government of civilians was supposed to replace the military. Even if the civilian elements could get together to choose a leader and a Cabinet, which seemed highly unlikely, and even if the religious as well as the political climate became peaceful, which seemed even more unlikely, the formula for implementing the new institutions of democracy, including the establishment of a new National Congress, was bound to be difficult to apply. As the situation stood early in September, the clock had more or less been turned back to August 15th, before Khanh promulgated his constitutional charter that had caused all the trouble. In an odd sort of way, however, he had emerged as a less lonely and a somewhat more heroic figure than before, and he had gained the respect of people he had previously been unable to inspire. Almost everyone was glad to have him back after the fortnight of turbulence and uncertainty, and if he was not altogether the indispensable man of the hour, he was just about the only one with a chance of holding things together. It remained to be seen whether he would be able to get rid of the influences that had alienated the Buddhists, and of the elements that had been plotting against him.

Khanh was able to produce a letter pledging support and unity, signed by both Thich Tri Quang and Thich Tam Chau. I was told by several reliable sources that this letter was paid for by the government to the tune of 22,000,000 piastres ($230,000, at the official rate). It is not unusual in Vietnam for this sort of thing to take place, and the Buddhists needed money for their mass organization drive, in addition to which, having gained most of the concessions they wanted from the government and having established themselves more firmly in the central part of the country, they could afford to relax briefly and put up a show of unity before making new demands. It remained doubtful, however, that the Buddhists, at least the dominant Tri Quang elements, would really want to co-operate with Khanh; while they might pretend to on the surface, their basic aims to establish Buddhist supremacy in the country remained paramount. Despite the letter of support given to Khanh, Tri Quang's well-disciplined organization soon let it be known that such support would continue only if the government proved itself to be "really revolutionary and democratic." "The revolution is not yet complete," Tri Quang himself had told me in an interview I had with him. If the regime did not prove satisfactory—and the Buddhists established themselves as the sole judge of this—they threatened to provoke more demonstrations and, in conjunction with the students, to call national strikes, including closing down the Saigon markets. Confidently, the Buddhists announced that they considered themselves "directly related to anyone joining the ranks of the people ready to sacrifice himself for Buddhism and the Fatherland." These were bold and broad pronouncements that the Vietcong could only welcome, and there was certainly no doubt that the Communists would continue to do what they could to encourage more discontent and rebellion; in fact, from this time on, Vietcong infiltration of agents into Saigon picked up noticeably. Most significantly, the Communists had begun to send south a number of high-ranking military and political men who had relatives in the Saigon government and in the Army. It is common in Vietnam for families to be divided, and many southerners have brothers and sisters and other relatives in the north. The fact that the Communists were now, for the first time, using family relationships in making a direct or indirect approach to South Vietnamese leaders was an indication of how shaky they believed the government to be, and of how close to victory they thought they might be.

Khanh did succeed, upon his return to office, in getting rid of one troublemaker: he forced Dr. Hoan's resignation as Vice-Premier, and the Dai Viet leader went abroad to Japan. For the moment, Khanh also had the assurance of all his top Army commanders that they would back him; he flourished a letter they had all signed, too. Nevertheless, the government obviously stood on shaky foundations. Unity in the Army, if it lasted—a big "if" always—was only one prerequisite for a successful effort to appeal to the masses over the head of Tri Quang and the Buddhist agitators, and, in effect, to neutralize them. The government still faced the task of creating an image of its own, and of formulating an institutional framework for the nation that the bulk of people in the countryside could comprehend and believe in.

In retrospect, this was probably the most crucial moment in Vietnam since the coup that overthrew Diem. Unless further disruption and violence were met firmly, while simultaneously the government responded to the legitimate demands of the religious, student, and political groups for more civilian control and for the safeguarding of individual liberties, then indeed there was scant hope for the future. The paradox was a built-in one. A nation at war, and fighting an uphill battle, had to be forcefully led, and the military had to play the key role. At the same time, the democratic aspirations of the people, whether naturally expressed or enunciated for whatever motives by pressure groups, had to be served. More than one nation had fallen in the attempt to walk such a tightrope, and for Vietnam the problem was all the more difficult because a disciplined and effective enemy already controlled a good part of its territory.

CHAPTER X

❦

Vietnam in Limbo

Almost from the moment General Khanh had seized power, the American position had been that he was "our boy," and it was made clear, in repeated statements both in Saigon and in Washington, that we were ready to back him fully in his efforts to sustain a government and conduct the war against the Vietcong. The chief architect of this initial policy of staunch support had been Secretary of Defense McNamara, who no longer objected to the war being described as "McNamara's war." A stepped-up schedule of American aid had been initiated to include more economic and military assistance, and more American rural affairs experts and technicians as well as military officers had been sent out to work on pacification in the provinces and to help out in the already overstaffed Saigon administration. But what we had failed to do, particularly during the August crisis, as noted, was to render the sort of firm on-the-scene political guidance that Khanh, whose dependence on the Americans was enhanced by his lack of close Vietnamese associates, so desperately needed. This was one of those irretrievable moments when it might have been advisable to go beyond persuasion and to hold out to the impulsive Khanh, about to embark on his dismal dictatorial adventure, the possibility of withdrawal of American support for him if he persisted in his course. But the Americans were uncertain themselves at this juncture, and as a result United States diplomatic efforts were as much off in their timing, and in their technique, as were

283

Khanh's ill-conceived and rather juvenile maneuvers and actions. It didn't matter, in the final analysis, whether this was the fault of Ambassador Taylor or of the State Department, of the Pentagon or of the White House in Washington—diplomacy just failed. It was obvious that the relationship between Taylor and Khanh was not nearly as close as the one that had existed between Khanh and Ambassador Lodge and that this had already led to the suspicion that the United States might have overreached itself in backing Khanh so strongly. If this suspicion was justified, then personal diplomacy on Taylor's part alone should have been fully invoked.

What came out of it all was the feeling, among other diplomats and among correspondents in Saigon, that American policy contained some fundamental flaws of its own, and that the United States was prone to make as many political mistakes of judgment, and errors of commission or omission, as the French had made in earlier days. In the second half of 1964, though the Americans were to play a more active role in the worsening situation, increasing criticism was forthcoming from the various embattled Vietnamese factions, none of whom seemed to approve of what the United States was doing; and charges of American "interference" became part of the deepening internal political struggle. This was purposeful—in terms of Vietnamese propaganda—and ironic in a diplomatic sense. It was ironic in that, on the one hand, the United States still failed to spell out what kind of political program or policy it was willing not only to talk about but to act on in Vietnam, while, on the other hand, it continued to "interfere" by backing one man or another, naïvely hoping that a panacea would somehow evolve. When the man of the moment either disappointed or turned against them, or both, the Americans were left out on a limb, having failed to provide themselves with an alternative. As a British diplomatic friend of mine put it, "The trouble with you people is that you always think only of Plan A, and if that doesn't work you never seem to have any Plan B or Plan C in mind."

Part of this general flaw seemed to be the inability to look both behind and beyond the extremely complex events and anticipate some of the more undesirable outcomes, in terms of group motives and reactions as well as individual ambitions. This is not to say that, in the confusing months that followed Khanh's return to power in September, 1964, the United States Embassy did not follow events carefully. Although events were followed, what was too often lacking, it seemed to others who were also following them, was an understanding of their underlying causes. This required, above all, a cultivated and intimate association with the Vietnamese who were more deeply concerned with events, as well as with those who were playing important subsurface or shadow roles. It was particularly unfortunate, in the opinion of many non-official observers, that the one or two Americans who knew most about what was going on, and who had, through their own efforts, built up close friendships with Vietnamese leaders over a period of years, left Saigon during this time. The departure of one such man who incurred Ambassador Taylor's displeasure was felt especially keenly because he had been the sole intimate link with Khanh and with many other officers, as well as with some of the civilians most deeply involved in the series of crises between September and mid-February, 1965. This misuse, or nonuse, of men whose personal friendships, knowledge, and experience make them particularly qualified to understand and to interpret the meaning of events—and who could be in a good position to help determine their consequences—seems to be a peculiar American diplomatic failing. It often appears to be due to bureaucratic as well as personal jealousy or animosity, but in *purely* bureaucratic terms there is something else, too, which another foreign diplomatic friend of mine has summed up as follows: "The whole American system has become so cumbersome in its own right, so convoluted and involuted, that it's practically impossible nowadays for you people to make a decision in a hurry and to act on it, despite your rapid-fire communications system. Too many matters, it seems, have to be referred to Washington, where they go through myriad channels, from the White House to the State Department to the Pentagon to the Central Intelligence Agency, and so on. The result is that practically nothing gets done in time. The same thing is true, I suppose, of all of us to a degree, but the American system of government is especially geared to provoke such uncertainty and delay." This appraisal, in the case of Ambassador Taylor and of his several predecessors in Vietnam is, to a greater or lesser degree, I think, a valid one. While Taylor, a military man without much political experience or comprehension, made some decisions on the spot, the complicated nature of the Vietnamese problem, and the fact that the whole issue of Vietnam, in an election year back home, was one in which the Johnson administration took a special interest, resulted in much of what was done or not done in Saigon being based on Washington's prior approval or disapproval. Resilience and the application of imaginative diplomacy in the field consequently were inhibited.

None of this criticism can in any way minimize the main reasons for the further disintegration that took place in Vietnam in late 1964 and early 1965; namely, the inherent jealousy and mistrust that existed among almost all Vietnamese generals, politicians, and religious leaders and that virtually precluded any cohesion in the war effort. As one high American diplomat, newly arrived on the scene, asked almost ingenuously, "Is there any Vietnamese who has a good thing to say about another one?" Certainly the divisiveness that had been flagrant ever since the overthrow of the Diem regime reached new limits of destructiveness at this time. Some of my friends kept citing an old Vietnamese saying, "At times like these, insects turn into human beings." Individual was pitted against individual, and group against group, in the manner of the jungle, and greed for power and money and the desire for self-preservation, rather than the preservation of the country in time of war, appeared to be paramount concerns.

The "Troika" Falls

In the wake of the mid-August and late-August crisis, after the Americans had urged General Khanh to return to power as Premier, General Minh again became, in effect, Chief of State, though he didn't hold the title. As chairman of the so-called "troika" of generals that included himself, Khanh, and Tran Thien Khiem, he signed legislation, gave out and received diplomatic credentials, but, most important, he was made responsible for appointing a new High National Council to represent all elements in the population. The Council was to prepare a new constitution for Vietnam preparatory to the government's return to civilian leadership, hopefully within a month or so. Minh's appointment did nothing to lessen the tension between him and Khanh, which the previous crisis had brought to a head, but it at least gave him a specific task that was in line with Khanh's own pledge to hand the government over to civilians again as soon as possible.

At the end of the first week in September, Ambassador Taylor returned to Washington, where he gave what was described as a "cautiously optimistic" report on the Vietnam political and military situation. The latter, he said, had not been too seriously affected by the former, and while General Khanh faced "a very hard task" of creating a new provisional regime in a short time, "he is very sincerely committed to principles of getting the military out of the government" and had already dismissed the Ministers who were military men from the Cabinet. The degree of Khanh's "sincerity" on the issue of military withdrawal from politics could be highly doubted, and the generals he let out of the Cabinet were simply incompetent or untrustworthy. On September 13th, when Ambassador Taylor was in Honolulu on his way back to Saigon, a bloodless coup was conducted by one of these deposed Ministers, General Lam Van Phat, who had been Minister of Interior, and by General Duong Van Duc, who was scheduled to be removed as commander of the Fourth Corps, in the Mekong Delta. General Duc's troops, aided by some tanks, appeared at first to have captured the key points in the city, including Khanh's headquarters—Khanh himself was in Dalat—and to be in control of the capital. Within twenty-four hours, however, the coup completely collapsed and General Khanh was back in power. His return was mainly engineered by a younger group of officers who remained loyal to him. They included Air Commodore Nguyen Cao Ky, head of the Air Force, who sent his planes flying low over the city and threatened to bombard it, and Sub-General Nguyen Chanh Thi, commander of the 1st Division, in the northernmost First Corps. The Americans, including Deputy Ambassador Johnson and some senior military advisers, had apparently helped bring Khanh back by urging a negotiated settlement between the coup leaders and the group headed by Ky and Thi that remained loyal to Khanh. Soon after the coup began, Washington had announced that the United States supported the "duly constituted" regime headed by Generals Khanh, Minh, and Khiem.

The circumstances of this coup remained somewhat obscure. On the surface, it looked like another attempt by a group of disgruntled officers who had just been fired to seize power in behalf of themselves and in support of the Catholics and the Dai Viet Party at the expense of the Buddhists. When the coup started, General Phat had described it as "just a little operation against some politicians." Phat, who had been close to President Ngo Dinh Diem and had not played a part in the November, 1963, coup against him, had been a relatively obscure officer with a "playboy" reputation, and his military promotion and elevation to the Interior Ministry under Khanh was largely due to the fact that he was a Catholic and presumably would balance the Buddhists in the Cabinet. When the coup was over, General Duc, who was regarded as a good officer but also somewhat eccentric, declared that it had been motivated by "the transfer to the capital of some neutralist elements, and by some pro-Communists in the government." This was an obvious allusion to Khanh's efforts to conciliate Generals Don, Xuan, and Kim—the three men Khanh had originally declared to have been plotting a "neutralist" peace with the French and with North Vietnam, and who, after receiving a mock trial and being more or less exonerated, had been brought back to Saigon as part of Khanh's efforts to establish unity.

What the coup chiefly did was to establish the authority of the new group of younger general officers who came to be known as the "young Turks," headed by Ky and Thi. There was some indication afterward that the Americans had not been as completely in favor of restoring Khanh to power as they had intimated. They had no choice but to disavow the temperamental Generals Phat and Duc, but they did not so much support the return of Khanh alone as the re-establishment of the Khanh-Minh-Khiem triumvirate. Thus the American position now seemed to be moving away from exclusive support of Khanh as a desirable "strong man" in favor of a balance-of-power formula. The argument was even made, by Vietnamese observers in Saigon, that the coup had been "staged," with the knowledge of Americans, to achieve this end. This theory subsequently gained some credence when the leading conspirators, including Phat and Duc, were acquitted after a brief trial. It was pointed out that the mechanics of the coup had been so badly arranged that it couldn't succeed; the real creator of the "puppet show," it was said, had been General Nguyen Van Thieu, the Chief of Staff, who was also close to the Dai Viet Party, and Thieu's function had been to "neutralize" not only his friend General Khiem, the pro-Dai Viet Commander in Chief of the Army, but the Americans as well. Thieu succeeded; he got Khiem to stay out of the coup, which for the moment served Khiem's private purposes as a potential opponent of Khanh's. It was later learned that a number of Americans had been aware that the coup was in the works the day before it took place and had played an odd catalytic role on both sides, canceling each other out. It is conceivable that this coup was several things at once: first, a badly conceived attempt by the deposed officers to grab power—an attempt that was smelled out by their superiors, who then, with the knowledge of the Americans, allowed the coup to take its course, knowing it would fail, in order to clip General Khanh's wings; a second objective might have been the creation of a new power balance by making Khanh beholden to the emergent younger generals, such as Ky and Thi; and, third, its purpose, as conceived by all of those involved, apparently was to weaken the power of the Buddhists, whom Khanh was mollifying. The results, unfortunately, created fresh sympathy for the Buddhists, and fashioned something of a Frankenstein in the young officers' group. "There are now two ropes around Khanh's neck," one Vietnamese observer afterward remarked. Henceforth there would be a growing alliance between the militant Buddhists and at least one strong element among the so-called "young Turks," the group led by General Thi, who was close to Thich Tri Quang, still the Buddhist leader in Central Vietnam and generally regarded by now as at least an incipient "neutralist." As such, whether staged or not, the September 13th coup did nothing to increase political stability and instead served to sow more seeds of chaos; no one benefited from it more than the Vietcong.

Two weeks after the coup of September 13th, amid further rumblings in Saigon and a Vietcong-inspired tribal rebellion in the highlands, the new High National Council, composed of seventeen elderly professional men, was inaugurated. The Council's tasks, in addition to writing the new provisional constitution, included the convening of a national convention to act as an interim legislature and to frame a permanent constitution, and the establishment of national institutions, whatever they might be. As the new civilian Council labored away, the atmosphere of crisis did not diminish. A group of regimental officers who had supported General Khanh in the mid-September coup crisis reiterated their demands that he dismiss and punish "all corrupt and dishonest" officials left over from the Diem regime. In Hué, despite the fact that he had been named a member of the High National Council, Dr. Le Khac Quyen, a sometime tool of both Tri Quang and General Thi, was forging ahead with his own political plans by setting up yet another group called the National Salvation Council, with branches in ten provinces. As it turned out, this new party was more of a threat than a reality, but it didn't help Khanh's unity efforts; Khanh himself had to intervene to settle the tribal rebellion, which he blamed on Communists and "foreigners," apparently meaning the American Special Forces that had been working among the tribes, and while he denied that his rift with the Americans was growing, he remarked to a correspondent, "I am young and I have my own way to go for the good of my people and Vietnam."

Despite the charge that the High National Council was composed of older men said to be too remote from current realities (it was disparagingly referred to as "the High National Museum") it fulfilled its promise to deliver a new constitution at the end of October. It then selected Phan Khac Suu, an elderly nonaligned politician who had been its chairman, to become the new Chief of State. It had been expected that General Minh would retain this job, but the Buddhists and other religious groups, including the Hoa Hao and Cao Dai sects, persuaded the Council members to choose a civilian in keeping with the pledges that had been made by the generals in September. Suu, an agricultural engineer, had served under Emperor Bao Dai and in Diem's first Cabinet, and was jailed by Diem after the unsuccessful 1960 coup. He was in poor health as a result of his imprisonment, but his principal assets were his cheery disposition and his political independence. The fact that he was nominally a member of the Cao Dai did not deter the other religious groups from supporting him, possibly because the Cao Dai religion itself was an almost incomprehensible mixture of Buddhism, Christianity, Taoism, and animism. Suu immediately chose as the new Premier a sixty-one-year-old former Mayor of Saigon named Tran Van Huong, who, like himself, had at first worked with the Diem regime and then turned against it. A schoolteacher by profession, Huong, like many other ardent nationalists, had co-operated briefly with the Vietminh in 1945 before he realized the movement was Communist-dominated. Except for two brief tenures as Mayor, first under Diem and then under Khanh, he had held no political office. "I'm not sure whether I should be congratulated or offered condolences," he said when he was named Premier, but he promised that his administration "would not indulge too much in politics but would aim at stabilizing the situation." It was a futile promise; from the very start, Huong was beset by political problems. He kept five of fifteen Cabinet Ministers from the previous caretaker regime and appointed technicians, rather than politicians, to the other posts—a decision that immediately subjected him to criticism from both the Buddhists and the Catholics, who resented the fact they had not been consulted. "The government is not going to be the prisoner of any pressure groups," Huong declared, but he was widely accused of having "betrayed the revolution" by choosing a number of civil servants who had been active in the Diem regime as Ministers. It quickly became apparent that the real power behind the throne was still Khanh, who seemed to have the proverbial cat's nine lives. He now took over as Commander in Chief from General Khiem, who was sent to Washington as the Vietnamese Ambassador, thereby being eliminated from the national political scene. General Minh was out of a job, and would also soon go abroad on a good-will tour; thus both of Khanh's chief rivals were out of the way. He had part of the Army behind him, and had gained the neutrality or support of the Buddhists. His relations with the Americans, specifically with Ambassador Taylor, while still tenuous, were no worse and, if anything, a bit better since he had belatedly made good on his promise to install a civilian government.

The Young Generals

The Huong regime, which was to last three months, was never out of trouble and was constantly on the defensive. Within a month, there were new riots in the streets of Saigon, led by students and fomented by some of the same Vietcong agents who had been active in August. The Buddhists at first remained on the sidelines, but soon made it clear that they joined in the opposition to the new regime because of its "pro-Diemist" make-up; by the third week of November, they were declaring that the government should resign "because it does not command the sympathy of the population." Initially, Huong, reluctant to face fresh accusations of police measures, had allowed the new demonstrations to take place, but as they continued, and were joined in by some Buddhist elements, he reestablished martial law. This served to fan the flames further, which was just what the Vietcong wanted. Communist agents had by now infiltrated many branches of the city's life—labor unions, newspapers, student bodies, college faculties, and some government agencies—and their avowed purpose, as expressed in captured documents, was to play one group off against another, in traditional Communist fashion, and to keep the demonstrations rolling. Late in November, while Huong mixed firmness with pleas that he be given a chance to prove the validity and sincerity of his civilian government, General Khanh made vague promises of supporting the new regime, with Army troops if necessary. There was considerable skepticism as to the sincerity of his backing; many observers still felt he was simply biding his time, waiting for the "experiment" in civilian rule to prove unworkable.

In the meantime, the war continued to be waged without any noticeable improvement in the government's position. A strong effort was being made in the area around Saigon to initiate pacification measures along the lines of those that had proved successful in the Communist crisis in Malaya in the early nineteen-fifties. The Vietnamese effort was based on an intensive campaign to break down Communist centers of intelligence, tax collection, and terrorism in a gradual series of concentric circles, and then to establish and maintain government security in those regions. But the main pacification program in the countryside was still foundering. This was primarily due to intensive Vietcong offensive actions that prevented the strategic hamlet scheme from making much progress; more and more lines of communication were cut, and assassinations and kidnapings of government officials continued to make the population reluctant to support the government. It was estimated by the Americans that the Vietcong during 1964 had infiltrated at least 10,000 fresh hard-core elements from North Vietnam into the south, and that the hard core now totaled at least 30,000 (most Vietnamese authorities privately put the figure at 45,000). The Communists were obviously emboldened in the rural areas by the lack of political stability, which was reflected in the constant changes still being made among provincial and district officials. A series of floods in Central Vietnam, in which approximately seven thousand persons died and several-score thousands were left homeless, added to the government's woes, and the Communists were quick to take advantage of this natural calamity. The boldness of the Vietcong was demonstrated by a mortar attack on the Bien Hoa airbase, just north of Saigon, during which four Americans were killed and nineteen wounded, and five B-57 bombers were destroyed. While the attack did not bring any immediate American bombing reprisals on the north, the issue of renewing such attacks, on a larger scale, was raised in Washington. Ambassador Taylor was arguing in favor of such a step, and he pressed his cause during another one of his periodic visits home at the end of November. Taylor was now considerably less optimistic than he had been previously, and he admitted that the outcome of the war was "very much in doubt."

By the time Taylor returned to Saigon and announced a policy of more military aid for the Huong government, including funds and personnel to add 100,000 soldiers to the 615,000 already existing Vietnamese forces, the political crisis had begun to boil again after a week of simmering. The Buddhists declared that the Americans were responsible for keeping Huong in power against "the just desires of the Vietnamese people and the Buddhist church." In the face of this threat of an anti-American campaign, the United States had apparently decided to go ahead and strengthen the government militarily, in the hope that such a program would also help it gain political strength; previously, the Americans had been reluctant to move until political stability was created. As three leading Buddhist monks, Thich Tam Chau, Thich Tri Quang, and Thich Thien Khiet, started a forty-eight-hour hunger strike to demonstrate their anti-government views, Premier Huong seemed to take heart from the Americans' backing and declared that he could not give in to Buddhist pressures because "I cannot admit a state within a state." Huong was also encouraged in his stand by another statement of support he had received from General Khanh and twenty-one top Army officers.

New jockeying among the generals had now become a factor, one that would soon become paramount. The younger generals who had helped save Khanh in the September 13th coup demanded that the High National Council fire nine generals and some thirty other officers who were alleged to be pro-Buddhist or simply "old guard" elements; this group included Generals Minh, Don, Xuan, and Kim and others of the original post-Diem junta who were still in a state of limbo, since they no longer had any jobs but retained their Army rank and pay. The Council refused to sign the necessary legislation implementing their dismissal. Spurred by the Council's refusal, and by the declaration of the Buddhists that they were now openly engaged in a "life and death struggle" against the Huong regime, the young generals, led by Thi and Ky, conducted a "purge" that amounted to a coup against the Council on December 20th. By this time, the Council itself had become rent by political differences— only nine of its original seventeen members were meeting even semi-regularly. Five of the nine were now arrested, and fifteen other politicians accused of being "political agitators" were also imprisoned.

It later became known that, in addition, about a hundred suspected pro-neutralist members of the National Salvation Council in Central Vietnam—Dr. Le Khac Quyen's new political party, which was being supported by Thich Tri Quang's militant Buddhists—had also been arrested as part of this December purge. On the surface, this indicated a split between General Thi, who had now taken over the command of the northern First Corps, and Tri Quang; but it seemed more likely that Thi had not broken so much with Tri Quang as with Dr. Quyen, who had overextended himself, and now saw his separatist movement nipped in the bud; there was evidence that neither Thi nor Tri Quang was unhappy about dropping him. The importance of the young generals' purge of the civilian High National Council, beyond its avowed purpose of curbing political elements that were described as disruptive, lay in the fact that it sired still another council—the Armed Forces Council—which was created to curb the domination of the other generals by General Khanh. Although Khanh was named head of it, the organization of the Armed Forces Council was to prove the first step in his downfall.

The young dissident generals of the A.F.C. immediately offered to mediate the political conflict—some of the Buddhists' complaints against the Huong government were said by air chief Ky to be "justified." But Ambassador Taylor, obviously taken by surprise by the purge of the High National Council, issued a veiled warning that the United States might reconsider its new program of military support unless "the fabric of legal government" was restored. Once again, it seemed, the Americans had been unable to have any influence over events because they had had no idea of what was about to take place; they had no close contact with those who were responsible. Consequently, the United States was reduced to the embarrassing role of a spectator.

The real irony of the American position now became clear. Ambassador Taylor advised Premier Huong to defy the purge of the High National Council. Huong, however, initially expressed his willingness to co-operate with the generals and to reorganize his government to their partial satisfaction. Taylor thereupon found himself the object of a bitter attack brought against him for having "interfered" in Vietnam's political affairs. This attack was mounted by General Khanh, who, in an interview with Beverly Deepe, of the New York *Herald Tribune,* declared that Taylor had engaged in "activities beyond imagination," and said that if the American Ambassador "does not act more intelligently, the United States will lose Southeast Asia and we will lose our freedom." Vietnam could not be made over "in the image of the United States," Khanh added, and Taylor "is not serving his country well." In an order of the day, Khanh also officially excoriated the Americans. "We make sacrifices for the country's independence and the Vietnamese people's liberty, not to carry out the policy of any foreign country," he declared. He defended the action of the Armed Forces Council against the High National Council, which he said had been "exploited by counter-revolutionary elements who placed partisan considerations above the homeland's sacred interest." He insisted that the country's military leaders retained the responsibility of "acting as an intermediary to settle all disputes and differences if they create a situation favorable to the common enemies—Communism and colonialism in any form." The Embassy in Saigon defensively denied that Taylor had done anything "improper," while in Washington the State Department also backed Taylor and, in turn, accused the Vietnamese generals of having engaged in "improper interference" with the civilian government. The Washington statement amounted to a warning that the United States would reconsider its program of support to Vietnam, which at the time amounted to about $1,500,000 a day, if the Vietnamese generals did not stop meddling in politics.

The issue was now joined between Khanh and Taylor. Khanh was said to have urged the Armed Forces Council to help mount an open anti-American campaign in the streets and to declare that American aid was not necessary. The position of Taylor and the Americans was to call Khanh's bluff, in the belief that Khanh had become a front man for the younger group of generals who would not go along with him on curtailment of American aid. Taylor was reported to have told Khanh, over the telephone in *advance* of Khanh's anti-American declaration, that he, Khanh, had outlived his usefulness. To back up their position, the Americans announced that they would not guarantee delivery of military items already in the pipeline once they arrived in Saigon, and that American participation in the "planning of non-routine military and civilian operations" would be temporarily suspended. It was a mild enough action, under the circumstances, and one that might better have been taken earlier, in the August crisis, before the conflict between the military and the civilian leaders had come to a head and when the lever of American assistance held over Khanh might have forced him to create a civilian government that would have had a better chance of fostering stability than the shaky Huong regime had ever had. Now, as Khanh met with Huong, Chief of State Suu, and Interior Minister Nguyen Luu Vien to try to rebuild some kind of government structure, the issue was clouded by uncertainty over what kind of new national legislature, if any, should be established in accordance not so much with the Americans' wishes as with the rational needs of the situation.

At the turn of the year, while the Vietcong was gaining a series of significant victories both north and south of Saigon, there were some signs that the political crisis would be at least temporarily resolved. First, Premier Huong and Chief of State Suu, while they belatedly declared their opposition to the generals' action of December 20th, appealed to the Army's "good will" to help find a fitting solution to the governmental problem. The statement represented a mild victory for Ambassador Taylor. On January 9th, after fresh riots had taken place in the city and Thich Tam Chau's Buddhists had again made clear their intention to oust Premier Huong, a communiqué was issued, signed by General Khanh and Huong and Suu: the Army promised to abide by its decision of the past August to turn over the government to civilians; it was agreed to call a national convention "in a short time" to re-establish civilian legislative responsibility (the convention, to be chosen or elected on a limited basis, would act as an interim legislature until a new permanent constitution was written and a regular assembly was elected); the five High National Council members still under arrest, as well as other politicians not suspected of being pro-Communists, were to be released; and "all genuine patriots" were to be "earnestly assembled" to help formulate a plan to defeat the Vietcong. Nothing

L

was said about restoring the High National Council, as such. Though Ambassador Taylor saw the communiqué before it was issued, and approved it, the Americans considered it a poor compromise; in Washington, the State Department blandly announced that "it appears to represent some improvement in the situation." What remained unclear was the real role of the Armed Forces Council, whether it would remain a "watchdog" and intervene whenever it wanted to or whether it would allow a civilian government really to function. The question, as before, underlined the essential issue of just how much chance at all there was to create a strong civilian government, or for that matter a stable military one. It had become apparent, as the crisis had progressed, that the issue of civilian or military rule at the top bothered the Vietnamese less than it did the Americans, who had made it a matter of principle without being certain just how far they were willing to go in cutting back the aid programs, or without being clear what sort of guarantees against military intervention they thought a new civilian government should, or could, feasibly obtain. "You Americans took this whole thing a lot more seriously than we did," one Vietnamese commentator said afterward. "I suppose you were reacting against the criticism that you hadn't done enough to stem the tide of events before. I'm not sure, the way it's all turned out, that either you or we accomplished very much."

Khanh's Next Try

Within three days of the compromise formula that re-established the legitimacy of Premier Huong's civilian rule, the Buddhists were again insisting that Huong had to go. A Buddhist-inspired student and general strike in Hué, the long-time center of militant Buddhist activity, where Thich Tri Quang still held sway, coincided with declarations by Thich Tam Chau in Saigon that the Huong government was continuing to engage in "criminal persecution" of the Buddhists. This two-pronged renewed Buddhist offensive again demonstrated that whatever rivalry might exist between the two top monks for gaining control over the southern Buddhists, and whatever tactical differences might exist between them on the surface, they would always co-operate in a crisis affecting the Buddhist movement as a whole, and that at such times it would be Tri Quang who would call the signals as the movement's supreme strategist. The Buddhists now rejected offers to have a greater voice in the existing government; General Thi was among those who urged this, and he underlined his views by refusing to curb the Buddhist demonstrations in Hué and Danang. The Buddhists, however, kept insisting that the Huong government had to be overthrown, and they refused to sign a joint communiqué of the Interfaith Committee, consisting of Hoa Hao and Cao Dai representatives as well as the Catholics, calling for national unity. Premier Huong, now at bay, announced that he would convene the proposed new Constituent Assembly in the third week of March, and at the same time he moved to bring some members of the Armed Forces Council into his government. On January 18th, as General Thi indicated he would no longer tolerate antigovernment demonstrations in view of the Buddhist hierarchy's adamant stand of not co-operating with Huong, the embattled Premier announced that four military men would be added to the Cabinet. The four were Air Marshal Ky, who agreed to take over as Minister of Youth and Sports only when he was allowed to continue as Air Force commander, too; General Nguyen Van Thieu, who become Second Deputy Premier; General Linh Quang Vien, who become Minister of Psychological Warfare; and General Tran Van Minh (known as Little Minh to differentiate him from General Duong Van Minh, who had gone off on a good-will tour to Europe), who was made Minister of the Armed Forces. What was interesting about this move was not only Huong's appeasement of the military but the fact that General Khanh was ostensibly being outmaneuvered by the other generals. It was said that Khanh had been offered Little Minh's defense post but that he had declined it, anticipating that he would in due time be summoned to take over the government. As the four generals joined the Cabinet, five of the top Buddhist bonzes, including Tri Quang and Tam Chau, went on another hunger strike to force the ouster of the Huong government.

What now took place was one of those special opportunistic alliances that have proved so common in South Vietnam in recent years. The partners in this one were the Buddhists and General Khanh. Despite their protest meetings and hunger strikes, the Buddhist leaders had found their popular support on the wane; the crowds at the pagodas were not what they had been during the height of the protests against President Diem and afterward, and there was some resentment on the part of the ordinarily passive Buddhist masses at the "politicalization" of the movement by its ambitious leaders. The meetings held at the Vien Hoa Dao, the newly constructed Buddhist headquarters in Saigon, had resulted in command orders being handed out to militant pagoda squads throughout the city, and to some extent in the provinces, but the response had not been nearly as great as Tri Quang and Tam Chau had wished. Whatever the ambitions of the top bonzes, and especially of Tri Quang, to play important political roles, they were not understood by the ordinary Buddhist population. Consequently, to maintain his self-appointed position, Tri Quang was ready to make an alliance with General Khanh, who saw himself being outflanked by the younger generals on the Armed Forces Council.

On January 23rd, the Buddhist leaders, frustrated by the lack of response to their hunger strike by both the Huong government and the American Embassy, ordered an all-out anti-American campaign. In Hué, a mob of five thousand students who responded automatically to Tri Quang's orders sacked the United States Information Service library and burned eight thousand books. They demanded the immediate recall of Ambassador Taylor and described Premier Huong as Taylor's "lackey." In Saigon, demonstrations in front of the Embassy and the U.S.I.S. library resulted in the arrest of more than two hundred persons. Faced by these fresh Buddhist demonstrations, the newly appointed generals in the Cabinet expressed reservations about the solvency of the Huong regime. General Khanh, playing his own daring game, promptly used the Buddhist uprisings to strengthen his own position. As the Buddhist monks kept up their hunger strike, Khanh declared sententiously, "We must talk with the Buddhists—you can't kill them all," adding, "The Buddhists talk against Ambassador Taylor, but that is only a form of anti-Americanism, which, if it goes on, will slow down our war against the Communists." Cryptically he asserted that "a more definite settlement is needed."

On January 27th, Khanh won his gamble of the moment. The Armed Forces Council ousted the Huong government, declaring it had proved itself "unable to cope with the present critical situation," and Khanh was appointed to "deal" with it. Almost exactly a year after he had overthrown the junta that had overthrown Diem, he was back in power, and this time he cast himself in the role of the great compromiser, promising to convene "an Army-Peoples Council" of twenty representatives of the religious groups, the armed forces, and important personalities from all over the country to advise the government "in all its important decisions." Unbelievably, the United States once more seemed to have been taken by surprise; when the move against Huong occurred, Ambassador Taylor was away on a brief trip to Laos and Thailand. It was not inconceivable that the generals, and particularly Khanh, had chosen that moment to act.

The reaction in Washington was typically hand-wringing. In a story in the *New York Times*, John Finney wrote: "Now the Administration has concluded that it must accept Saigon's power struggle as inevitable in a nation still emerging from colonial control. Partly as a result of lessons learned in the December crisis, Washington was no longer trying to impose Western political solutions. The hope here was that at least a facade of a continuing civilian government could be maintained." There was no more talk of disposing of Khanh or of suspending aid. It seemed apparent that whatever degree of leverage the Americans had still hoped to use had been taken away from them by the quick new turn of events. For the moment, it all seemed up to Khanh again. One experienced Vietnamese politician commented: "Khanh has learned his political ABC's well; he's much more mature. He came to power clinging to the Americans; now he's built the image of being mildly anti-American and a more independent anti-Vietnamese leader." At first, this seemed to be true. He declared the day after he was back in power that the generals would restrict themselves to mediating the political crisis, and he announced that Phan Khac Suu would remain temporarily as Chief of State while

Nguyen Xuan Oanh, who had been Third Deputy Premier, would again become the stopgap acting Premier, as Khanh had named him to be the previous August. On the surface, by his statements and actions, Khanh seemed to have learned a lesson—that he could not grab power for himself in blatant fashion—but essentially he was still trying to do just that.

Everyone now sat back to see what Khanh would do. The Americans made no comment, although when Khanh saw Ambassador Taylor on January 29th—the meeting was reported to have been cordial but stiff—he made it clear that he intended to dominate whatever kind of government emerged. Warned of his previous failure, he insisted he had benefited from that experience. He said the Buddhists had agreed to stop demonstrating against the government, and for the time being this was so—the five monks ended their hunger strike—although Khanh's claims that he obtained the agreement of Tri Quang and Tam Chau to leave the country proved false. Tri Quang made his continued presence very much felt; when asked if Khanh could become Premier again, he replied sharply, "He is too bad a man." In an interview in the Saigon *Post*, Tri Quang disavowed any anti-American policy. "The Vietnamese Buddhists resent America only for misunderstanding the whole problem," he said, which was a fair enough statement. If there had been a deal between Khanh and the Buddhists, as was probable, Tri Quang and his principal lieutenants were now obviously biding their time. When two generals visited them at the Vien Hoa Dao, they denied they had made an agreement with Khanh for him to rule Vietnam as military chief for two years; Khanh had boasted to his colleagues on the Armed Forces Council that he had obtained such an agreement. "Monks are religious people and do not make agreements or engage in politics," Tri Quang smilingly told the two generals who came to ask for his formal blessing. The militant monks could afford to be as blasé as they had been belligerent; they had been responsible for bringing down three Vietnamese governments in little more than a year—the regime of Diem, the first government of Khanh, and the administration of Huong.

In this new atmosphere of uncertainty, two more foreign figures now suddenly emerged. One was McGeorge Bundy, President Johnson's special assistant, who made his first trip to Saigon to get a personal estimate of the touchy situation at a moment when Ambassador Taylor was being criticized in Washington for his inability to avert coups and half-coups and for his failure of personal diplomacy with Khanh. The other important foreign figure who suddenly came upon the Vietnamese scene, but in an obviously altogether different way, was Premier Aleksei N. Kosygin, of Russia, who announced on the last day of 1964 that he would head a Soviet delegation to Hanoi. The fact that Kosygin himself would go to North Vietnam, at the request of the Hanoi government, and the composition of the Soviet delegation, including top economic, military, and foreign affairs specialists, clearly showed that the Russians were about to re-evaluate their policy of generally ignoring the Vietnamese war in the interests of achieving co-operation with the United States in Europe. The role of the Chinese Communists, while more loudly propagandistic than indicative of the desire to give Hanoi any sizable amounts of military assistance, had apparently prompted the Russians to take steps, partly in view of their ideological battle with the Chinese over "wars against imperialism"; more significant than pure ideology, however, was Moscow's power-play decision to re-enter the Asian arena in order to fight for the support of some of the Asian Communist movements, which, like North Vietnam, were veering more and more toward Peking.

The General Is Fired

Events now took place with such rapidity that they must be related in chronological order. After stopping off in Peking, where he was courteously but not enthusiastically received, Premier Kosygin arrived in Hanoi on February 7th, 1965. The North Vietnamese gave him a warm welcome, and both they and he were careful to maintain the fiction that the Vietcong was a separate instrumentality; this was expressed despite the obvious expectation that Kosygin's trip would produce fresh Soviet assistance to North Vietnam. Premier Pham Van Dong hailed Kosygin's visit as "a powerful support for North Vietnam" and an "inspiration" to the Vietcong, while Kosygin described North Vietnam as an "inspiring example" to the South

Vietnamese engaged in their "struggle against American interventionists and their puppets." The following day, as discussions began between Kosygin and his experts and the North Vietnamese on the kind of aid required, eight Americans were killed and more than a hundred wounded in a night attack by the Vietcong on the American barracks at Pleiku, in the South Vietnamese central highlands; simultaneously, Camp Holloway, the airbase at Pleiku, was attacked, while two other installations on the coast, at Tuyhoa and Nhatrang, were hit by the Vietcong. Twelve hours later, in response to what President Johnson called "provocations ordered and directed by the Hanoi regime," forty-nine planes from American aircraft carriers bombed and strafed barracks and what the United States described as major staging areas at Donghoi, just beyond the Seventeenth Parallel in North Vietnam; from these areas, Washington charged, North Vietnam had been sending men and supplies to help the Vietcong in the south. Because of Kosygin's presence in Hanoi, Washington informed Moscow that the air attacks were retaliatory and were not meant to expand the war. The following day, since bad weather had kept some additional planes from reaching their targets, twenty-four South Vietnamese bombers, escorted by American jet fighters, struck at another base near Donghoi.

Whether Hanoi specifically ordered the daring attack at Pleiku or not, it seems doubtful that the Vietcong would have made it, under the circumstances of Kosygin's visit, without informing Hanoi first. This would normally have been done through the Central Office in charge of the Communist military campaign in South Vietnam from headquarters believed to be in the Tay Ninh forest. The Central Office would have radioed the Commission of Reunification, attached to the Council of Ministers in Hanoi, or the Reunification Department of the Central Committee of the Laodang Party, both of which are headed by General Nguyen Van Vinh, who is said to direct all Vietcong strategy under the supervision of General Vo Nguyen Giap, Commander in Chief of North Vietnam's armed forces and Minister of Defense. On the assumption that Hanoi at least knew the Pleiku barracks would be assaulted, it can be surmised that no objections were raised. Certainly North Vietnam had more to gain than to lose by having the attack take place while Kosygin was present, even though it might embarrass him, as it very likely did. If the Americans failed to respond, the North Vietnamese could argue that the United States was indeed a paper tiger, and that all that was needed for the war to be brought to a successful conclusion in the south was some additional military assistance. If the United States did respond, the North Vietnamese could claim that more aid was necessary to prosecute the war under more difficult circumstances, and they could then reasonably ask for planes and defensive missiles with which to protect their own cities, too. Since Kosygin was wooing North Vietnam for Russia's own purposes as much as Hanoi was wooing him to help it regain some balance between Moscow and Peking, the Russian Premier was hardly in a position to leave Hanoi in a huff, which besides would have made him look foolish. After the American air attacks, Kosygin, in a speech in Hanoi, declared that the situation was "fraught with serious complications." The Chinese, beyond staging huge protest rallies in Peking and an attack by Chinese and Vietnamese students on the American Embassy in Moscow, did not officially react with anything stronger than a reiteration of their oft-repeated statement that Communist China would "definitely not stand idly by" in the face of such "undisguised war provocation," although a week later Foreign Minister Chen Yi called for "concrete action" against the United States, asserting that peaceful coexistence was "out of the question" and that "United States imperialism is the most ferocious enemy of the people of the whole world." There were reports at the time that two Chinese battalions had moved into North Vietnam. Moscow took advantage of the attacks, in the days that followed, to hold out a mild olive branch to Peking by asserting that Soviet Russia might be "forced, together with its allies and friends, to take further measures" to help North Vietnam defend itself from American air attacks, and by making mention, for the first time in several months, of the possibility of invoking the Chinese-Soviet Friendship Treaty, relating to the maintenance of peace and security in the Far East. The Chinese did not respond to this overture.

It was apparent that the war was entering a new phase. Three days after the Pleiku attack, on February 11th, the Vietcong again managed to pull off a sneak attack on an American installation in South Vietnam by blowing up the barracks at Quinhon, on the central coast, and killing twenty-one American officers and servicemen. North of Quinhon, which is the capital of Binh Dinh Province, the Vietcong also severely mauled South Vietnamese forces in a major battle. The following day, the United States again attacked military bases and supply depots in North Vietnam, employing a hundred and sixty planes, mostly jet fighter-bombers from carriers, and some United States Air Force planes based at Danang and Saigon; the South Vietnamese also joined in this series of raids. While the White House again described the attacks as a "response to further provocations by the Hanoi regime," the statement this time was less clear in defining the potential limits of the American response, and the implication was that future air attacks might be provoked by general Vietcong attacks on South Vietnamese targets, whether or not Americans were the object. It was at this point that plans were set in motion, and deliberately obscured, to send additional American troops to South Vietnam and to mount a general air war against North Vietnam in an effort to force Hanoi to negotiate; but, for the moment, the air attacks stopped.

During this week-long war crisis, South Vietnam was still attempting, once more, to form a government. Amid reports that some of the younger generals, notably Nguyen Chanh Thi, might take steps to curb General Khanh in his attempt to regain power, Khanh was having trouble persuading the bickering political and religious factions to form a temporary legislative and advisory body; Catholic, Hoa Hao, and Cao Dai leaders were unwilling to join the Buddhists on the new legislative group, which was also supposed to help pick a new Premier and Chief of State. Neither McGeorge Bundy, who was still in Saigon when the American air attack took place after the Pleiku bombing, nor Ambassador Taylor was able to persuade the Vietnamese to bury their differences and form a government of unity. Finally, on February 16th, after two other candidates had turned the job down, Dr. Phan Huy Quat, who had been Foreign Minister under Khanh the previous summer, accepted the Premiership.

Dr. Quat, a northerner, and a former leader of the Dai Viet Party in the north—his Dai Viet ties were no longer close—appointed a twenty-one-member Cabinet that included three military men designated by the Armed Forces Council, included General Nguyen Van Thieu, who retained the title of Deputy Premier and became Defense Minister, too. The Cabinet altogether contained four Catholics including General Thieu, one member each of the Cao Dai and Hoa Hao sects, and the rest were all Buddhists, including Dr. Quat, although only two of the Ministers were close to the official Buddhist hierarchy; Thich Tri Quang and Thich Tam Chau maintained a discreet silence and neither approved nor disapproved of the new regime. The Armed Forces Council also appointed a twenty-man National Legislative Council that included two representatives from each of the four religions, two selected from each geographical area of the country—north, central and south—and six military men.

Although the American air attacks on North Vietnam had momentarily lifted morale in Saigon, the new Quat government was greeted more with a sense of relief than with enthusiasm, and no great expectations were held out for it; it was the ninth attempt to form a government since the overthrow of Diem. It was obvious from the outset that it would be under the domination of the Armed Forces Council, which, in its statement announcing Dr. Quat's appointment, made clear that it would continue "to act as a mediator until the government is popularly elected."

Rumblings within the Council about Khanh's leadership, which had begun about two weeks before, had continued during the final days of the new government's formation. They now culminated in one of those explosions that had become so typical in Vietnam during the past year, and this time the circumstances of the coup that took place, and that resulted in the ouster of Khanh and his departure from the country, were particularly dramatic and ironic. Some of the young generals of the A.F.C. who had been instrumental in saving Khanh in September undoubtedly wanted to oust him because they feared that, despite his protestations to the contrary, he was again moving toward the re-establishment of a one-man dictatorship. They had no plan yet formulated, however, and it is by no means certain that they would have succeeded in creating one, since they were not in full agreement and were beset by their own rivalries.

At this point, matters were taken out of their hands by another group of plotters who were to serve as catalysts. These plotters were directed by Colonel Pham Ngoc Thao, one of the original group of conspirators against Diem, organized, it will be recalled, by Dr. Tran Kim Tuyen and Colonel Do Mau. Following that coup, during which he had led the tank attack on Diem's palace, Thao had been among those purposefully sidetracked by the ruling junta and had spent six months studying conventional warfare tactics at Fort Leavenworth, after which, on his way back to Vietnam, he had spent a month in England. Upon his return, he had become Khanh's press officer, but unofficially he served as a close political adviser, too. When Khanh became involved in his power struggle with General Minh and General Khiem, Thao found himself in the middle, between Khanh and Khiem—he was a close friend of Khiem's—and when Khiem was finally defeated and sent to be Ambassador to the United States, Thao was also sent to Washington to be Khiem's press attaché.

In the third week of December, 1964, Thao had suddenly received a cablegram from the Foreign Minister in Saigon summoning him home. He suspected that Khanh was setting a trap for him, and it appears that the cablegram was inspired by an article I wrote in the New York *Herald Tribune* of December 20th, in which the theory was projected, as held by a number of American and Vietnamese observers, that Khanh and the Buddhists, particularly Thich Tri Quang, were using each other in an effort to grab power in Vietnam and that both men might at some point be willing to make a neutralist deal with the National Liberation Front, or with Hanoi. As it turned out, after the generals had begun to whittle away at the Huong regime by abolishing the High National Council on December 20th, Khanh did get back to power late in January, when Premier Huong was deposed, and as we have seen, he did use the Buddhist opposition to Huong as a means of accomplishing it. Although I had known Thao, my article was not written on the basis of information from him, as Khanh suspected, but it was enough for Khanh to decide to get rid of Thao, which he had wanted to do anyway, realizing it was a mistake to have two of his enemies, Khiem and Thao, plotting against him in Washington. He apparently planned to arrest Thao as soon as Thao got back to Saigon. Aware that a trap was being sprung for him, Thao decided to accept the bait and to spring a trap of his own. He arrived back in Saigon at the end of December and almost immediately went underground. In mid-January, the Foreign Minister issued a "wanted notice" for him, warning him that he would be "considered guilty of abandoning his post, with all the consequences of such a situation," if he failed to report. Thao had no intention of surfacing.

Since, in all respects, Thao was one of the most unusual and remarkable Vietnamese around, being a conspiratorial revolutionary figure straight out of a Malraux novel and, at the same time, a politically astute man as well as an experienced guerrilla fighter, some additional background on him is required. He was one of eleven children of an educated Vietnamese Catholic family named Thuan that held French citizenship but was strongly anti-French. His father, whose name was Adrien Pham Ngoc Thuan, was an engineer who once headed a Communist underground organization in Paris and worked with the Vietminh. After attending good French schools in Saigon, Thao, for reasons known only to himself, kept his family name of Pham but changed Thuan to Thao, and renounced his French citizenship. In 1942, he went to work for the Vietminh as a resistance leader in the south; as such, he was the man who gave political indoctrination to Khanh and his fellow cadets of the class of 1947 when they joined the Vietminh. By 1949, he was in charge of the entire Vietminh espionage apparatus around Saigon and had the job of organizing guerrilla companies in the countryside. He also maintained contact with Bishop Ngo Dinh Thuc, Diem's brother, and kept him informed of the progress of the resistance movement. After the 1954 Geneva settlement, Thao helped evacuate Communist elements from South Vietnam and Cambodia in accordance with its terms. He then more or less broke with the Vietminh, though he was still in touch with its southern leaders; he remained in touch with Bishop Thuc, too, who had become his spiritual mentor, and with the heads of the Cao Dai and Hoa Hao sects. For a time, he taught school in Saigon and then worked in a bank there, and during this interval he refused to turn over to the Diem government the names of his former fellow resistance workers, claiming they were not Communists but, like himself, simply patriots. By 1956, however, Thao had begun to ally himself with Diem, mostly as a result of his friendship with Bishop Thuc, and he was soon working in various Army units as a propagandist for the government-created Can Lao Party. Next, he became a trouble shooter for Diem in the provinces, and was named province chief of Kien Hoa, where, by using his intimate knowledge of Vietminh tactics to win the support of the peasant population and organize resistance against the Vietcong, he distinguished himself as a counter-insurgency leader. In the months before the coup against Diem, he was inspector of the strategic hamlet program, and this, as noted earlier, enabled him to make valuable contacts for the execution of the coup.

Now, back in Saigon, between mid-January and mid-February, 1964, Thao was plotting his own coup, as he had done in 1963 before he joined the amalgamated one against Diem. Shortly before 1 P.M. on February 19th, employing about fifty tanks and mixed elements of battalions he had worked with before, Thao seized control of the military headquarters area in Saigon, of the post office and the radio station, and surrounded the homes of Chief of State Suu and General Khanh. Khanh, who was supposed to have been captured at headquarters and spirited out of the country, managed to escape through a gate that had accidentally been left open by one of the conspirators and, after returning briefly to his house, flew in his private plane to his retreat at Cap St. Jacques, on the coast. In a radio announcement in midafternoon, Thao declared that the sole objective of the "military operation," as he termed it, was to get rid of Khanh, whom he described as "a dictator," and he indicated that he would bring his friend General Khiem back from Washington to be head of the Army but that the civilian government headed by Dr. Quat would be retained. After Thao went off the air, some of the dominant Catholic supporters of the coup broadcast some comments that gave rise to reports it was mounted by followers of the late President Diem, which was not true, although there were such elements in the conspiracy. One of the leaders who had been close to Diem, for example, and whom Thao was forced to use because he needed more strength, was General Phat, the leader of the abortive coup of the previous September. It was Phat's assignment to grab the Bien Hoa airfield, north of Saigon, and to keep Air Marshal Ky from putting up his planes against the coup, as Ky had done in September. Phat failed to carry out his assignment completely, though he and his troops did seize part of the airbase. Ky, however, got some planes in the air, and they buzzed the city, but his threats to bomb the installations at the airport held by the dissident troops were allayed by the Americans, who pointed out that there were several thousand American troops in the area. At 8 P.M. on February 19th, Phat and Thao, under a safe conduct arranged by the Americans, met with Ky and offered to negotiate but insisted that Khanh had to go. The coup forces still held most of Saigon at this point, and had imposed a curfew. In the meantime, General Khanh had been traveling around the delta in his plane, trying to line up support; he discovered that most division and regimental commanders were willing to support the Armed Forces Council, but not necessarily him.

By midnight, loyal Army troops from the south had begun moving on the city, and by dawn they entered it. At the same time, troops sent from Bien Hoa by Air Marshal Ky reached the capital, and these elements were apparently pro-Khanh, which at first seemed to indicate that Ky was again standing behind Khanh, as he had done the past September. The dissidents quickly gave up when confronted by superior strength. Colonel Thao slipped back into the government radio station shortly after the loyal forces had recaptured it, and after broadcasting "a final message to the nation" to the effect that the coup had succeeded in its aim of getting rid of Khanh, he stole the crystals necessary for running the station and disappeared. (This later was referred to as the "crystal coup.") General Phat also vanished. A tape-recorded message from General Khanh was broadcast throughout the morning, and it appeared that Khanh had again demonstrated his capacity for survival. But this was not so. At 10:30 A.M. on February 20th, a majority of the Armed Forces Council adopted a vote of "no confidence" in Khanh. The leader of the anti-Khanh forces was General Thi, and Marshal Ky now went along with him. Khanh was not present at the meeting, nor was he present at an afternoon press conference, at which Thi indicated that no "final decision" had yet been reached on Khanh's future. According to some of the generals, Khanh was on an "inspection trip" northeast of Saigon, where a heavy cache of Vietcong weapons had just been captured; but apparently he had got wind of what the Council was about to do at its midmorning meeting and had flown in his plane to Cap St. Jacques, where he began telephoning all around the country to rally support, promising young officers promotions and older ones top jobs if they would come to his rescue, but none did. He then flew to Nhatrang, and finally to Dalat, where his plane ran out of gas and could not be refueled in the middle of the night. Near midnight, in Saigon, the Armed Forces Council met again, and, having voted Khanh definitely out, prepared to take precautionary measures against his return, aware of his capacity to counterplot. Shortly before dawn, his efforts to rally support frustrated, Khanh telephoned to the headquarters of the Armed Forces Council in Saigon and said he would abide by the Council's unanimous decision to fire him as its chairman. The Council had already voted for General Tran Van Minh (Little Minh) to take over as Commander in Chief, but no successor to Khanh was selected as Council chief.

Three days later, after some mock farewell performances that were calculated to enable Khanh to save face, he left Vietnam to become Ambassador-at-Large, starting at the United Nations in New York. At the airport to see him off, in addition to high-ranking Vietnamese officers and politicians, was Ambassador Taylor, who had managed to survive Khanh. The two men were glassily polite. Not unexpectedly, one of those absent was Colonel Thao, who was chiefly responsible for Khanh's exit. Thao was in hiding near the city, and he was not yet through conspiring.

CHAPTER XI

The New American Commitment

The end of the Khanh era in South Vietnam coincided with some of the most momentous decisions and actions taken by the United States since the Korean War. There was no direct relationship between Khanh's departure and these new developments, which vastly increased America's involvement in the Vietnamese conflict, although the coup against Khanh did delay the major implementation of plans that had been formulated and set in motion in Washington by mid-February. The day before the coup, in response to a request by the Vietnamese government when Khanh was still at the head of it, one phase of the new plan was introduced. This was the employment of American B-57 jet light bombers and F-100 supersonic jet fighter-bombers, for the first time manned solely by American crews, against massed Vietcong troops in South Vietnam. The bombing and strafing took place in Binh Dinh Province, where the Communists were mounting a successful offensive that threatened to cut South Vietnam in two. This air attack, and a series of follow-up raids in the next two days, marked an important departure from the so-called "advise and assist" policy under which Americans had accompanied Vietnamese pilots on "training missions" against the Vietcong, not only in South Vietnam but also—though it was never officially admitted—on bombing sorties in Laos, to interdict Vietcong supply routes there. The new, exclusively American action in Vietnam, it was explained, was in accordance with the resolution passed by Congress the previous August, after the incidents in the Gulf of Tonkin, which permitted the President "to take all necessary steps, including the use of armed force" in defense of South Vietnam as a means to secure the "vital" peace and security of Southeast Asia. There was some irony—and some embarrassment for the United States—in the fact that the raids in South Vietnam were announced on the same day that Secretary General U Thant of the United Nations disclosed that he had sent "concrete ideas and proposals" to a number of nations involved in Southeast Asia, including the United States, in order to encourage "dialogues" that he hoped would "enable the United States to withdraw gracefully" and bring peace and stability to South Vietnam. The immediate reaction to Thant's proposal was varied. France, which had been urging peace and the neutralization of Southeast Asia for some time, was sympathetic; Great Britain, aware that her American partner in the Atlantic Alliance was loath to start any inconclusive negotiations and had already rejected a proposal of Thant's to reconvene the Geneva Conference of 1954, did not indicate any formal support for Thant's new offer, though privately the British were said to see some merit in it. The initial response of the North Vietnamese, who had everything to gain and nothing to lose by pretending to be interested, was reported to be favorable, though nothing was said officially. In view of the victories the Vietcong were achieving in South Vietnam, no climate for serious negotiation could be said to exist, and Thant's tactics, which seemed somewhat contrived, may have been calculated to preclude what he must have known was forthcoming in Washington and considered, out of his own special Asian orientation, to be a dangerous move.

On the last day of February, the United States issued its fourteen-thousand-word White Paper on Vietnam—which Thant certainly must have had some advance knowledge of—that represented a full-scale indictment of North Vietnam's long-time aggression against the south. The document, entitled "Aggression from the North—the Record of North Vietnam's Campaign to Conquer South Vietnam," accused the Hanoi government of having infiltrated large numbers of troops into the south. (Since 1959, it was charged, some twenty thousand officers, soldiers, and technicians had been sent into the south from the north, and these had now become the "backbone" of the Vietnam forces.) Hanoi was also accused of having smuggled increasing amounts of weapons from Communist arsenals all over the world into South Vietnam, and of directing the Vietcong's political and military campaign in the south. The White Paper was obviously designed to prepare the way for a resumption of American and South Vietnamese air attacks against the north, and two days later more than a hundred American jets bombed a North Vietnamese munitions depot and provided air cover for an attack by South Vietnamese planes on a Communist naval base. These attacks, which marked the real beginning of the air war against North Vietnam, were described in Washington as part of what President Johnson had already said would be a continuing effort—"measured, fitting, and adequate"—to resist aggression. It was made clear that they were not in retaliation for specific North Vietnamese actions, as the first American air attack the previous August and the three attacks on February 7th, 8th, and 11th had been, but signified the end of American "restraint" and a fresh determination to force the North Vietnamese to halt their aggressive actions against South Vietnam by ending the infiltration of men and supplies and calling off the guerrilla war. Simultaneously, it became known in Washington that the first American combat units would be sent to South Vietnam to guard important airbases, and a few days later the first elements of two reinforced Marine battalions, to total 3,500 officers and men, landed at Danang.

The State Department, in a further effort to establish legal sanction for the new American policy of military support in South Vietnam, denied that "a state of war" existed, in any legal sense, and maintained that the United States and South Vietnam were engaged "in collective defense" against "armed aggression" in accordance with Article 51 of the United Nations Charter. Once again, the United States went out of its way to inform the Soviet Union of its limited intentions in resuming the air raids against North Vietnam, and it was soon apparent that on the diplomatic front Washington was seeking, with Great Britain's help, to persuade the Russians to adopt a non-militant position vis-à-vis South Vietnam and, in effect, to co-operate with the West in seeking a solution to Southeast Asia instead of with China. Although Moscow had held some discussions with the French about the possibilities of calling a new conference or creating another mechanism to establish peace in Southeast Asia, the Russians were obviously caught in the middle on the matter; they maintained a pained silence when the British sought to elicit their response to diplomatic overtures about calling another Geneva conference, which London had previously suggested. Ten days after the White Paper was issued, the United States formally thanked U Thant for his "suggestions" about peace and added the hope that "all channels will be held open." In effect, however, the Secretary General's peace proposals were rejected by America's insistence that any peaceful solution would have to await "some indication that the aggressors are prepared to stop trying to take over South Vietnam by violence."

The determination of the United States to maintain pressure on North Vietnam by bombing selected targets, first in the lower part of the country and then, as it became necessary, farther north, served to stiffen the Saigon government's backbone, but there was considerable skepticism from the start about just how effective the bombings would be in persuading Hanoi to call off the infiltration of South Vietnam and the subversion of its people. Because of this, and also because of the usual imponderables that were besetting the South Vietnamese government, there remained a good deal of confusion in Saigon about the aims and the likely outcome of the many-faceted conflict. Somewhat paradoxically, the bombings and the arrival of the American Marines at Danang, amid reports that more American troops were soon coming, had the effect of strengthening the defensive but not the offensive posture and mood in South Vietnam. Many South Vietnamese and Americans, too, felt that if the bombings continued and were restricted to less important targets, and were carried out only sporadically, they would simply encourage the North Vietnamese to step up their attacks in the south, where the Vietcong, despite being reinforced from the north, was still very much a southern revolutionary force in their own right, and were moving toward what appeared to be a showdown reminiscent of the one against the French in 1953, in the same crucial central plateau and coastal areas. The possibility loomed that more and more of the countryside would fall to the Communists and that the South Vietnamese and the Americans would be reduced to holding on to Saigon and certain heavily guarded provincial capitals and cities like Danang. In other words, if so-called "limited" bombing of the north was not accompanied by political and military measures in the south calculated to deal aggressively with the guerrilla war, which was still the vital fight, the air assaults would have a purely negative effect.

If the bombings were extended to targets farther north in North Vietnam—important bridges and railheads, roads leading into China, factories and other installations relatively close to Hanoi and Haiphong, including airfields and the Red River dikes—the possibility of direct Chinese and perhaps even Russian involvement, and the virtual certainty of increased material help from China and Russia, would have the same effect as limited bombings in hardening the resolve of Hanoi neither to give up nor to go to the conference table. Either way, the bombings thus represented a calculated risk, and one that was bound to have obvious repercussions in a number of important capitals, not only in terms of diplomacy but also of public opinion, which was already turning against the United States throughout the Asian-African world. Despite these handicaps and dangers, Americans and Vietnamese alike were gratified that a first step had been taken—not only because the war on the ground was going so badly that something new had to be devised to rally resistance (the American air attacks against the Vietcong in South Vietnam did that immediately), but also because it was believed there was at least an outside chance that if the North Vietnamese were sufficiently hurt by the bombings, they might welcome an opportunity to halt hostilities. This would then enable them to trade with the south for rice, to achieve a better balance in their relations with Russia and China, and to consolidate their strength for the next big move. Such a move would undoubtedly be a political one, aimed at the further undermining of the South Vietnamese government and at capturing it from within, through the instrumentality of the National Liberation Front.

If South Vietnam was to have any chance of avoiding this, it obviously was in dire need of a strong national government with sufficient popular support, and with the ability to contain all the disparate elements that, wittingly or unwittingly, had been tearing the country apart in the year and a half since the overthrow of Diem and his family oligarchy. In March, 1965, there appeared to be some slight promise of stability. The most disruptive figures of the immediate past had managed either to eliminate each other or to defeat themselves; the three top-ranking generals—Khanh, Minh, and Khiem—who had been bitterly fighting each other for control, were now all out of the country ("We have our own three sputniks," one Vietnamese editor remarked), while some of the other important generals who had been in the first junta, and had become subjects of continued political dispute, were now out of the Army and were engaged in the export-import business in Saigon. However, other generals were sitting on top of the civilian government, and were inhibiting it. The most important of them, and the man regarded as the worst potential troublemaker, was General Nguyen Chanh Thi, the impulsive paratrooper who was already rumored to be plotting against those he considered possible rivals, in or out of the government. Part of the danger Thi represented derived from his continued close association with the militant Buddhist leaders, who had started a curious movement for peace while privately saying that they were ready to support the full prosecution of the war, including American bombing of North Vietnam, if their efforts to bring the Hanoi and Saigon governments together failed.

The Buddhist peace campaign was regarded by most observers who had followed the ups and downs of the political-religious movement for the past two years as a tactical maneuver by Tri Quang, Tam Chau, and Quang Lien, another activist priest, to re-establish their still-diminishing control over the nominally Buddhist masses. Since the Vietnamese Buddhists had never been as pacifist-minded as Buddhists elsewhere in Southeast Asia, the militant bonzes appeared to be using the peace issue primarily as a political weapon. The situation was a dangerous one because the Vietcong, for its own disruptive purposes, had created a "peace offensive." The Buddhists, whatever tactical differences they had among themselves, still seemed determined to control any government, or else to bring it down. They did not, at first, take any stand toward Dr. Phan Huy Quat's new regime, undoubtedly because it included so many nominal Buddhists, but it was apparent that Dr. Quat was embarrassed by the Buddhist clamor for peace. As soon as the unrest caused by the coup and its aftermath was over, and it had become certain that he would be allowed to stay in power, Dr. Quat issued a firm declaration insisting that there would be no peace until the Communists in the north stopped their infiltration of the south. The government, Dr. Quat said, would take "all necessary measures to smash the fallacious propaganda maneuvers that the Communists are waging with a view to deceive public opinion, sow confusion among the population, take advantage of the credulous . . . and carry out their Machiavellian maneuver to take over all of Vietnam." There would be no negotiations for peace that the Communists would simply exploit, he added, and none that would not contain "concrete, efficient, and appropriate means" for guaranteeing the security of South Vietnam.

The Quat government moved discreetly but forcefully to break the Buddhist peace movement—it managed to drive a wedge between the official Buddhist church and Quang Lien, who assumed the leadership of the peace movement, and he was shortly ordered to stop his activities. Meanwhile, Tri Quang and his aides quietly gained control of most of the pagodas in Saigon; they purged the monks who refused to go along with them, established a tight vertical chain of command that went down to the block level, and created a broad horizontal front of women's and youths' organizations, and of special departments. (Despite Tri Quang's gains in Saigon, there were some indications, by April, 1965, that his influence in the Buddhist hierarchy had somewhat waned. Following the suicide of a Buddhist woman and a bonze in protest against Vietcong terrorism, the secular branch of the Buddhist movement, at a meeting in the capital, voted to issue a statement denouncing Communist acts of terror against the population and Vietcong efforts to subvert the Buddhist masses. The motion, carried over the objections of Tri Quang, was initiated by Thich Tam Chau. It marked the first time the two top monks had openly disagreed about tactics, and it indicated that perhaps the Buddhists had begun to realize that they had moved too far to the left in the opportunist and pacifist orientation.) However, at this point, as always, it remained hard to gauge the sincerity and real intentions of the Buddhist leaders. They still seemed dominated by motives of self-preservation and aggrandizement of their new political role; it was hard to believe, at any rate, that they were serious in their declared intention of supporting the war in earnest if their peace offensive proved fruitless. Many observers had become convinced that whatever they said, the Buddhist militants were thoroughly xenophobic, and especially anti-American, and that they were ready to make some sort of accommodation with the Communists in the north, hoping then to be left in peace in a neutralist south. Such a hope, at best, had to be regarded as naïve.

As for the minority Catholics, they, too, had to be reckoned with; from the outset of the Quat government, they felt shunted aside, and they resented the fact that they were blamed, as a group, for the unsuccessful coup. The Army remained another source of uneasiness; it contained some strong Buddhist elements, like General Thi, but there were also many officers and men, Catholic or neutral, who resented the attempts of the Buddhists to seek political power, and there was a danger that these elements could become rebellious. In this touchy situation, Prime Minister Quat and his Cabinet were treading cautiously—too cautiously, some warned—in hopes of keeping peace among all the factions and creating some semblance of orderly government. Quat was generally respected, if not universally admired, as a long-time nationalist, even though he had served as Minister of Defense under the French-sponsored regime of the former Emperor Bao Dai; he had joined the opposition against Diem, but had managed to stay out of jail. A quiet, urbane northerner, he established his own small brain trust composed mostly of fellow northerners or men from Central Vietnam, and he was soon charged with selecting too many northerners to fill administrative posts—an accusation he countered with the comment that he couldn't find enough able southerners willing to work with him. However, he made a fairly good first impression on most Vietnamese, as well as on the Americans, who tended to regard him as probably the best man they could support under the circumstances. He issued another one of those broad platforms full of promises about the country's future, and about reinvigorating the war effort. One of his first declared tasks was to control the prices of rice, sugar, water, and electricity, and this was not easy to do in a climate of corruption that was growing increasingly worse. He announced that the elections supposed to be held for a National Congress on March 21st would have to be postponed; in view of the decisions of the Armed Forces Council creating the new National Legislative Council, a new election law would have to be drafted, he said. In the meantime a conference of provincial representatives would be summoned to discuss local and regional problems, and then with the help of the Legislative Council a system would be set up to hold preliminary elections for municipal councils in controlled areas. If Dr. Quat were allowed to go his own way for a few months, without interference from the Buddhists, the Catholics, or the generals, it was felt that he might have some chance of clearing up the messy situation, but skepticism remained. "In a way, after all the pent-up years under the French and under Diem, we are like children letting off steam," one Vietnamese political observer commented. "Maybe there will have to be yet another half-dozen coups before we settle down—even though we know we can't afford them."

It was not long before the rumors of another coup started. The Buddhists formed a new group, the National Front for a True Revolution, and openly began talking again of the need to get rid of the "many henchmen" and "dog generals" of the Diem regime, ostensibly to "preserve the new national spirit," "force the Quat government to carry out truly a real democracy," and "preserve security for the Buddhists." On one side were the Buddhists and the generals favorable to them, and on the other were the forces coalescing anew around the conspiratorial Colonel Thao. When I got back to Saigon, a few days after the February 19th coup, I managed to see Thao several times, though he was in hiding. He expressed his eagerness to co-operate with the Quat government if the officers—some fifty in all—who had joined him in the coup were amnestied. "After all, we simply wanted to get rid of Khanh, and we did," Thao told me. "Everyone else, including the Americans, wanted the same thing, but now we're being blamed and punished for what we did." Thao told me that if an amnesty was declared, he would be willing to leave Vietnam and return to the United States, where his family was still living. I passed his offer along to the American Embassy, and to Dr. Quat. There was some interest in it, but nothing was set in motion, and Thao grew increasingly impatient. The impact of the kind of skirmishing going on was naturally felt throughout the countryside, where it inevitably disrupted the war effort by provoking fresh uncertainties among both military and civilian leaders. Each time there had been a new coup, or each time there was talk of another one, things ground to a halt in the provinces because, among other reasons, province chiefs became uncertain of their tenure and tended to cling to the funds allotted them by the Saigon government out of fear that a new government would accuse them of waste or, even worse, of malfeasance. As one astute Vietnamese officer I knew put it, "If the civilians don't trust their leaders, and if the troops don't trust their officers, how can you fight?"

Johnson Defines Our Role

The combination of the influx of more Marines, of a few government victories that followed the American bombing support within South Vietnam, of the evolving pattern of bombings against North Vietnam's communication and transportation systems, and, finally, of the speech President Johnson made at Johns Hopkins University, in Baltimore, on April 7, 1965, all served to bring the war into new focus. In this speech, Johnson clearly defined the United States stake in Vietnam. "Let no one think for a moment that retreat from Vietnam would bring an end to the conflict," he said. "The battle would be renewed in one country and then another. The central lesson of our time is that the appetite of aggression is never satisfied. To withdraw from one battlefield means only to prepare for the next. We must say in Southeast Asia—as we did in Europe—in the words of the Bible: 'Hitherto shalt thou come, but no further.'" He added, "We will not be defeated. We will not grow tired. We will not withdraw, either openly or under the cloak of a meaningless agreement." In a phrase that, in an odd kind of way, summed up the whole American moral predicament, Johnson said: "I wish it were possible to convince others with words of what we now find necessary to say with guns and planes. Armed hostility is futile— our resources are equal to any challenge—because we fight for values and for principles, rather than for territory or colonies." The President then went on to offer what many Americans with long-time experience in Southeast Asia, and particularly in Vietnam, had wished had been offered sooner. He said he would ask Congress to "join in a billion-dollar American investment" program in the Southeast Asia area that would include the development of the Mekong River Valley "on a scale to dwarf even our own Tennessee Valley Authority," and he pledged to make available American surplus agricultural products "to assist in feeding and clothing the needy in Asia." Eugene Black, former president of the World Bank, was designated by the President to head a team of Americans "to inaugurate our participation in these programs," in which Johnson emphasized that North Vietnam, as well as South Vietnam, would share once peace was established.

In Saigon, the President's speech caused a strange reaction: it was praised by Prime Minister Quat and Foreign Minister Tran Van Do, but an undertone of worry was detectable, prompted by the fear that President Johnson had gone too far in declaring "We are ready . . . for unconditional discussions." Whether he meant it or not, it was felt, he had opened the path to actual negotiations, even though other American spokesmen had made it clear that the United States would not negotiate until it was satisfied that aggression from the north had ceased. The South Vietnamese, of course, had received a great deal of American aid for many years, so the prospect of peacetime aid for other countries in the area, including North Vietnam, carried less weight than it might elsewhere. The government's worries aside, though, the reaction of the Vietnamese to the speech was generally good, though guarded, and it was apparent that the United States was eager to obtain a more significant reaction from North Vietnam and other Communist nations when it briefly halted its air bombardment of the north. Hanoi, however, reacted as might have been expected, as did Peking; the Johnson offer amounted to nothing more than a bribe, both capitals asserted, and it was described as dishonest and insincere.

The feeling in South Vietnam was that there was still a long way to go in the war, and that under no circumstances would North Vietnam surrender its long-term objectives in the south. Most South Vietnamese felt that the United States had overplayed its secondary role in Southeast Asia, and had not made it sufficiently clear that it was engaged in Asia in order to defend its *own* position in the basic world struggle against Communism just as much as to defend South Vietnam's. What was more important than big economic and social plans, no matter how splendid, the South Vietnamese indicated, was the determination of the United States to handle first things first; that is, to continue to deal with the war itself, and then, during and after any discussions or negotiations, to protect South Vietnam from renewed Communist encroachments or subversion.

South Vietnam's role in this defense was still certainly far from successful. Although the military picture had taken a momentary turn for the better, the picture remained pretty grim. The Communists controlled almost two-thirds of the country, including whole new chunks of territory they had gobbled up where they were currently consolidating their political position and regrouping their military strength. There was every indication that when the rainy season started, in a month or so, and it became harder for planes to fly, a new Vietcong offensive, possibly aimed simultaneously at some of the provincial and district capitals in the highlands and at some of the major towns along the coast, would tax to the utmost the government's capability to resist with the forces it had available. Most of the regular government battalions in the nine Army divisions were still twenty-five per cent or more under strength as a result of combat losses; there were still only eleven reserve battalions that could be moved about quickly to deal with emergencies, and these were obviously not enough to help handle a multiple Vietcong offensive. The recruitment of new manpower for the important secondary elements—the Regional (provincial) Forces and the Popular (local) Forces, whose ranks had been decimated in battle and by large-scale desertions during the Vietcong offensives in 1964 and in the first part of 1965—was not proceeding nearly as fast as the government and the Americans had hoped.

In recent months, the difference between victory and defeat had been the improved mobility provided by the American air effort. In particular, an influx of helicopters—still more were due to come—had enabled the rapid movement of company-size attack forces and, when necessary, reserves to follow up on what were called "Eagle Flight contacts." Eagle Flights represented one of the true innovations of the war in Vietnam.

Eagle Flights

Early one morning, in the town of Phucat, in the coastal province of Binh Dinh, I climbed aboard an Army helicopter to accompany such a flight, which consisted of six helicopters, each with an American pilot and co-pilot, each guarded at its two open doors by American machine gunners, and each carrying six Vietnamese soldiers, whose mission was to attack and destroy a fortified Vietcong village fifteen minutes' flying time away. Shortly before we reached the objective area, two American Skyraiders strafed and bombed the village, which lay in a shallow valley below a long range of hills, and as we approached the site, two additional rocket-carrying helicopters, known as gun ships, flying alongside us, made another attack around the landing area and on the village itself. When the troop-carrying ships set down in the field designated as the landing zone, about two hundred yards from the village, the pilots found it had been staked with dozens of short tree trunks, the purpose of which was to prevent just such a landing. They managed to ease the helicopters in carefully among the stumps, and they set down, debouched their troops, and took off in the remarkable time of ten seconds, which is thirteen seconds less than the time of flight of an average shot of mortar, a weapon the Vietcong now have in considerable supply. While the pair of gun ships and the auxiliary one I was in hovered overhead to provide added protection and to attack any Vietcong flushed from their hiding places, the three dozen government soldiers and a young American lieutenant who was their adviser—all of whom wore red sashes over one shoulder, so they wouldn't shoot each other by mistake—dispersed through the village, which was surrounded by a moat filled with two- and three-foot-high sharpened bamboo spikes, called "*punji* sticks." There was little sign of life, the inhabitants apparently having fled, but eight bodies were found in the adjacent ditches and alongside the many foxholes that had been dug. After carefully searching the twenty houses in the village, the troops set fire to all of them. Then, deploying through the fields, they found seven women and children cowering in or around the canals, and took them as prisoners. The operation, as is customary with Eagle Flights, lasted a little less than an hour, after which the helicopters, which had been circling nearby, landed again, picked up the troops, and returned to Phucat, with their fuel tanks almost empty. The prisoners, who were frightened and weeping, were immediately questioned by Vietnamese interrogators, who sought information about the men of the village and the movements of the Vietcong contingents in the area. Afterward, I was told, the seven would be set free and sent to one of the government-held villages, of which there were few in Binh Dinh, where the Vietcong controlled ninety per cent of the provincial area and about seventy per cent of its nearly one million population.

Eagle Flights were essentially quick response actions aimed at meeting emergency situations and at baiting the Vietcong into a fight, and many of them had proved more successful in both objectives than the one I accompanied. For example, early in February, 1965, when the Vietcong had attacked the American barracks at Pleiku, fast-pursuing Eagle Flight troops had caught up at dawn with the fleeing terrorists and, with the help of additional government troops brought in by helicopter, had killed twenty-seven Vietcong. There was little doubt that the combination of fast troop movement and aerial assaults against enemy troop concentrations and bases within South Vietnam, especially quick reaction strikes by the B-57 light bombers, had forced the Vietcong to alter their basic plan to attain victory in 1965. This plan, conceived in mid-1964 as the beginning of the so-called third, all-out stage in the Communists' long-term strategy, was predicated on the continuing instability of the Saigon government and on the seeming demoralization of government troops in South Vietnam. The scheme was based on a series of projected assaults down from the mountains onto the central coastal plains, the establishment of enclaves along the shore to receive new Chinese-made Soviet-type weapons brought in by sea, and the use of forces up to regimental size to cut the country in two. This left the southern delta, already mostly held by the Vietcong, as the lower part of the vise in which to enclose Saigon, while the northern mountainous part, above the central plateau and just below North Vietnam, would also be isolated and then attacked.

Until March, 1965, it seemed the Vietcong plan might succeed. Regular and local elements of the Vietcong, bolstered by the new hard-core infiltrators from North Vietnam, had moved boldly onto the plains of the two most important coastal provinces, Binh Dinh and Phu Yen, formerly held by the government, and had completely disrupted earlier pacification efforts there. Then, however, primarily because of American air attacks, the Vietcong had been driven back into the mountains or been forced to lie low in the villages and swamps near the coast, and they had learned that any assaults they made in the open were likely to be costly. At the same time, government forces had become more aggressive and had won a series of victories, both in repelling Vietcong attacks and in initiating their own. These victories, which resulted in some seven hundred Vietcong killed, had taken place not only in the plateau and coastal areas but also in the delta and up north. The arrival in early April of three thousand more American Marines in the northern corps area, bringing the total to about eight thousand, or half a reinforced division, with their own air and missile support, had probably nipped in the bud any immediate Vietcong plans to launch a major attack in the region around Danang. The added Marines were to be used, it was announced, for offensive patrol work over a wider area extending inland from the city of Hué, just north of Danang and close to the Seventeenth Parallel, to a point below Danang, and perhaps even farther south and west. These troops thus represented the first sizable American ground units for offensive as well as defensive action in South Vietnam, and sooner or later, it was surmised, they would tangle directly with the Vietcong; in fact, it was obvious from the outset that in an emergency they would be airlifted to other areas away from their base.

The Military Adviser System

Despite the added American support, and the government's seemingly new offensive spirit, the South Vietnamese forces had still not gained much ground because, as most experts were quick to point out, the major roads that had been recaptured remained subject to easy interdiction, and mere mobility and the use of special techniques were not enough. The application, for example, of such expedients as chemical sprays to kill rice crops in Vietcong-controlled areas, of defoliation sprays and fire bombs to chase and burn the Vietcong out of forest bases, and of tear-and-nausea gas to flush the enemy from caves, did not provide the real answer to the greater problem of winning the war in Vietnam; in fact, even when preceded by warnings to the population, which were given in the case of the sprays and in the use of napalm and ordinary bombs in what were now called "bomb-free" zones, their value as legitimate weapons of war was doubtful when set off against the basic need "to win the hearts and minds of the people," a phrase that had by now become pretty shopworn but remained the key to the situation. To be sure, all things might be fair in war, but the conflict in South Vietnam was so much political and social as well as military that certain practical military measures, taken by themselves, could have the opposite from the desired effect and do anything but make people love the South Vietnamese and their American allies, even if for the moment, out of fear of being killed, some of the guerrillas renounced the Vietcong and switched sides. Moreover, the Vietnamese are extremely superstitious people, and when a forest fire set by napalm in a Vietcong zone was extinguished by a sudden freak rainstorm, and when attempts to spray a Vietcong rice area and to use tear gas against a Vietcong hide-out failed because of winds and bad weather —all within the space of a fortnight—the failures were widely commented upon and discussed in Saigon as "heavenly omens" favoring the Communists.

Any kind of warfare is grotesque, and in a war as messy and fluid as the Vietnamese one, where the elements of hide-and-seek were predominant, the civilian population was bound to suffer more and more as aerial attacks, acts of terror like the Vietcong bombing of the American Embassy in Saigon at the end of March, and other measures of interdiction and reprisal increased. Escalation tended to breed escalation, and if, notwithstanding the President's April speech, the continuing attacks against North Vietnam did not achieve their desired effect, it was believed inevitable that additional American troops would be committed as fighting units in South Vietnam and that the United States would have to assume greater operational control of the war through the formal establishment of a joint command. Such a step might not be popular either in the United States or in Vietnam, it was said, but it would be the logical and the unavoidable consequence of what had taken place—or, rather, had *not* taken place—in the previous four years. To a large extent, it would be an admission of what was widely felt to be the failure of the American advisory system, whereby American officers in the field trained, and served as consultants to, the Vietnamese down to the battalion level and down to the administrative districts that were the paramilitary subdivisions of the country's forty-four provinces.

The advisory program, while it had been a tribute to the politeness of both parties, had failed in its primary aim of persuading the Vietnamese officers to get their men out into the countryside and to *stay* there, if necessary, day and night, for weeks on end in order to beat the Communists at their own game. This view of the failure of American efforts at persuasion was privately expressed to me by most of the advisers I spoke with during my trip through the vital plateau

M

area, and it was reinforced by what advisers from other battle areas told me. The consensus was that the system was inherently anomalous and unworkable in that it reflected the American predilection for trying to get a difficult and probably impossible job done in what a British friend of mine described as "your typical nice American way."

There were many reasons why the South Vietnamese were unwilling to take advice and fight the war in what we regarded as the right fashion, and these reasons were constantly discussed and debated not only by the Americans but also by the relative handful of Vietnamese who had their own ideas about how to deal in counter-guerrilla terms with a guerrilla war; these were invariably men who had spent several years with the Vietminh during the war against the French. The chief reasons cited for the failure of the South Vietnamese forces consistently to do better than they had were lack of leadership and a lack of motivation. There was a big difference, it was emphasized by those who had watched the situation for some time, between courage and leadership, and between morale and motivation. The individual Vietnamese soldier, these observers acknowledged, was brave and potentially aggressive if he was properly and imaginatively inspired and led; but too many of the senior officers and most of the junior officers thought of fighting the easy instead of the hard way, of going out on an action in the morning and returning for dinner and a relatively comfortable bed at night, in camp or in a village, where, under the Vietnamese system, the families of all troops, officers and men alike, lived with them, following them about from place to place. The Americans had for several years been urging the regular forces to stay out on patrol and fight at night, but they had been unsuccessful, except in the case of a few elements such as the Vietnamese Special Forces, with whom American advisers had established a unique role that was much more co-operative and participating; it was significant that these troops, usually operating in squads or platoons and sometimes in company size, had done the best job of interdicting the various mountain, valley, and river-bed trails used by the Vietcong along the Laos border and the central Annamite mountain range to infiltrate men and supplies into South Vietnam from the north.

While tactically, in point of communications and transportation as well as in aerial combat assistance, the greater American involvement had obviously strengthened the South Vietnamese, there had tended to be too great a reliance on American support, especially on the helicopters, and on other new techniques and new forms of assistance. This was where the question of motivation versus morale also came to bear. Morale, so low in 1964, undoubtedly had been lifted as a result of the new display of American air power; attack planes were now even encouraged to buzz Vietnamese troops during actions to enhance their confidence, and the Vietnamese responded to air strikes both in the north and in the south with almost child-like glee. Significantly, though, there was still no desire on the part of the troops to remain in the woods and swamps and to search for the enemy by setting traps for him, clobbering him, and then pursuing him relentlessly; nor was there any concomitant willingness to live in strange villages among strange people and protect and get steady intelligence from them—"from girl friends in place of wives, if need be," as one American senior officer bluntly put it to me.

This matter of motivation was essentially a Vietnamese problem that American persuasion could do very little about, although the Americans kept trying. The problem had to do with many subtle aspects of Vietnamese life, with the long French orientation of the army, with the whole system of rewards and punishments that reflected political and family influences in the structure of the Vietnamese officer corps and civilian administration—most of these had been created and had flourished during the nine years of the dictatorial Ngo Dinh Diem regime—and with the continuing lack of confidence in the countless governments that had come and gone after the fall of Diem and the constant shifts they provoked.

In trying to cope with the military problem that involved so many fluctuating psychological and emotional as well as political and social factors, the American advisers, who represented the top ten per cent of the United States Army officer corps, were subject to countless daily doses of frustration and exasperation. Invariably, either their patience tended to wear thin or they subjected themselves to the rationalization that they were accomplishing more than was actually the case, that agreement by their counterparts to do something they recommended, for example, acually meant it would be done. The task of the advisers was not made easier by what was a standing order from the top American command to remain optimistic; pessimism was not countenanced, and any man who consistently complained, legitimately or not, was characterized as a "loser." I do not wish to overstate the case; the relationship of American advisers in the field to their superiors in Saigon had become much better in March, 1965, than it had ever been before, and false optimism was now no longer a factor. Furthermore, in four years of covering the war in South Vietnam I had seen numerous instances where a a particularly close relationship between an American officer and his Vietnamese counterpart had achieved commendable results, both in battle and in the field of civic action—co-operation between troops and the civilian administration, province and district chiefs, to protect villages from the Vietcong and turn them into viable anti-Communist molecules. By and large, however, the advisory system didn't work, many advisers themselves felt, because Americans and Vietnamese could not possibly, in the short time of a year in which advisers stayed in Vietnam, understand each other's ways of thinking and action. The Americans could not comprehend all the intricate aspects of Vietnamese history and culture that play such a prominent part in the waging of the war in that country, in personal and bureaucratic terms. It was undoubtedly too much to ask that they should. The language difficulty alone was a paramount one, and while a growing number of advisers sent to Vietnam were receiving some Vietnamese-language instruction back home, the huge majority still had to work through interpreters whose knowledge of English was rather limited and whose knowledge of military strategy and tactics, the basic things advisers and their counterparts talk about, was nil. The lower the echelon, and particularly at the battalion level, where good interpreters are most scarce, the more difficult this matter of communication became.

While many advisers also felt that a two-year term instead of one year would accomplish more, since it took so long to get close to their counterparts, others maintained that one year was enough of a drain on their emotions. "You effectively advise your counterpart only an hour a day, but the interchange of ideas is very taxing," one captain, who was an assistant sector, or province, adviser told me. "By the end of the day, you know you've lived it." Most of the advisers I spoke with agreed that the year of service tended to fall into a pretty firm pattern. "For the first three months, while you're feeling your way, you're inclined to be optimistic and full of beans," one man told me. "Then the curve starts going down, and it reaches its low point after about eight months. And then, oddly enough, maybe because you've grown wiser and expect less, or just because you know you're soon going home, the curve starts going up again, and by the eleventh month your sense of hope returns. That's why a surprisingly large number of officers and men volunteer to come back." It was during the five months or so in the middle that an adviser was most apt to blow his top. Most of all, he got fed up with Vietnamese work habits, which include a two-and-half-hour lunch-and-siesta break and a disinclination to work in the evening. Another man I met, a lieutenant colonel, walked into a division headquarters one evening a day or so before a large operation was scheduled and found eight American officers busily at work but none of their Vietnamese counterparts. He angrily ordered the eight to quit and go to bed; shortly thereafter, the Vietnamese division general appeared and wanted to know where the Americans were. When told what had happened, he roused his Vietnamese officers out of their quarters and everybody, Americans and Vietnamese, went back to work until midnight.

Vietnam was not the first place where the United States had played an advisory military role, but the rules of the game there made it the most subtle and complex. In Korea, it had been more direct; Korean elements were, in fact, augmented to American units, and there had been a true joint command; not only was there more American decision-making but, as one adviser who had served in Korea told me, "The Koreans were more persuadable than the Vietnamese." The same had been true, other advisers pointed out, of the Greeks, who had American advisers with them during their war against the guerrillas in 1948 and 1949. "There were no American helicopters and bombers in Greece," one of the Greek veterans recalled, "but we gave the Greeks some good Missouri mules. I spent six months in the field with a mountain division, climbing around and lugging howitzers on muleback. We chased the guerrillas night and day and never lost contact with them, as happens here. In Greece, too, we were able to force political reforms. There were other factors, of course, that turned the tide. When the borders with the neighboring Communist satellites were sealed and no more military assistance came in, victory over the local Communists became possible. We never have been able to seal the borders here in Vietnam, and men and supplies are still coming in from the north."

Both in Korea and Greece, there had been a great degree of mutual adaptation on the part of Americans and their counterparts to each other's ways. The same was not true of Vietnam, and the fault may have been as much that of the Americans as of the Vietnamese. There were many military experts who felt that in the first phase of American assistance—starting in 1954, when there were a few hundred advisers in Vietnam, and increasing measurably after 1961, when the figure started to rise into the thousands—the Americans had tried to re-create the shattered South Vietnamese Army in their own image, as too much an American-type organization. This pertained not only to administration but to ways of fighting; many Vietnamese junior and senior officers at the time were sent to American war colleges for training, where for the most part they received courses in conventional warfare scarcely suited to the type of guerrilla warfare being waged in Vietnam. This, as much as the previous French influence, undoubtedly accounted for the predilection of too many Vietnamese commanders to commit their forces in large numbers to so-called "sweep actions," where whole battalions and even regiments were flown by American helicopters to areas where the Vietcong, according to intelligence reports, were supposed to be located; the time it took to mount such operations, and their very size alone, almost always gave the Communists a chance to escape. Even though the Eagle Flight technique tended to reduce the number of such large-scale maneuvers, they were still being attempted; I went on one, during my March, 1965, trip, in Binh Tuy Province that involved elements of five different outfits totaling more than a thousand troops, and the net result after three days was half a dozen Vietcong killed. The Americans strenuously opposed such tactics, but Vietnamese general officers were invariably sensitive about such matters and were defensive about the whole question of accepting advice. One of them I talked to, who was considered to be one of the two or three best generals in the country, praised the early American reorganizational effort of the Vietnamese Army, but added that in the current stage of the war "The help of American advisers is not always valuable, because we Vietnamese feel we know more about the situation in the countryside than our American friends."

It is at this point, of course, that exasperation set in on both sides. While the Americans agreed that they naturally knew less than the Vietnamese about village life, they did not accept the excuses given them by Vietnamese battalion or regimental commanders for not moving promptly and efficiently against reported Vietcong elements. "I can't use a club on my counterpart," one battalion adviser said. "All I can do is try to influence him, even coax him, and if I go too far or too fast, our relationship, which perhaps is just beginning to be a close one, is spoiled." Involved in this were other intricate aspects of the relationships both between the American and his counterpart and between the Vietnamese officer and his superiors. Frequently, because he had been educated that way under the old French system, an officer would not pass on American advice to his immediate superior; this was due partly to subservience, but also to a feeling of independence and pride, as well as self-protection, on his part. Many incompetent officers stayed in their jobs for years by following this careful practice, and there was very little, under the circumstances, the Americans could do about it. Sometimes, influence could be brought to bear nearer the top, at the division and corps levels, and sometimes changes were made, but more often they were not and things just slid on as before.

When exasperation gave way to dissillusion and fatigue, an adviser's usefulness was obviously impaired. I once heard a weary senior American officer say, only half in jest, "I could do a better job out here advising the Vietcong." The tedium of the job, the fact that every bit of progress brought about by advice called for the utmost amount of patience, was particularly disturbing to most Americans, who by nature tended to be impatient, a quality of national character that, in turn, upset the Vietnamese, who were anything but impatient. The relationship of an adviser and his counterpart was as much a psychological game as anything else—and sometimes it degenerated into a kind of psychological warfare. One of the more enthusiastic officers I met, a colonel who was a deputy corps adviser and, perhaps because he was an older man, was also one of the more patient, handled matters of funneling supplies to the Vietnamese, of getting them to use certain things the right way, and of gently rejecting their appeals for other things he felt they didn't really need or may simply have wanted to distribute as largess or rewards. "The way I see my job," this officer said, "is to get my counterpart to want the things he knows I have that I think will help him, and to keep him from asking for anything else. I find it a rather stimulating challenge."

The job of being an adviser was regarded by many of the men holding it as a challenging one, and whatever success they had was due as much to luck as anything else—the luck of the draw in the selection of their counterpart. In Pleiku, for example, one of the central provinces where the Vietcong was strongest in the spring of 1965, Captain William Zaldo, of El Paso, Texas, who took part in the successful chase of the Vietcong terrorists after they attacked Pleiku barracks and the airfield in February, had what he called "a tremendous relationship" with a Vietnamese captain, whom he advised on the training and use of Regional and Popular Forces. "He was a wonderfully aggressive guy, who never got tired of doing his job and doing it well," Zaldo said. "We got to be great friends and did everything together—eat, drink, and go out on dates and dance. When we traveled around the villages and hamlets, we always stayed in the same room. But then he was transferred to go to staff and command school. I realized it was for his own good, but I haven't been able to establish nearly as close a relationship with either of his two replacements since then." Zaldo, when I saw him, was engaged in the difficult job of building up the Popular Forces in Pleiku, where there had been many desertions, and in organizing them into company- instead of platoon-size outfits in the hamlets, so they wouldn't be mangled by the Vietcong and be panicked into surrendering or throwing away their weapons before regular Army elements could come to their support. His problem, as everywhere else in Vietnam, was to find one good leader for each hamlet force, and he felt that his job would be a lot easier if he had been able to keep his original counterpart with him.

The importance of the single leader was borne out time and again. In March, near Phucat, in Binh Dinh, two American captains and a sergeant accompanied a Regional Force of three companies on an early-morning search for a reported Vietcong battalion in the area. Moving on two villages in three columns, one of the companies was ambushed, its commander killed, and the American sergeant wounded. Instead of quickly appointing a Vietnamese sergeant to take the place of the dead company commander, the lieutenant who was the task force commander in charge of the whole operation bolted, and the whole second company he was with turned and ran with him, severely jeopardizing the position of the isolated third company and ruining whatever chance the task force had for a successful mission. A Vietnamese major, in charge of the Phucat training camp, sat on a nearby hill and laughed as he watched the rout through a pair of binoculars. "All it takes is one bad egg like that lieutenant," Captain Kenneth Wright, of Louisville, who was advising the third company, later told me. "Despite the report we wrote, neither the lieutenant nor that major who thought it was so funny was transferred, though no Vietnamese in the camp would even talk to them."

The Battle of Binh Dinh

The battle of Binh Dinh, up to that point one of the most important of the war, began early in December, 1964, when the Vietcong moved down from the hills and captured a district capital in the northern part of the province after ambushing a government battalion. Government forces then retreated and built a strong fortified position and an airstrip above the town of Bongson, on Route 1, the north-south coastal road. The fort and strip, atop a hill, were the most strongly defended spots I had seen in Vietnam, with bunkers and parapets and blockhouses built all over the top and the surrounding slopes. Although the airfield was necessary for supplying the whole area, and had to be protected, the place reminded me rather dismally of the French forts I had seen fifteen years earlier. In March, Bongson was still totally isolated and could be reached only by air. This was the result of the big Vietcong offensive that began early in February, just after Tet, the Vietnamese New Year, when the Vietcong took advantage of a self-declared truce to move their troops into position. When they again struck, the Communists seized control of all of Route 1 in Binh Dinh—they already had control of it in the provinces of Phu Yen to the south and Quang Ngai to the north. At the same time, they seized the lateral east-west road, Route 19, from Pleiku across to Quinhon, the Binh Dinh capital. Late in February, the government began to hit back and, with the help of American air support, including the almost perfectly co-ordinated use of bombers, rocket gunships, and troop-carrying helicopters, landed troops on Route 19 to attack the Vietcong, gave them protective fire, and then lifted them out again after a series of battles that hurt the Communists, who began moving back into the hills. Then on March 9th, when the Vietcong attacked the Special Forces camp of Kannack, just north of the road, they suffered a stunning defeat, losing a hundred and thirty hard-core dead against the barbed wire of the encampment and at least another hundred and fifty as a result of air attacks. After Kannack, Route 19 was successfully reopened to convoys, and in mid-March the government started its campaign to reopen Route 1, the north-south road, too. By early April it had done so, with a minimum of resistance, up as far as Bongson; the Vietcong apparently was willing to let Route 1 be opened that far without a major fight, figuring they could always cut it again, as they had done before, by digging deep ditches and placing rail ties from the adjacent railway across it. I saw their handiwork when I walked up the road during the clearing operation, watching the same poor villagers who had been ordered by the Communists to dig the holes in it and place the rails across it now following the orders of the government troops to fill the holes up and drag the ties away.

While it was undoubtedly important, for supply purposes as well as for strategic and psychological reasons, to keep the lateral Route 19 open, many American military observers felt that the government was putting too much emphasis on Route 1, which they probably wouldn't be able to keep open all the time anyway, and that it should be concentrating more on the vital valleys eastward of this road, to the sea, and westward toward the mountains. It was in these areas that the Vietcong was entrenched in the villages—including fortified villages like the one attacked and burned out by the Eagle Flight company I had accompanied. "Route 1 by itself doesn't mean a damn thing," one American adviser told me. "If they just stick to that, they're right back to where the French were. They have to get out into the villages where the people are." Although the Vietnamese Marines moving north of Bongson on Route 1 toward the Quang Ngai border had been killing a large number of resisting Vietcong, other troop elements farther south in Binh Dinh were still conducting futile large sweep operations and were not probing the countryside. "It's meaningless," another adviser declared, "for troops to move out, make contact with the Vietcong, take a casualty or two, and then call for an air strike, which may kill some Communists along with other people but surely will settle nothing in these crucial rural areas."

The Grass Roots

As long as the war in Vietnam lasted, the ability to deal with the Vietnamese situation at its grass roots, first militarily and then politically and socially, would remain basic to the problem of winning the war, and it would be just as important in winning any peace. Millions of words had already been written and spoken about pacification programs and psychological warfare, and so on, but very little actually was being done, particularly as more and more of the country was coming under Communist control. It was the firm belief of a handful of Vietnamese and their American supporters I knew that the only way to reach the people was to start not from the top, but from the bottom, from among the thousands of scattered hamlets of the country, and to reorganize them politically and militarily, so that the men who speak and fight for them would be truly representative of them and not of government-appointed officials and higher military echelons. To do this, according to one high Vietnamese official I knew in a key province, a real "People's Forces" had to be organized, consisting of local partisans who would be responsible only to the province chief, who would be both the military and the civilian head of the province. This would entail something that many American military advisers privately admitted would be a good thing—the abolishment of corps and divisions and the creation of brigades and battalions operating, as the Vietminh did and the Vietcong was doing, in special zones and in individual provinces. "In many respects, I think we should look upon the war as being lost, and we should consider ourselves the true guerrillas," this Vietnamese official told me. "The Communists have sown many seeds in the last ten years, but if we do things right, we can still reap them. We must think in social revolutionary terms, the way the Communists pretend to do, and in terms of true social justice in the villages and hamlets. Up to now, despite all the talk, there has never been any real village democracy or any real land reform. The members of the hamlet militia protected the government's hamlet chief, and when the Vietcong killed him, they ran away or deserted to the enemy. If a village is liberated by the government, the landlords, who were the first to flee, are always the last to come back, and they collect all the back taxes they can. There must be a true village democracy. One way we can start, I think, is to establish small village governments-in-exile among the refugees from the Communist areas, and then, when we can get these people back to their villages, let them take over as the heads of new cooperative village councils. There is not enough arable land for everyone, but it should be distributed to those who till it, and those who protected and supported the Vietcong should be sent to virgin lands in the highlands, where they can raise new crops and create new homes, working with the mountain tribes—perhaps, in a generation or so, integrate themselves and the mountain people back into the national society. We will need the help of the United States in mechanizing agriculture and in other ways, just as we need your help now, logistically, to fight the war, but it must be a Vietnamese fight."

In the early spring of 1965, there were a few quietly conceived and functioning American-backed programs in some key areas of South Vietnam where ideas such as these were being slowly introduced. They were based on the injection of native elements, often refugees from specific villages, into areas the Vietcong now control. A well-armed platoon of these "black commandos" in Vietcong-type black pyjamas not only sought out and fought the enemy but then remained in a village, if it was recovered, and worked with the people, helping them harvest their crops, dig wells, and so on. These programs, which were outside the pale of the major war effort, were making some headway. The question was would there be time for them to expand and have a real impact? If they didn't, most impartial observers of the Vietnamese scene who had been watching the slow process of erosion and retrogression for a long time were convinced that, whether in war or under conditions of armed peace, the battle in Vietnam would be lost, and such bold schemes as those outlined by President Johnson would never have a chance of being implemented.

More Catholic-Buddhist Friction

While the government forces, with close American air support, were holding their own against the Vietcong during the dry season, the Communists were obviously lying low and regrouping, waiting for the monsoonal rains to start in May, when the air operations against them would be slowed down and they would be able to regain the initiative. Even before the new Vietcong push began, a serious new political crisis arose in Saigon, and once again the United States might have done more than it did to ward off the consequences.

When I returned to Saigon from my military trip to the highlands and to Binh Dinh, I discovered that nothing had been done to improve relations between the Buddhists and the Catholics and to avert another possible coup attempt by preparing an amnesty for Colonel Thao's junior officers, who were still in jail for having taken part in the February 19th coup. Two members of the Quat government told me that plans were "underway" but would "take time." The Americans, because of a basic distrust of Thao, seemed less interested in prosecuting such plans, but some "inquiries" were being made behind the scenes. The Americans' resentment of Thao stemmed from his allegedly having claimed they were behind his coup effort. (He denied to me that this was so, but even if it was true, he had simply done what any coup-master had to do if he was to have a chance of success.) Now, in considering arranging an amnesty, the Americans were afraid of General Thi, the pro-Buddhist northern commander, who was a bitter enemy of Thao's and whom the Americans were afraid of offending. Thi was known to have "killer squads" looking for Thao, who was still in hiding and who enjoyed the protection of a number of police officials and of the Army's military security section. On several occasions when I saw Thao, he professed to be increasingly disgusted with the failure of the government, and the Americans, to arrange an amnesty; it was apparent that soon he would no longer be interested in any arrangement, and would, by choice, stay underground and prepare another coup. I passed these warnings on, as I had done before, emphasizing that whether Thao succeeded or not, there was bound to be more trouble unless something was done to avert it, and that any further disruptions would obviously hurt the war effort. Early in May, after I had left Saigon, it was suddenly announced that a military tribunal had passed death sentences on Thao, General Phat, and a civilian leader of the February 19th coup. This ended whatever hopes there had been for an amnesty of the younger officers, and for the plan that had also been posed to give Thao a light sentence and then get him out of the country, which he had initially proposed himself. General Thi had had his way with his fellow officers and with the Americans. Around the same time, the Armed Forces Council announced that it would disband and thereby give Dr. Quat more freedom as the civilian head of the government; Thi had been against the disbanding, and his condition for accepting it, as one of the A.F.C. leaders, apparently had been the meting out of the death sentence to Thao.

Dr. Quat had spent a great deal of his first two months in office cultivating the generals on the Armed Forces Council and persuading them to allow him to run the government without military interference. A number of his most intimate advisers felt that he had done so to the exclusion of other matters, including the reorganization of his

Cabinet, the maintenance of good working relations with Chief of State Suu, and the creation of better harmony between the Catholics and the Buddhists. Although the Buddhists were having internal troubles of their own—including a renewal of the contest between Thich Tri Quang and Thich Tam Chau for control of the movement in the south, and of a long-simmering dispute between lay-Buddhist leaders and the official hierarchy—they were still unified enough to make their political strength felt. They now forced a number of changes in the military command. They obtained the dismissal of General Pham Van Dong as Governor of Saigon and chief of the capital military district; Dong, although nominally a Buddhist, had opposed the militant Buddhists in their uncompromising fight to overthrow Premier Huong, and he had incurred the Buddhists' opposition because of his close relationship to the Americans, who thought well of him. The Catholics reacted strongly to this new Buddhist pressure, which they saw as a fresh attempt to reduce the influence of Catholic officers in the Army; several such officers, in fact, including the Commander of the Navy, were suddenly dismissed at the same time as General Dong. This militant Catholic response, under the leadership of Father Hoang Quynh and organized under the banner of the Central Movement of the Catholic Struggle, quickly became directed at Dr. Quat. Father Quynh's group attacked him for being "too soft on Communism" and for giving in to the renewed Buddhist "neutralist" aims. Priests in a hundred and twenty parishes in the Saigon area were encouraged to arm their parishioners with knives and sticks in self-defense against a possible neutralist deal between the Buddhist and the Vietcong. The official Catholic hierarchy, as represented by the regional Bishops and by Archbishop Nguyen Van Binh in Saigon, remained aloof from Father Quynh's direct action group, but privately they gave it their blessing.

It is unlikely that the high Catholic clergy aligned itself with Colonel Thao directly, but other militant Catholic leaders may have. With a death sentence on his head, Thao was now virtually forced into plotting another coup. He and General Thi were trying to trap each other into striking first. On May 20th, in what was described by the generals and the Quat government as the defeat of another coup effort, a half-dozen junior officers and some forty civilians, mostly Catholics, were arrested. According to the official charges, the plotters had planned to assassinate Premier Quat and to kidnap General Thi and Air Marshal Ky. To the majority of observers, it looked as if the government had initiated the action, in anticipation of a coup by Thao, and had fabricated at least some of the charges. It was particularly doubtful that Dr. Quat was scheduled to be assassinated, although his personal bodyguard had been suborned. Several of the fifty-odd people arrested were known supporters of Thao, who had played key roles in the previous coup effort, and one of the military men apprehended was the head of the military security section, who had been protecting Thao in his movements around the city. Another officer, a captain who had been sentenced to twenty years' imprisonment in absentia for his part in the February 19th coup, was shot and killed trying to escape from civilian police in the round-up. Colonel Thao again managed to evade arrest. A price of $30,000 was now placed on his head. (In July of 1965, Thao was reported to have died of injuries en route to Saigon in a helicopter after having been captured by Vietnamese security forces north of Saigon. It seemed apparent that he had been murdered. In a letter to an American friend, a few days earlier, he had written of the need for a form of "humanitarian Socialism" to curb Communism in Vietnam.)

If Thao's alleged second "coup" was indeed phony and represented an attempt by General Thi and his group to crush Thao and his co-conspirators, it did not succeed in subduing the Catholics. Within a week or so, Catholic pressure mounted against Quat, and Father Quynh's militants were openly seeking the government's overthrow, charging Quat with being incompetent and with "plotting with the colonialists [i.e., the French] to negotiate," which was commensurate in falsity with Quat's similar accusation against the Catholic "coup" leaders. Various Catholic delegations regularly began visiting the office of Chief of State Suu to present resolutions calling for Dr. Quat's ouster, and they obtained the support of some Hoa Hao and Cao Dai sect representatives. The issue had now come to a head over some Cabinet changes Dr. Quat wanted to make in order to bring more southerners into the government. The Premier's motives were honorable enough, but he had spent so much time trying to placate the generals that he had made the mistake of forgetting about the need to maintain close relations with Chief of State Suu. When two of the five Cabinet members Dr. Quat wanted to have resign refused to do so, Suu backed their refusal as "legal." The Catholics quickly took advantage of the differences between Suu and Dr. Quat to push their attack against the Quat regime. On June 9th, Dr. Quat paved the way for his own ouster by asking the generals "to play the role of mediators" in his dispute with Suu. He apparently expected the generals to support him against Suu, but three days later the generals forced Dr. Quat to resign and again took over the South Vietnamese government.

The United States, while it had supported Dr. Quat and had hoped that he might be able to weather the storm, was "gratified" that the new change-over had at least been accomplished peacefully. The Embassy urged the generals to set up a new government as quickly as possible, particularly in view of the serious war situation, and, somewhat forlornly, it requested that it be kept better informed than it had been about the various negotiations that were going on among the generals, the politicians, and the religious leaders. Once again, Ambassador Taylor had been out of the country when a government fell; he was back in Washington reporting to President Johnson. The generals quickly established a new National Leadership Committee, headed by General Nguyen Van Thieu, who had been Defense Minister. The forty-two-year-old Thieu, a moderate converted Roman Catholic who had been involved in the 1964, Dai Viet Party coup attempts, had fought with the French against the Vietminh during the Indochina war and had worked his way up slowly through the Army chain of command. He was considered to have the best chance of keeping peace among the generals and of obtaining the support of the two main religious groups. Initially, Air Marshal Ky and General Nguyen Huu Co, commander of the II Corps, joined Thieu on the National Leadership Committee, but this triumvirate was then increased to ten members, including General Thi. General Co was named Commissioner General of the armed forces—in effect, commander in chief—and the thirty-five-year-old Air Marshal Ky was given supervision of a new Executive Council, in charge of the day-by-day administration of the country. A dispute immediately arose as to whether Ky would also become chairman of the Executive Council, which was in effect a "war Cabinet," and thus be cast in the role of Premier. The Americans, who regarded Ky as a satisfactory Air Force officer but doubted his political acumen or his administrative ability, sought to preclude Ky's appointment to the chairmanship, and relations between Ky and Ambassador Taylor became touchy in a manner reminiscent of Taylor's 1964 feud with General Khanh. The Buddhists and the Catholics also urged that a civilian chairman of the Executive Council be chosen, and religious leaders of both groups spoke out against the complete resumption of power by the military, even though the Catholics and some of the moderate Buddhists admitted that another civilian government might open the door to negotiation with the National Liberation Front. Nevertheless, Ky did become Premier. He immediately moved to emphasize the seriousness of the situation by announcing that Vietcong terrorists as well as black-marketeers, speculators, and corrupt officials would be summarily shot without trial if judged guilty, and a large outdoor execution area was blocked off in the Saigon central market to emphasize that they meant business. Ky also banned all newspapers for a time and made it clear that Saigon was to be considered in a state of siege, a condition he did not exaggerate since in a matter of weeks the capital was cut off by road from such nearby areas as the airbase at Bien Hoa, as well as from Dalat and the coast.

The war had indeed become serious. During May and June, in a series of swift, furious actions that involved multi-battalion attacks, counterattacks, ambushes, and counterambushes, the Vietcong had inflicted more punishment on the government troops, and on their American supporters, than in any comparable period in the war to date. During this time, an estimated thousand to fifteen hundred government soldiers had been killed or were missing, and some three dozen Americans lost their lives, in the ground fighting or in the air. For a period of six days in mid-May, after President Johnson made another speech in which he offered the North Vietnamese "unconditional discussions" and economic assistance, the United States suspended its bombings of the north, in the hope that the Hanoi government would respond to the American offer in disregard of Chinese advice; but when no reaction was forthcoming, the bombing attacks were renewed, and targets closer to Hanoi were hit. No effort was made, however, to change the basic targets from bridges, roads, military barracks, and radar installations to factories, dikes, or airfields around Hanoi, where the Russians were reported to have sent some Ilyushin 28 bombers and to have begun building sites for ground-to-air missiles. In July, when one American plane was shot down, apparently by one of these missiles, the Americans did destroy one of the seven missile sites believed to have been set up around Hanoi.

Most of the fighting in South Vietnam was concentrated in the central highlands and on the coast, particularly in the provinces of Binh Dinh and Quang Ngai. The biggest battle, however, took place in mid-June in Dongxoai, in Phuoc Vinh Province, northwest of Saigon, where in a violent four-day fight government forces lost an estimated seven to eight hundred men, and nineteen Americans were killed. It was the largest engagement of the Vietnamese war, and for the first time American forces were committed to combat action when a battalion of American paratroopers flown in took up positions in support of the shattered Saigon troops. This followed by a few days the announcement by President Johnson that General Westmoreland, the American military commander in Vietnam, had been given permission to send American forces, then numbering more than 53,000 and including approximately 15,000 combat elements, into action in response to requests by the Vietnamese government. Actually, American Marines engaged in patrolling operations around their coastal bases had already fought some small engagements against the Vietcong, but the announcement by the President marked an open departure from the earlier American policy of non-engagement and made it clear that henceforth American soldiers would, whenever necessary, fight alongside the Vietnamese under a loose system of joint regional command, but in separate units. The President's disclosure was followed up by Secretary of Defense McNamara's announcement that six more American combat battalions, plus supporting units, would be sent to Vietnam, thereupon bringing the total American troop commitment there to approximately 75,000, of which a third were combat troops. McNamara said there was fresh evidence that the Vietcong had infiltrated elements of nine regular North Vietnamese battalions into South Vietnam, and he now estimated that the Vietcong had 65,000 "full time" or hard-core men fighting in the country, which was about 20,000 more than the Americans had been estimating only a week or so before. Part-time guerrillas, he figured, amounted to about 100,000, and the Vietcong also had some 30,000 engaged in "political and propaganda activities."

Significantly, McNamara noted that the South Vietnamese forces, including regular Army, paramilitary, and police contingents, totaled 574,000, which was about 50,000 less than had been estimated a few months before, when it had been announced that 100,000 additional Vietnamese would be recruited. The new figure was an implied admission of the gravity of the number of government desertions that had been taking place, and of the failure to recruit as many additional men as had been anticipated. It brought the over-all ratio of total government troops to total Vietcong forces to just under 4–1, which, according to standard estimates of what is necessary to fight a guerrilla war—generally 10–1—was far too low. The Pentagon in Washington hedged the 4–1 figure somewhat by claiming that only one out of three of the Vietcong regional and local guerrillas had weapons; this seemed a doubtful claim in view of the success the Vietcong had been having, but even if it was accepted, the government still had no more than a 6–1 ratio of troops in its favor. It was obvious, in any event, that the whole shape of the war had now altered, that the North Vietnamese and the Vietcong were clearly intent on prosecuting their advantage to the utmost in gaining, if not complete victory in South Vietnam, at least an advantage that would enable them to hold the upper hand in any "discussions" or "negotiations" that took place. In the words of General Giap, the minimal aim of the Vietcong was not to fight to the bitter end but "only to the point that the enemy can be brought to the conference table and there defeated."

CHAPTER XII

ᘓᘛ

The Lost Revolution

It is doubtful that any crisis since the end of the Second World War has confounded and bedeviled the United States so much as the one in Vietnam. This has been due, primarily, to the nature of the Vietnamese ideological and political struggle itself, and, secondly, to its significance as part of the larger power struggle in Asia and in the world. The Vietnam tragedy represents many things, not only to the Vietnamese people, who have suffered most from the twenty-year conflict, but to the United States, which has also suffered from it and whose conscience, in a certain sense, Vietnam has become. By mid-1965, the war had turned into a military contest of wills; the United States was ready and willing to negotiate itself out of an impossible situation but would do so only on terms it deemed "honorable." The word "honorable" had many connotations and applications. It implied a settlement that would give the South Vietnamese some guarantee of remaining independent, and of not being sacrificed to the Communists in the Southeast Asian political jungle, although eventual reunification with North Vietnam was not opposed if it represented the popular wish. And for the United States an honorable settlement, somewhat less tangibly, meant one that would preserve and protect its own prestige and position, not only in Asia but—as a result of the heavy American commitment in Vietnam, morally and politically as well as militarily and financially—in Africa, Europe, and Latin America, too. In view of our long and complicated involvement, it could not justifiably be said, as some maintained, that the superior strength of the United States naval and air power in the Pacific was the prime factor in protecting the American position, and that neither South Vietnam nor other Southeast Asian states were in themselves important enough in the grand strategy of the nuclear age to warrant further aggravation or risk on the Asian mainland. The importance of the long struggle in Vietnam far transcended strategic military concepts alone. Whether we liked it or not, or wished that we had never become involved as thoroughly as we had, the far deeper issue in Vietnam was and remained a revolutionary one, and its political meaning could not be denied or evaded, now or tomorrow. It was in this sense that Vietnam had become part of the American conscience, and it was herein, too, that the importance of the contest appeared to transcend other major postwar crises—in Berlin, Korea, Greece, Lebanon, the Suez, etc. To be sure, ideological issues were involved in those crises, too—as they were even more specially in all of Western Europe when the Marshall Plan was created—but most of the other struggles had been essentially clear-cut power contests, some of them of the eyeball-to-eyeball variety, as in Berlin during the period of the airlift. They were, by and large, resolvable through the use of military power or the threat of it, and some of them, from the outset, contained a built-in stalemate potential that the various antagonists accepted, tacitly or otherwise. The one exception, perhaps, was the Cuban missile crisis, but it cannot be said, even there, that a stalemate potential did not exist; it was simply a matter of whether or not the United States would call the Russian bluff, and once the bluff *was* called, the Russians backed down.

All along, Vietnam has been different. The issues, from the outset, were more subtle and complex, and they raised the fundamental question of the age: What kind of revolution, guided by which elements in the world political society, would succeed there? It was not a case of Soviet armies sweeping over Eastern Europe and installing Soviet satellite governments in one country after another—countries that, only now, are beginning to drop out of the Soviet orbit in many fascinating ways. Nor was it a matter, as in China, of a revolutionary army with a firm dogma of its own slowly crushing an outworn, incompetent, and corrupt bureaucratic and autarchic dynasty that was already deteriorating. Vietnam in 1945, in an odd kind of way, was "virgin" revolutionary ground. As we have seen, there were elements of Communism, both Stalinist and Trotskyist, and there was above all a vibrant nationalism that was stirring and waiting to be developed. There were the dying embers of colonialism waiting to catch fire again. And there was the promise of a democratic revolution, as represented by the new victorious power of the United States after the defeat of Japan and by the wartime pledges that had been made to support new independence movements, in the image of American's own great revolutionary tradition. Nowhere else in the world was there such a revolutionary microcosm, except perhaps in Indonesia, whose revolution, for better or worse, at least would develop under its own dynamic thrust. Thus it may be said that Vietnam was perhaps the most pristine postwar revolutionary area, where in the beginning the odds were even. Would the United States, working with the French or separately, be able to help foster a viable Vietnamese nationalism that would result in the already nascent revolution being taken away from the Communists? Or would the Communists win the revolution in that crucial part of Asia? In mid-1965, it seemed that no matter what happened in Vietnam, the revolution was lost as far as the West was concerned, because the opportunities to help encourage and guide it had been irretrievably overlooked.

The details of these lost opportunities have been discussed earlier in this book. The end results were graphically summed up by Senator J. W. Fulbright, Chairman of the Foreign Relations Committee, in the concluding paragraphs of his speech in the Senate on June 15, 1965: "The tragedy of Vietnam is that for many reasons, including the intransigence of a colonial power and the initial failure of the United States to appreciate the consequences of that intransigence, the nationalist movement became associated with and largely subordinate to the Communist movement. In the postwar era, it has been demonstrated repeatedly that nationalism is a stronger force than Communism and that the association of the two, which has created so many difficulties for the United States, is neither inevitable nor natural. In the past, it has come about when, for one reason or another, the West has set itself in opposition to the national aspirations of the emerging peoples. It is to be hoped that we will not do so again; it is to be hoped that the United States will leave no country in doubt as to its friendship and support for legitimate national aspirations. If we do this, I do not think that we will find ourselves in another conflict like the one in Vietnam."

The Decisive Summer of 1965

The importance of Senator Fulbright's speech, which he first discussed with President Johnson, lay in the fact that it spelled out United States aims and intentions at a time when Americans were becoming increasingly disturbed over their role in Vietnam and confused and uncertain about what could be done about it. The speech followed several declarations by President Johnson himself, and by other administration spokesmen, in which it had been re-emphasized that the only purpose of the "continuing" bombing of North Vietnam was to persuade the North Vietnamese to stop their aggression in the south and to negotiate an equitable solution. It had been made quite clear so far by the Hanoi government, and been echoed both in Moscow and in Peking, that despite the bombings the Communists were not interested in negotiations, except on their terms, and that they had every intention of letting the war in South Vietnam continue, especially in view of the considerable gains the Vietcong were making during the new monsoon season. Fulbright said that it was no longer possible for the United States to think in terms of complete military victory in Vietnam (it had not been too long ago that such a victory was just what a number of prominent American officials had been claiming was not only possible but probable); that "unconditional withdrawal of American support . . . would have disastrous consequences"; and that "our policy therefore should remain one of determination to end the war at the earliest possible time by a negotiated settlement involving major concessions by both sides." To withdraw, said Fulbright, would "betray our obligation to people we have promised to defend," would "weaken or destroy the credibility of American guarantees to other countries," and would, in effect, prove that Peking's plan to expand Communism through guerrilla wars was sound. Further escalation of the war was also unwise, Fulbright added, since the bombings hadn't achieved their aim so far, and extending them might only provoke more large-scale infiltration or even invasion of the south by regular North Vietnamese elements, in time involving the United States "in a bloody and protracted jungle war in which the strategic advantages would be with the other side"; the sole alternative then, he warned, would be a further extension of the air attacks that might bring in the Chinese and even start a general nuclear war. What Fulbright consequently counseled, and what was, in fact, American policy at the moment, was to demonstrate "continued restraint and continued patience." What this meant, in military terms, was the intention of the United States to support the South Vietnamese with sufficient troops of its own—beyond the 75,000 that were already in Vietnam —to continue to give the government forces strong air support within South Vietnam, and to continue the limited bombings in the north. It appeared to be the hope of the United States that this limited conventional war approach, kept short of a Korean-type commitment, would hold the fort until the monsoons ended in November. Then, if it had not already been accomplished, the North Vietnamese could be persuaded that the Vietcong offensive could not be sustained in the dry season, when the guerrillas on the ground would be more vulnerable again to air attacks, and that it was time to negotiate.

At the end of July, following another trip to Saigon by Secretary of Defense McNamara and by Ambassador Lodge, who had been newly designated to replace Ambassador Taylor, President Johnson announced his new program for increased aid to South Vietnam. In effect, the program spelled out what Fulbright had said. Johnson announced that an additional 50,000 Americans would be sent to Vietnam, raising the total to 125,000, and also announced a doubling of the selective service draft in the United States. This was less than the "hawks" in Washington had wanted and more than the "doves" had recommended. Though the American bombing of North Vietnam had been moving closer to Hanoi and the Chinese border, there was no indication that Johnson was yet prepared to bomb Hanoi itself, or attack the Chinese supply railheads—the possibility was held out, however. At the same time, Johnson made it clear that American aid, including more military assistance if necessary, would be forthcoming, and that the United States was as determined as ever to remain in South Vietnam indefinitely.

More and more, American policy, even though determined, seemed caught in a fresh paradox. We would stay and fight with our own troops alongside the South Vietnamese, but we wanted to negotiate more than ever too. As the tone and temper of the war grew more militaristic—hardly anyone talked any more of political reforms in South Vietnam—we began almost to beg for negotiations. President Johnson himself, while breathing fire at one moment, all but pleaded for negotiation in the next, pointing out, in an injured tone, that the United States had sought some fifteen times to bring Hanoi to the conference table, but had been steadily rejected. Where earlier the President had abruptly dismissed the peace efforts of Secretary General U Thant of the United Nations, he now went out of his way to seek Thant's support for any conceivable UN effort that might help produce an atmosphere of negotiation. It was obvious that Johnson would go to almost any limits that were still "honorable" to bring about a peace in Vietnam, but it remained equally clear that both sides were far apart, and that Hanoi was unwilling to sit down and talk so long as it thought the war could be won on the ground: its purpose, in response to the American stand in behalf of "honor," was clearly to humiliate the United States, to force it to withdraw from Vietnam, and thereby to prove to the world that "wars of liberation" could be won.

In outlining the various possibilities that existed in Vietnam in the summer of 1965, we then could say that they were as follows:

A. A conventional war defense by the United States in support of South Vietnam as long as it was necessary—a defense that, backed both by gathering ground and air strength, would prove to the North Vietnamese and the Vietcong that they couldn't win the war any more than we could, and that the best thing for all concerned was fair negotiation.

B. Continued disintegration of the military and political situation in South Vietnam to the point where either a new government in Saigon would express a desire to negotiate with the National Liberation Front, or with Hanoi, or the way would be paved for such negotiations by the establishment of a coalition regime in South Vietnam that would include some neutralist and/or National Liberation Front elements. If this happened, the United States might effectively be "negotiated out" of the picture by being asked to leave, which presumably it would have to do unless it decided to go on fighting in defense of a rump government of anti-Communist Vietnamese established either somewhere in Vietnam or outside the country. While in July, 1965, the chances of these things occurring were not immediately likely, no experienced American or Vietnamese observers of the political and military disintegration of the preceding two years would say they were impossible. There were some Vietnamese politicians, and some military men, who believed that such a settlement might be the only solution, and who favored the proposal of the French, as set forth by President de Gaulle, for the establishment of peace and the "neutralization" of the entire former Indochina area. A coalition government in South Vietnam presumably would quickly be followed by a move to unify the south with the north, under conditions that would be tantamount to handing South Vietnam over to the Communists. The machinery for such a program would be set in motion within South Vietnam and/or outside the country. For example, such a solution could be prepared by discussions between neutralist South Vietnamese and representatives of the National Liberation Front in Algiers, Prague, Cairo, Havana, Jakarta, Moscow, or Peking, where the N.L.F. had branch offices. Among the participants could be men such as Professor Nguyen Van Hieu, the roving "Foreign Minister" for the N.L.F., or former Premier Tran Van Huu and other spokesmen for the "neutralist" group of Vietnamese in Paris. As a corollary to this in South Vietnam, negotiations might then be conducted in the jungle, in a captured district town, or even in Saigon.

C. A modified form of the negotiations outlined above, which would obviously favor the Vietcong and would represent a victory for Hanoi in implementing the resolutions adopted at the second session of the third National Assembly of the Democratic Republic of North Vietnam. As a "basis" for a settlement, the Hanoi government at that meeting in April, 1965, set forth four points: (1) complete United States withdrawal from South Vietnam and an end of air attacks on North Vietnam; (2) respect of the 1954 Geneva agreements anticipating reunification of North and South Vietnam, and permitting no foreign bases or troops in either half of Vietnam in the meantime; (3) determination of the affairs of South Vietnam "by the South Vietnamese people themselves" without "foreign intervention" and "in accordance with the program of the South Vietnamese National Front for Liberation"; (4) unification to be achieved by the people of North and South Vietnam without any foreign intervention. These four points were interpreted in some Western quarters as offering some hope for discussion, since Hanoi perhaps was not insisting on withdrawal of American troops as a precondition of starting a dialogue. When they were first announced, the basic stumbling block in the four points was the insistence that any discussions or negotiations developing out of them be conducted with the National Liberation Front and the Vietcong. Both the South Vietnamese and the United States had all along adamantly refused to do this, but by mid-1965 the feeling was growing, in Washington as well as in Saigon, that the Vietcong or the N.L.F. would have to be included in whatever discussions were ultimately held, either directly or as observers seated alongside the Hanoi delegation. If such discussions took place, they would almost certainly have to be preceded by a cease-fire in South Vietnam and a suspension of the American bombings in North Vietnam. Here again the United States would want assurances that North Vietnamese infiltration of the south had stopped first. The whole theory of this approach, with the faint glimmer it held of discussions starting at a time and place that would suit the United States, was based on the rejection by both sides of any so-called "preconditions"; but there remained much difference of opinion as to what constituted a precondition, and what didn't.

D. A conference under the sponsorship of a group of nations such as the seventeen "non-allied" ones or the British Commonwealth nations that sought, in the spring and summer of 1965, to prepare the way for discussions to start without any preconditions. Another possibility under this heading remained a peace move initiated by the United Nations, which began to look a little more possible in August, 1965. However, the chance of any such a meeting being summoned would, again, have to depend on a preliminary definition of preconditions, and the chief value of such an attempt by non-allied elements would be in creating the atmosphere for behind-the-scenes discussions among the key participants, who would be able to confer informally, and perhaps even secretly, without committing themselves to anything.

E. The summoning of another Geneva conference on the problem of Vietnam, and an attempt to return, at least in part, to the atmosphere and situation of 1954. This suggestion was one that had provoked shifting responses among the major powers over many months. The French had been most consistent in supporting it. By the summer of 1965, the United States had veered from opposing such a conference to accepting its "purposes," in 1954 terms, if the necessary preconditions were met. The British were willing to go along with this idea; the Russians had at one point been willing to consider it but had rejected it once the American bombings of the north began, and the Chinese and North Vietnamese were against it. As co-sponsor of earlier Geneva agreements, Russia's position here was the key one. While the Soviet Union was eager to maintain and develop its policy of coexistence with the United States, it did not want to be in the position of supporting a settlement in Vietnam too enthusiastically in view of its new determination to re-enter the Asian scene and to contest China for influence in North Vietnam and in other nations of the area. The Russians were themselves caught in a dilemma when the Chinese accused them of "selling out to the imperialists," by secretly favoring negotiations on Vietnam. The Sino-Soviet dispute had thus become an important factor in the Vietnamese situation, and one that might become increasingly significant the longer the war lasted and the more determined the United States showed itself to be. The possibility loomed of Chinese volunteers entering the war more as a challenge to Russia than as a source of help to the Vietnamese, and such a step might embarrass the Hanoi government walking its tightrope be-

tween Moscow and Peking. In June, 1965, when the Chinese intensified their attack on the Russians over the Vietnamese issue, the
Russians struck back and accused China of refusing to formulate a
joint policy of assistance to North Vietnam. There was still a possibility of such a joint policy being created, but it seemed unlikely. All
in all, the Russians were being forced to make a difficult decision—
either to continue their coexistence policy with the United States and
take their chances on regaining influence in Asia, or to go it alone with
limited assistance to North Vietnam and risk further aggravation of
the Sino-Soviet conflict. In either event, the prospects of a successful
Geneva conference at best seemed slight. Moreover, it did not seem
likely that the negotiatory conditions of 1954 could be re-established
or that, even if they could, they would produce any results, especially
in view of the inherent weakness of the old Geneva agreements,
which, except for the cease-fire clauses, were left unsigned by all the
participants, who simply "took note" of them.

Few Vietnamese were ingenuous enough to believe that even a
new Southeast Asia agreement with "teeth" in it—presumably American ones—would convince the Communists that they should renounce their long-term objective of reunifying Vietnam to their own
advantage. In this respect, the situation of 1965 was far more complex
than the one in 1954. The Communist apparatus in the south was now
much larger and more effective, and no matter what terms might be
agreed upon, one could hardly expect that all the hard-core Vietcong
could be got out, that all the guerrillas would turn in their arms, or
that the National Liberation Front could or would be broken up.

F. A conference at Geneva or somewhere else that would use
either the Laotian or the Cambodian problems, or both, as a catalyst
in discussing the Vietnamese situation. The idea would be that, in
conferring formally about the restoration of a unified Laotian government or the guaranteeing of Cambodia's neutrality, informal discussions on Vietnam could be held in the corridors among the powers attending. An international conference on Cambodia was proposed in
mid-March, 1965, by Prince Norodom Sihanouk, who suggested it be
attended by the nine Geneva participants. The United States, Great
Britain, and Russia all expressed some interest in the idea, but, under

pressure from the Chinese, Prince Sihanouk then insisted that only the Vietcong or the National Liberation Front and not the Saigon government be allowed to represent South Vietnam. This was, naturally, unacceptable to Washington. Subsequently, late in May, Sihanouk indicated that a compromise might be possible under which both Saigon and the N.L.F. would take part.

The Laotian and the Cambodian problems are so closely related to the Vietnamese situation that they will probably be part of any settlement eventually reached on Vietnam. Some background of the situation in those countries is consequently necessary.

Stalemate in Laos

To the Western observer familiar with the repeated South Vietnamese crises, the Laotian military and political skirmishing of the last several years has looked a lot like the exaggerated swordplay and gesturing of masked warriors in traditional Chinese opera. Almost everyone in the country's backwater capital, Vientiane, agrees that what ultimately happens to Laos hangs on the outcome of the turbulent events in Vietnam, where Laos has played a vital role by serving as a funnel for Communist supplies and troops sent through the jungles and mountains to the Vietcong guerrillas in the south. Laos, of course, has been the source of much international debate in its own right; in fact, it is doubtful whether the future of any small section of the globe has occupied so many nations so much of the time during the past decade with such inconclusive results. Nevertheless, these attempts to resolve the stalemate among Laotian neutralist, Communist, and rightist factions may yet pay off in larger diplomatic terms. In the summer of 1964, representatives of the three groups got together in Paris for talks, in the hope of ending once and for all the sporadic fighting between government troops and those of the Communist Pathet Lao and of re-establishing the coalition government that collapsed in 1963. The talks produced no final results, but their aim— the convening of another multi-power conference on Southeast Asia, such as the conferences that took place at Geneva in 1954 and 1962— may yet be realized. Ultimately, another conference on Laos, similar to the one in Geneva in 1962, seems bound to take place; the question is how and when. Too much delay could prove disastrous for Laos. For one thing, American and Laotian bombing of Vietcong supply lines through Laos, which started late in 1964, could eventually provoke Communist counterattacks on Laotian soil. And if Communist troops should ever reach the Mekong River, which separates Laos and Thailand, the Thais and the Americans would, in their turn, probably be forced to counterattack.

For the present, Laos remains, as it has ever since it was accorded international recognition as a nation in 1950, the most artificial entity in Southeast Asia. During a stay there in the summer of 1964, I found that people in the government, though weary of their country's anomalous role as a kind of non-nation and international pawn, had become quite fatalistic about the whole thing. This attitude had produced an odd condition in Vientiane; it seemed that almost nothing had changed in the two years since I had last been there, and I felt that I had come back to visit a region somewhere in space. The sense of unreality and frustration was increased both by a complex political situation, which many people felt might result in the eventual partition of the country, and by the indecisive military maneuvering that has been going on since the spring of 1963 around the Plaine des Jarres, a strategic plateau north of the capital. Strangely, in a part of the world where guerrilla warfare is the predominant mode of fighting, and has been brought to a high point of development by the Vietcong, the battles—if one can describe them as such—that have taken place in Laos have been fought largely along conventional lines, most frequently for the control of a few major roads or for the ridges that command them. The action has usually been initiated by Pathet Lao contingents of battalion size or less, with North Vietnamese weapons, including some artillery. The government troops have been supplied by the Americans with weapons that include a few tanks and planes. Each outburst of fighting has invariably ended quickly with the retreat of one side or the other. The government has retained control of the most populous part of the country, including the strategic Mekong River Valley, and while the Communists have claimed about two-thirds of it geographically, most of the territory they ostensibly control is actually mountainous no-man's land where the sparse villages are visited only occasionally by local guerrillas rather than Pathet Lao regulars or Communist officials. By the same token, government troops seldom venture out of their headquarters in the towns, and if they do occupy a village area, to offset a real or imagined Pathet Lao threat, they simply sit tight there for a while and then move back to town. Consequently, most of the Lao are not only almost totally ignorant of the larger political forces swirling around them but have hardly been touched by the war.

One thing that makes generalizations about Laos risky is the fact that it is not really a country at all but, rather, a mélange of about three million people. (No one knows what the actual total is, since no proper census has ever been taken.) Roughly half the population is composed of Lao, who migrated from China about a thousand years ago. They have a considerable affinity with the Thais, who compose another fourth of the population, for both speak a Sino-Tibetan language and have been largely influenced by Indic culture. Except for sixty or seventy thousand Chinese and Vietnamese, the rest of the population is made up of other tribal peoples, most of whom speak primitive Mon-Khmer languages, and all of whom are looked down upon by the Lao. The most numerous of these are the Khas, whose name is a Laotian word meaning "slave," and the Lao tend to apply this derogatory term to all the tribal folk other than the Thais. There are about twenty separate groups of actual Khas, who comprise a sixth of the total population and mostly live a primitive existence in the mountains, where they hunt game and cultivate rice and other vegetable crops. The remaining tribes are the Meos, the Mans, the Hos, and the Thos, almost all of whom live in the north and almost all of whom are of Chinese origin. Except for the Meos, who have mingled with the Lao, and have even been represented officially in Vientiane, these tribal people live remote and separate lives, and have no sense of nationhood or any common outlook. The bulk of the Pathet Lao's support comes from the tribes, especially the Khas, who form most of the leftist Army. One American who has traveled around the country distributing aid explained to me how illusory it was to think of the tribesmen as having any political orienta-

N

tion at all. "They think of their situation solely in terms of their own ridgelines," he said. "They know when and where they're likely to be shot at, and that's it." The Lao themselves, although they are more enlightened in other ways, have scarcely more awareness of the purpose of politics. Historically, the issues that have united them have been negative ones—resentment of the French, for instance, and hatred of the Vietnamese, who are the traditional invaders. Their feeling for their King, Savang Vathana, is more a matter of respect for the rituals of coronation and cremation than for the man or for the throne. The Lao's lack of interest in broader issues is the product of a live-and-let-live philosophy. As uninvolved with practical affairs as any people in the world, the Lao wish only to remain that way, if the rest of the world will let them.

Except for the city dwellers, the inhabitants of Laos are hardly aware of the nation's principal contending elements, or of the three men who have headed them and shaped the country's recent history— the neutralist Premier Prince Souvanna Phouma; his leftist half-brother Prince Souphanouvong; and the rightist General Phoumi Nosavan, who went into exile in the spring of 1965. Souvanna, who turned sixty not long ago, is a suave French-educated engineer and architect, perhaps more European than Oriental in his outlook. In 1931, upon finishing his schooling in France, he returned to Laos, and soon decided to devote himself to fighting for his country's freedom—a more urgent task, he felt, than building bridges. When the struggle for independence began in earnest, fourteen years later, Souvanna chose persuasion rather than violence as his weapon against the French, and his efforts were rewarded when, in 1949, an agreement was signed in Paris giving Laos its autonomy within the French Union. Souvanna is both proud and vain, and his political career has been mercurial; as a result of various coups and counter-coups, he has been Premier on four separate occasions. Those who know him recognize his intelligence but say that he lacks forcefulness and tends to ignore details, frequently handing them over to incompetent subordinates and taking no further interest in them. Though Souvanna is surely a non-Communist, he has gone through periods of co-operating with his half-brother, and in 1961 for a time he accepted a subsidy from Hanoi for his shaky neutralist party, the Lao Pen Kang.

Souphanouvong is probably the most intelligent and most complex member of the trio. He is at once lucid and cryptic, affable and withdrawn, impassioned and bland. His essential motivations seem to be those of an ardent nationalist and xenophobe, and extreme ambition seems to be the reason he has nevertheless submitted to Communist direction. Now a little over fifty, he was born in Luang Prabang, and was educated first in Hanoi—where he proved to be a brilliant student—and then in Paris. He has an astonishing, electric memory, and the French wanted him to become a classical scholar, but, like Souvanna, he insisted on being practical and studied engineering. (There are only four qualified Laotian engineers in Laos today; Souvanna and Souphanouvong are two of them.) When he came back to Indochina, he was assigned by the French government to an engineering post at Nhatrang. He soon became disillusioned, for although he was far more capable than his French associates, he was given an unimportant job at a low salary. In an obviously autobiographical sketch he wrote at the time, he described a young Lao who had studied abroad and then returned home under similar circumstances. "Bitterness, rebellion, and discouragement disabled this young man," he said. In 1945, Souphanouvong made contact with the Communist Vietminh, and he has been under Hanoi domination ever since. He is married to a dynamic, politically conscious Vietnamese woman, who has borne him twelve children. Unlike Souvanna, he refused to have any dealings with the French, and between 1949 and 1953 he exiled himself, moving back and forth between North Vietnam and Thailand for much of that time, in order to prepare his Pathet Lao resistance movement for an eventual take-over of Laos. In 1951, he went to Communist China for a year of indoctrination. At the 1954 Geneva Conference, the control his Pathet Lao units exercised over the two provinces of Sam Neua and Phong Saly was formally acknowledged. While his life as an outlaw was presumably ended, he was arrested in Vientiane in 1959 by the right-wing regime of Phoui Sananikone, and he remained locked up for almost a year, until he escaped.

Although the propaganda of the Vietcong bills Souphanouvong as the political head of the Pathet Lao, he is probably no better than No. 4 or No. 5 in the secret hierarchy of his party, the Neo Lao Hak

Xat, which is itself subservient to the North Vietnamese Workers Party. His two immediate political superiors are Nouhak Phoumsavan, who is the secretary of the Central Committee of the Neo Lao Hak Xat, and Kaysone Phomvihan, a top propagandist and hatchet man. Whatever Souphanouvong's exact rank and prerogatives may be, he seems content to continue to do the Vietcong's bidding, whatever it may be.

Phoumi, a headstrong and wilful man in his forties, whose military career began in the war against the French, depended on military strength and American backing in attempting power grabs in 1959 and 1960. Though the Americans subsequently made it clear to him that they supported the coalition formula for a Laotian government, he persisted in his ambition of becoming a local strong man. His direction of several economic monopolies—notably those for the import of gold, perfume, and alcoholic beverages—and his association with the people controlling the opium trade and the four nationally operated gambling casinos aroused the opposition both of politicians and of many of his fellow Army officers.

In the spring of 1964, two of the latter, General Kouprasith Abbay and General Siho Lanphouthacoul, attempted a coup with the purpose of ousting Souvanna and cutting Phoumi down to size. Souvanna, with the backing of American Ambassador Leonard Unger and of the King, who, although largely a figurehead, enjoys national prestige, managed to survive and even emerged with his position greatly strengthened. Not only was Souvanna's flagging zeal spurred and his personal pride restored, but he was, for the first time, given a real opportunity to govern as the head of a coalition of neutralist and rightist groups—groups that had theretofore been divided in their willingness to back him. So Siho and Kouprasith, who had wanted to eliminate Souvanna because he wasn't showing enough authority and forcefulness, ended by helping him obtain the authority he needed. The "young Turks"—about eighty officers who had aided Siho and Kouprasith in plotting the coup—were given the job of cleaning up the Cabinet, and it was reorganized to remove the corrupt elements that had gathered around General Phoumi. The gambling casinos were closed, and a number of new committees were formed to control the government monopolies. General Phoumi, however, retained his Vice-Premiership—and his capacity for plotting. Finally, in February, 1965, after Phoumi failed in another attempted coup, he was forced to flee to Thailand—where he continued to plot. Another revolt by pro-Phoumi forces in March was also crushed. The net result of both these failures was to strengthen further Souvanna's position as head of the new neutralist rightist coalition.

In mid-1964, the war against the Pathet Lao took a turn for the better. By midsummer, the Communist threat to grab full control of the north-south road between Vientiane and Luang Prabang and then drive all the way to Vientiane and the banks of the Mekong was effectively countered, and, with the help of United States Navy reconnaissance planes and a strengthened complement of American fighter-bombers flown by Laotian pilots and some hired Thai pilots, the government forces kept the Pathet Lao from reinforcing its troops along the east-west road running across Laos from the Vietnamese border to the Thai border. Next, government troops counterattacked to keep the Pathet Lao confined to the Plaine des Jarres. Subsequently, a new Pathet Lao drive south of Vientiane toward the Mekong was thrown back. For the time being, the government's position in the Mekong Valley was thus secured. The success of the government's military operations, limited though they were, was confirmed by the fact that several Pathet Lao contingents surrendered—something that had never happened before—and by increasingly shrill and angry pronouncements of the Pathet Lao radio, which kept repeating that the United States was "holding Souvanna Phouma in its clutches like a puppet" and that Vientiane was "under strict control of hangmen."

In the spring of 1965, following the various coup failures, the United States decided to meet the Pathet Lao challenge on its own terms as a violation of the Geneva agreements. By mid-1965, large supplies of American weapons were being sent to the neutralist forces around the Plaine des Jarres in northwestern Laos, and Air America, the C.I.A.-sponsored "private" airline, was playing a leading role in strengthening the pro-Western Meo tribesmen as well as the forces of neutralist commander Kong Le. At the same time, American planes from Vietnam and from aircraft carriers in the Gulf of Tonkin, as well as from airbases in Thailand, stepped up their attacks on Viet-cong supply lines into Laos. The Pathet Lao was thereby placed on the defensive everywhere except in southeastern Laos, where it still dominated the tribes and protected the supply trails into Vietnam.

Siho, Kouprasith, and the other officers concerned now seem to realize that, for all its imperfections, the government of Laos has to remain under the leaky 1962 Geneva umbrella, still held up by Prince Souvanna Phouma. The suave Prince, who will never be a man of the people and who has been compared by members of the Vientiane diplomatic community to an aristocrat on the eve of the French Revolution, nevertheless is a man whose courage is equal to his vanity; he is dedicated to the cause of Laotian independ-ence and to the creation of an effective political structure. Although he can no longer pretend to be the head of a national union embracing all elements, but only of a combination of neutral and rightist fac-tions, he remains, certainly more than anyone else on the scene, the symbol of compromise in the country of the detached center. When, in 1964, I spoke with General Kong Le, who had played along with the Pathet Lao until the Communists turned on him in April, 1963, and drove his forces off the Plaine des Jarres, he admitted that Souvanna Phouma's position as a coalition leader had been altered, but insisted that the Prince was the only leader he and his men could look up to, and that the Pathet Lao had become his enemy. "The Communists once did everything they could to buy me, but now I have learned about Communism and I will use all my force to fight it," he said. "The morale of my troops is still very high. If we get more American help, we can recapture the Plaine des Jarres."

The possibilities of strong American intervention in Laos are still being considered, but any further commitment would be designed primarily to redress the situation enough to facilitate the start of equitable negotiations on both Laos and Vietnam. Meanwhile, Laos remains relatively calm, as the Communists are apparently determined to devote most of their effort to Vietnam. In an election held in July, 1965, at least ten of the sixteen candidates who ran on the Young People's party ticket were chosen. The party led by Sisouk Na Champassak brought the thirty-seven-year-old Finance Minister to the forefront as a new power in the faction-ridden neutralist and right-wing political spectrum. The pro-Communist Pathet Lao, which is theoretically still supposed to share control of the government with the neutral and right-wing groups, boycotted the elections. Sisouk has pledged his support for Prince Souvanna Phouma.

Cambodia Is Sihanouk

His Royal Highness Prince Norodom Sihanouk, a self-deposed king who, as Chief of State of Cambodia, prefers the ambivalent title of "Lord Comrade" or the simple designation "Monseigneur," is probably the most unpredictable and articulate one-man government in the world. He likes to explain, with a disarming laugh, that there is no need for spies in Cambodia because all anyone has to do is pay attention to what he says. Because Sihanouk has always had a lot to say, this advice may at first sound reasonable, but because Cambodia has for some time been engaged in a particularly delicate balancing act between East and West, much of what Sihanouk has said in his effort to prove his neutrality has been so contradictory and confusing that even the shrewdest and most assiduous spy would have a terrible time figuring it out.

At the end of 1963, Prince Sihanouk terminated all American military, cultural, and economic aid, amounting to some thirty million dollars annually, and ordered his Embassy in Washington closed. For some time, he had been making it increasingly clear that among all the nations of the world he regarded the People's Republic of China as his best friend and chief protector. The game of guessing just how seriously Sihanouk meant such threats, if threats they were, became the main preoccupation of diplomats, correspondents, and businessmen in Cambodia, and the difficulty of gauging the Prince's true aims was soon further attested to by more instances of hedging and retracting. In mid-January, 1964, he suddenly decided to keep his Embassy in Washington open after all, declared that he could never make Cambodia a Chinese satellite, and indicated that he might deign to go on accepting certain forms of American aid to supplement assistance that he was arranging to get from France and China. But the situation continued to deteriorate. First, it became apparent that the United States had no intention of resuming any form of aid to Cambodia unless Sihanouk settled down and gave some firm indication that he would negotiate with the West on other than his own stubborn terms. Then, in mid-March, there were three other developments. After he had proposed a four-power conference to be attended by Cambodia, South Vietnam, Thailand, and the United States, the Prince reneged on the idea. Next, following an attack on the American Embassy in Phnom Penh by demonstrators, who, obviously encouraged by the government, did considerable damage, and a small peaceful demonstration that took place in front of the Cambodian Embassy in Washington a day or so later, Sihanouk decided to bring his Ambassador, Nong Kimny, and all his Embassy personnel in Washington home, leaving only a small delegation at the United Nations to represent him in America. A few days later, a conference between representatives of South Vietnam and Cambodia to deal with border questions fell apart when it coincided with an open violation of Cambodian soil by South Vietnamese forces, accompanied by American military advisers, during which sixteen Cambodian villagers were killed. Sihanouk refused to accept the quickly proffered apologies of both Saigon and Washington.

There are a number of theories about Sihanouk's multiple gyrations, and he has been variously described as a psychotic with a persecution complex, a frightened rabbit about to be devoured by Communist tigers, and a brilliant political strategist who is doing his best to disprove the concept of the survival of the fittest by effecting, through a mixture of monumental pride and astute opportunism, the survival of one of the weakest and most vulnerable nations on the seething Southeast Asian peninsula. It should be noted that those people who have had the best chance to study Sihanouk, including Westerners who have watched him at work in Cambodia, express more respect and admiration for him than those who have observed him only from a distance. If his tactics and his manner seem mystifying and exasperating, his fundamental strategy seems realistic enough when viewed in the light of his own prognosis of what is likely to happen in Southeast Asia. Like a number of other people, including de Gaulle, Sihanouk is convinced that the war in South Vietnam cannot be won by the anti-Communist forces, and that all of Vietnam, plus Laos and Cambodia, and perhaps eventually Burma and Thailand as well, should become a neutralized bloc, whose identity can be preserved only by some sort of international guarantee against interference from either China or the West.

Sihanouk's attitude is basically not pro-Communist, despite his efforts to make it appear so. Rather, it is a logical outgrowth of present realities considered in the context of the recent past—a past that includes Sihanouk's and Cambodia's postwar struggles for independence (the two are virtually synonymous), the collapse of the French-colonial heritage in Southeast Asia, France's efforts to regain influence there, a history of always difficult relations between Cambodia and her Vietnamese and Thai neighbors, and the presence of the United States in the area since the end of the Second World War. Sihanouk is well aware of all these situations and events, for he has been actively engaged in the affairs of his country for half his life; indeed, his story is the remarkable one of a once carefree young monarch whose political consciousness and, to some extent, social conscience have grown with each successive crisis and each new responsibility. As his curiosity and his desire to make closer contact with his people, the Khmers—the indigenous Cambodians, who make up ninety per cent of the country's population of nearly six million—have also grown, he has emerged as one of Asia's most dynamic nationalist leaders. A born extrovert, he has tackled his job with boundless energy and the flair of a showman.

The first phase of the Prince's public career began in April, 1941, when his grandfather, King Sisowath Monivong of Cambodia, died and Sihanouk, although only nineteen, was chosen by the French to succeeed to the throne in preference to his father, Prince Suramarit, and several other male relatives. If the French thought Sihanouk would be easier to handle, they were quickly proved wrong. The new King was immediately embroiled in a crisis. The French, fighting to hang on to their Far Eastern empire under the Vichy regime, were trying to stave off nationalist rebellions in Cochin China and Annam, and to check the Siamese, who had become allies of the militaristic

Japanese and were taking advantage of France's troubles to nibble territory from both Laos and Cambodia. In May, 1941, after a brief flurry of naval warfare between the French and the Siamese, Siam seized three of Cambodia's rich rice-growing provinces—Battambang, Sisophon, and Siem Reap. The Japanese compelled Vichy to accept the loss and take the occasion to secure the right to establish bases and to station troops in Indochina, and were accorded some economic concessions; in return, they permitted the French to retain administrative control. This tenuous and difficult relationship lasted until March 9, 1945, when the Japanese, with defeat in sight, interned the French and themselves took over. Three days after that, King Sihanouk announced Cambodia's "independence"—with Tokyo's blessing. The Premier in the new government, and the man actually behind its creation, was a Cambodian nationalist named Song Ngoc Thanh, who is now in exile and is the one Cambodian who represents a threat to the Prince's power. In mid-October of 1945, when British, Indian, and French units moved into Phnom Penh following the Japanese surrender, the French seized Thanh as a collaborator. He was taken to Saigon and tried, convicted, and sentenced to twenty years at hard labor, but the sentence was later commuted to house arrest in Paris. Many Cambodians still regarded him as a national hero, and some of them organized Issarak bands in the provinces of Battambang and Siem Reap, where the Siamese, still in control, allowed them to operate. In January, 1946, Sihanouk agreed to a *modus vivendi* whereby Cambodia as a kingdom within the French Union would theoretically have a degree of internal autonomy; in reality, the French, through their High Commissioner and a host of advisers at every level of government, continued to run the country much as they had in the prewar era. In the fall of 1946, under a treaty negotiated in Washington with the help of United States diplomats, Cambodia regained the three provinces Siam had taken in 1941. In the same year, Cambodia, as a constitutional monarchy, became one of the Associated States of Indochina within the French Union. Although the Cambodians were now allowed to elect a popular assembly and to choose their own Cabinet, the French still maintained effective administrative control, and, along with indigenous Chinese and Vietnamese, still dominated Cambodia's economy. The majority in the new Parliament was held by the Democratic Party, which regarded Son Ngoc Thanh as its head despite his exile, and which kept urging Sihanouk to get tougher and demand real independence. In October, 1951, to appease his opponents, Sihanouk arranged for the return of Son Ngoc Thanh. Thanh began delivering inflammatory speeches, and within five months Sihanouk again decided that he had had enough. Thanh fled into the forests of Siem Reap, where he started a clandestine radio station and sought, with only indifferent success, to consolidate the various Issarak guerrilla bands, which by now had split into pro- and anti-Communist factions. In the spring of 1953, when Thanh was momentarily weakened and isolated in the jungle, Sihanouk took a real gamble. He left Phnom Penh on what he described as a "vacation trip" to Europe and America. After a stay in Paris, during which he failed to convince the French that Cambodia must have full freedom, he came to the United States and announced that unless this was granted "within a few months," his people would very likely go over to the Communist Vietminh. Having returned home by way of Canada and Japan, he shut himself up at a retreat in Siem Reap, declaring that there he would stay until independence was won. The following year, at Geneva, France and eight other Western and Asian nations met to draft the treaty that terminated the Indochina war by setting up two separate Vietnams and that led to the creation of Laos and Cambodia as free states.

Back in Phnom Penh, the hero King, still only thirty-two years old, was ready to embark on the second phase of his career. In February, 1955, he fulfilled his earlier promise by conducting a national referendum on whether or not he had achieved freedom and security for Cambodia. The "ayes" had it resoundingly, to the tune of 99.8% of a total of 927,000 ballots cast. Shortly afterward, Sihanouk jolted the nation by announcing his abdication as King. "I want to renounce the throne in order to show that I do not cling to power, authority, and privileges for my own person, for my happiness, and for my private well-being," he declared, and went on to say that as King he had been too isolated and too revered: "I could only see the flowers and hear the lies." Sihanouk's father, Suramarit, replaced him on the throne, and since Suramarit's death, in 1960, the sovereign has been Sihanouk's mother, Queen Kossamak. By thus formally renouncing his royal role, Sihanouk arranged to gain the best of both worlds, the divine monarchical and the temporal, and he has been extraordinarily successful in representing himself to his people as the examplar of each.

After his abdication, Sihanouk spent several months traveling around the countryside, delivering folksy, down-to-earth talks on his plans for social and economic improvement. Having established his new image, and obviously having come to relish his new role, perhaps as a kind of game that was both educational and fun, Sihanouk announced the creation of thé Sangkum Reastr Niyum, or People's Socialist Community. Though he insisted, then and later, that this was not a political party but, rather, a "movement for the expression of the will of the poor classes," the Sangkum soon became —and remains—the only effective political machine in Cambodia. In 1957, in order to counteract charges by the dwindling opposition that the Sangkum was under the thumb of the entrenched nobility, with the backing of the conservative country people and the Buddhist priests, the Prince established a more liberal-minded auxiliary organization, called the Socialist Youth of the Khmer Kingdom. In spite of this, among younger Cambodians there remained strong intellectual ferment and outright discontent—not necessarily unhealthy signs in a new country, though the Communists were quick to try to take advantage of them. The racial composition of Phnom Penh—a city of half a million, divided equally among Chinese, Vietnamese, and Cambodians—offered the Communists good openings for propaganda and infiltration, especially since Communist sympathizers were numerous among the Chinese, in particular, and most of the newspapers, in all three languages, tended to be leftist. Sihanouk, though, like the late Prime Minister Nehru of India, has never allowed his cordiality toward foreign Communist governments to weaken his vigilance toward domestic Communists, so whenever he has felt, for instance, that certain papers were dealing too sharply with local issues, he has slapped them down by threatening to close them.

Regardless of what official title or post he has held at any given time, Sihanouk has kept the passive and reverential Cambodians under his sway by virtue of the fact that he is always the acknowledged Chief of State—as well as a former King who may reascend the throne someday. In essence, then, the Sangkum has served as a perfect example of paternalism in action. Sihanouk's program of social and economic reform has had a more qualified success, for while it has undoubtedly brought some benefits to the Cambodians, especially in the field of education, it has so far done little or nothing to alter the basically feudal political and social structure of the nation. Sihanouk's proudest accomplishment, which he refers to, without false modesty, as "a masterpiece of this atomic age," is the creation of a new port, Sihanoukville, on the Gulf of Siam. Carved from virgin forest and mangrove swamp, Sihanoukville was opened in 1960, and since then, in addition to serving as Cambodia's only major seaport (in 1963 it handled almost three hundred thousand tons of merchandise), it has became a popular resort. It has been connected to Phnom Penh by a new hundred-and-forty-mile highway, mostly the work of American engineers using American funds. A number of other new communities, including cities and model villages, have sprung up in outlying areas, and hundreds of miles of roads and irrigation canals have been built—the latter stimulating the production of rice, Cambodia's major crop, and also of cotton and maize. Just about every Cambodian village has some sort of project underway these days, and much of the work is done by voluntary manual labor; government officials, led by the indefatigable Prince, bare-chested and wearing shorts, step up the volunteering a bit by helping the peasants with their work on roads, dikes, bridges, health clinics, and, perhaps most notably, schools. In comparison with other underdeveloped nations, Cambodia has an outstanding record in education—a hopeful omen for constructive social change in the future. The illiteracy rate is still about at fifty per cent, but in the past eight years the number of primary schools has been increased from twenty-five hundred to thirty-five hundred, the student population has risen from three hundred thousand to six hundred thousand, and the number of secondary schools has risen from ten to seventy-five, including a dozen college-preparatory *lycées*. A new normal school, built by Americans, and a new technical institute, built and staffed by Russians, have greatly increased the opportunities for professional instruction, and there is a newly organized Royal University of Phnom Penh, with four faculties—liberal arts, science, law, and medicine—attended by a thousand students. However, there are still many young unemployed Cambodian intellectuals, and they have become the spearhead of opposition to the Sangkum, which they have charged is corrupt. These young intellectuals are subject to Communist propaganda, a fact that Sihanouk has openly admitted, and they represent probably the most serious internal threat to his regime.

When Sihanouk began his program, in 1956, he relied mainly on the Cambodian budget, plus some aid from France and the United States, to pay for it. The Russians had meanwhile initiated an aid program, too, and as Sihanouk's projects grew more ambitious, he turned more and more to the Soviet Union and then to China. Since 1957, China has given Cambodia thirty-five million dollars' worth of help, including materials and equipment for textile, plywood, cement, and paper plants, as well as assistance in building them; the two countries have also carried out annual trade agreements. The value of Russia's aid since 1955 has come to twenty-five million dollars, the most noteworthy contributions being the technical school, a modern five-hundred-bed hospital that can also take care of five hundred outpatients, and the promise of a long-term loan for a major hydroelectric project. By comparison, the United States has given Cambodia two hundred and sixty million dollars' worth of economic aid in the past ten years, plus ninety-five million dollars' worth of military assistance. At first, the United States mostly underwrote large-scale projects like bridges, roads, and irrigation works; then it began to concentrate on education and, more recently, on specialized training in agriculture, public health, and internal (police) security. While the Cambodians remained grateful for the large amount of American assistance—Sihanouk himself once described it as "the oxygen that keeps Cambodia alive"—they became steadily critical of the fact it had not been supplied in the form of outright grants, as the

Communists' assistance was, and of the fact that Washington had consistently imposed limitations and restrictions on the use of it.

It is Sihanouk's aim to socialize sixty per cent of Cambodia's trade and industry, and he estimates that twenty per cent is socialized now. Late in 1963, he declared his intention of nationalizing the Cambodian banking system, as he had just nationalized the country's import-export trade, and said that his decision was prompted by a desire to wipe out corruption—specifically, corruption that had arisen as a result of the manipulations of middlemen handling agricultural products, and corruption that had been the result of the manner in which American economic assistance was granted. About half of this aid was in the form of money raised by the sale of United States goods sent to Cambodia. Some of this money, called counterpart funds, was used to meet the country's military payroll, but unfortunately the profits accruing to the merchants selling the counterpart goods were used to import autos, phonographs, wrist watches, and other luxuries that could be quickly disposed of to the small segment of Cambodia's population able to afford them. While the whole concept of American aid may have overemphasized the principle of forced feeding, giving such nations as Cambodia too many things too quickly, it is certainly true that Sihanouk could have prevented much of the corruption if he had established and enforced strict import quotas and cracked down on the process of obtaining licenses by bribery.

Much of the criticism of the American aid program stemmed from Cambodia's resentment of Washington's often awkward efforts to induce her to make some sort of avowal of support for the West, either by issuing a unilateral declaration or by joining the Southeast Asia Treaty Organization, which extends what is called a "protective umbrella" over South Vietnam, Laos, and Cambodia. Sihanouk, however, has thus far regarded the umbrella as more of an embarrassment than a protection. On a number of occasions, the Cambodians accused the United States of having delayed execution of economic and military aid agreements by insisting on impossible conditions, with the result that even after Washington backed down, an attitude of suspicion and resentment was retained. The idea—so frequently expressed in Congress—that American aid ought to be used as an immediate means of securing American political advantage was never appreciated in Phnom Penh, and it undoubtedly contributed to Sihanouk's decision to renounce United States help and consider closer ties with the Chinese.

Sihanouk had his first contact with the Chinese—and with Premier Chou En-lai in particular—at the conference of Asian and African nations that was held in Bandung, Indonesia, in 1955, and about ten months later the Prince made the first of four state visits to Peking. Although on that trip, as on the subsequent ones, he received the red-carpet treatment, and though he returned with glowing accounts of Chinese economic progress, he certainly gave no indication afterward that he had any notion of taking Cambodia into the Communist camp. His most notable comment, in fact, was to the effect that "human life is of no importance" in China, where people "work day and night with hardly any respite." Sihanouk also observed that Cambodia's Buddhist tradition made it antipathetic to Communism, and suggested that his country "remain neutral in the same way that Switzerland and Sweden are neutral, not neutralist, like Egypt or Indonesia." It may have been inevitable that, having once accepted economic aid from the Communists, Cambodia would establish diplomatic relations with Peking. Early in 1958, the Prince declared cryptically, "I know the Communists are going to cut my throat, but I am ready to die for my country." A few months later, he warned the West that circumstances might force him to "invoke aid from the opponents of our aggressors." In this case, he referred to recent incursions by South Vietnam, and most impartial observers now agree that our government might have delayed Cambodia's *rapprochement* with China and stopped her drift to the left if we had acted more boldly, or at least more flexibly, at that time. In June, 1958, as the culmination of a number of border incidents, South Vietnamese troops, pursuing some escaped Communist prisoners, apparently entered Cambodia and tried to conceal their entry by moving some border markers about four kilometers back from the agreed-upon boundary line. Sihanouk instantly appealed to Washington to mediate, and Washington replied that it couldn't do so because the Saigon government hadn't also asked for mediation. Driven by historic Cambodian fear of the Vietnamese, and also by despair over American impartiality, Sihanouk thereupon sent a letter to Chou En-lai recognizing the Peking government *de jure*. In August, 1958, Ambassadors were exchanged.

Relations between the United States and Cambodia continued to deteriorate. Sihanouk, in his propaganda, associated the deterioration with the increasing hostility between Cambodia and its neighbors, South Vietnam and Thailand, with which, in 1960 and 1961, it severed diplomatic ties. Thereafter, he kept repeating that his worst enemies were the late Premier Sarit Thanarat, of Thailand, and the late President Ngo Dinh Diem, of South Vietnam, and he pointed out that the United States was their protector. As his anger—or his paranoia, as some people describe it—became more intense, he accused the three nations of a conspiracy to mount a *coup d'état* against him. Moreover, he was able to muster evidence to back up the accusation with the discovery, in 1959, of two plots against him, both linked to Son Ngoc Thanh. Sihanouk charged that "American bungling," stemming from attempts to force him into a Western alliance, had been a factor in both plots, and that the plots had served only to encourage the Cambodian Communists.

Thus far, despite the increase of Chinese Communist influence—and the increase among Sihanouk's entourage of left-wing advisers, some of them French-born, most others Chinese—the local Communists are still biding their time politically, and the only serious opposition that Sihanouk faces is still that of Son Ngoc Thanh and the movement he heads, which is now known as the Khmer Serai (Free Khmer) and which Sihanouk claims is secretly supported by the C.I.A. Although there is some reason to believe this was true before, it is probably no longer true. It is estimated that two thousand members of the Khmer Serai are at large, armed mostly with old French guns—equipment issued to them by the Vietnamese government for the purpose of helping to subdue the Vietcong in the southwestern Vietnamese provinces adjacent to Cambodia and populated largely by Cambodians. The majority of these Khmer Serai troops, though under Cambodian leaders, are considered part of the South Vietnamese paramilitary organization, and they are known to have had some association with American Special Forces contingents that have been acting in a training and advisory capacity in South Vietnam. Between 1954 and 1960, the Khmer Serai obtained some financial and material support from the Vietnamese government of Ngo Dinh Diem, whose hatred of Sihanouk was as strong as Sihanouk's was of him, and this aid undoubtedly included some American equipment that had been given to Diem. Presumably, the Americans were aware then, as they are now, that the Khmer Serai's ultimate aim has always been to overthrow the Sihanouk regime and establish a government that, while maintaining neutrality, would lean toward the United States and the West.

A visitor to Song Ngoc Thanh's secret headquarters in Saigon early in 1965 found the Khmer Serai leader still confident that he would take over in Cambodia eventually, though obviously worried about the growing role played by the Chinese Communists there. Thanh, who is a muscularly built, bespectacled, youngish-looking man in his mid-fifties, with a crew cut, was particularly disturbed over the recent arrival in Phnom Penh of half a dozen Chinese economic advisers, allegedly to help in the implementation of Sihanouk's newly announced nationalization plans. The Chinese, Thanh claimed, were being much more "realistic" than de Gaulle's French, who are continuing to act as military advisers and who have also announced a stepped-up program to furnish Cambodia with transportation equipment. While biding their time until the Americans were forced out of Cambodia completely, Thanh said, the Chinese were quietly pushing Sihanouk down the economic path toward Communism, and he predicted that eventually they would try to overthrow Sihanouk forcibly or turn him into a puppet. The only way this could be avoided, Thanh maintained, was for Sihanouk to institute a basically free economy, one that would do away with all the old feudal relationships and thereby really benefit the peasants. According to Thanh, Sihanouk has patronized the peasants with economic gifts, instead of making any attempt to awaken their social conscience or encourage them to increase their productivity for their own advantage. Thanh repeatedly emphasized the point that he regarded his dispute with Sihanouk as one between Cambodians, and that he wished to avoid involving any other country, including the United States, in the argument.

Sihanouk won't let Thanh off that easily. He is equally emphatic in charging that Thanh, the Vietnamese, the Thais, and the C.I.A. are still all engaged in a vast conspiracy against him. In the fall of 1963, before he formally demanded that all United States military, economic, technical, and cultural aid be ended, he carried on a highly emotional campaign on the radio, in the press, and at political meetings and public rallies, playing adroit variations upon the theme of persecution and showing himself, in the words of one observer, as "alternately humorous, abusive, self-pitying, bawdy, frantic, and dramatic." Sihanouk, as usual, appeared to have a variety of motives, the most important one probably being his growing conviction that the tide of war in South Vietnam was going against the Vietnamese and their American backers. A second motive undoubtedly was the murder of South Vietnam's President Ngo Dinh Diem and his brother Ngo Dinh Nhu. Convinced that the coup had been instigated by the Americans, Sihanouk also believed that he was next on their list. A third motive was the revelation of serious corruption in the Cambodian economic community, which embarrassed the Prince domestically and led him, in his anti-American mood, to blame most of his economic troubles on the misuse of counterpart funds. And, finally, he had become incensed when we refused to give him armed jets and anti-aircraft guns as part of our military aid program.

Between 1955 and the end of 1963, the United States supplied a Cambodian Army of thirty thousand men with small arms, recoilless rifles, machine guns, mortars, howitzers, scout cars, trucks, halftracks, and light tanks. An American military advisory group, composed of sixty-three officers and men, plus several mobile training teams of experts and thirty technicians under special contract, was supposed to be supervising the distribution and use of this equipment, but the Cambodians consistently refused to take any military advice, or even to permit the Americans to go out into the field. Many of the weapons were never uncrated, many of the vehicles were badly maintained, and many of the men in the Cambodian Army seemed to spend their time building accommodations for themselves and their families. The French, with a staff of two hundred and fifty, were supposed to be doing the actual military training, but they had scarcely more success than the Americans. When Sihanouk asked the Americans to install guns on four training jets that he wanted to use for patrolling the Vietnamese border, the Americans told him this was technically impossible. Sihanouk turned to the Russians, who gave him not only three armed jets but also some twenty-five-year-old anti-aircraft guns. Sihanouk then got furious at the Americans all over again, because Congress had placed a prohibition on "commingling" (as the Pentagon puts it) our aid with the Russians'—for example, using our gasoline to fuel the Russian-built jets. In his anger, Sihanouk called American equipment "so old that it can be used only in theatrical performances or military parades."

As time went on, Americans and other Westerners in Phnom Penh who sought to explain Sihanouk's philippics were forced to conclude that it was useless to subject them, or·him, to rational analysis. The Prince, as if aware of the problems he was creating and enjoying every moment, began to sound rather like a man who has become used to being mentioned in gossip columns and wants to keep the items rolling. When the Khmer Serai underground radio station criticized his personal life, for instance, he picked up the charges with relish and expanded upon them: "This radio accuses me of having numerous mistresses, including a beautiful Chinese for whom I have sold out to the People's Republic. It is true that from 1941 until 1952, when I was King, still young and handsome, certain pretty specimens of the feeble sex liked my company and it came about that I sinned. But I am able to swear that since 1952 . . . my personal life has been beyond reproach. . . . I back China's legitimate rights, but not because of the beautiful eyes of a Chinese girl who exists only in the stupid and morbid imagination of traitors." (In point of fact, Sihanouk has had six "favorites," including two "permanent" wives, and of his dozen children five are the offspring of one wife, who happens to be the half-sister of his mother. The other wife, who has been his chief companion since 1952, is a beautiful Italian Laotian named Monique, whom he first saw at a beauty contest in Phnom Penh when she was seventeen years old.

He has had two sons by her, who are studying in Moscow and Prague. Another child, Prince Norodom Naradipo, who is being educated in Peking, was named by Sihanouk last November to be his successor as president of the Sangkum "in case I am assassinated.")

Since all attempts to persuade him to phase out the American aid program gradually, in a sensible way, were met with persistent invective, the Americans decided to take him at his word and get out, lock, stock, and barrel, by January 15, 1964, as he had demanded. Upon belatedly realizing how much damage he had done, Sihanouk seemed ready to swallow some of his pride, but he could hardly have been termed contrite. When the abrupt termination of American aid threatened Cambodia's economy by depriving it of such desperately needed items as jute bags for the rice crop that was about to be harvested—to say nothing of gasoline—the Prince accused the United States of trying to "asphyxiate" Cambodia by making "an abusive and erroneous interpretation" of his request for us to leave. When he realized that the French had no intention, despite General de Gaulle's grandiose pronouncements about re-establishing France's role in Asia, of giving aid to Cambodia on anything like the scale the United States had employed, and that stepped-up Russian and Chinese aid would not be adequate substitutes either, he grew panicky. He faced not only the termination of supplies of military equipment and spare parts for such equipment but also the abandonment of some twenty major building projects, including the resurfacing of the highway to Sihanoukville and the construction of half a dozen educational institutions he very much wanted. He was further upset by a flurry of inflation that sent the Cambodian riel sky-high on the black market and brought home to him the realization that his economic reform program, which was to be implemented largely through new state-owned concerns, would require a lot more belt-tightening than he had anticipated. Then Sihanouk indicated that he was willing to extend his deadline for the termination of American aid beyond January 15th, and negotiations were quietly started to see what could be done. However, they bogged down in technicalities, and almost all the American staff was gone or getting ready to go by then anyway.

In the second half of 1964 and in early 1965, Sihanouk became further angered by incursions of Vietnamese ground forces and American planes into Cambodian territory, and in several instances Saigon and Washington acknowledged that mistakes had been made because of confusion of just where the border between Vietnam and Cambodia lay. As Sihanouk issued more warnings, he became more hostile toward both South Vietnam and the United States and veered more toward Hanoi and Peking. The complexity of the border situation was demonstrated by the fact that Cambodia charged Vietnam with as many as fifty violations in a single month, while Vietnam, in turn, accused Cambodia of invading Vietnamese territory as many times. While Sihanouk had denied the right of pursuit to either Vietcong or South Vietnamese troops, Saigon and Washington claimed that he still harbored the Vietcong and allowed them to establish rest camps in Cambodia, a fact Sihanouk denied. Out of his growing skepticism of the chances of the South Vietnamese to survive, the Prince made moves to deal directly with the National Liberation Front and with Hanoi, and obtained their pledges not to violate his borders. In March, 1965, Sihanouk sponsored an Indochina People's Conference, attended by National Liberation Front spokesmen and some North Vietnamese representatives, as well as by some of the Paris group of neutralists and the Pathet Lao. He hoped to use the conference not only to obtain guarantees of Cambodia's territorial integrity, but also to form the nucleus of an alliance of neutral Indochina states. However, the Communists quickly dominated the conference and it degenerated into an attack against American imperialism. The end results were inconclusive. Nevertheless, on May 3rd Sihanouk announced that he was severing diplomatic ties with the United States. He offered to permit the continuance of consular ties, which Washington rejected. Thus ended, for the time being, the degenerating recent history of American-Cambodian relations. In the months that followed, Sihanouk resumed his customary game of blowing hot and cold. While he moved closer to the Communist orbit, he made overtures to the West and indicated that eventually relations with America might be re-established. But because he felt that South Vietnam would lose the war and that the National

Liberation Front would become the dominant force in South Vietnam, he maintained close ties with the Front, as well as with Hanoi and Peking.

Overshadowing the whole situation is the question of whether or not there will eventually be some sort of international conference to guarantee Cambodia's neutrality—something that Sihanouk himself has been seeking since 1962, when he succeeded in arranging the conference to "guarantee" the neutrality of Laos. Although Washington admitted that the political and military picture in Cambodia was not nearly as fragmented as the one in Laos, the State Department seemed afraid, despite Sihanouk's assertions to the contrary, that a conference attended by the Soviet Union and China would inevitably be a debate over President de Gaulle's idea of neutralizing all the former Indochina area, and would aggravate rather than help the Vietnamese situation. At first Washington had favored a smaller conference, such as the four-power one briefly advocated by Sihanouk, that could deal specifically with the problems of the Cambodian-Vietnamese and the Cambodian-Thai borders and seek to reduce or eliminate both the violations of Cambodia's borders and the traffic in men and supplies carried on by the Vietcong across those borders. Sihanouk's rejection of the four-power idea that he himself had originally suggested apparently stemmed from his objection to a recommendation by Washington that the conference consider establishing mixed commissions to demarcate the disputed borders; Sihanouk wanted his definition of the borders accepted, he wanted fixed control posts established to prevent future violations, and he wanted the United States to pay for the control posts. In recent months, the whole question of a Cambodian conference was revived more in the context of Vietnam, as discussed in the preceding section of this chapter.

Sihanouk obviously believes that if he shouts long enough and loud enough and makes enough threats, some sort of conference is bound to take place, and that it will give him his best chance of remaining both neutral and independent, but there are those who fear that in the meantime he is getting himself so far out on a limb in the direction of China and North Vietnam that he may not be

able to crawl back. On the other hand, there are still some Westerners in Phnom Penh who, though they readily acknowledge the difficulty of dealing with the volatile Prince and wish he was not quite
so ill-mannered and irascible, remain convinced that he will never let
Cambodia go Communist. They hope his fierce passion for survival
will yet succeed in forcing a solution that will not only satisfy him
but may, in time, provide a formula for Vietnam and possibly for
other countries in the area as well. Perhaps more clearly than anyone
else in Southeast Asia, Sihanouk, supreme realist that he is, recognizes
that what will happen there in the long run depends on future relations between China and the United States, and his furious maneuvering may yet serve to make those relations more realistic.

If Sihanouk, in one way or another, should turn out to be the
Southeast Asian catalyst, he would be a self-perpetuating one, since
his own salvation, as he has been the first to imply, will ultimately
depend on an accommodation between the United States and China.
The chances of such an accommodation taking place soon are obviously not great, and the Communists may effectively capture
Cambodia long before there is even a possibility of Peking and Washington coming to terms. Nevertheless, the time must obviously come
—perhaps in one generation, perhaps in two—when China and the
United States are once again capable of dealing with each other
diplomatically and, one would hope, culturally and politically, too.
And eventually, if there is to be any chance of permanent peace
or adjustment in Southeast Asia, it will probably be of the sort
envisaged by Sihanouk; a neutral bloc of Southeast Asian nations
might be able to exist, and perhaps thrive, only because, with the
passage of time and the modification of Chinese Communist imperialist aims, a transition will take place in this area similar to the one that
has occurred in Europe. How far Chinese imperialism will reach in the
meantime is the looming question. And whether a process of "de-satel-
lization" comparable to Europe's could occur before Laos, Vietnam,
Cambodia, Thailand, and Burma had lost much of their national iden-
tities as well as their freedom would also be problematical. There
are many aspects of the Chinese revolution that fill one with trepida-
tion, and the fact that the Chinese are not yet capable of waging a

protracted and successful war on the Asian mainland against the United States and its Western allies does not mean that China would not be ready to do so in a decade or even less. Nor does it mean that the "balance of terror" that existed between Soviet Russia and the United States in the forties and fifties, and that has since veered to coexistence, could be repeated vis-à-vis China and the United States. There are signs that the Chinese, at least in their present orientation, will go to great limits to inhibit the American-Russian relationship, tentative as it is, and that China will remain hardheaded and determined in its form of Communism.

The "Lost Revolution"

All of this, of course, underlines the tragedy of the Vietnamese situation. The "lost revolution" in Vietnam represents more than the failure of the United States to capture a revolution from the Communists. It demonstrates that we were incapable, over the period of the last twenty years, of encouraging and supporting the cause of a true nationalism against a spurious one. What might be termed "our failure of revolutionary nerve" is bound to have an effect that far transcends the salvation of Vietnam alone, or of Cambodia and Laos. It is in this sense, once again, that Vietnam has become both the conscience and a belated cause of the United States, and it seems a pity that so much of the frustration that has been encountered in the last few years was not avoided by an awareness of the need to meet the challenge sooner and identify ourselves with the cause. This is not to say, aside from the imponderables presented by white people trying to deal with a yellow or a black race—and these problems are admittedly great—that the United States should attempt to "export" revolution any more than it would "export" the American way of life. But we can act in such a way that the people and leaders of a country such as Vietnam will have respect for American revolutionary motives and methods, and then respond and react to them in their own ways and in their own terms. It seems to me that we have consistently approached Vietnam negatively—"to prevent" its military conquest and subversion, and "to preserve" freedoms that have never actually existed—and have failed to deal with it creatively and with authority. This has inhibited our understanding of the real difficulties, and at the same time of the potentialities. There were no comparable possibilities in China in the middle and late forties, where nothing we could have done would have altered the inevitable Communist victory under the circumstances of the Kuomintang collapse from within, a collapse that was as deeply social as it was political and military. But Vietnam *could* have been saved *if* we had responded to the initial challenge of nationalism affirmatively, rejected colonialism once and for all, and lent our firm and continuing support—including military support, if necessary—to a newly emerging nation. Far beyond questions of strategy in the years ahead, the ideological and power-prestigial impact of the final loss of Vietnam, if and when it occurs, will seriously be felt for a long time, no matter how gracefully or ungracefully we manage to extricate ourselves.

We come then, finally, to the difficult question of what is wrong with the American diplomatic and political enterprise. Why *is* it that we have proved so incapable of dealing in revolutionary terms with a revolutionary situation? How much of the incapacity has been due to inherent failures of national character, of leadership, of policy, of bureaucracy, of timing, or, for that matter, how much of what has happened has been due simply to bad luck? It no longer, somehow, seems enough to say that we were simply "not prepared" to cope with a situation as complicated as the one in Indochina at the end of the Second World War. This was undoubtedly true, but it should not have precluded as completely as it did the willingness to learn and then to make gambles if need be, to realize, by 1948-49 at the latest, that the courting of the French in Europe, at the cost of losing the respect of a vital part of Asia, by supporting the French in Indochina, was at first foolhardy, then dangerous, and finally destructive. Of the various turning points that I have discussed in this book, some strategic and some simply tactical, none was as significant, in my estimation, as our failure to influence the French to grant the Vietnamese in the south a decent amount of independence before it was too late. In this context, it might even be said that the revolution in Vietnam was lost in Ha Long Bay, in 1947 and 1948, when the first unsatisfactory agreements were signed between the French and Emperor Bao Dai.

The American lack of background and preparation to deal with the Indochina situation after the Second World War reflected our historic policy of isolation. There were probably no more than a handful of people in the State Department who knew anything about Indochina during and immediately after the war. President Roosevelt's brave words about a postwar trusteeship and ultimate independence were more the broad phrases of a libertarian leader than the thoughtful appraisal of a student of international affairs, and Roosevelt's careful instructions to have nothing to do with Vietnamese nationalists were indicative of a lack of conscious appreciation of the situation on his part. But in the years that followed, certainly by the late forties, there was ample opportunity to familiarize ourselves with Indochina, and to some extent, of course, we did, though we failed to realize what its ultimate importance would be, especially after the Communists had so obviously begun to win the Battle of China. The deeper and more pressing question remains: How *interested,* let alone *involved,* were we really in the revolutionary possibilities, and the revolutionary dangers, in Indochina? This, in turn, raises questions that go to the very root of the diverse and often self-driven and self-immolated American society. Americans, privately and officially, are surely generous, and this generosity has been demonstrated time and again in many parts of the world, including Vietnam. United States economic and social assistance has not always been as graciously or gratefully received as we have felt it should be, or, put another way, our aid has sometimes been received with caution because our motives or purposes in giving it were suspect. This suspicion or rejection has helped account for our inordinate desire to be esteemed and respected more than has been necessary in the tough cold-war arena of the modern world. But this is not what I mean by the societal problems in America that affect our way of dealing with foreign situations, although these questions of aid often become part of a complex diplomatic and political approach. The sad truth of the matter, it seems to me, is that we have lost our revolutionary zeal; we tend not to think so much in terms of change and revolution as of adjustment and accommodation. The latter are commendable objectives, as in our relations with the Soviet Union today, but, unlike the Russians, who still retain their revolutionary aims and ardor and make it very clear that they simply differ with the Chinese on methods, we don't seem to think politically or philosophically about revolution. Economic revolutions—the development of Mekong Valley programs, and so on—are fine and important revolutionary adjuncts, but they are scarcely a substitute for a positive political policy. Such things as "free elections" and "coalition governments" are also commendable formulas and objectives sometimes, but they, too, are more palliative and ameliorative than inspirational where a fundamental policy of change seems advisable. This is not to say, again, that we can go around the world inspiring or fomenting revolutions—our few attempts to do so (i.e., the Bay of Pigs)—have been pitiful in their execution. But we can learn much more than we now know about the technique of revolution. It was not very long ago that even the best of our universities did not have courses on Marxism or Asian revolutionary history. There are today numerous centers of international relations where such things are studied and discussed, and these are worthwhile. But beyond teaching Marines and some of our other troops the military techniques of insurgency, would it not be logical to establish a School for Revolution somewhere, which Foreign Service officers would have to attend, as they now often attend the Army and Navy war colleges?

American Shortcomings

Much has been said and written about the structure and operation of America's diplomatic enterprise. It is one of the healthier signs of the times that some of our lawmakers and executives are now studying these problems and attempting to come to grips with them in a systematic way. For example, in the last year the Subcommittee on National Security Staffing and Operations, of the Senate Committee on Government Operations, held a number of hearings under the chairmanship of Senator Henry M. Jackson and heard some highly critical and productive testimony from Ambassadors and former Ambassadors, from Secretary of State Rusk and Undersecretary of State W. Averell Harriman, among others, about what is wrong with the way our foreign missions are run and with the whole process of decision-making and implementation in the foreign field. One of the questions that particularly concerned the subcommittee dealt with the role of the Ambassador today. In one of its staff reports, it commented that, despite the great volume of telegraphic traffic between the State Department and its Embassies—a daily total of some four hundred thousand words—there is "a frequent failure of Washington to provide a timely, coherent, approved policy line and to give the reasoning behind its action—and inaction. Ambiguity of policy is bound to result in missed opportunities to protect our position in situations abroad." This is what has frequently happened in Vietnam in the last two years, as I have noted in earlier chapters, and the mere advantage of having established rapid-fire communications between Saigon and Washington has not solved the problem. As the subcommittee also pointed out, speaking generally there are "too many cooks" in Washington, what Robert Lovett has described as "the foul-up factor" in our methods, whereby so many executive agencies become involved in policymaking that nothing gets decided before it is too late or conflicting instructions are sent to the field. "It is obvious that an Ambassador's first job is to carry out his instructions," the subcommittee wrote. "The problem is to find a balance between the extremes of overinstruction, on the one hand, and free-wheeling, on the other. On many occasions, an Ambassador can usefully indicate to Washington that he intends to act in a certain way by a certain date, 'unless otherwise directed'—a practice known in the Navy's books as UNODIR." The subcommittee also criticized the growing custom of sending special emissaries out from Washington; Vietnam has been a notorious victim of this habit. "The practice of commuter trips by special emissaries is now clearly overdone," the subcommittee declared, "and a serious consequence is to erode the Ambassador's prestige and authority in the eyes of the local government." Several former Ambassadors criticized the "caution and timidity" demonstrated by Chiefs of Mission in the field, as a result of their being inhibited by Washington. "No amount of instructions and visits from the Department can replace the exercise by an American representative abroad of independent judgments under field conditions," former Ambassador Gullion testified. Former Ambassador Samuel Berger, now Deputy Commandant of the Army War College, testified similarly, "It is poor operation to keep referring matters to Washington for decision: an Ambassador has the responsibility for resolving problems in the field in the light of general policies set by Washington. On the rare occasions when an issue must be referred to Washington, it is the Ambassador's responsibility to define it, submit the different views, and make his own recommendation. Likewise, when a Washington general policy is no longer valid or workable, it is the Ambassador's responsibility to seek a revision or adjustment. . . ." The subcommittee, guided largely by testimony from Secretary Rusk and others, suggested that one way of achieving better liaison between Washington and Ambassadors in the field was to upgrade the status of the so-called Desk Officer, in charge of a specific country at the State Department. Rusk testified, "It seems to me that the man in Washington who spends all of his time brooding about a country like Brazil ought to be a man comparable in competence to the man who is Ambassador to Brazil." If the Desk Officers were given more freedom to study and formulate policy, it was pointed out, the regional offices above them could be eliminated, and the Assistant Secretaries, in charge of whole areas such as the Far East, would be the principal link between the Ambassadors in the field, the creative Desk Officers at home, and the Secretary of State at the top policymaking level. All of this, of course, presupposes that the Department of State resumes its full Constitutional function and responsibility in conducting Foreign Affairs, and does not take a back seat to the Department of Defense or the White House Executive Staff, which has happened in the case of Vietnam.

These suggestions of the Jackson subcommittee were good ones, as were others it made, including a revision of the reporting system in the Embassies: for too long, the rule has been to "report everything," which takes up far too much time. "Despite the volume of reporting, Washington often feels and is poorly informed," the subcommittee said. "The reason is largely that the decision-making process is not understood well enough for headquarters to identify a need before it arises." This, of course, is what has happened over and over again in Vietnam, and the fault has been both Saigon's and Washington's. The tendency to report too heavily has often been at the expense of reporting well. Far too much time has been devoted to paper work generally, instead of to the establishment and nurturing of important contacts among the Vietnamese. I have already mentioned the fact that at the request of a number of Vietnamese friends of mine, whose positions and views were important, I introduced them to the American Embassy. It is hard to believe that these contacts should not have been made by the Embassy itself. In this way, and only in this way, could the Embassy have created the sort of close associations with Vietnamese that would have put it in a position to know what was likely to happen before it happened, not afterward, as was so often true. As a friend of mine who has watched the Vietnamese situation closely for some time has commented, "My basic complaint is that when a vital dispute comes along between two Vietnamese leaders or two factions, all we can say is 'Now, now.' Surely we can do more than that. It isn't a question of wielding a big stick at all, it's a question of patiently building up relations with a broad spectrum of people over a long period of time, and this can't be done by sending out the third secretary to see someone at the last minute. It must be an American whom the Vietnamese we want to talk to has known for a long time."

Certainly it is undeniable that much of our failure in Vietnam has been due to our lack of close association at the Embassy level with enough Vietnamese of varying rank and opinion, and even when efforts have been made to talk to people—for example, through the provincial reporting system established by the Embassy political section—the result has been such a plethora of written reports as to overburden the political section itself, the Ambassador, and the State Department back home. Embassies, in fact, have become far too large and cumbersome. Former Ambassador Ellis O. Briggs cogently related to the Jackson subcommittee his experience in Czechoslovakia some fifteen years ago, following the Communist seizure of the country. He had been unable to cut the Embassy staff from eighty to forty, as he had suggested and the State Department had approved, because other government agencies that had representatives in Prague expressed "outraged protests" at having them eliminated. It was only when the Communists ordered most of the official Americans out of the country that Briggs achieved more than his aim, and he was left with a staff of only thirteen. "It was the most efficient Embassy I ever had," he said. Much of our diplomatic hardening of the arteries is due to the oversupply of personnel, which simply impedes the flow of blood in the conduct of our foreign affairs and leads to complications from an overlap of functions. In Vietnam, as I have pointed out earlier, there once were one or two men with long experience in the country who knew more people than anyone else and who could achieve more in an hour than the rest of the Embassy could get done in a week, if at all, but unfortunately these men were forced to leave, largely because it was thought "they had outlived their usefulness."

None of these faults by themselves contributed drastically to "the lost revolution" in Vietnam, but collectively they have played an important part. Their significance has been symptomatic in inhibiting the diplomatic process as a whole and in making it virtually impossible for intelligent policy to be formulated and implemented on the scene, preferably by the Ambassador. It was no accident that Ambassador Lodge, during his first tenure in Saigon, accomplished more in this respect that any other postwar Ambassador we have had in Vietnam, and provoked the strongest amount of American involvement in Vietnamese affairs, culminating in the part we played in overthrowing the Diem dictatorship. Lodge was less encumbered than anyone else by the yards of bureaucratic red tape emanating from Washington and fed back from Saigon. He was, in the traditional sense, the representative of one man—President John F. Kennedy. Now that, at the eleventh hour, he was being sent back as Ambassador by President Johnson, in a less political climate, it remained to be seen how much he could accomplish. It was at least encouraging that Lodge was taking with him a small, tight team of his own that included General Lansdale, who would be Lodge's assistant, and a number of other counter-insurgency experts with previous experience in Vietnam, among them the men who were declared only a year ago to be no longer "useful" because they knew too much.

The saga of Vietnam is not yet over. It will undoubtedly continue for a long time. It is unlikely, however, that the opportunities we had during the last twenty years to use our diplomatic leverage, apart from military leverage, will be offered us again. The importance of what has happened in Vietnam lies in our being persuaded by the experience not to make the same sort of mistakes of omission and commission in other places. The world, approaching the last third of the twentieth century, is still a highly combustible and revolutionary one. We cannot afford to abandon or remain aloof from the revolutionary struggles in any region, including our own, nor can we afford to be cautious when caution is only calculated to bring about the defeat of our own democratic objectives and those of our allies. The taking of risks and gambles is just part of operating out of a revolutionary context. We must reformulate our own revolutionary inheritance and redefine it to cope with today's problems. Such a reappraisal must be essentially political. Castros and Tshombes will appear and disappear along with Diems. But unless we understand what they represent, before as well as after their arrival on the scene of power, and unless we direct our diplomatic enterprise to sound and affirmative political concepts that can be honestly applied, we will inevitably suffer more "lost revolutions."

Index

Acheson, Dean, 66
Advance Guard Youth, 4
Africa, 84
Agrovilles, 142-43, 165
Air America, 365
Air Ground Aid Service (AGAS), 34
Allied Southeast Asia Command, 31
Ambassadorial responsibilities, 389-90
American-Vietnamese Friendship Association, 98
Anh, Nguyet (alias), 16-17, 18, 24-25, 26
Annam, xii, 3, 11, 12, 35, 108, 369
Anti-Americanism, 300-01
Argenlieu, Admiral Thierry d', 9, 13, 14, 58
Armed Forces Council, 295, 296, 298, 299, 300, 301, 302, 307, 312, 321, 342
Asian and Australian Trade Union Conference (1949), 53
Asian revolution, xiii, xx
Associated State of Vietnam, 61, 62, 65, 67, 72, 75, 81, 93, 100
Associated States of Indochina, 370
Atlantic Charter, 6
Attentistes, 67-68, 69, 79, 81, 156
Au Phu Dong, 23
Auriol, Vincent, 62

Bamboo Dragon, The, 36
Bandung, Indonesia, 376
Bank of Indochina, 9, 14, 50, 76, 80
Banmethuout, South Vietnam, 78
Bao Dai, Emperor, 3, 21, 52, 59-65, 67, 74, 78, 79, 90, 93, 97, 100, 101, 108, 119, 126, 127, 129, 387; Diem and, 111, 112, 113, 123-24, 129
"Bao Dai" formula, 59, 60
Bator, Dr. Victor, 95-97
Bay of Pigs disaster, 388
Bencat, South Vietnam, 179
Bengiang outpost, 182
Bentuong, South Vietnam, 180
Berger, Samuel, 390
Berlin Conference (1954), 95
Biarritz, France, 46, 47
Biau, Tran Van, 5
Bien Hoa airbase, 293, 311, 346
Binh, Archbishop Nguyen Van, 15, 343
Binh Dinh, battle of, 337-39
Binh Dinh Province, South Vietnam, 135-36, 313, 325, 327, 347
Binh Duong Province, South Vietnam, 179
Binh Thuan Province, Annam, 108
Binh Tuy Province, South Vietnam, 334
Binh Xuyen (gangster group), 8, 103, 116, 117, 119-20, 121, 123-26